John F. Hart

The Industries of Buffalo, N.Y.

A résumé of the mercantile and manufacturing progress of the queen city of the

lakes

John F. Hart

The Industries of Buffalo, N.Y.
A résumé of the mercantile and manufacturing progress of the queen city of the lakes

ISBN/EAN: 9783337328559

Printed in Europe, USA, Canada, Australia, Japan

Cover: Foto ©Suzi / pixelio.de

More available books at **www.hansebooks.com**

THE

Industries of Buffalo

A RÉSUMÉ OF THE

Mercantile and Manufacturing Progress

OF THE

Queen City of the Lakes,

TOGETHER WITH A

CONDENSED SUMMARY OF HER MATERIAL DEVELOPMENT AND HISTORY

AND A

SERIES OF COMPREHENSIVE SKETCHES

OF HER

REPRESENTATIVE BUSINESS HOUSES.

BUFFALO, N. Y.
THE ELSTNER PUBLISHING COMPANY.
1887.

PREFACE.

IN preparing the historical chapters of this work, and those treating of the commerce and material interests of Buffalo, the editor has been guided by a regard for plain facts plainly stated in concise and intelligible terms rather than by affectation of a florid style. As a result that department of "THE INDUSTRIES OF BUFFALO" will be found a mine of valuable information such, we believe, as has never before been crystalized into so brief a space for the instruction and entertainment of those already interested, or whom it may be desirable to interest in the Queen City of the Lakes, her varied resources, attractions and advantages as a place of residence and of business.

Necessarily our space is limited, and matters of minor importance have as a rule either received only cursory attention or have been passed by in silence as having no bearing upon the subject in hand. At the same time we must confess that Buffalo offers a most inviting field for the exercise of literary talent, there being ample material here both of fact and legend to employ the pens of historian and novelist for years to come.

In this connection we desire to publicly tender our acknowledgments for favors and assistance to those obliging and public-spirited citizens who have extended to us that aid and encouragement without which our efforts must have come to naught. Conspicuous among these are ex-President Wright and Secretary Thurstone, of the Merchants' Exchange; President Sweet, of the Third National Bank; Barnes, Hengerer & Co., Geo. W. Tifft, Sons & Co., Root & Keating, Walbridge & Co., John F. Moulton, David S. Bennett, Alonzo Richmond, John Wilkeson, P. P. Pratt, W. W. Walker, Frederick W. Bell, Cosack & Co., The Courier Company, and many others.

With these few prefatory remarks we submit the result of our labors to an indulgent public, and hope the reader may enjoy its perusal as well as we have its compilation.

CONTENTS.

PROMINENT ILLUSTRATIONS.

CITY AND COUNTY HALL.—(SEE "OUR ILLUSTRATIONS.")

PHOTO-ENG. CO. N.Y.

THE PAST.

ABORIGINAL OCCUPANTS—ADVENT OF THE WHITE MAN— SETTLEMENT AND DEVELOPMENT.

GREAT cities are never the result of accident, but invariably the out-growth of natural and artificial conditions clearly defined and un-questionable in their existence and influences. The most important natural conditions are salubrity of climate, convenient geographical loca-tion, fertility of soil in the adjacent agricultural region, and, above all, accessibility to navigable waters—for all history bears witness that no rich, populous and prosperous community has ever flourished and grown power-ful without commerce, and, hitherto at least, commerce has always been dependent upon riparian communication with the outside world. In all of these things Buffalo has been and is peculiarly blessed. Her climate is a delightful one at all seasons, the excessive heats of summer and killing blasts of winter so much dreaded by the inhabitants of less favored regions being almost unknown, as are also the sudden and dangerous changes of temperature common to most latitudes. Mr. Alonzo Richmond, a leading citizen, who for many years has been a close student of the weather, recently said : " Buffalo has a remarkably fine climate as compared with some inland localities, and it is not generally known how much we owe to our geograph-ical position. We are located at the foot of Lake Erie, which is immediately southwest of us, and as the prevailing winds in this latitude are from the southwest, we have, even in summer, moderately cool weather, and the same conditions modify our climate in winter. The lake, once it is thoroughly warmed, takes some time to cool, and it is only in the latter end of the winter season, or the early spring, that we have anything like severe weather. Probably no city in the Union has a more equable climate, or one where the seasons glide more imperceptibly into each other. Our coldest winds are from the northeast, but our climate is cooler in summer and milder in winter than that of either Cleveland or Chicago. And why ? Because they receive their winds over land; we receive ours tempered by a sheet of water. I maintain that for manufacturing as well as for residence purposes no city on this continent is more favorably situated than Buffalo. Rarely do we hear of a case of sunstroke in this city, and we never have a zero temperature in winter to extend over many successive days. Both east and west of us the climate is much more severe. At Albany, Syracuse, and south as far as Binghamton, they have colder weather than we. From our geographical position we are also free from cyclones. Ourselves about 600 feet above sea level, we are protected by the hills southwest of us at Chautauqua, at least 1,200 feet above the level of the sea. Lake Erie is, I believe, about 300 feet higher than Lake Ontario. Well, a cyclone or whirlwind needs a level country, needs to have a free circuit, but any breeze coming around from the lake necessarily strikes the Chautauqua hills, which break the force of the wind and send it harmlessly over our heads. Winds coming around by Lake Ontario are also broken by the hills intervening between Ontario and Lake Erie. That is my explanation of why the devastating winds that play such havoc in other places are not experienced in Buffalo. We have occasionally, it is true, a pretty high wind, giving us high water for a while, but the force of our winds is no greater than the average of cities in this latitude. With her fine supply of pure Niagara water, Buffalo ought to be one of the cleanest, as she is one of the healthiest of American cities. In 1873 the wind's velocity in this city aggregated 76,555 miles, as against 87,921 for New York, 86,120 for Philadelphia, 86,760 for Chicago, and 79,766 for Cleveland."

Sergeant Cuthbertson of the signal service says the average rainfall is not more than thirty-seven to forty inches for the year. The lowest temperature since 1870 in Buffalo was 13.5 below zero on January 25, 1884, and the next lowest was 13 below on February 9, 1875. The maximum temperature in 1873 was 85.5, and in 1886 it was 86.7, showing but little difference in the character of the summers. Rarely does the summer temperature of Buffalo go into the nineties. There are but two instances of this on record during the past sixteen years, viz.: June 30, 1878, when the mercury rose to 92, and August 28, 1881, when it reached 90.8.

Her location from a commercial point of view, midway between the teeming East and the productive West, is a source of constant self-gratulation on the part of those who are so fortunate as to live and do business here. No more fertile or productive region exists than that comprised in the counties composing Western New York, while the vast iron, coal, oil and natural gas resources of Western Pennsylvania and the broad grain fields of Ontario lie at her very doors. Stretching away to the southwest glitter the blue waters of Lake Erie, of which she holds the key and through which she reaches by means of her fleets of steam and sailing vessels the heart of the golden Northwest, the granary of the world. She is the natural outlet for the ores, lumber, wheat, barley, corn and provisions of half the continent on their way to the Atlantic and a market, and so wisely has she exercised her prerogatives in this matter that, notwithstanding unfair discrimination on the part of various railroad lines and the industrious jealousy of rival ports, she continues to maintain her supremacy at this end of the lakes, and if the State Legislature were half as much interested in developing the best interests of the State as they are in party politics, Buffalo would to-day be the most important grain port in the world. Further along, under the head of "The Grain Trade," this subject is treated more at length.

A HISTORICAL SUMMARY.

As long ago as 1620 the French missionaries who penetrated the Canadian wilds as far as Lake Erie found this entire region occupied by warlike tribes of aborigines, the most powerful of whom were the Mohawks, Cayugas, Onondagas, Oneidas and Senecas, the latter the strongest, most crafty and ambitious, and through whose influence the famous confederation known as the Five Nations was organized, further strengthened at a later period by the accession of the Tonawandas. The Six Nations held almost undisputed sway until the French had established a chain of military and trading posts extending from Montreal via Detroit to St. Louis and down the Mississippi to New Orleans, when the jealousy of England at last, in 1756, precipitated a war in which the Indians, much against their wishes, were persuaded to take up arms and aid in the conquest of their original friends, the French. This act, however, proved the destruction of Indian supremacy hereabout, for the English at once occupied both Canada and New York and ruled the savages with a rod of iron, varied only by occasional bloody outbreaks which were quelled, the last one occurring in 1763, when an army train was ambushed by a band of Senecas, a few miles below the falls, and the entire escort of ninety-six men killed with the exception of four. The redskins took no important part in the revolution, and in 1779–80 most of the Senecas settled about four miles up Buffalo creek and engaged in agriculture. Some ten years later the first actual white settler of Erie county located at the mouth of Buffalo creek, about where Washington street now ends, and began trading with the Indians. He was a Hollander named Winne, and to him unquestionably belongs the honor of founding the city of Buffalo.

Previous to this time Robert Morris, the celebrated revolutionary financier, had become possessed, by purchase from the Indians, of vast tracts of lands in this vicinity, including fifty-nine square miles lying within the present limits of Erie county, and upon which now stands this splendid city, which cost the old patriot just one-third of a cent per acre. Two square miles, however, now lying in the heart of the city, had previously been ceded by the Senecas to a Lieutenant Johnson of the British army, who had joined the Senecas at their settlement on Buffalo creek and married a squaw. These lands were afterward purchased by the famous Holland Land Company, Johnson accepting in part payment forty acres bounded by Buffalo creek, Washington, Seneca and Michigan streets. This Holland Land Company (which, by the way, never was incorporated) was composed of Hollanders, whose American agents negotiated the purchase of about four-fifths of Morris' holdings, the Indian titles being finally extinguished in 1797 and the property being known long after as the "Holland Purchase." The actual owners being aliens, an act was passed by the Legislature in 1798 to enable them to hold the property in their own names. They were thirteen in number, and their plan of operations in respect of sales was cautious and complicated in the extreme, requiring the individual signature of each member to all deeds of transfer, the last survivor only having the right to devise by will what might remain. Terms of payment on purchases were made so lenient that at last when claims were pressed the occupants rebelled and serious troubles ensued. All difficulties were, however, finally smoothed away, probably by mutual concessions, and all just titles confirmed. Joseph Ellicott, brother of the then Surveyor-General of the United States, was employed by the Holland Land Company as surveyor, and to him is due the blame or praise of the city's odd topography, which was not original with him, but copied to a great extent from the curious plan of Washington city. He had sufficient penetration, however, to perceive the advantages of the location, and in 1803 made the plat from which the city has grown. Previously the hamlet had been called, first, Lake Erie, later Buffalo Creek, but,

1*

by authority as representative of the owners, Ellicott rechristened it New
Amsterdam, which clung to the place like a Dutch nightcap until 1810,
when the present name was adopted and legalized by the General Assembly
of the State. Ellicott was a queer bundle of qualities—at once a man of
common sense and eccentric to a degree, republican and democratic in
theory and aristocratic and imitative in practice, original and servile, wise
and ridiculous, as may be supposed from the peculiar and labyrinthine plan
of his city and his personal notions. It is related of him that he reserved
to himself a large piece of ground with its chief front in the centre of the
town, from which three of the principal streets radiated, named Vollenhoven
avenue, Stadnitski avenue and Schimmelpennick avenue, but now known
by the more euphonious names of Erie street, Church street and
Niagara street. This ground comprised one hundred acres, and had a semi-
circular boundary in the central part of the western side, as was well said,
like a mighty bay window. Here Mr. Ellicott expected to build his palace,
and enjoy his look-out over the great avenues after they should be lined with
splendid buildings and become the marts of trade or the abodes of fashion. All
this was done in 1803, when there were only about thirty-five families in the
village, and exhibits either a most extraordinary foresight in Ellicott or else
something akin to insanity. Happily, though the city has had to endure
the perpetuation of most of this old-time crank's queer ideas in the matter
of intricate streets and catty-cornered open spaces, his palace never was
built, and the town authorities in 1809 took the bull by the horns and
straightened Main street without regard to Ellicott's bay-window. Reform
seems to have stopped there, however, and nothing short of a second edition
of the Chicago fire will ever make way for a reconstruction of the manufacturing district and its remodeling upon a basis of convenience and common sense. In view of the foregoing it is not surprising to learn that five
years after Ellicott resigned his direction of the Holland Land Company's
interests, and the consequent loss of his only special claim to consideration
as the leading spirit of this section, he became a melancholy misanthrope
and ended his career by suicide in 1826.

By special act of the Legislature in 1807 Buffalo, then a village of
scarcely more than forty houses, mostly log, was made the seat of justice of
Erie county, conditional upon the ceding of half an acre of ground and the
erection of a court-house and jail thereon within three years by the Holland
Land Company. The proposition was accepted, and the close of 1809 saw
a comfortable frame temple of justice and stone prison completed and ready
for occupation, on a half acre of ground on Onondaga (Washington) street.
Pending the erection of these buildings the courts of common pleas and
general sessions were held at Landon's tavern, which stood upon the corner
of Exchange and Main streets. The conveyance of the court-house, jail and
lot to the county supervisors is dated November 10, 1810, and here Mr.
Ellicott got in his fine work again, the plot of ground, surveyed by him,
being in the form of a perfect circle, with the centre located exactly in the
middle of Washington street.

The first mechanic known to have located here was Asa Ransom, who
came in 1796, a silversmith. He made every description of rude ornaments
for the Indians, and obtained great influence over them. He afterward removed to Clarence Hollow, where he kept a tavern under the auspices of the
Holland Land Company, and also engaged in farming, raising the first regular crops in that vicinity. He was an energetic and capable man, and by
1807 had risen to the position of lieutenant-colonel of the Erie county

militia, in which capacity he gave such satisfaction that he was appointed sheriff in 1808, again in 1812, and for the third time in 1816. Another conspicuous figure of those times was Dr. Cyrenius Chapin, who came from Oneida county in 1803, and was the first to practice the healing art as a profession in Erie county. Besides being an excellent physician the doctor was an enterprising, bold, impetuous man, a born leader, and popular with his fellow-citizens. He it was who organized and led the night expedition of boats from this side which in October, 1812, cut out and captured two armed British vessels lying at anchor off Fort Erie. Two Americans were killed and five wounded, while the British loss was seventy-one. Some forty American soldiers, captured at the River Raisin, were recaptured, and the vessels brought safely to this side of the river. It was a brilliant achievement, and all engaged in it acquitted themselves most creditably. The next year Dr. Chapin was appointed sheriff, a position which he resigned to accept a commission as lieutenant-colonel of militia, serving with distinction until his capture by the British at the time of the burning of Buffalo. He was kept a prisoner in Canada for a year or more, returning upon the restoration of peace, when he took an active part in the rebuilding and advancement of the town, never relaxing his interest in all that concerned her welfare until the hour of his death, in 1839. Many other noble men made their way to Buffalo in those early days of the century, and we have been thus particular in our reference to Mr. Ransom and Dr. Chapin because they were typical pioneers and good examples of the earnest, brave and energetic class who rescued this now rich and powerful section from the wilderness and caused it to blossom as the rose.

. The Buffalo *Gazette*, the pioneer newspaper, was first issued in October, 1811, and unquestionably exercised great influence in the development of the town for many years, discussing questions of public policy with great ability, encouraging the struggling citizens, urging public improvements, and carrying to distant centers of civilization the news of the frontier and a cordial invitation to the young, the strong, the skillful and the hopeful to come hither and help in the work of erecting a commercial and industrial metropolis. The breaking out of the war of 1812 interrupted the progress of affairs for some years, but the good seeds already sown sprang up with the return of peace and the resumption of peaceful avocations. The public schools, established in 1811, were re-opened as soon as suitable provision could be made, manufactures, ship-building and all the useful arts were fostered, and an era of unexampled prosperity followed the withdrawal of the opposing armies. It is interesting, however, to note the part taken by Buffalo and Western and Northern New York in that memorable struggle, several of the fiercest fights on the northern frontier having taken place within hearing distance of the then village, and at least one—the successful defense of Fort Erie by an American garrison—within sight of the excited citizens. The battles of Chippewa and Lundy's Lane were fought on the Canada side of the Niagara river, between Buffalo and the falls, and in both the American arms were successful. As before stated, however, Buffalo was burned to the ground, with the exception of the jail and two residences, December 30, 1813, a strong force of British regulars and Indians having crossed at Black Rock the previous night with that object. The militia, under Lieut.-Col. Chapin, made an ineffectual resistance, but most of them escaped, carrying with them a portion of the government stores. Rebuilding was commenced in 1815.

The village had been chartered in April of 1813, but it was found necessary to secure a new charter, which was obtained April 5, 1816, and from that time dates the real growth of the place, which was truly wonderful for those times. A pier was built and the harbor formally opened to commerce in 1823, a third charter having been granted the previous year. The citizens were fully awake to the advantages of the place as related to navigation, and cheerfully contributed of their means for the removal of the bar and the permanent maintenance of harbor facilities—a work in which they were in later years aided by liberal appropriations by Congress.

In 1822 Millard Fillmore, a Cayuga county farm lad, who had served an apprenticeship to the tailoring business, arrived here. He had already made some progress in the study of law, and devoted himself to the profession, teaching school to maintain himself meanwhile. In 1828 he was elected to the Legislature, again in 1829, and again in 1830. He was afterward elected thrice to Congress, in 1832, in 1835 and in 1838. In 1847 he was made State Comptroller, and in 1849 nominated for the vice-presidency on the ticket with Zachary Taylor. The Whigs were victorious, but in July General Taylor died, and Mr. Fillmore became President. His administration was marked by conservatism throughout, the most exciting event being the passage and approval of the famous fugitive slave law—a piece of legislation that unquestionably had a mighty bearing in a passive way upon the subsequent history of the country—the organization of the Republican party, the Kansas troubles, the John Brown raid into Virginia, secession, the great civil war, and emancipation. Mr. Fillmore returned to Buffalo upon the inauguration of his successor, James Buchanan, and resumed the practice of law, enjoying the confidence and respect of his fellow-citizens generally up to the time of his death, March 8, 1875.

The most remarkable Buffalonian of his time—early in the '30s—was Benjamin Rathbun, who made his *debut* here as proprietor of the Eagle Tavern. He was mentally constructed somewhat on the order of Law of South Sea bubble notoriety, and had visions of wealth and grandeur such as few men have ever entertained. He was full of enterprise, but the story of his operations reads like a chapter from the "Arabian Nights." He speculated in lands upon a vast scale, planned mammoth improvements, and had the rare faculty of interesting others in his ill-advised ventures. Mr. Howells writes of him : "One of his buildings, of which he actually laid the foundation, was a vast hotel and exchange (on the very spot that Joseph Ellicott had reserved for himself, whereon to erect his mansion, at the time of laying out the town), which was to occupy the whole square between Main, North and South Division and Washington streets, the rotunda of which was to be 260 feet high. This hotel was to stand opposite the churches, where the three grand avenues, Erie, Church and Niagara streets, give a character of imperial magnificence to the view. Rathbun also laid out a great city at Niagara Falls, the lots of which were to be sold at auction, the sale to continue as many days as might be necessary to dispose of them all. This was in 1836, when the flush times were at their height, but in the midst of the sale he was arrested on the charge of committing some stupendous forgeries on a Philadelphia capitalist. When confronted by his victim he confessed that those were not a tithe of what he had perpetrated. He had been going on for years in this business, taking up one set of forged notes, as they became due, by the substitution of another set of forged notes. All his building projects were immediately dropped, but the workmen received their pay, though it absorbed nearly the whole of the assets of the estate. Rathbun was brought to trial, convicted and sentenced to five years in the State prison. After serving his full time he took up his old business of hotel keeping in New York city, and again became comparatively a rich man. The panic in Buffalo occasioned by the disastrous termination of Rathbun's enterprises, and the destruction of confidence between man and man, brought on a condition of hard times here without a parallel either before or since; even the long season of depression commencing with 1873 was trifling as compared with it. Rathbun may then well be characterized as the evil genius of the place."

So far as Buffalo's material interests are concerned, the year 1825 was the greatest she ever saw. A former historian writes : "That year marked the completion of the Erie canal—Dewitt Clinton's monument—a work that did more for the future of the place than any one thing ever attempted since. Nearly twenty years before (1807), the great project of uniting the Atlantic with the lakes was discussed, but the country was yet too new and too poor to plunge into such a mighty work. The idea, however, that such was possible gradually gained strength. It took ten years, though, from its first inception till ground was broken for what proved to be one of the most important works of internal improvement that had up to that time been made in any country. Governor De Witt Clinton, the acknowledged champion of the scheme, gave it untiring support, and succeeding in removing all obstacles, although its enemies were earnest in opposing it. For a long time it remained undecided where its western terminus should be placed, as Buffalo and Black Rock were about equally divided in their advantages and disadvantages. At length it was ascertained that the harbor of Buffalo could be satisfactorily improved in depth and safety, and the canal was ordered to terminate there. At the time of the opening, in 1825, it was generally known as the Grand canal, but shortly afterward it became known as the Erie canal. At this time Buffalo contained a population of 2,412, but the opening of the gates of the canal at once gave its progress a new vigor. The canal became the medium of shipment between the rapidly settling West and the East, and as Buffalo was the western entry port to the great highway, it naturally increased in population, resulting in the census of 1830 showing that there were 8,668 inhabitants within the town limits. On every hand evidences of advancement were manifest, and people poured in until the numbers made the reorganization of the village necessary. A city charter was applied for, and the act incorporating the city of Buffalo was passed April 20, 1832, which divided the city into five wards. The charter provided for the formation of a common council, consisting of two members from each ward, who elected the mayor, which this body continued to do until 1840, since which time he has been elected by the people. The mayor acted as president of the council, and so continued until 1853, at which date the charter was revised, Black Rock annexed, and the council empowered to elect one of their own body as president. The city, being then greatly enlarged, was redistricted and divided into thirteen wards, with two members of council from each, said members being the board of aldermen. The city was now placed upon a substantial foundation, and the future looked bright and prosperous. Buffalo, in common with all industrial and commercial communities, suffered severely from the panic of 1837, but, like other enterprising towns, gradually recovered from its effects and became more bustling and prosperous than ever."

In 1842 the grain elevator was first adapted to steam power and applied to the unloading of lake vessels and canal-boats by Joseph Dart, a fuller

14   THE INDUSTRIES OF BUFFALO.

account of which revolution of methods will be found in our chapter
entitled "The Grain Trade."

In 1847 it became evident that the harbor accommodations were becoming daily more and more inadequate to the rapidly increasing demands of
an expanding commerce. consequent upon Western development. Hon.
George W. Clinton writes that in this emergency all classes, regardless of
party and private ends, concurred in sanctioning an enlarged system of
improvement, which when completed would suffice for the ever-expanding
commerce of a century to come. This system, having been carefully
matured by a joint committee of the citizens and of the common council,
was adopted at a general meeting of the citizens on the 21st and by the
council on the 24th of August, 1847. The plan contemplated primarily the
completion by the State of the Main and Hamburg Street canal, and two
large basins, the Ohio and the Erie, with slips connecting them with the
canal, the Ohio basin to have an area of ten acres, and to be connected with
the Buffalo creek about a mile from the mouth ; the Erie basin to be three
hundred feet wide and a half mile in length, extending from the north side
of the entrance of the harbor toward Black Rock—both to be of a depth
sufficient for the largest craft. The State made appropriation for the execution of these great works contingent upon the city's extinguishing the
individual titles to the necessary lands, which was done, and contracts were
immediately let and active operations at once begun upon a series of improvements that when completed more than quadrupled the shipping capacity of
the wharves. The succeeding ten years were the most active Buffalo had
ever seen, and trade and manufactures, navigation and railroad building
flourished. Elevators, factories, mills, mercantile blocks, residences,
churches and school-houses went up as by magic, and the proud and
ambitious city became the intra-continental and international metropolis to
which all eyes were directed. Fleets of splendid steamers and sailing craft
brought to her doors the teeming products of the West, which were from
here transferred by canal and rail to the seaboard, the returning trains and
boats bringing machinery and manufactured goods in a thousand forms for
transportation to consumers in the forests of Indiana or the prairies of Illinois, and for the use of pioneers further west. Buffalo held the key to the
only great artery of trade, and levied a legitimate tribute upon all that
passed. Her population grew at an amazing rate. The increase is thus
stated from official figures, beginning with 1830, when the census showed
8,668 residents ; 1835, 15,661 ; 1840, 18,213 ; 1845, 29,773 ; 1850, 42,261 ;
1855, 74,414. The receipts of western grain for 1850 aggregated 6,000,000
bushels ; for 1855, 20,000,000 bushels, and business in all lines partook of
the same wonderful augmentation in a greater or less degree.

The period from 1855 to 1860 was the most depressing that has ever
overtaken Buffalo. The panic of 1857 was ruinous in its consequences to
many of her most energetic and enterprising men, and trade and manufactures were paralyzed. The railroads were gradually absorbing the carrying
trade when the completion of the canal enlargement again opened that
grand artery, and aided more than any other one cause in the restoration of
confidence and the resuscitation of public spirit—the inauguration of an era
of prosperity which continued, with a temporary check at the beginning of
the great civil war, up to the tremendous financial panic of 1873, and from
which Buffalo, already dependent upon railroads and manufactures for her
business welfare, was one of the severest of sufferers. She had but little
more than recovered from the effects of that siege of adversity when the

last season of business depression, lasting from 1880 to 1884, began, but her merchants, financiers, manufacturers, shippers and industrial classes generally had learned much in the past; they were prudent, conservative and cautious, and Buffalo was among the first of progressive communities to feel and profit by the returning tide of healthful business activity that has characterized the past two years and presents such hopeful prospects for the future.

The war period was one rather of political excitement than of material progress, yet Buffalo made considerable advances in population and wealth, besides contributing generously of men and means for the preservation of the Union. But in all the past, wonderful as has been her progress at times, Buffalo has never given such evidences of substantial growth and improvement as during the last semi-decade, and more particularly within the two or three years just concluded, the building operations for 1886 involving an outlay of not less than $5,000,000, with which street extension and improvements necessarily kept pace. Referring to this latter phase of improvement, the *Express* of January 9, 1887, says : "There were opened since January 1, 1886, 12,162 lineal feet of streets. That is to say, the legal proceedings taken by the city to acquire the necessary lands completed and the awards of the appraising commissioners made, with one or two exceptions, and confirmed by the courts. In most cases the actual opening of the streets to public traffic awaits only the confirmation of the assessment rolls to pay for the improvement. Lineal feet to the number of 12,162 opened this year for streets! More than in any single year before. In New York City, where growth in its northern parts continues to be very brisk, there were opened during 1885, 7,900 feet. Besides all this there was considerable widening and straightening of streets to keep in the line of growth and progress, and there were taken by the city fourteen acres of land to furnish new breathing spots for the increasing population. The Rumseys gave up twelve acres adjoining the park for $30,000, and the Bennett park property cost $104,577.90."

Unquestionably much of Buffalo's recent rapid advance and growing fame is due to the enfranchisement of Niagara under an act of the Legislature, which passed the Assembly March 14, 1883, and the Senate April 18 following, under the provisions of which appraisers were appointed and $1,433,429.50 awarded the owners of " Goat Island, Bath Island, the Three Sisters, Bird Island, Luna Island, Chapin Island, the small islands adjacent to said islands in the Niagara river, the bed of the river between said islands and the New York mainland, the bed of the river between Goat Island and the Canadian boundary, and a strip of land beginning near Port Day in the village of Niagara Falls, running along the shore of said river to and including Prospect Park and the cliff and *debris* slope ; and including also, at the east end of said strip, not exceeding one acre of land for purposes convenient to said reservation, and also including all lands at the foot of said falls, and all lands in said river adjoining said islands and the other lands described." The grasping owners, who for three-quarters of a century had enjoyed a monopoly of this mighty wonder of nature, with its vast water power and speculative possibilities, demanded a total of about $20,000,000 for the property, which, it is pleasant to know, they failed to get. The result of the State's firm assertion of the right of eminent domain is that Niagara is free to all who choose to visit and enjoy its awe-inspiring beauties. It was appropriately inaugurated and dedicated July 15, 1885, with religious, civic and military exercises, in the presence of the governors of New York and Ontario and a brilliant assemblage of eminent statesmen, clergy, civilians and soldiers. The State of New York holds, and will for all time continue to hold, control of this grand property, in trust for mankind, that it may be preserved in all of its wild and startling beauty for the enjoyment of remotest generations. It was a noble work, nobly done.

The Tugby building and the pulp mill, the only buildings remaining on the shore of the river in the Niagara Falls reservation, will soon be removed. By next summer the toll-house on the bridge and the restaurant on Goat Island, as well as the mill, will have disappeared, and Niagara will be practically restored to its natural conditions so far as possible. The administration of the reservation-trust continues enlightened and governed by good taste and public spirit.

THE PRESENT.

GEOGRAPHICAL POSITION, GENERAL APPEARANCE, POPU-
LATION AND CORPORATE EXTENT—LOCAL INTERESTS—
BANKS—MANUFACTURES, ETC.

THE beautiful and powerful city of Buffalo is situated most eligibly at
the foot or eastern end of Lake Erie at its junction with the Niagara
river, in latitude 42 deg. 53 min. north and longitude 78 deg. 55 min.
west, 293 miles northwest of New York city. The navigable waters of the
great lakes stretch away from her feet westward and northwestward for a distance of more than 1,200 miles, while the various railroads centering here provide communication directly or through their branches and connections with
every portion of the North American continent accessible to the iron horse
—the Canadas, New England, the Middle and Southern States, the vast
Northwest, the Pacific slope, the far Southwest and Mexico. She has a
superb water front of some six or seven miles, and a secure and excellent
harbor extending about two miles along the Buffalo river, which empties
into the lake and the Niagara in front of the city. A fine government
breakwater 4000 feet in length, supplemented by a similar city work of 1,500
feet, protect the entrance to the harbor, whose shores are lined from end to
end with vast elevators, warehouses and factories. Basins, docks, slips and
other conveniences, including the Erie canal itself, provide ample conveniences for the handling of all kinds of craft, and it is estimated that the
navigable water front is at least eighteen miles in extent, kept in excellent
condition throughout the season by means of dredges and a regular system
of repairs. In point of commerce and manufactures Buffalo ranks second
only to New York, while in population she is the third city in the State, a
careful estimate making her the home of about 245,000 souls at this time.
The residence portion of the city (comprising beautifully built, broad, well-
shaded and handsome streets, public parks and open squares, with many
grass-grown triangular spaces—left vacant by Ellicott's topographical
vagaries) is to the full as attractive as can be found anywhere, and in summer no more delightful place of sojourn could be desired, while even the
winter season, with its copious snows and comparatively moderate temperature, is full of healthy pleasure. The architectural attractions of the
principal business streets are many, and constant improvement bids fair to

THE BUFFALO LIBRARY.—(SEE "OUR ILLUSTRATIONS.")

render them in time the peers of any thoroughfares in America. The public buildings, embracing the City and County Hall, the Library building, the Music Hall, Postoffice, etc., we illustrate and describe in their appropriate places.

Buffalo embraces within her corporate limits a little more than thirty-nine and a half (39.599) square miles of territory, intersected by 651.96 miles of streets, of which 151.96 miles are paved (30.75 with asphalt, the remainder with stone), and 500 miles are still to be completed. There are within the city 163.93 miles of sewers, many miles of track operated by the New York Central, Erie, Lake Shore, Belt Line, Buffalo Creek and other railroad companies, and some twenty-five miles of street railways.

The total valuation of real estate for taxation, as shown by the assessors' report, foots up $113,963,445; total personal, $8,405,225; total collections $2,113,685.24 ; total receipts for licenses (*vide* Comptroller's report), 1886 $14,198.33; total bonded city debt, January 1, 1887, $8,283,775.67, less $176,721.53 in the treasury. Total taxes and assessments for 1886, $3,844,-096.02 ; street extension, park and sewer bonds issued, $312,844.03 ; increase of bonded debt for year, $233,041.74 ; premiums on sales of bonds, $17,-496.10. The Treasurer's report shows total receipts from all sources, 1886, $5,914,128.16 ; disbursements, $4,653,639.20; cash on hand December 21, $1,260,488.96. The Engineer reports 18.2-5 miles of streets paved with stone and asphalt at a cost of $1,006,784.84; in addition to which sixteen miles of sewer were constructed, a large amount of dredging done, sidewalks laid, and repairs made, at an expense of $197,454.65. The cost of street cleaning and sprinkling for the year was $85.078.93 ; other expenses of street department, $27,844.94.

The School Department is worthy of special attention. We find that the available fund for this department for the year was $751,754.41; total expenditures, $538,820.38. Number of public schools, 45 ; of private schools, 45. Attendance—public schools, 28,372; private schools, 11,995. Licensed teachers employed, 583, of whom 43 were males and 540 females. Total value of public school property, $1,073,935. In addition, some 1,400 pupils attended the night schools at a total expense of $8,224.

Expenses of Poor Department for the year, $84,412.32.

The report of the Health Department shows 6,476 births and 3,861 deaths; ratio of the former, 308 per thousand of population ; of the latter, 18.4.

The Police Department, first and last, comprises 334 men, and cost for its maintenance last year about $340,000. Arrests for the year, over 9,000. The patrol wagon and police alarm system is about to be inaugurated.

The Fire Department employs 228 men, 19 engines, 15 hose carts, 4 hose wagons, 5 chemical engines, 5 hook-and-ladder trucks, 97 horses, and 32,000 feet of hose. There were about 500 fires and alarms during the year. A fire-boat will be ready for use next May.

The water service is first-class and extends to all portions of the city. A new pumping engine of 15,000,000 to 20,000,000 gallons daily capacity is soon to be added to the present equipment, which will make the works equal to any in the country, superior to danger of temporary disability from accident, and enable them to meet all demands from fire department and private consumers for many years to come. The quality of water supplied is the best, such as is unknown save along the lakes. Receipts for the year, $480,000; expenditures, $460,923.36.

Total expenditures on public buildings for 1886, $70,371.57.

From the Mayor's message we quote as follows concerning the parks—which, by the way, are among the city's chiefest attractions:

"The only important improvement in the park system during the past year has been the paving of Fillmore avenue with Barber's Trinidad asphalt pavement, extending from the southerly line of Genesee street to the north line of Seneca street, a distance of nearly two miles. This work has been done at a total expense of $174,491.18, one-half of which was paid from the park fund appropriated by the Common Council and the other half assessed upon the abutting property. This was a much-needed improvement, and has proved a great benefit to the eastern section of the city. A considerable portion of the parkways have also been stoned and graveled, and the road-ways generally kept in good condition. The grounds and plantations have received careful attention. The parks never appeared to better advantage than during the past season. Important additions of territory have been added to the park system during the year—notably the portion bordering the south line of the park known as Rumsey's Grove, and two blocks of land on the lake shore opposite "The Front." All the public parks and squares in the city have been formally turned over to the Park Commissioners, who will doubtless at the proper time submit a recommendation for their improvement. These additions will involve a corresponding increase in the appropriation for park maintenance. I learn from the secretary that the receipts from all sources during the year up to the 22d of December were $150,607.87, and the expenditures $147,080.96, with some liabilities unliquidated."

The city is well lighted, there being on January 1st a total of 6,763 gas lamps and 546 electric lights distributed in the improved portions and along the principal boulevards.

A revision of the city charter to meet the demands of the times has been agitated from time to time, and as we write "a self-constituted committee of public-spirited citizens," as the Mayor characterizes them, is engaged upon that work, the result of their labors to be submitted to the Legislature for adoption or rejection when completed.

EDUCATIONAL.

The educational advantages of Buffalo are many and varied. Besides the ninety schools, public and private, mentioned in the above summary, a superb high school supported by the city, and State normal school, there are nineteen Catholic parochial schools, and a number of institutions devoted to higher education, as follows : State Normal School, Jersey street, between Thirteenth and Fourteenth ; Buffalo Female Academy, Delaware avenue ; St. Joseph's College, corner Church street and Delaware avenue ; Canisius College, No. 651 Washington street; St. Mary's Academy, No. 74 Franklin street ; Buffalo Classical School, No. 335 Franklin street ; the Heathcote School, No. 310 Pearl street ; Mrs. Curtis' Select School, No. 157 Butler street ; Mrs. Williamson's School for Young Ladies, No. 254 Franklin street ; English and Classical School for Boys, No. 94 Johnson place ; Kindergarten and Training School, No. 623 Delaware avenue ; St. Stephen's Church School, No. 300 Adams street ; Evangelican Lutheran St. John's Church School, No. 283 Hickory street ; German Lutheran Trinity School, corner Goodell and Maple streets ; St. Margaret's School for Girls, corner Franklin and North streets; St. Andreas' School, No. 173 Sherman street ; St. Marcus' German Evangelical School, No. 400 Oak street; German Evangelical Friedens Church School, Eagle street, foot of Monroe; St. Mary's Academy and Industrial School, Franklin street, near Church; St. Peter's Evangelical School, corner Genesee and Hickory streets; Martin Luther College, Maple street, near Virginia. There are also seven convents. Of churches there is no lack, and many of them own and support fine temples of worship. The congregations comprise 11 Baptist, with four missions; 148 Catholic, 14 Episcopal, 12 Presbyterian, 2 Congregational, 16 Methodist, 21 Lutheran and German Evangelical, 4 Jewish, 10 miscellaneous, and one Methodist, one Baptist and one Presbyterian church extension, supporting numerous benevolent and charitable societies.

CHARITY ORGANIZATION SOCIETY.

The most conspicuous and effective charity here, however, is the Charity Organization Society of Buffalo, for the subjoined sketch of which we are indebted to Secretary Rosenau : "The Charity Organization Society of Buffalo, N. Y., was founded in the fall of 1878 by a number of public-spirited citizens for the purpose of introducing advanced methods in the dispensation of public and private charity, the repression of mendicity and the prevention of pauperism. It is modeled after the Charity Organization Society of London, England, and was the first of some sixty similar societies to be established in America. Its aim is not to give actual relief, but to aid the worthy poor to become self-supporting, and by a system of registration and thorough investigation to discover and exterminate fraud in begging. In 1881 it was made the recipient of a large gift in trust from Benjamin Fitch of New York city, estimated to be worth about $300,000. In pursuance of the terms of the gift the society erected the Fitch Institute, a magnificent fire-proof building at the southwest corner of Swan and Michigan streets, containing, besides rooms for various purposes, a lecture hall capable of accommodating one thousand people. The cost of the building was about $140,000. In it the society now maintains a medical dispensary for the free treatment of the worthy poor and a hospital for the immediate and temporary treatment of the injured. The society also has in operation a wood-yard to give employment to men who have no work and no means of support, a labor bureau for women working by the day, and also the Fitch Creche, a day home for the children of working women, which is located in the building adjoining the institute on Swan street. As soon as its income is available the society will, in addition, maintain in the institute classes in mechanical drawing, a free reading room, a school for the instruction of domestics, a provident laundry, a penny savings bank, and free lecture courses for working people.

"For the purposes of its regular work the society maintains two offices, one at No. 10 Court street and one in the Fitch Institute. It systematically pursues its work of investigation, and has in the course of its existence effected a saving to the citizens of Buffalo in the reduction of the expenditures of the poor department of nearly $500,000. The present officers of the society are : Edwin T. Evans, president; T. Guilford Smith, vice-president; Nathaniel S. Rosenau, secretary and treasurer. Trustees—One year—Edward Bennett, Thomas Cary, Sherman S. Rogers, George P. Sawyer, E. Carlton Sprague ; two years—James H. Dormer, Edwin T. Evans, Josiah G. Munro, T. Guilford Smith, Ansley Wilcox ; three years—John H. Cowing, Josephus N. Larned, Jewett M. Richmond, Solomon Scheu, Sheldon T. Viele."

The libraries and reading rooms embrace the grand Buffalo Library, whose magnificent building is illustrated in this work, located between Washington, Ellicott and Clinton streets and Broadway; the free Grosvenor Library, corner Broadway and Washington streets; the Young Men's Christian Association Library and Gymnasium, corner Pearl, Mohawk and Genesee streets; the Buffalo Historical Society Library, lately removed to the Buffalo Library and Art building; the Law Library, room 23, City and County Hall; Erie County Medical Society Library and Buffalo Medical Library Association, University of Buffalo; Women's Educational and Industrial Union Library, No. 25 Niagara square; Guard of Honor Library, No. 620 Washington street; German Young Men's Association Library, Music Hall building (illustrated); Catholic Institute Library, Main and Chippewa streets; Lutheran Young Men's Association Library, No. 659 Michigan street; Young Men's Catholic Association Library and Gymnasium, corner Swan and Franklin streets, and Erie Railway Library Association, Michigan and Exchange streets.

The medical societies include the University of Buffalo, corner of Main and Virginia streets; Medical Department of Niagara University, Ellicott street; Buffalo Obstetrical Society, Alumni Association, Medical Department University of Buffalo, Homeopathic Medical Society of Western New York, Medical Union, Buffalo Medical and Surgical Association, Erie County Medical Society, Homeopathic Medical Society of Erie County, Medical Club, Physicians' Club, Erie County Board of Pharmacy and Buffalo College of Pharmacy, University of Buffalo.

There are six hospitals, viz.: The Buffalo General Hospital, No. 100 High street; Buffalo Homeopathic Hospital, corner Cottage and Maryland streets; Buffalo Hospital of the Sisters of Charity, No. 1883 Main street; Buffalo Maternity Hospital, No. 334 Seventh street; the Emergency Hospital, corner of South Division and Michigan streets, and St. Francis Hospital, No. 337 Pine street. The Buffalo State Asylum for the Insane, one of the most extensive, costly and well-conducted establishments of the kind in the United States, is located in the suburbs, near the City Park. The Buffalo Quarantine Hospital is at No. 762 East Ferry street. In addition there are no less than twenty-one homes and asylums for all classes of unfortunates.

There are two regiments of militia and one battery of artillery here, besides an independent company of military. Fort Porter, the celebrated government post, sadly decayed, is garrisoned by a detachment of regulars. Through the efforts of Hon. John M. Farquhar, M. C., a liberal appropriation has been secured and the works and buildings are to be restored at once.

Buffalo is well supplied with social, literary, dramatic, political, sporting and other clubs, conspicuous among which may be named the "Buffalo," "City," "Acacia," "Press," "Gentlemen's Driving" (owners of the driving park), "Oakfield," "Audubon," "Republican League," "Cleveland Democracy," "Democratic Legion," "Buffalo Yacht," etc., while all the leading beneficial orders and societies, Masonic, A. O. U. W., Knights of Honor, etc., and labor organizations are well represented. No less than fifteen vocal and instrumental musical societies are supported.

Of literary and scientific societies there are many, the most prominent being the Buffalo Society of Natural Sciences, Buffalo Fine Arts Academy, Buffalo Historical Society, Young Men's Association, German Young Men's Association, Buffalo Civil Service Association, Buffalo Horticultural Society,

Buffalo Dental Society, Buffalo Architects' Association, and the Women's Educational and Industrial Union.

There are three gas light companies—the " Buffalo," " Buffalo Mutual" and " Citizens"—one natural gas fuel company, and one electric light company—the Brush, of which a more extended account is given in another portion of this volume.

BANKS AND BANKING.

The foundation of all commercial and industrial prosperity is a sound banking system, prudently and honestly administered. The people of New York State are to be envied in this respect, for they have the option of patronizing either the secure and unquestionable National system or the State system, conducted under such laws and restraints as make it in all respects equal, and, some believe, superior to the government plan. Here in Buffalo the State banking system is the favorite, and is represented by no less than fifteen regular, savings and private houses, while a single National institution enjoys the distinction of being the only bank of issue—the Third National, capital $250,000, surplus $60,000, of which Mr. Charles E. Sweet is president and Mr. Nathanial Rochester cashier. The State banks are the Bank of Attica, capital $250,000, surplus $75,000; the Manufacturers and Traders, capital $900,000 ; the Merchants, capital $300,000; the Marine Bank of Buffalo, the German, the Bank of Commerce, the German-American, the Farmers and Mechanics, and the Bank of Buffalo. Savings banks —the Buffalo, the Western, the Erie County and the National. Private— American Exchange (late White's Bank of Buffalo), Donaldson & Co., Buffalo Loan, Trust and Safe Deposit Co.

The local insurance companies are six in number—the Buffalo German, the Erie County Mutual, the Union and the Harmonia Mutual, fire associations; the Life and Reserve Association, and the Buffalo Mutual Accident Association.

The aid and savings associations are thirty-one in number, all well managed and prosperous.

MANUFACTURES.

Notwithstanding Buffalo is concededly a manufacturing center of the first class, it is impossible to obtain reliable data upon which to predicate statistics showing the number and extent of her factories of various kinds, the number of operatives employed, or the volume and value of annual output—all owing to the lack of organization and non-recognition of community of interests among those who, in their individual capacity, do so much toward creating the material wealth and extending the fame of the city. We are therefore constrained to refer the seeker after knowledge on this subject to the second part of this volume, where will be found special mention of most, if not all, the representative manufacturers, to whose enterprise and industry the Queen City of the Lakes is indebted for her unquestioned eminence in the mechanic arts.

A PERMANENT EXPOSITION.

January 7 last an association of prominent business men was formed and $200,000 guaranteed for the establishment and support of a permanent exposition. Grounds have been secured and buildings will be erected this spring for continuous exhibition of all the industrial products of the city. In the summer or early fall an agricultural and dairy exhibition will be given. Fine stock will be a prominent feature. The exposition will be partly mechanical in character, and partake of some of the attributes of a county fair. It will be a mammoth affair, and will attract many people to the city, and interest all the citizens of Buffalo as well. The proximity of Buffalo to the Dominion will permit the exposition to be of an international character, and the accessibility of Buffalo by railroad and boat will serve to draw many people here from all the surrounding country. Buffalo seems peculiarly well situated and favored for the success of such an enterprise, and with her extensive manufacturing interests, and the rich farming and grazing lands in her immediate environment, there will be plenty of material out of which to make exhibits.

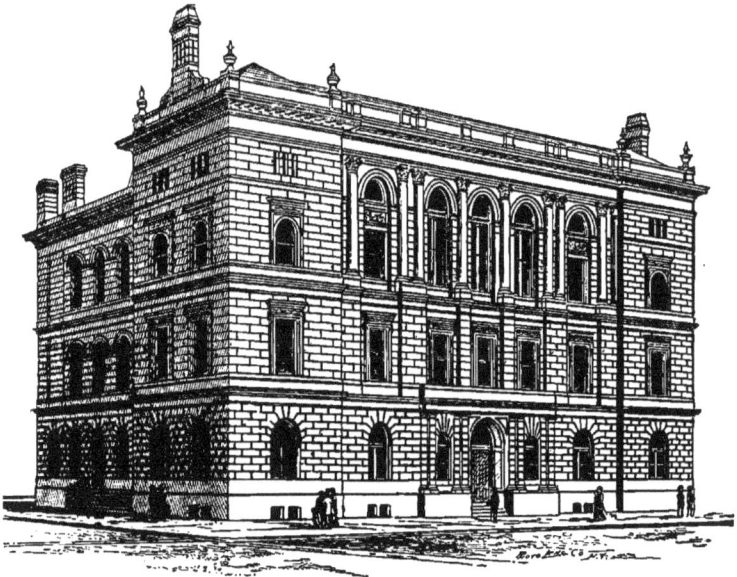

NEW GOVERNMENT BUILDING.

The above illustrated handsome new building (or, more properly, extension of the former custom-house and postoffice) was recently completed and occupied by the United States courts, internal revenue officials and post-office. At her present rate of growth Buffalo will require largely increased facilities for the transaction of government business within a few years. Value of imports for 1886—Dutiable, $4,367,845 ; free, $1,349,466 ; total collections, $965,819.61 ; increase of collections over 1885, $100,000.

THE PRESS.

FOR some unexplained reason the editor of this work has experienced extraordinary difficulty in securing from publishers historical data upon which to predicate as full and satisfactory a chapter on this subject as he could have desired. The subjoined sketches were prepared from such information as could be obtained. For the rest, mere mention of the names and character of the various publications is all we can offer.

THE COURIER COMPANY.

The genealogy of *The Buffalo Courier* is turned back to the first daily paper printed in this city, *The Daily Star*, which shed its mild light in the year 1831. From the humblest beginnings it long ago became a power, and the institution from which it is now issued is of enormous extent and almost unlimited resources. Dignity and enterprise are characteristic of The Courier Company's publications, while their influence is second to that of none in Western New York. Its establishment is justly claimed to be the greatest show and general printing house in the world.

In 1855 Joseph Warren became identified with the management of *The Courier*, which was destined to be directed into channels of prosperity by the influence of his character and ability. From that time it has continued the leading Democratic paper of this part of the State, with some of the ablest journalists of the country at different periods in managerial charge of its columns. With the advent of Mr. Warren also began the upbuilding of the job and show printing business of the establishment, which has since attained colossal proportions. He secured a proprietary interest in 1859. Years of growth followed, and on the first of January, 1869, the large printing houses of Joseph Warren & Co. and Howard, Johnson & Co. were consolidated, and a stock company formed under the title of The Courier Company. On the first of December, 1874, Charles W. McCune, a gentleman of splendid business talent and unbounded energy, entered the office as general manager. Mr. Warren died on the 30th of September, 1874, regretted by the entire community. He was a political director of great discernment, a strong man in the Democratic councils of the State, and accomplished much for the advancement of Buffalo. As president of the company he was succeeded by the Hon. William G. Fargo. He in turn was followed in that capacity by Mr. McCune in March, 1880, and three years later the latter became sole proprietor of the institution, which under his control had obtained the solidest of financial foundation, and had in every department thriven and enlarged. Its work became world-famous. Its newspaper publications extended their influence and had their facilities

2

increased. In the zenith of his success, and with his business in magnificent order, Mr. McCune, after a very brief and unexpected illness, died March 14th, 1885. His loss was mourned throughout the State and nation. Especially was it deemed severe in Buffalo, where he was recognized as a most worthy and valuable citizen whose enterprise had an important bearing on the city's industrial growth.

Mr. George Bleistein, a young gentleman whose business training had been obtained in the establishment, became president of The Courier Company, with Mr. J. W. Bridgman, an experienced financier, as vice-president. Under their management the institution has continued its course of great and uninterrupted prosperity. In its many departments the perfection of the different branches of the printer's and engraver's arts has been obtained. To convey an idea of the magnitude of the establishment in few words cannot be better effected than by enumerating the buildings owned and occupied for its business, and which contain a vast aggregation of the most approved machinery, and an invaluable accumulation of materials: The five-story and basement building No. 197 Main street, used for the stationery store, offices, etc.; No. 199 Main street, four stories and basement; Nos. 202 and 204 Washington street, six stories and basement, the highest and finest perfectly fire-proof industrial building in Buffalo; Nos. 188 and 190 Washington street, five stories and basement, devoted to the company's newspaper publications; Nos. 208, 212 and 216 Washington street, four stories and basement; and the lithographic department building, seven stories and basement, between Main and Washington streets.

THE BUFFALO EXPRESS.

This handsome eight-page journal is issued from the Matthews' block, corner of Exchange and Washington streets, every morning and weekly, by James N. Matthews, editor and publisher. The publication of the *Express* was begun January 15th, 1845, by A. M. Clapp & Co., and the present owner, Mr. Matthews, helped set the type for that issue. The politics of the paper were then Whig, and it has been consistent in opposition to the Democratic party from the first, espousing the cause of the Republicans on the organization of that party, and remaining faithful thereto until the present. Many able and brilliant men have occupied the editorial chair of the *Express*, but it is questionable if any more vigorous, terse or forcible writer ever presided over its columns than Mr. Matthews, who has made it one of the ablest, most fearless and trenchant of interior morning newspapers. Under his direction it has become a real power here at home, loved and supported by its friends, hated and feared by its enemies, and has performed yeoman service for the city in the exposure and correction of official misconduct as well as in the advocacy of improvement, and in attracting hither enterprise and capital in search of employment and investment.

THE EVENING AND SUNDAY NEWS.

The *Evening News*, one of the most influential and widely circulated papers in this State, dates its origin with the establishment of the *Sunday News* in 1873. There were then no Sunday papers in Buffalo, but the experiment proved a success. The paper was from time to time enlarged, and there seemed to be no limit to its popularity. Bright, vigorous, enterprising and entertaining as it was, its influence with the people increased until it wielded such power in politics that in the election of 1875 a people's ticket, put forward by it, was elected with few exceptions. In 1880 Edward H. Butler, the editor and founder of the *Sunday News*, carried into effect a plan he had long cherished, that of printing a cheap and interesting evening paper. It appeared on October 11th as a four-page, six-column folio, and on the first night the sales were 7,000 copies. The circulation steadily increased until now the average daily circulation is 37,500. The largest number of papers sold of any one issue was 48,539. The circulation of the Sunday edition averages 18,000. *The News*, among other things, suggested and boomed Grover Cleveland for Governor and President.

The News occupies its own well-appointed building at No. 218 Main street, and is the only paper which does not have a job printing attachment. In the mechanical department the best machinery is used, and the editorial department is well equipped. Besides the United Press service, the paper has special correspondents at New York, Albany, Chicago and Washington, as well as in all the towns in Western New York.

E. H. Butler is the editor and proprietor of the paper. He is ably aided by his brother, J. Ambrose Butler, as business manager.

THE DAILY TIMES,

One of the liveliest and newsiest papers in Western New York, was started by Norman E. Mack as a five-cent Sunday paper September 7th, 1879, from the office located at No. 200 Main street, the present site of the Exchange building. Six months later the offices, composing and editorial rooms were removed to No. 50 Seneca street, where in February, 1883, the stock and plant were almost entirely destroyed by fire. For a short time the paper was published from new offices secured at No. 272 Washington street. May 13th, 1883, the offices were removed to No. 191 Main street, whence *The Times* is still issued. On September 13th, 1883, *The Daily Times* was started as a cheap morning paper, selling for two cents, with the Sunday edition at the regular price. The daily flourished and prospered until December 2d, 1886, when it was decided to publish it as a morning and afternoon one-cent paper. The first edition appears at 10.30 A. M., and the fifth at 5 P. M. It made its appearance on that day, and its cordial reception by the public ever since encourages the publishers to claim that it is destined to be *the* organ of the people in the future. The Daily and Sunday *Times*, the latter being a mammoth 16-page edition, is now published by The Times Company, Limited, which was incorporated June 15th, 1885, with the founder of both the Daily and Sunday *Times*, Norman E. Mack, as president.

BUFFALO COMMERCIAL ADVERTISER.

This is the oldest, and ranks high among the prosperous and influcutial Western New York journals—the lineal descendant of Buffalo's pioneer newspaper, the *Gazette*, founded in 1811. The first number of *The Daily Commercial Advertiser* appeared January 1st, 1835, *The Weekly Patriot*, from which it sprung, being continued for some years. After various changes of ownership the establishment was purchased April 9th, 1861, by Rufus Wheeler, Joseph Candee and James D. Warren. December 8th, 1862, James N. Matthews succeeded to Mr. Candee's interest, and April 29th, 1865, Mr. Wheeler retired, the firm becoming Matthews & Warren. In October, 1877, Mr. Warren became sole proprietor, continuing in that position until his death in December last, when his sons, O. G and

W. C. Warren, succeeded. September 28th, 1868, the *Commercial* printing house was burned to the ground, but publication was continued without interruption. July 1st, 1871, the paper was enlarged to its present size—forty columns. April 11th, 1882, the establishment occupied a splendid new five-story building, which was burned in the following December. Not an issue was lost, however, and October 1st, 1883, the *Commercial* occupied its present elegant quarters—a superb fire-proof structure and an ornament to the city. The price of the *Commercial Advertiser* was reduced to two cents February 1st, 1886, a move which has added largely to its popularity, the sales at this time reaching nearly 12,000 daily. The equipment is very complete, embracing, besides full supplies of new and stylish types, a fine Hoe perfecting press of 12,000 per hour capacity.

THE SATURDAY MERCURY.

This neat and newsy hebdomadal was established in April of 1886 by W. J. McCahill & Co., and is already looked upon as the leading distinctively weekly newspaper of Western New York, full of entertaining reading for people of every class, and a welcome visitor to thousands of homes in all the region roundabout. Its success has been phenomenal, beginning without a subscriber, and at this time printing and circulating nearly 20,000 copies every Saturday. The management is excellent, both in the business and editorial departments, and as a result the *Mercury* is bright in appearance and contents, handsomely printed, and noted for its pointed and telling editorial paragraphs, whether aimed at current follies or treating of the serious side of things. The *Mercury* is on the right path to a career of honor and usefulness, and bids fair to become a power in the land.

Buffalo Daily Evening Democrat and *Weekly Weltburger* (German); office, No. 509 Main street.

Buffalo Daily and Weekly Volksfreund; German Printing Association; office, Nos. 46 and 48 Broadway.

Buffalo Daily and Weekly Freie Press and *Sunday Tribune;* Reinecke & Zesch, No. 500 Main street.

Daily, Tri-Weekly and Semi-Weekly Mercantile Review; C. H. Webster, No. 16 Nichols street.

Daily, Tri-Weekly and Semi-Weekly Price Current and Live Stock Reporter; W. G. Webster, No. 244 Main street.

Farmers' Review and Live Stock Journal, weekly; C. H. Webster, No. 16 Nichols street.

Milling World, weekly; American Industry Press, No. 13½ Swan street.

Lumber World, monthly; American Industry Press, No.13½ Swan street.

Iron World, monthly; American Industry Press, 13½ Swan street.

Roller Mill, monthly; A. B. Kellogg, No. 128 Washington street.

Buffalo Christian Advocate, weekly; Nos. 41 and 43 Franklin street.

Catholic Union and Times, weekly; Catholic Publication Co., Franklin and Swan streets.

Sunday Truth, labor weekly; Hausauer & Rappold, No. 200 Washington street.

People's Saturday Evening Pictorial Press; Matthews, Northrup & Co., No. 179 Washington street.

Matthews-Northrup Official Railway Guide, monthly; Phin. M. Miller, manager, No. 42 Exchange street.

Popular Gardening, monthly; Popular Gardening Pub. Co., room 23, No. 202 Main street.

Church Home Quarterly ; Church Charity Foundation, No. 752 Niagara street.

Saturday Tribune ; Crotts & Hurley, No. 4 North Division street.

The Argus, A. O. U. W. monthly; R. C. Hill, No. 200 Washington street.

Medical Press, monthly ; Medical Press Association, No. 137 W. Tupper street.

Buffalo World, weekly ; David Paine, No. 271 Washington street.

Ojczyzna, Polish weekly; Polish Pub. Association, No. 46 Broadway.

Our Record, monthly ; managers of Home of the Friendless, No. 1500 Main street.

Independent Practitioner, medico-dental monthly; W. C. Barrett, M.D., D.D.S., No. 208 Franklin street.

Buffalo Medical and Surgical Journal, monthly; office, No. 260 Pearl street.

Iron Review, monthly; C. L. Sherrill & Co., Nos. 41 and 43 Franklin street.

The XVIth Amendment, prohibition weekly. W. H. H. Bartram, Coal and Iron Exchange.

Queries, literary, art, scientific and educational monthly ; C. L. Sherrill & Co., Nos. 41 and 43 Franklin street.

Railway Magazine, monthly; Geo. E. Allen & Co., No. 177 Main street.

Triumphs of Faith, Christian monthly; No. 260 Connecticut street.

Chautauqua Tourist; John Laughlin, No. 191 Main street.

The North and the South, emigration monthly; J. T. McLaughlin, Academy of Music.

Pioneer Co-Operator ; L. J. Hedges, manager, No. 555 North Division street.

Fashion Quarterly; A. E. Rose, No. 260 Main street.

MERCHANTS' EXCHANGE.

ORIGIN, PROGRESS AND INFLUENCE—OFFICERS AND COM-
MITTEES.

As long ago as 1844 the necessity for an organization of Buffalo merchants, manufacturers and shippers became manifest, and the Board of Trade was organized. In May of the following year its building, at Prime and Hanover streets, w a s completed, a n d occupied in June. For reasons not necessary to recount, the board did not receive the support and encouragement it had a right to expect, and was not therefore i n c o r p o r a t e d until 1857. The same year, marked by a great panic as it was, afforded opportunity for a manifestation of usefulness and strength which added vastly to the prestige of the organization and secured for it the co-operation of most of the city's progressive business men. In 1862 a removal was effected to Central Wharf, and the Board of Trade continued to flourish until 1880, when a reorganization was accomplished under better auspices than ever, and with a largely increased membership, as the Buffalo Merchants' Exchange. In 1881 began the movement which resulted in the erection of the present stately Board of Trade building, corner of Seneca and Pearl streets, designed by M. E. Beebe & Son, architects, of which we present an engraving. It was completed in 1883, at a cost of $250,000, and occupied with appropriate inauguration ceremonies January 1, 1884. It was erected under direction of the Board of Trade trustees, and is the property of that body. The building, fire-proof throughout, is seven stories in height, with basement, fronts 132 feet on Seneca and 60 feet on Pearl street, and rises 100 feet above the sidewalk. The facade is of cut stone, terra cotta, pressed brick and iron, and in all respects the structure is a substantial, handsome and imposing one. The principal entrance is on Seneca street. The board room and Merchants' Exchange occupy the entire fourth floor, the remainder of the edifice being devoted to office purposes, thus bringing in a handsome revenue.

The officers of the Exchange, elected January 12, 1887, are as follows : President, James R. Smith ; Vice-President, Charles H. Gibson ; Treasurer, Henry S. Sill ; Secretary, William Thurstone. Trustees—Daniel E. Newhall, Geo. Urban, jr., John C. Graves, Albert J. Wright, Horace J. Harvey, Peter C. Doyle, Henry D. Waters, Henry C. Zimmerman, H. G. Nolton, W. C. Cornwell. Committees for current year: Finance—Charles H. Gibson, John C. Graves, H. G. Nolton. Rooms and Fixtures—H. C. Zimmerman, Wm. C. Cornwell, Henry D. Waters, Wm. P. Andrews, Harrison N. Vedder. Floor—Albert J. Wright, Daniel E. Newhall, Horace J. Harvey. Reference—Roswell R. Buck, Chas. B. Armstrong, Harris Fosbinder. Arbitration (elected)—P. P. Pratt, John Satterfield, Jewett M. Richmond. Transportation (until 12th May)—Henry Montgomery, F. H. Tyler, E. B. Wilber, Thomas Hodgson, John G. Kerr, W. H. H. Newman, J. Adam Lautz, John P. Irish, Charles G. Curtiss, Robt. B. Adam, Philip Becker, C. W. Hammond, N. W. Ransom. Real Estate and General Information— Henry C. French, Henry W. Box, G. Barrett Rich, Chas. A. Sweet, George H. Lewis, John Otto, John L. Williams. Lumber—Harvey J. Hurd, W. W. Brown, W. W. Tyler, George P. Sawyer, Alfred Haines. Coal— T. Guilford Smith, Thomas Hodgson, Thomas Loomis, George H. Lewis, J. J. McWilliams. Oil—George F. Southard, A. S. Holmes, William R. McNiven, John A. Donaldson, S. A. Wheeler. Groceries, Produce, etc.— Leroy S. Oatman, George W. Hayward, J. H. Gail, Charles E. Selkirk, Henry Hearne. Live Stock—John G. Kerr, N. W. Ransom, John Hughes, M. F. Windsor, M. Danahy. Flour and Grain Inspection—W. C. Newman, George B. Mathews, N. C. Simons, F. J. Henry, Charles G. Curtis, S. S. Brown, Wilson H. Sherman. Grain—W. W. Sloan, George Sandrock, Stephen F. Sherman, E. B. Wilber, F. J. Sawyer, Charles F. Sternberg, Milton Brown. Call Board—William Meadows, Warren F. Chandler, H. V. Burns. Introduction—George Urban, jr., Peter C. Doyle, S. S. Guthrie, Frederick Truscott, Charles Kennedy. Meteorological—N. C. Simons, Frank W. Fiske, Willis C. Jacus. Harbor Improvement—John C. Graves, Peter C. Doyle, E. D. Hedstrom, ———— ————, Charles W. Goodyear.

The blank in the Committee on Harbor Improvements is due to the death of Mr. Alonzo Richmond on the morning of March 2d. The vacancy was not filled when this part of our work went to press. The *Express* says of Mr. Richmond:

" Alonzo Richmond was the son of Anson Richmond, of Syracuse, and was born in that city December 4, 1821, being in his 66th year at the time of his death. He was first cousin to the famous Dean Richmond. His early years were spent in Syracuse, where he was educated in the public schools. For a time he studied law, but, having a delicate constitution, it was deemed best that he should have outdoor employment. The leading industry in Syracuse was the production of salt, and Alonzo became associated with his brothers, Moses and Jewett, in that business. After a few years the salt interests of Syracuse were consolidated in a concern known as the Onondaga Salt Company, which Mr. Richmond represented in Chicago until 1864 or 1865, when he took up his residence in Buffalo, where his brothers had established themselves in the grain and commission business.

Again the brothers united their interests, and Alonzo remained a partner until about four years ago, when he retired with a handsome competency. For the last twenty years his face and figure have been familiar in and about the Board of Trade, of which body he has been president and always a prominent member. At the time of his death he was a Civil Service Commissioner, appointed by the mayor. He never married. Alonzo Richmond enjoyed the respect of every one who knew him. A purer character, a more unselfish nature, a more kindly disposition, a sweeter temper, a more genial soul than his it has never been the good fortune of this writer to know. His life was blessed by his own good deeds. Simple in his habits, and preferring domestic retirement rather than public or social recognition, he had not a personal acquaintance with one in a hundred of those who knew him by name. He was devoted to the public good. No man has thought more, few in a quiet way have done more to advance the prosperity of Buffalo, or to promote the best welfare of her citizens. He was always on the watch for opportunities in this direction. He was a man of ideas. No one understood the transportation question better than he, and none has contributed more material facts for an intelligent discussion of it. His special regard was for the water route, but he was not in favor of hampering the railroads with unjust restrictions. He was eminently a fair-minded, clear-sighted man. His contributions to canal literature were many and valuable, though seldom published over his own name. He ranked with the Seymours as an authority on canal subjects and a champion of its interests."

RAILROADS.

BUFFALO is a terminal point of eleven trunk line railroads radiating north, east and south, and one of the greatest railroad centers on the continent. In addition the Buffalo Creek railroad connects the island, the canal, the harbor, the elevators and the stock-yards with the various main lines; a belt line passenger road encircles the city, and several short roads are in course of construction or projected to various tributary points.

NEW YORK CENTRAL AND HUDSON RIVER RAILROAD

The consolidation of the New York Central and the Hudson River railroad companies was consummated November 1st, 1869. The former company was organized in 1853 under a special law authorizing the consolidation of the roads extending from Albany to Buffalo, as follows: The Albany & Schenectady, the Schenectady & Troy, the Utica & Schenectady, the Mohawk Valley, the Syracuse & Utica, the Syracuse & Utica Direct, the Rochester & Syracuse, the Buffalo & Rochester, the Buffalo & Lockport, and the Rochester, Lockport & Niagara Falls. The new company took possession August 1st, 1853. The Hudson River Railroad Company was chartered May 12th, 1846, and opened from New York October 3d, 1851. Since the consolidation to East Albany the N. Y. C. & H. R. Railroad has built, bought, leased or chartered the following-named roads: The New York & Harlem, the Spuyten Duyvil & Port Morris, the Dunkirk, Allegheny Valley & Pittsburg, the Syracuse Junction, the Buffalo Junction, the Geneva & Lyons, the Troy Union, the West Shore, and three-fourths of the ownership of the two Hudson river bridges at Albany. The capital stock of the company is $89,428,300; funded debt, $56,424,333.33; current liabilities, $6,635,514.64; cost of road and equipment, $146,630,682.19; cost of additions and betterments, 1886, $555,846.39; total miles of tracks, 3,688.25, of which 374.50 are laid with iron, leaving 3,313.75 miles of steel rails. Lineal feet of bridges, 178,320. Number of engine-houses, 58; shops, 19; elevators, 5, of 3,450,000 bushels capacity. Number of employes, 19,260; aggregate salaries and wages, $10,502,460.01. The equipment comprises 273 passenger engines, 349 freight engines, 221 switch engines and 10 dummy engines, 940 passenger coaches, and 32,280 box, platform, cattle, oil-tank, coal, conductors', tool and service and derrick cars, and a total floating equipment of 65 boats, including 12 propellers and steam tugs. Number of miles run in 1886 by passenger trains, 7,918,201; by freight trains, 12,502,729; by switching and working trains, 8,206,817. Through passengers carried between New York, Buffalo and the bridges, 168,188; way passengers, 14,493,930. Tons through freight carried north and west, 389,390; east and south, 1,435,515; way freights, both ways, 10,893,196. Gross earnings, $30,506,360.92; charges against same, $29,433,394.41. Surplus, 1886, $1,072,966.51; deficit for 1885, $953,647.90. The income account shows a surplus, September 30th, 1886, of $11,473,469.38, against $10,508,332.39 at same period of 1885.

Chauncey M. Depew, of New York, is president of the company; Charles C. Clarke, first vice-president; Horace J. Hayden, second vice-president; James Tillinghast, assistant to president; Edwin D. Worcester, secretary; E. V. W. Rossiter, treasurer; Isaac P. Chambers, comptroller; John M. Toucey, superintendent; Henry Monett, general passenger agent; Edson J. Weeks, general agent, Buffalo, No. 1 Exchange street. The board of directors is composed of Cornelius Vanderbilt, William K. Vanderbilt, Fred'k W. Vanderbilt, Chauncey M. Depew, Charles C. Clarke, Horace J. Hayden, Samuel F. Barger, J. Pierpont Morgan and Cyrus W. Field, of New York; William Bliss, of Boston, Mass.; Erastus Corning of Albany, N. Y.; George C. Buell, of Rochester, N. Y., and Sherman S. Jewett, of Buffalo, N. Y. The election for directors is held on the third Wednesday in April in each year.

NEW YORK, LAKE ERIE AND WESTERN R. R. CO.

This powerful corporation operates, in addition to its own magnificent four-track road from Buffalo to New York, branches, leased lines, etc., as follows: The New York, Pennsylvania & Ohio road, the Hawley branch, the Conesus Lake road, the Middletown & Crawford road, the Montgomery & Erie road, the Chicago & Atlantic road, the Pavonia Ferry, Pavonia Horse railroad, and Erie Express—the latter organized May 15th, 1886, to succeed the United States Express Company on all roads controlled by the Erie Railway Company. The total stock of the N. Y., L. E. & W. Railroad Company September 30th, 1886, aggregated $86,536,900. The gross earnings for the year ending on that date were $22,500,047.73; working expenses, $16,388,-638.14; net earnings, $7,057,869.23; interest on funded debt, rentals of leased lines, etc., $7,043,258.28; surplus, $14,610.95—against a deficit of $1,376,943.55 in 1885. The road proper, with all its appurtenances, equipment, etc., and those of its branches and leased lines, are in superb condition. The officers are: John King, president; S. M. Felton, jr., first vice-president; Charles Paine, second vice-president; A. R. McDonough, secretary; Edward White, treasurer; James A. Buchanan, attorney; L. P. Farmer, general passenger agent; G. H. Vaillant, freight traffic manager; J. S. Hammond, general freight agent; Stephen Little, comptroller; A. J. McDowell, auditor of traffic; W. G. Fuller, purchasing agent—all of New York; B. Thomas, general superintendent; J. H. Barrett, superintendent Eastern division—all of Jersey City; E. Van Etten, superintendent Delaware division, Port Jervis, N. Y.; D. H. Blackham, superintendent Susquehanna division, Elmira, N. Y.; W. B. Coffin, superintendent Western division, Hornellsville, N. Y.; G. W. Bartlett, superintendent Rochester division, Rochester, N. Y.; W. J. Murphy, superintendent Buffalo division, Buffalo; W. C. Rinearson, general northern passenger agent, Buffalo; J. Deuel, division freight agent, Buffalo. The Erie's board of directors is composed of Messrs. Henry H. Cook, William B. Dinsmore, William N. Gilchrist, James J. Goodwin, Jacob Hays, Morris K. Jesup, John King, William Libbey, John G. McCullough, Ogden Mills, Courtlandt Parker, George W. Quintard, William L. Strong, J. Lowber Welsh, William A. Wheelock and William Whitewright. Buffalo offices, No. 177 Main street, cor. Exchange.

BUFFALO, ROCHESTER & PITTSBURG RAILROAD.

This road, already completed, was purchased by the present company under a charter granted October, 24th, 1885. The total length is 283.95 miles, single track, steel rails. The equipment consists of 13 engines of all classes, 42 passenger coaches, and 5,277 box, platform and other freight and service cars. During the year ending October 24th, 1886, 318,779 passengers and 1,326,084 tons of freight were carried; the gross earnings were $1,393,013.31; gross expenses, $1,410,891.25; deficit, $17,877.94. The common stock of the company aggregates $4,800,000; preferred stock, $6,000,000; funded debt, $8,091,070, less redemption fund, $1,778,000; total, $6,313,070. The officers of the company are: President, W. H. Brown; secretary, Thomas F. Wentworth; treasurer, Fred. A. Brown—all of New York city; general manager, George E. Merchant, Rochester; general superintendent, James T. Gardner, Buffalo; auditor and assistant treasurer, John F. Dinkey; chief engineer, Wm. E. Hoyt; general freight and passenger agent, I. S. Emery; superintendent of motive power and machinery, C. W. Mills—all of Rochester. General offices, No. 20 Nassau street, New York, and Rochester.

BUFFALO, NEW YORK & PHILADELPHIA R. R. CO.

This company was organized February 14th, 1883, by the consolidation or lease of the following railroads: The Bradford road, the Buffalo Coal Company's road, the Kinzie road, the Kendall & Eldred road, the Genesee Valley road, the McKean & Buffalo road, the Mayville Extension, and the Olean, Bradford & Warren road, with the Buffalo, New York & Philadelphia and Pittsburg & Western railroads. The capital stock is $50,000,000, and the total length of track operated is about 674.16 miles—mostly steel rails. The rolling stock comprises 116 locomotives, 49 first-class and 64 second-class passenger coaches, and about 5,000 freight and service cars of all kinds. Number of employes, 2,500. Gross earnings for 1886, $2,367,937.83; total expenses, $1,844,364.50. The principal offices are in the Mills building, New York, and at No. 242 South Third street, Philadelphia. Officers: President, G. Clinton Gardner, New York; secretary, Joseph R. Trimble, Philadelphia; treasurer, John Dougherty, New York; auditor, W. L. Doyle, Buffalo; general superintendent, Geo. S. Gatchell; general passenger agent, J. A. Fellows; general freight agent, E. T. Johnson; chief engineer, R. D. McCreary—all of Buffalo. Buffalo offices, Nos. 82 and 84 Exchange street.

MICHIGAN CENTRAL RAILROAD COMPANY.

This prosperous company was originally organized in 1836, under the name of the Detroit & St. Joseph railroad. Before completing any portion it was sold in 1837 to the State of Michigan, and constructed as follows: Detroit to Ypsilanti in 1838; Ypsilanti to Ann Arbor in 1839; Ann Arbor to Jackson in 1841; Jackson to Marshall, 1844; Marshall to Battle Creek, 1845; Battle Creek to Kalamazoo, 1846. About March 28th, 1846, the present company (Michigan Central) was incorporated under a special charter, and the railroad and property purchased from the State, taking possession thereof September 24th, 1846, and completing the road as follows: Kalamazoo to Niles in 1848; Niles to New Buffalo in 1849; New Buffalo to Michigan City in 1850; Michigan City to Chicago in 1852. The main line extends from Buffalo to Chicago, via Niagara Falls and Detroit, 536 miles, with branch lines connecting all important towns and cities in the State of

Michigan, aggregating 1,027, making the mileage of the entire system 1,563, with 140 miles of second and 576 miles of side track—in all 2,259 miles—all steel rails. * The motive power consists of 293 freight and 126 passenger engines—total 419. Of passenger coaches there are 293, of dining cars 7, of freight cars 12,997 ; total cars, 13,297. Number of employes averages 9,500. Through passengers carried in 1886, 93,058 ; way passengers, 2,826,381. Through freights, 1,607,557 tons; local freights, 3,928,719 tons. Income for year, $12,250,000; outlay, 8,350,000 ; profits, $3,900,000.

The Michigan Central Railroad Company is comparatively a new institution in the city of Buffalo, having gained an entrance into this city through the acquisition of the Canada Southern Railway Company three years ago, and in order to show its importance it seems but proper to state that it has on its schedules during the winter months 96 passenger trains, and during the summer months about 110. It runs five through trains daily between Buffalo and Chicago. The time consumed by the fastest trains between Buffalo and Chicago, a distance of 536 miles, is fourteen hours and forty-five minutes, an average speed of about thirty-eight miles per hour, which fact is sufficient evidence that the track and equipment is first-class. The Michigan Central's principal eastern connections are the New York Central & Hudson River and Boston & Albany roads, over which through cars are run between Boston, New York & Chicago via Buffalo. Connections at Buffalo are also made with the West Shore, New York, Lake Erie & Western, Delaware, Lackawanna & Western, Lehigh Valley, Buffalo, Rochester & Pittsburg, and Buffalo, New York & Philadelphia, and at Suspension Bridge with the New York Central and Rome, Watertown & Ogdensburg roads. Hence it will be observed that the Michigan Central is the connecting link between Buffalo and Chicago in the great through line across the American continent. At Chicago connections are made with all lines diverging. The general offices of the road are at Grand Central depot, New York ; Central depot, foot of Third street, Detroit; Nos. 183 to 189 Dearborn street, Chicago ; No. 57 Exchange street, Buffalo. Officers: C. Vanderbilt, chairman board of directors, New York; H. B. Ledyard, president and general manager, Detroit ; E. D. Worcester, vice-president and secretary, New York ; Henry Pratt, treasurer, New York ; D. A. Waterman, auditor, Detroit ; E. C. Brown, general superintendent, Detroit ; John E. Crampton, general Eastern freight agent ; W. R. Busenbark, Eastern passenger agent, Buffalo.

DELAWARE, LACKAWANNA & WESTERN.

This company was chartered in 1853, and the road, 888.86 miles in length, completed in 1882. It is double track, all steel rails, and superbly constructed, the equipment consisting of 505 engines, 369 passenger and 34,231 freight cars. A branch road to Rochester is projected. General offices of the company, New York city. President, Samuel Sloan ; general manager, W. F. Hallstead ; assistant superintendent, Buffalo division, F. A. Seabert ; general Western passenger agent, Ira S. Beers, No. 11 Exchange street, Buffalo.

LEHIGH VALLEY RAILROAD.

This road is Buffalo's chief source of anthracite coal supply, and is a most important adjunct to the manufacturing and shipping interests of the city. Its total coal tonnage for the year ending November 30th, 1886, was : Anthracite, 6,656,474; bituminous, 45,262; total, 6,701,736 tons, an increase of 109,090 tons over 1883, the previous year of heaviest shipments. Miscellaneous freight carried, 3,041,016.66 tons; number of passengers, 2,664,235; total gross earnings, $8,744,756.48; expenses, $5,293,816.56; net receipts, $3,450,939.92. The total miles of steel track are 619.14. The equipment consists of 329 engines, 120 passenger and parlor cars, 1 pay car, 62 baggage, express and combination cars, and 42,089 cars of all other classes. The officers are: Elisha P. Wilbur, president; Charles Hartshorne, vice-president; Robert H. Sayre, second vice-president; Wm. C. Alderson, treasurer; John R. Fanshawe, secretary; H. Stanley Goodwin, general superintendent. General offices, Bethlehem, Pa.

WEST SHORE RAILROAD.

(N. Y. C. & H. R. R. Co., LESSEE.)

J. D. Layng, general manager; E. V. W. Rossiter, treasurer, Grand Central depot, New York; P. B. McLennan, general counsel; J. W. Musson, traffic manager; F. L. Pomeroy, general freight agent; Chas. E. Lambert, general passenger agent; Isaac P. Chambers, comptroller, Grand Central depot, New York; C. W. Bradley, general superintendent, Weehawken, N. J.; L. S. Greves, general Eastern freight agent, No. 363 Broadway, New York; H. B. Jagoe, general Eastern passenger agent, New York; A. A. Smith, New England passenger agent, Boston, Mass.; Edson J. Weeks, general agent, Buffalo; Wm. Caldwell, general Western passenger agent, Chicago, Ill. General offices: No. 5 Vanderbilt Avenue, New York; freight and passenger office, No. 363 Broadway, New York. Buffalo passenger office, No. 1 Exchange street, corner Main.

LAKE SHORE & MICHIGAN SOUTHERN RAILROAD.

John Newell, president and general manager, Cleveland, Ohio; E. Gallup, assistant general manager, Cleveland, Ohio; Edwin D. Worcester, secretary and treasurer, New York; C. P. Leland, auditor, Cleveland Ohio; P. P. Wright, general superintendent, Cleveland, Ohio; C. B. Couch. superintendent Eastern division, Cleveland, Ohio; J. T. R. McKay, general freight agent, Cleveland, Ohio; A. J. Smith, general passenger and freight agent, Cleveland, Ohio; E. C. Luce, assistant general passenger and ticket agent, Cleveland, Ohio; L. H. Clarke, chief engineer, Cleveland, Ohio; Geo. W. Stevens, superintendent motive power, Cleveland, Ohio; William Kline, superintendent telegraph, Toledo, Ohio; J. A. Burch, Eastern and Southern passenger agent, office over No. 178 Main street, Buffalo, N. Y. General office, Cleveland, Ohio; New York office, Grand Central depot: Buffalo offices—D. Kenyon, freight agent, Louisiana street and Hamburg canal; F. W. Burrows, ticket agent, No. 21 Exchange street; J. Q. Adams, ticket agent, Exchange Street depot.

GRAND TRUNK RAILWAY.

General offices, Montreal, Canada; London office, 9 New Broad street, London, England. Officers—Joseph Hickson, general manager, Montreal: L. J. Seargeant, traffic manager, Montreal; W. Wainwright, assistant manager, Montreal; James Stephenson, superintendent, Grand Trunk section, Montreal; C. Stiff, superintendent Southern section, Hamilton: E. P. Hannaford, chief engineer, Montreal; Joseph Hopson, chief engineer. G. W. section, Hamilton; William Edgar, general passenger agent, Montreal;

John Porteous, general freight agent, Montreal; T. Tandy, through traffic general freight agent, Detroit, Mich.; Robert Wright, treasurer, Montreal; T. B. Hawson, traffic auditor, Montreal; H. W. Walker, accountant, Montreal; John Taylor, general storekeeper, Montreal. Agents in Buffalo— Thomas D. Sheridan, passenger agent, corner Exchange and Washington streets; S. S. McCrea, freight agent, No. 177 Washington, corner Exchange; also River Street and Black Rock freight depots.

NEW YORK, CHICAGO & ST. LOUIS (NICKEL-PLATE) RAILROAD.

Runs from Buffalo to Chicago, 524 miles. General offices, Cleveland, Ohio. Officers—D. W. Caldwell, receiver, Cleveland, Ohio; Wm. K. Vanderbilt, president, New York; F. W. Vanderbilt, secretary and treasurer, New York; J. P. Curry, auditor, Cleveland, Ohio; Lewis Williams, general manager, Cleveland, Ohio; G. B. Spriggs, general freight agent, Cleveland, Ohio; B. F. Horner, general passenger agent, Cleveland, Ohio; G. H. Kimball, superintendent Eastern division, Cleveland, Ohio; C. D. Gorham, superintendent Western division, Fort Wayne, Ind.; P. G. Murphy, commercial agent, No. 23 Exchange street, Buffalo; F. J. Moore, ticket agent, No. 23 Exchange street, Buffalo.

BUFFALO, NEW YORK & ERIE RAILROAD.

Daniel N. Lockwood, president; John C. Gray, secretary and treasurer, New York. Buffalo office, over Western Savings Bank.

BUFFALO CREEK RAILROAD.

Forming a line of road from the cattle-yards at the New York Central railroad to the lands on the south side of Buffalo harbor. Officers—F. L. Danforth, president; R. F. Goodman, general superintendent; Wm. H. Sayre, secretary and treasurer. Office, Hamburg turnpike.

COMMERCE.

THE LAKES AND THE CANALS—EXTENT AND IMPORTANCE
OF WATER COMMUNICATIONS.

THE
GREAT WATER ROUTE
FROM
THE ATLANTIC TO THE PACIFIC,
E. B. GUTHRIE, C.E..

FROM the above map (for which we are indebted to the courtesy of John Wilkeson, Esq., one of Buffalo's oldest and most public-spirited citizens) it will be seen that this is the focal point at which meet the direct and shortest lines of trade and travel between Boston, New York, Philadelphia, Baltimore and all North Atlantic ports, the lake cities, and, via the Northern Pacific railroad, the great Northwest and the Pacific coast. By way of Buffalo also lies the shortest and most practicable route to Canada and British Columbia. The vast hard wheat regions of Northern Minnesota, Dakota and British America are brought into almost direct water communication, through Buffalo, with all principal Atlantic ports, and the products of Eastern Oregon and Eastern Washington must seek a market via this route. Much of the Japanese and Chinese trade must also pass over the same route to the Eastern States and Europe. The grain of Nebraska, Wyoming and Idaho naturally seeks an outlet via Duluth to the East.

One of the great needs of the cold Northwest is fuel, and anthracite is the favorite. Buffalo is the only lake port from which it can be profitably shipped, for the reason that returning wheat and ore vessels can carry it at very low rates, thus making a profit both ways and offering vessel-owners an inducement which will enable them to influence shipments to this port in preference to any other, and particularly in slack times when freights are scarce. This is an advantage of which no other lake port can ever deprive Buffalo, and cannot but insure her continued ascendancy. For the same reason vessels carrying ore for the Pennsylvania furnaces will eventually prefer to unload here and carry return cargoes of coal to Lake Superior ports. A project is on foot to connect the St. Louis river with the Mississippi, and another to connect Lake Winnipeg with the Red River of the North. It is claimed the expense will be comparatively small, and if ever accomplished the scheme will be in line with the far-reaching plans of De Witt Clinton when advocating the construction of the Erie canal, and extend our navigable waters to the eastern base of the Rocky Mountains, bringing through the lakes to Buffalo, and through the canal and the Hudson to New York, at moderate cost for freight, the bulk of agricultural and mineral products of all that mighty territory.

THE LAKES.

It would be difficult to overestimate the value to commerce, or the beneficent influence exerted upon the progress and prosperity of the whole country, of the magnificent chain of fresh water lakes—appropriately called inland seas—that stretch away for many hundreds of miles from Buffalo to Duluth, bearing upon their broad bosoms the peaceful fleets of two mighty insular empires, carrying the products of a domain greater and grander than all Europe. A severe storm last October did serious damage to the Government breakwater and to the Buffalo harbor improvements. Both members of Congress from this county have labored for an increased appropriation, not only for repairs but for the deepening of the harbor and river channel to Tonawanda, and were successful, a dispatch of March 2d informing the public that the sums appropriated in the River and Harbor bill, as finally passed, for New York waters were : Buffalo $225,000, Dunkirk $5,000, Gowanus bay $10,000. The "Cullom amendment," with respect to the Hennepin canal, was incorporated in the bill. Unfortunately the hour at which the bill was passed prevented its formal engrossment in time to receive the President's official approval, and it consequently failed to become a law.

An intelligent appreciation, widely extended, of the value of the lakes to the commerce of the nation would dispel all factious opposition to the appropriation of all the funds requisite to render them the most valuable and useful inland waters on the globe.

Referring to Buffalo's breakwater and harbor facilities, some time ago, Capt. Mahan, an old lake skipper, said: " Let us compare our situation with that of cities in the Old World. Antwerp is a city of Belgium not quite as large as Buffalo. It had 205,000 people at the last census. But the commercial activity there ! In 1885 I visited its great docks and learned that for thirty years the city had spent $500,000 a year in harbor improvements alone, independent of about three times that amount given by the Belgian

Government. Now Buffalo not only does not spend a cent for such things, but it is not even making a live effort to secure a fair appropriation from Congress. Here is Cleveland going away ahead in this respect. The breakwater there was begun after the Buffalo breakwater, yet it is now considerably the longer, and the harbor is much better protected."

At a meeting of the Merchants' Exchange, held on the 3d of the present month (March), Gen. Graves presented a report of the harbor committee, which set forth that a visit had been paid to Capt. Mahan, U. S. Engineer in charge of the harbor. They had been shown the plans for repairing the breakwater with stone two feet below and twelve feet above low-water mark. The report speaks of the inefficiency of the breakwater, refers to the great storm of October 14th last, and adds that wharves are expected to be built along the lake and that vessels are to lie behind the breakwater. " Suppose," it continues, "that such had been the case last October, who can estimate the damage that would have ensued?" The new structure should, in the opinion of the committee, be made five feet higher than the highest part of the present structure. The following was appended to the report, which was adopted and forwarded as indicated :

"*Whereas,* The United States has spent in times past large sums of money for the improvement of the harbor of Buffalo, N. Y.; and

"*Whereas,* The northern end of the superstructure of the breakwater at Buffalo is to be rebuilt of stone ; and

"*Whereas,* The height of the proposed new superstructure is, in view of the very poor anchorage afforded by the bed of the lake, and in view of the very probable near construction of piers and wharves on the lake front, wholly insufficient to protect the vessels lying inside the breakwater during heavy gales, such, for example, as the one which raged here on October 14, 1886 ; therefore be it

"*Resolved,* By the Buffalo Merchants' Exchange, that the honorable the Secretary of War be petitioned to reconsider the plans which he has approved for the reconstruction of the superstructure of the breakwater at Buffalo, N. Y.; and be it further

"*Resolved,* That the Buffalo Merchant's Exchange protest as strongly as may be against the lack of height proposed for said superstructure ; and be it further

"*Resolved,* That the honorable the Secretary of War be petitioned to cause the height of the proposed superstructure to be increased at least five feet, so that vessels lying behind the breakwater may be adequately protected ; and be it further

"*Resolved,* That the honorable the Secretary of War be petitioned to cause to be taken such action as may be necessary at the earliest possible moment, as the engineer in charge of the improvement of Buffalo harbor is now engaged on the estimates for carrying on the work according to the present plans.

" *Resolved,* That a copy of the foregoing be sent to the Chief of Engineers at Washington."

Gen. Graves supported the report in a speech of some length, and it was adopted without opposition.

Further along will be found the tables showing Buffalo's interest in lake commerce. In this place we wish merely to present some interesting figures showing the increase of tonnage in seventy years, from

3

1816 to 1886. In the former year, according to David Thomas' "Travels through the Western Country," the following list comprised all the craft plying these waters:

VESSELS.	TONS.	VESSELS.	TONS.
American Eagle	48.67–95	Leopard	18.00–95
Aurora	31.69 "	Michigan	132.36 "
Black Snake	21.08 "	Monroe	28.70 "
Boxer	16.60 "	Maria	24.28 "
Dove	13.55 "	Miami	10.46 "
Commodore Decatur	49.14 "	Merchant	21.51 "
Diligence	32.38 "	Nautilus	23.00 "
Diana	8.00 "	Neptune	61.64 "
Experiment	29.69 "	Olive Branch	14.19 "
Erie	77.41 "	Commodore Perry	42.50 "
Eagle	28.03 "	Salem Packet	27.00 "
Eliza	23.82 "	Buffalo Packet	12.00 "
Franklin	73.00 "	Paulina	27.25 "
Firefly	24.09 "	Pilot	27.05 "
Friendship	50.10 "	Perseverance	28.65 "
George Washington	99.73 "	Ranger	16.79 "
Governor Cass	30.58 "	Superior	70.73 "
General Scott	20.28 "	Lucy Jane	15.00 "
General Jackson	60.00 "	Traveler	22.23 "
General Brown	31.22 "	Union	104.30 "
General Wayne	85.39 "	Unknown	35.08 "
Hannah	48.73 "	Venus	14.00 "
Hercules	59.18 "	Widow's Son	40.79 "
Hornet	11.64 "	Wasp	18.00 "
Industry	"	Wolf	28.78 "
Independence	21.00 "	Not enumerated	200.87 "

Total lake tonnage.. 2008.00

In comparison with the above the appended table, showing the number and total tonnage of lake craft of all kinds for 1886, must be very gratifying to all interested in navigation and shipbuilding. It is proper to state that the figures are collated from the Inland Lloyd's Reports, and that several new vessels have been built and put into commission since their compilation —notably the Susquehanna, the largest, costliest and finest iron screw steamer on the lakes, built at Buffalo:

BUILD AND RIG.	TOTAL.		BUFFALO.	
	No.	TONNAGE.	No.	TONNAGE.
Side-wheel Steamers	42	12,580	..	......
Propellers	879	240,342	94	65,971
Schooners	704	185,142	21	9,502
Lake Barges	319	121,565	29	11,608
St. Lawrence River Barges	2	375	..	......
Totals	1946	560,004	144	87,381

The year 1886 was one of unusual misfortune to lake craft, as will be seen from the appended table, which includes only vessels sailing from United States ports. Of Canadian craft wrecked there were 33 schooners, 9 propellers, 6 barges, 1 steamer and 1 tug. The loss of life was 138, against 85 for 1885.

Date	Rig	Name of Vessel	Tonnage	Owner	Port of Hail	When Bl't	Lives Lost	Where Wrecked	Class	Value
April 1	Barge	Star of Hope	267	Pickle	Algonac	1864		Point au Pelee	† 1	$ 2,500
July 6	Propeller	Oconto	447	Colwell	Port Huron	1872		St. Lawrence R.	†	18,000
July 8	Propeller	Milwaukee	192	Howard	Manistee	1886		Lake Michigan	B 2	8,000
July 14	Schooner	Hercules	80			1854		Lake Michigan	*	
July 14	Schooner	Coaster	85	Nelson	Chicago	1867		Chicago	*	
July 18	Propeller	A. Booth (tug)	38	A. Booth	Buffalo	1882		Lake Superior	A 1	14,000
Aug. 27	Propeller	H. Carr	107	Carr	Chicago	1877		Port Colborne	†	2,000
Sept. 1	Schooner	J. F. Tracy	161	Smith	Chicago	1855		Beaver Island	A 2	
Sept. 2	Schooner	F. J. King	266	Dunham	"	1867		Lake Michigan	*	9,000
Sept. 15	Schooner	John Bean	149	McDonald	"	1867		Muskegon	A 2	9,000
Sept. 30	Schooner	G. M. Case	327	Morton		1874	3	Lake Erie	A 2	7,000
Oct. 14	Schooner	Nevada	303	Barker	Oswego	1867	8	Fairport	A 2	9,000
Oct. 14	Schooner	Belle Mitchell	304	Lefevre		1874	2	Lake Erie	A 9	9,000
Oct. 14	Schooner	O. M. Bond	259	Bradley	Cleveland	1873	5	Rondeau	A 2	7,000
Oct. 14	Propeller	S. Chamberlain	964			1873		Lake Michigan	A 2	65,000
Oct. 14	Steamer	Lizzie Sutton	93	Whitney	Detroit	1870		Lake Superior	A 2¾	7,000
Oct. 19	Schooner	Eureka	314	Brown	Green Bay	1872		Lake Superior	A 2	7,000
Oct. 30	Schooner	W. L. Brown	295	Bradley	Cleveland	1880		Green Bay	A 2	25,000
Oct. 21	Schooner	S. J. Tilden	382	Mitchel		1869		St. Clair River		25,000
Oct. 23	Propeller	S. Neff	198	Van Anken	E. Saginaw	1872		Edward's Island	A 2	9,000
Oct. 24	Propeller	William Rudolph	209	Pelton	Vermilion	1860		Lake St. Clair	A 2½	6,000
Oct.	Propeller	M. Stalker	956	Murphy	Detroit	1863		Clay Banks	A 2	
Nov. 5	Schooner	Sea Star	95	Fellows		1855	1	Lake Michigan	*	8,000
Nov. 5	Schooner	Detroit	300	Mitchell	Detroit	1872		Lake Michigan	A 2	6,000
Nov. 5	Schooner	City of Sheboygan	246	Keith	Chicago	1871		Lake Michigan	A 2	24,000
Nov. 5	Schooner	Ellen Spry	316	Becker	Chicago	1873		Iloe Island	A 2	10,000
Nov. 7	Schooner	Lafrinier	395	Nicoll	Cleveland	1862		Kelley's Island	B 1	50,000
Nov. 12	Propeller	Northwest	1638	Blanchard	Detroit	1876	3	Skillagalee	B 1	3,000
Nov. 17	Barge	P. M. Dickinson	371	Gilchrist	Detroit	1860		Kewaunee	B 1	8,500
Nov. 17	Barge	Emerald	273	Corrigon	Detroit	1808	1	Kewaunee	B 1	9,000
Nov. 18	Schooner	Florida	294	Brezeinmeister	Vermillion	1869	10	Marquette	A 2	10,000
Nov. 18	Schooner	Lucerne	682	Menea Bros.	Cleveland	1873	7	Lake Superior	B 1	2,500
Nov. 18	Schooner	Helen	113	Finley	Chicago	1867		Muskegon	A 2	2,500
Nov. 18	Schooner	South Haven	114		Milwaukee	1867	7	Muskegon	A 2	13,000
Nov. 18	Schooner	Pathinder	603	M. H. L. Co.	Racine	1869	7	Two Rivers	A 2¾	15,000
Nov. 18	Barge	Minnekanne	480	M. B. Line	Racine	1873	5	Frankfort	A 2	23,504
Nov. 18	Schooner	Marianette	659	O. C. & T. Co.	Ogdensburg	1873	7	Frankfort	A 2	3,000
Nov. 18	Barge	Mady	100	Allen		1877		Brighton	B 2	
Nov. 18	Schooner	Ida Walker	217	Congar		1867		Brighton	*	5,000
Nov. 18	Schooner	Queen of the Lakes	347	Smith	Muskegon	1858	5	Brighton	B 2	3,000
Nov. 18	Schooner	L. J. Conway	86	Powers	Chicago	1873		Whitehall	*	3,000
Nov. 18	Schooner	Milwaukee Belle	251	Chavaley	Chicago	1856		Sheboygan	B 2	3,000
Nov. 22	Schooner	Belle Walbridge	237	Merrick	Detroit	1857		Beaver Island	*	7,000
Nov. 25	Schooner	Republic	298	Rice	Chicago	1854		Grand Island	*	3,000
Nov. 25	Schooner	North Star	215	Hend	Chicago	1855	1	Lake Ontario	B 1	7,000
Nov. 25	Schooner	Metropolis	234	Quonce	Oswego	1857		Old Mission.	A 2	6,000
Nov. 28	Schooner	Comanche	306	Osweyo	Oswego	1867		Sackett's Harbor	A 2	6,000
Nov. 29	Schooner	Forest Queen	167	Nicol	Detroit	1853		Indian Point	*	8,000
Nov. 29	Schooner	A. P. Wright	23	Dumpsey	Detroit	1877		Manistee	*	8,000
Dec. 1	Tug	Matilda	299	Pinet		1863		Saginaw Bay	*	3,500
Dec. 2	Barge	Ariadne	172	Ure	E. Saginaw	1867	4	Mexico Bay	*	3,000
	Schooner									
Totals			**23,781**				**138**			**$549,000**

* Not insurable; value estimated.   † Vessel loaded, or survey not allowed by owners.

RECEIPTS AND SHIPMENTS BY LAKE AND CANAL.

The subjoined figures are from advance sheets of the official reports of the Merchants' Exchange :

THE LAKE.

The amount of grain and flour received at Buffalo by lake during the season of 1886 has been exceeded but once in the history of Buffalo; that was during the season of 1880, yet in 1878 and 1879 more grain of all kinds was received than in 1886. Every year shows increased milling facilities out West, and a consequent increase in the movement of flour. In 1886 there was an increase of 1,381,432 barrels of flour over 1885. Compared with the year last named, there was an increase of 13,694,930 bushels of wheat, an increase of 5,249,068 bushels of corn, an increase of 174,257 bushels of oats, an increase of 186,167 bushels of barley, and a decrease of 86,879 bushels of rye. The total increase in all grain over 1885 is 19,217,548 bushels, and in all grain, flour reduced to wheat, 26,124,703 bushels. The receipts of lumber compared with 1885 show an increase of 46,656,952 feet; in lath and shingles there is also a large increase, but a decrease in staves. With the steady growth of agricultural operations and increase of products of the forest and mines at the West, the prospect of a steady augmentation of lake shipments in the future is very bright indeed. An assurance of the maintenance and improvement of the canals is all that is necessary to render Buffalo the principal lake port in point of receipts.

Statement showing the receipts of most articles by lake during the season of lake navigation, 1886 :

Flour, bbls ...	2,041,933	Logs, ft	4,729,150
Flour, scks...	2,348,275	Lard, tcs......	205,193
Wheat, bu....	40,921,205	Lead, pigs....	104,391
Corn, bu... .	25,494,838	Lead, tns.....	90
Oats, bu......	864.356	Malt, bu... ..	19,042
Barley, bu....	755.184	Metal, scks...	114,954
Rye, bu......	151,025	Oatmeal, bbls.	5,414
Peas, bu......	34,808	Oilcake, scks.	205.450
Beans, bu ...	1,700	Oil, bbls......	4,797
Alcohol, bbls.	393	Pig iron, tns..	18,376
Ashes, caks ..	337	R. R. ties, No.	48,833
Bullion, bars.	880	Rags, scks	3,091
Bacon, tcs....	305	Shingles, No..	66,204,450
Copper, tns ..	21,899	Stavebolts cds	9,199
Copper, bbls.	697	Seed, flax, bu.	54,454
Copper, pigs..	81,790	Spelter, plates	41,752
Copper, plates	2,300	Stearine, bbls.	797
Cotton, bls ..	1,786	Sugar, bbls...	375
Coal, tns . .	520	Starch, bxs...	10,521
Cornmeal, bbl	3,188	Starch, bbls..	300
Feed, bgs ...	353,688	Silver ore, sck	38,277
Feed, tns.....	780	Silver ore. tns	900
Fish, pkgs ...	25,083	Tallow, bbls..	8,046
Glucose, bbls.	11,343	Staves, No.....	860
Grease, tcs...	5,709	Tobacco, pkgs	10,416
Hides, bls....	1,024	Wool, bls	10,786
Hay, bls......	1,307	Wood, cds....	765
Hay, tns......	218	Zinc, csks. ...	106
Hair, bls	60		
Hoops, No.. .	406,000		
Iron ore, tns.	21,534		
Lumber, ft...275,586,051			
Lath, No..... 16,210,400			

Comparative statement showing the receipts of leading articles by lake at Buffalo during the season of navigation for three years :

	Lake opened April 25, 1884.	Lake opened May 2, 1885.	Lake opened April 16, 1886.
Flour, bbls	1,823 143	3,008,778	4,390,210
Wheat, bu.... ...	33,671,756	27,226,275	40,921,205
Corn, bu.........	16,051,163	20,245,770	25,494,838
Oats, bu.........	3,113.781	690.099	864,356
Barley, bu.	537,937	569.017	755.184
Rye, bu....	2,376,186	237,904	151,025
Coal, tons	1,841	522	520
Copper, tons	13,464	17,832	21,899
Copper, bbls......	3.317	731	697
Feed, bags.......	139,855	209,084	353.688
Hoops, No........	390,000	696,000	406,000
Iron ore, tons ...	8.863	8,071	21,534
Lumber, ft.	240,139,090	228,929,099	275,586,051
Lath, No.......	16,930,850	12,046,500	16,210,400
Lard, tcs..	34,777	45,120	205,193
Lead, pigs.... ...	63,637	72,229	104,391
Lead, tons........	1,250	70	90
Oilcake, sacks...	110,489	130.793	205,450
Oatmeal, bbls	1,500	6,944	5,414
Pig iron, tons....	6,575	10,974	18,376
Pork, bbls........	41,520	3,940	26,983
Railroad ties, No.	70 664	21,831	44,853
Staves, No.	797.115	2,940,559	1,490,500
Shingles, No......	41,358,500	53,495,250	66,204,450
Stavebolts, cds...	7,369	15,000	9,199
Seed, flax, bu ...	998,022	2,752,860	2,960,163
Seed, bags	58,423	40,749	54,454
Wool, bales	4,224	16,438	10,786

Comparative statement showing the aggregate receipts of flour and grain at Buffalo by lake, during the past three years:

	1884.	1885.	1886.
Flour, bbls........	1,823,143	3,008,778	4,300,210
Wheat, bu..... ...	33,671,756	27,226,275	40,921,205
Corn, bu...........	16,051,163	20,245,770	25,494,838
Oats, bu...........	3,113,781	690,099	864,356
Barley, bu	537,937	569,017	755,184
Rye, bu.......	2,376,186	237,904	151,025
Total grain, bu..	55,750,823	48,969,065	68,186,608

Statement showing the rates of freight on wheat and corn from Chicago to Buffalo on the dates given:

	1884.		1885.		1886.	
	Wheat.	Corn.	Wheat.	Corn.	Wheat.	Corn.
May 4.......	2¼	2	3	2¾	3¼	3
May 11.......	2¼	2	2¼	2	3½	3¼
May 18.......	2	1¾	1¾	1½	3	2¾
May 25.......	2¼	2	1½	1¼	2½	2½
June 1... ...	2¼	1¾	1½	1¼	2½	2¼
June 8.......	1¾	1½	1½	1¼	2¼	2
June 15......	2½	2	1⅛	1	2½	2¼
June 22......	2½	2¼	1½	1¼	3¼	3
June 29......	2¼	2	1⅜	1¼	3¼	3
July 6..	2	1¾	2	1¾	2¼	2
July 13.......	2	1¾	1½	1¼	2½	2¼
July 20	2	1¾	1¼	1	3	2¾
July 27	2	1¾	1	1	3	2¾
Aug. 3	1¾	1½	2	1¾	3	2¾
Aug. 10	1¾	1½	1¾	1½	3	2¾
Aug. 17	1¼	1⅛	1¾	1¼	3¼	3
Aug. 24	2	1¾	2¼	2	3¼	3
Aug. 31	2¼	2	1⅞	1⅝	4	3¾
Sept. 7.......	2¼	2½	1⅜	1½	5¼	5
Sept. 14......	2	1¾	1¾	1½	4½	4
Sept. 21......	2	1¾	1½	1¼	4	3¾
Sept. 28	1¾	1½	1½	1¼	4½	4¼
Oct. 5	1¾	1½	1⅞	1¾	5	4¾
Oct. 12.......	1⅝	1⅝	2½	2¼	5	4¾
Oct. 19.......	1¾	1½	2¾	2½	4¾	4¼
Oct. 26.......	2½	2	3	2¾	4¾	4¼
Nov. 2.......	2¾	2½	3¼	3	4¼	4
Nov. 9.......	2¼	2	2¾	2½	4½	4
Nov. 16......	2	2	2½	2¼	3¼	3
Nov. 23	2¼	2	2	2	4¼	4
Nov. 30......	4¼	4	3¼	3	5¼	4¾

Statement showing the aggregate receipts of grain and the total receipts of flour reduced to its equivalent in wheat at Buffalo for the past forty-five years:

	Grain, bu.	Grain, including flour, bu.
1842................	2,015,928	5,687,463
1843.......	2,015,025	6,642,610
1844................	2,365,568	6,910,718
1845............ ...	1,848,040	5,581,700
1846...............	6,493,522	13,386,167
1847...	9,868,187	19,153,187
1848....	7,396,912	14,641,012
1849................	8,028,013	14,665,183
1850................	6,618,003	12,059,556
1851................	11,078,741	17,740,781
1852......	13,392,937	20,390,504
1853	11,078,741	15,956,526
1854...	18,553,455	22,252,235
1855................	19,788,473	24,472,278
1856....	20,123,667	25,763,907
1857..	15,348,930	10,578,690
1858................	20,202,244	26,812,890
1859...	14,429,069	21,530,622
1860............ ..	31,441,440	37,053,115
1861..	50,682,646	61,460,601
1862.......	58,642,314	72,872,454
1863................	49,845,062	64,735,510
1864................	41,044,096	51,177,146
1865................	42,473,228	51,415,183
1866..	51,880,342	58,388,067
1867....	43,079,079	50,168,064
1868...	42,573,125	50,197,215
1869................	37,456,131	45,489,276
1870................	38,208,039	45,477,604
1871................	61,319,313	67,529,158
1872................	58,703,606	62,550,566
1873............ ...	65,499,955	70,962,520
1874................	55,665,198	62,525,153
1875........	52,883,451	57,967,661
1876.	44,207,121	48,184,036
1877................	61,822,292	65,145,407
1878...	79,823,548	84,540,863
1879................	74,105,455	78,547,578
1880................	105,184,136	110,465,866
1881................	54,288,351	58,088,071
1882........	50,321,841	57,298,316
1883................	64,264,483	73,126,028
1884................	55,750,823	64,866,538
1885.......	48,969,065	64,012,955
1886........	68,186,608	90,137,658

Comparative statement showing the shipments of a few leading articles from Buffalo by lake for thirteen years:

	Coal, tons.	Cement, bbls.	Salt, bbls.	Salt, tons.
1886.........	1,472,924	368,914	191,890	2,831
1885.	1,416,547	269,271	137,093	8,961
1884.........	1,359,980	195,640	64,510	7,246
1883.........	1,177,074	214,724	118,422	13,786
1882........	964,336	184,327	96,053	10,937
1881.........	841,312	164,521	112,812	12,341
1880.........	246,050	156,733	234,826	16,842
1879.........	513,580	114,802	253,647	26,385
1878.	325,676	85,093	243,308	18,107
1877.........	439,399	114,402	352,638	6,665
1876.........	356,970	156,410	261,640	2,220
1875	541,812	165,436	356,410	20,410
1874.........	396,564	156,371	461,512	5,000

Statement showing the opening and closing of lake and canal navigation at Buffalo during the past thirteen years:

	Lake opened.	Canal opened.	Canal closed.	Days open.
1874...	April 18	May 5	Dec. 5	215
1875..........	May 2	May 18	Nov. 27	194
1876	May 6	May 4	Dec. 5	216
1877	April 17	May 8	Dec. 7	214
1878.....	Mar. 16	April 15	Dec. 7	287
1879	April 24	May 8	Dec. 6	213
1880..........	Mar. 18	April 20	Nov. 21	215
1881..........	May 1	May 17	Dec. 8	206
1882....	Mar. 26	April 11	Dec. 7	212
1883.... ...	April 28	May 7	Dec. 1	209
1884... ...	April 22	May 6	Dec. 1	210
1885	May 2	May 11	Dec. 1	205
1886..........	April 16	May 1	Dec. 1	214

The Erie Canal.

The business of the canal during the season last closed has doubtless exceeded the expectations of its most ardent friends. Compared with 1885 there is an increase of 744 in the number of boats cleared; an increase of

13,857,943 bushels of wheat; a decrease of 186,202 bushels of corn; an increase of 145,104 bushels of barley; an increase of 129,512 bushels of flaxseed, and an increase of 10,325,492 feet of lumber. In the receipts, pig iron shows an increase of 84,413,164 lbs., the arrivals of this article being more than three times the amount which came to hand in 1885; the same is true of bloom and bar iron, which shows an increase of 76,636,130 lbs.

Comparative statement showing the shipments of most articles from Buffalo by canal for three years:

	1884	1885	1886
Lumber, ft..... ...	47,739,858	54,265,783	64,591,275
Staves, lbs..........	31,915,300	33,369,500	27,445,500
Shingles, M.	18,914	9,031	10,541
Flour, bbls	4,812	2,991	4,518
Wheat, bu...........	25,592,802	18,803,758	31,861,701
Corn, bu.............	6,941,741	12,731,611	12,545,408
Rye, bu..............	2,066,203	228,742	....
Barley, bu	205,603	138,190	283,294
Barley Malt, bu......	204,650	204,335	106,149
Oats, bu..	3,065,328	350,587	326,760
Bran, etc., lbs	1,795,574	1,331,491	924,000
Peas, bu.............	....	8,024	23,809
Clover seed, lbs	....	....	15,000
Flax seeds, lbs	16,347,965	84,080,948	91,851,705
Oil cake, lbs.........	1,575,000	628,000	2,073,000
Pig iron, lbs.........	5,375,010	7,637,780	11,520,480
Sundry mdse, lbs....	47,600	....	12,000
Stone lime, etc., lbs..	4,000,000	3,106,000	8,489,000
Bituminous coal, lbs.	63,915,781	54,064,066	39,352,687
Sundries, lbs........	3,383,792	3,370,500	5,285,460
Total boats cleared..	6,413	5,670	7,414

Statement showing the amount of grain shipped by canal from Buffalo, and points of destination of the same, during the season of 1886:

	Wheat.	Corn.	Oats.	Barley.
Lockport	348,229	16,488	....	...
Rochester	652,250	....	....	....
Utica	....	149,400	....	....
Geneva	....	....	.. .	96,911
Albion..........	500	3,000	....	....
Baldwinsville...	....	8,600	....	...
Ithaca	...	5,000	. ..	....
Gasport	2,500	3,000	....	....
Lyons..........	....	....	....	9,250
Fultonville.....	95,861	55,955	....	....
Oswego........	....	8,200	....	....
Phœnix........	15,979	....	....	....
Syracuse	157,808	148,937	....	2,959
Frankfort	....	16,000	....	....
Little Falls	....	91,925	...	....
Schenectady ...	26,800	790,922	61,700	....
Canajoharie....	....	33,855	....	....
Fort Plain	....	8,386	...	...
Troy.....	1,743,561	573,967	.. .	....
Albany	28,818,213	10,631,773	265,060	174,174
Totals	31,861,701	12,545,408	326,760	283,294
" 1885..	18,003,758	12,731,611	350,587	138,190

Shipments of flour and grain for three years:

Canal opened	May 7.	May 7.	May 1.
Flour, bbls.......	5,349	4,812	4,518
Wheat, bu.......	17,842,272	25,592,802	31,861,701
Corn, bu.........	18,472,804	6,941,741	12,545,408
Oats, bu.........	2,949,375	3,066,328	326,760
Barley, bu.......	283,962	204,603	283,294
Rye, bu..........	2,821,790	2,066,283	. ...
Total, bu......	42,370,223	37,871,757	45,017,163
Flo'r to wheat bu	26,745	24,060	22,590
Grand total, bu..	42,396,968	37,895,817	45,039,753

Receipts by canal for three years:

	1884.	1885.	1886.
Lumber, ft.. ...	1,554,894	124,278	1,030,074
Timber, cubic ft.	515,152	9,245	7,716
Barley, bu......	. ...	....	84,430
Apples, bbls.....	....	11,181	....
Dried fruit, bbls.	2,833,978	368,294	6,064,763
Pig iron, lbs....	61,562,711	39,095,910	123,509,074
Castings, etc. lbs.	399,-80	265,529	1,783,446
Bloom iron, lbs.	65,767,497	42,010,524	118,646,654
Phosphates, lbs.	83,290,653	68,575,092	107,712,279
Dom. salt, lbs...	50,156 570	24,517,300	14,742,225
Foreign salt, lbs.	24,476,793	28,993,906	26,676,265
Sugar, lbs.......	7,207,941	1,535,549	19,054,756
Molasses, lbs...	14,159,034	8,615,466	6,346,211
Coffee, lbs.	1,372,766	155,563	9,035,482
R. R. iron, lbs..	44,616,403	2,487,173	49,930,532
Crock'y, etc., lbs.	474,936	211,840	317,250
M'chandise, lbs.	94,000,951	50,798,945	115,267,550
Stone, etc., lbs.	308,689,853	295,909,676	342,297,632
Coal, lbs........	303,342,508	360,695,773	162,890,638
Sundries, lbs....	78,376,571	60,194,560	130,394,932

Statement showing the rate of freight on wheat, corn and lumber, from Buffalo to New York. on the dates named:

	1885.			1886.		
	Wheat, bu.	Corn, bu.	Lumb'r. ft.	Wheat, bu.	Corn, bu.	Lum'r. ft.
May 11...	5	4½	$2.65	5½	5	$2.50
May 18....	4½	4	2.65	6¼	5¾	2.50
May 25....	3¾	3⅛	2.30	5¾	5	2.50
June 1...	3¼	3	2.10	5	4½	2.50
June 8....	3¼	3	2.00	4¼	4	2.50
June 15....	3½	3¼	2.00	3¼	3	2.50
June 22....	3	3⅞	2.00	3¼	3	2.50
June 29....	3	3¼	2.00	3¾	3½	2 00
July 6....	3	2¾	2.00	3¾	3⅝	2 00
July 13....	3	2¾	2.00	3⅝	3¼	2.00
July 20....	3¼	3	2.00	4	3¾	2.00
July 27....	3⅛	2⅞	1.90	5	4½	2.00
Aug. 3...	3⅛	2⅞	1.90	5	4½	2.25
Aug. 10....	3½	3¼	1.90	4¾	4¼	2.25
Aug. 17....	3¾	3¼	1.90	5¼	4¾	2.15
Aug. 24....	4	3⅝	2.00	5¾	5¼	2.75
Aug. 31....	4¼	3⅞	2.00	6	5½	2.75
Sept. 7....	3⅝	3⅞	2.00	6	5½	2.75
Sept. 14 ...	3⅝	3⅛	2.10	6½	6	3.00
Sept. 21...	3⅝	3⅛	2.10	5⅝	5¾	3.00
Sept. 28...	3⅝	3⅛	2.10	5⅞	5⅜	3.00
Oct. 5....	3½	3¼	2.00	6	5⅝	3.00
Oct. 12....	3½	3¼	1.90	4¾	4¼	2.75
Oct. 19 ...	4	3⅝	1.90	5½	5	2.75
Oct. 26....	5	4½	2.00	5⅞	5¼	2.75
Nov. 2...	5½	5	2.50	5¼	5	2.75
Nov. 9...	5½	5	2.75	4½	4	2.75
Nov. 16....	4	3½	2.75	4⅜	4	2.75
Nov. 23....	5½	5	2.75	5¾	5	2.75

Canal clearances, 1886, 7,414.

Following are the shipments in bushels of grain by rail from the Buffalo elevators for the years noted :

	1886.	1885.	1884.
Wheat	7,792 632	4,832,616	3,360,152
Corn	12,380,886	5,928,151	8,503,104
Oats	484.717	462,259	249,233
Barley	219,064	90,610	67,131
Rye	42,000	6,900	217,629
Total bu	20,919,299	11,315,544	12,397,249

And total shipments for previous ten years:

1883	17,403,379	1879	16,308,526
1882	13,205,193	1878	19,136,668
1881	21,808,356	1877	14,235,805
1880	30,958,927	1876	13,672,782

The tonnage of the port of Buffalo, N. Y., for the fiscal year ending June 30, 1886, is shown by the following statement :

Iron propellers	8	Iron yachts	2
Iron tugs	2		—
Total			12
Total gross tonnage			14,365.17
Tugs	48	Propellers	50
Yachts	13	St'm canal b'ts.	9
Total			120
Total gross tonnage			64,598.83
Schooners			36
Total gross tonnage			18,312.87
Barges			25
Total gross tonnage			6,478.56
Canal boats			21
Total gross tonnage			2,772.13
Grand total, 1886	214 vessels—tonnage		106,517.56
Grand total, 1885	214 vessels—tonnage		112,011.60
Grand total, 1884	216 vessels—tonnage		110,304.56
Grand total, 1883	228 vessels—tonnage		118,347.62
Grand total, 1882	225 vessels—tonnage		110,180.50
Grand total, 1881	217 vessels—tonnage		100,815.43
Grand total, 1880	212 vessels—tonnage		99,543.69
Grand total, 1879	211 vessels—tonnage		97,734.46

Receipts and shipments of lumber were as follows for three years:

At Buffalo—receipts by lake—

	1886.	1885.	1884.
Lumber, ft	279,493,000	240,637,000	231,653,000
Shingles, No	58,582,000	52,716,000	37,616,000

Shipments by Canal.

| Lumber, ft | 64,591,250 | 54,264,750 | 47,739,850 |
| Shingles, No | 10,541,750 | 9,031,000 | 9,457,000 |

At Tonawanda—receipts by lake—

	1886.	1885.	1884.
Lumber, ft	505,425,400	408,631,000	493,268,200
Shingles, No	32,636,000		

Shipments by Canal.

| Lumber, ft | 347,932,840 | 355,230,400 | 384,455,640 |
| Shingles. No | 32,036,000 | 26,082,750 | 32,652,000 |

The following is a summary of the arrivals and departures of vessels, with their tonnage, in the district of Buffalo creek for the season of 1866 ; also, a comparative statement showing the aggregate figures for thirty-five years:

Arrivals—

Vessels in coastwise trade entered	2,928	2,239,477
American vessels entered from foreign ports	170	28,690
Foreign vessels entered from foreign ports	765	98,602
Total in 1886	3,863	2,366,829
Total in 1885	3,455	2,146,041
Increase in 1886	408	220,788

Clearances—

Vessels in coastwise trade cleared	2,984	2,267,174
American vessels cleared	166	23,603
Foreign vessels cleared	759	95,861
Total in 1886	3,909	2,386,638
Total in 1885	3,479	2,049,839
Increase in 1886	430	336,799

LIVE STOCK.

With one exception Buffalo boasts the largest and most complete stock-yards in the world—those at East Buffalo, under the superintendency of Mr. L. B. Crocker, of whom more extended mention is made on page 143. The comparative receipts and shipments for 1886, and for the six previous years, were as follows:

	RECEIPTS.					SHIPMENTS.			
Month.	Cattle, cars.	Hogs, cars.	Sheep, cars.	Horses, cars.	Month.	Cattle, cars.	Hogs, cars.	Sheep, cars.	Horses, cars.
January	2,156	2,842	1,162	77	January	1,868	1,971	931	50
February	1,757	1,913	713	121	February	1,634	1,398	683	120
March	1,895	1,655	639	217	March	1,726	1,267	626	214
April	1,893	1,833	602	199	April	1,840	1 371	477	178
May	2,086	2,330	504	201	May	1,954	1,701	512	185
June	2,208	1,863	775	155	June	2,084	1,387	559	152
July	3,170	1,758	775	127	July	2,700	1,200	612	103
August	3,234	2,111	824	137	August	2,902	1,397	629	115
September	2,796	2,137	799	124	September	2,464	1,476	634	109
October	2,990	2,979	929	114	October	2,727	2,249	734	105
November	3,199	3,367	801	77	November	3,918	2,547	619	76
December	2,697	3,126	987	79	December	2,446	1,924	665	87
Total	30,081	27,914	9,324	1,622	Total	27,362	19,898	7,681	1,494

RECEIPTS.—Continued.

Via	Cattle, cars.	Hogs, cars.	Sheep, cars.	Horses, cars.
L. S. & M. S. ...	15,816	16,247	4,063	1,200
N. Y. C. & St. L.	6,825	6,901	1,172	66
Grand Trunk....	2,640	1,510	2,594	182
Mich. Central....	4,631	3,090	1,416	163
B. & S. West.....	113	137	62	4
B., N. Y. & P....	53	16	15	7
N. Y., L. E. & W.	1	2	1	0
N. Y. C. & H. R.	2	2	1	0
Total, 1886.....30,081		27,914	9,324	1,622
Total, 1885.....25,228		22,721	10,053	1,244
Total, 1884.....29,860		21,120	7,562	1,375
Total, 1883.....35,515		20,692	8,110	1,004
Total, 1882.....37,115		17,902	7,300	1,094
Total, 1881.....38,653		16,357	5,562	1,022
Total, 1880.....46,258		19,581	5,156	1,293

SHIPMENTS.—Continued.

Via	Cattle, cars.	Hogs, cars.	Sheep, cars.	Horses, cars.
N. Y. C. & H. R.16,118	14,334	4,499	821	
Del. L. & W.....5,232	777	835	196	
N. Y., L. E. & W. 2,363	4,197	1,919	160	
West Shore 3,610	584	427	314	
B., N. Y. & P.... 39	6	1	3	
Total, 1886.....27,362	19,898	7,684	1,494	
Total, 1885.....21,346	16,594	6,654	1,160	
Total, 1884.....28,441	15,791	6,555	1,252	
Total, 1883.....32,735	15,730	6,916	999	
Total, 1882.....35,024	13,560	6,319	956	
Total, 1881.... 41,024	12,533	4,654	853	
Total, 1880 ...44,568	16,002	4,698	1,105	

GROWTH OF THE TRADE.

The following table shows the growth of the trade at this point from the year 1874 to 1886, inclusive:

Year.	Cattle, head.	Hogs, head.	Sheep, head.	Horses, head.
1874......	504,594	1,431,800	783,800	21,986
1875......	513,530	1,067,300	831,000	18,187
1876......	615,790	1,150,210	872,928	12,542
1877......	569,915	1,128,770	762,600	12,557
1878	657,809	2,063,765	1,032,225	13,602
1879......	633,556	1,916,015	1,019,600	20,976
1880	786,386	2,251,815	1,033,200	20,768
1881......	738,900	2,096,325	1,113,350	17,366
1882.....	630,955	1,965,350	1,460,000	17,376
1883	603,755	2,379,580	1,622,000	17,040
1884.....	507,620	2,428,500	1,512,400	22,000
1885	428,876	2,613,260	2,010,600	19,904
1886......	511,377	3,710,110	1,864,800	20,196

STOCK SLAUGHTERED.

The following table shows the estimated amount of stock slaughtered in this city from the year 1874 to 1886, inclusive:

Year	Cattle, head.	Hogs, head.	Sheep, head.
1874......	35,073	173,300	96,800
1875...	19,956	159,500	118,200
1876...	25,651	208,560	103,678
1877......	20,158	171,000	47,500
1878	53,025	386,210	175,255
1879................	23,511	310,845	87,600
1880	38,000	406,295	88,600
1881...	35,846	443,100	98,600
1882	35,547	406,180	196,200
1883	47,260	570,630	238,800
1884	24,123	612,835	201,400
1885	65,994	704,950	679,800
1886...	46,223	921,860	328,600

The following table shows the number of carloads of sale and through stock received at the New York Central stock yards for the year just closed as compared with the year 1885:

Through stock—

	Cattle, cars.	Hogs, cars.	Sheep, cars.
1886......	14,839	10,512	1,676
1885......	11,154	9,054	1,742
Increase....	3,685	858	....
Decrease....	....	......	66

Sale stock—

	Cattle, cars.	Hogs, cars.	Sheep, cars.
1886...	10,463	9,418	6,618
1885......	8,597	7,730	6,593
Increase....	1,866	1,688	28

The following figures give the approximate cash value of the total receipts of the live stock at this point, the value of the sale stock, and value of stock slaughtered in this city for the year 1886, estimating cattle $4.00, hogs at $4.40, sheep and lambs at $4.50 per cwt.:

Value of total receipts—
Cattle................................. $24,064,800.00
Hogs................................... 27,120,752.00
Sheep.................................. 6,291,700.00

Total $57,477,252.00

Value of sale stock—
Cattle................................ $ 8,460,800.00
Hogs................................... 9,249,240.00
Sheep 4,509,000.00

Total.................................$22,219,040.00

Value of stock slaughtered—
Cattle.................................$ 2,175,200.00
Hogs................................... 7,759,488.00
Sheep.................................. 1,069,025.00

Total $11,003,713.00

REGULATION OF LIVE STOCK TRANSPORTATION.

February 18th, State Senator Coggeshall introduced a bill providing, in substance, that on and after its passage it shall be unlawful for any railroad company, whose line of road is wholly or in part within the limits of this

State, to discriminate against any person, company, or corporation by declining to receive upon its road and haul to their destination, over a part or the whole of such line of railroad, any live stock in suitable condition for shipment which may be loaded in the car or cars of any person, company, or corporation, providing such car or cars are so constructed as to make them safe for the purposes for which they are employed; that when cars are constructed in such manner as to make them safe for transporting live stock in suitable condition for shipment, it shall be the duty of any railroad company, whose line of road is wholly or in part within the limits of this State, to receive and haul the car or cars to the desired destinations upon the same terms, subject to the same conditions and liable to the same obligations as it is then hauling similar car or cars for other railroad companies under like conditions; that whenever it shall become necessary to move any empty car or cars, owned or operated by any person, company, or corporation, from one place to another for the receipt of live stock to be shipped, the railroad company shall receive such car or cars and haul it or them to the desired destination or destinations upon the same terms and subject to the same conditions as it is then hauling empty cars for other railroad companies for the same purpose; that any railroad company whose line of road is wholly or in part within the limits of this State, who shall violate any of the provisions of this act shall be liable to the person, company, or corporation owning or operating said car or cars, for all damages which may result therefrom ; that said damages may be recovered in action prosecuted in any court having jurisdiction thereof, and that any railroad company, whose line of road is wholly or in part within the limits of this State, who shall violate any of the provisions of this act shall, in addition to the right of action given in the preceding section, be liable to the consignor or consignors or the consignee or consignees of such stock for all damages which may result therefrom. The same may be recovered in an action prosecuted in any court having jurisdiction thereof.

THE NIAGARA RIVER.

This stream, narrow, swift and dangerous for some distance below the inlet, connecting Lake Erie with Lake Ontario and supplying the vast volume of water that rushes in eternal thunder over Niagara Falls, is navigable and utilized for the needs of commerce as far as Tonawanda, twelve miles below Buffalo and the principal lumber port of the State. The river is a picturesque and romantic feature, dotted with islands of greater or less extent, the principal ones being Squaw Island, Grand Island and Strawberry Island.   Strawberry and Squaw Islands are flat and low-lying, but produce excellent crops ; Grand Island is partly under cultivation, and is adorned with a fine grove and provided with the necessary accessories of a popular pleasure resort, being reached by steamer throughout the summer.   A fine hotel is being built, which will greatly add to the attractions. The Niagara is spanned at Black Rock by the great International bridge of the Grand Trunk railway—one of the greatest engineering triumphs ever achieved. A ship canal extends from Buffalo harbor to Black Rock, and sailing vessels and barges towed to Tonawanda by way of the river are towed back past the rapids to the lake via canal. The following shows the number of lumber

vessels and rafts that passed and repassed through the International bridge
during the past season of navigation:

MONTH.	STEAMERS.	OTHER VESSELS.	RAFTS.	TOTAL.
April...............................	98	111	......	209
May.................................	436	360	......	796
June................................	771	323	.....	1,094
July................................	1,056	290	10	1,356
August.............................	1,007	318	7	1,332
September..........................	745	246	4	995
October............................	465	248	......	713
November..........................	282	166	......	448
December..........................	14	17	......	31
Total for season..................	4,874	2,079	21	6,974
Total for 1885....................	4,071	1,715	40	5,826
Increase for 1886.............	803	364	* 19	1,148

* Decrease.

INTERNATIONAL BRIDGE.—(GRAND TRUNK RAILWAY.)

THE GRAIN TRADE.

BUFFALO unquestionably owes her past prosperity and present prominence more to the Erie canal than to all other causes combined.
Projected in 1807, it was opened for traffic in 1825, and at once became
the great artery of commerce between the East and West, pouring into the
lap of Buffalo, directly and indirectly, untold wealth, accruing from the
handling of eastward-bound grain and westward-bound merchandise, bringing hither legions of industrious people of all classes—enterprising specu-
lators, merchants, manufacturers, bankers, shipbuilders, railroad projectors,
mechanics, laborers, and all the elements that combine to build up and
advance a community. The growth of this city from that date to the present
has been, if not phenomenal, at least steady and substantial, as is evidenced
by the statistics of population. In 1825, the year of inauguration of the
great water-way from the lakes to the Hudson and thence to the Atlantic,
Buffalo contained 2,412 souls; in 1830, 8,668; in 1835, 15,661; in 1840,
18,213; in 1845, 29,773; in 1850, 42,261; in 1855, 74,414; in 1860, 81,129;
in 1865, 94,502 ; in 1870, 117,714 ; in 1875, 134,573; in 1880, 163,506; in
1885, 232,440, and (estimated) in 1886, 240,604. Whoever may have originated the idea, it is certain that to Governor De Witt Clinton's unbounded
industry, energy and determination, more than to any other one cause, is
the city, the State and the nation indebted for the prosecution and completion of this then mighty work of internal improvement, undertaken under
the greatest discouragements and carried on to a triumphant issue in the
face of difficulties such as no other public or private enterprise on this continent ever encountered, means and resources considered.

Notwithstanding the powerful combinations to divert the grain trade to
the railroads, and to the Welland canal and St. Lawrence, the Erie canal has
bravely held its own under adverse circumstances, as will be seen by the
appended tables of imports and exports for the years 1883, 1884, 1885 and
1886, for which we are indebted to Secretary Thurstone, of the Merchants'
Exchange:

CANAL OPENED.	MAY 7, 1883.	MAY 7, 1884.	MAY 11, 1885.	MAY 1, 1886.
Flour, barrels.................	5,349	4,813	2,991	4,518
Wheat, bushels................	17,824,272	25,592,802	18,003,758	31,861,701
Corn, bushels.................	18,472,804	6,941,741	12,731,611	12,545,408
Oats, bushels.................	2,949,375	3,066,328	350,587	326,760
Barley, bushels.........,......	283,982	204,603	138,190	283,294
Rye, bushels..................	2,821,790	2,066,283	228,742	....
Total, bushels...............	42,352,223	37,871,757	31,452,888	45,017,163
Flour to wheat, bushels.........	26,745	24,065	14,955	22,590
Grand total, bushels..........	42,378,968	37,895,822	31,467,843	45,039,753

Previous to 1842 the commercial grain elevator was unknown, and the unloading of lake vessels and loading of canal-boats was accomplished by the slow and laborious process of carrying the grain on the shoulders of laborers from one craft to the other. In the year named Joseph Dart, an ingenious and far-sighted Buffalo mechanic, conceived and carried into practical effect the idea of a steam elevator, adopted from that of Oliver Evans, in use in merchant flour mills, East and West. Before the Buffalo Historical Society, March 1865, Mr. Dart stated, in a paper prepared for the occasion : " My experiment from the very first working, was a decided and acknowledged success. Within a month after I started, a leading forwarder, who had confidently predicted that shippers could not afford to pay the charges of elevating by steam, came to me and offered double rates for accommodation, but my bins were all full. The great saving of time by the use of the elevator was immediately seen. To give an instance that occurs to my mind, the schooner John B. Skinner came into port, with four thousand bushels of wheat, early in the afternoon, and was discharged, received ballast of salt and left the same evening ; made her trip to Milan, Ohio, brought down a second cargo and discharged it, and on her return to Milan, went out in company with vessels which came in with her on the first trip down, and which had but just succeeded in getting rid of their freight in the old way."

Never was an invention better timed. The great Northwest had just commenced her wonderful career of agricultural success, and the ever-increasing volume of her products sought an outlet through the lakes and the canal. Elevator after elevator was erected, until at this time some forty of these lofty structures of varying capacity line the Buffalo river and the canal, twenty-two of which are storage and ten transfer elevators, and five floaters ; and the demand is for increased facilities each year. Needless to say, railroad building, lake navigation and local improvement have kept pace with the commercial growth of the city, and she now stands in the front rank of inland business centers, with a bright vista of grand prospects before her—a future full of promise, to be realized only by continuing the policy of enterprise and commercial integrity that have already done so much for her. It is not, however, too much to say that the Erie canal is now, as heretofore, the key-stone in the arch of her hopes. Once let that superb work fall into the hands of its enemies, the railroads, or into desuetude, and the knell of Buffalo's commercial supremacy will soon be heard ; her glory will have departed, and from the proud position of Queen of the Lakes she will descend to a mere way-station on the trunk railroad lines ; her elevators will rot as they stand, her wharves go to ruin, and scarcely a sail will dot or a steam-tug ripple the bosom of her beautiful bay.

Among the first to realize the importance to Buffalo and the West of an enlightened policy in the management of the canals, and to perceive the necessity for enlarging and making them free, was Hon. David S. Bennett, one of the city's foremost business men. Mr. Bennett was born and reared on an Onondaga county farm, educated at the Onondaga academy, married and commenced life on a two-hundred acre farm transferred by his father, added to his gains by various trades, then entered the produce commission business at Syracuse, afterward organized the house of Bennett, Hall & Co., New York, and came to Buffalo in 1853 to represent it, purchasing the elevator erected by Joseph Dart, the first one in the world operated by steam. Not long afterward Mr. Bennett and the late George W. Tifft built another elevator on the Ohio basin, and subsequently the former joined A. Sherwood & Co. in the erection of still another on Coit slip, which was burned. In 1862 work was begun on the Bennett elevator (Mr. B.'s individual enterprise), which was completed in 1866, and which, with the "Union" adjoining, has a storage capacity of 700,000 bushels and can handle 20,000,000 bushels per annum. In recognition of his business ability, patriotism and public services in a private capacity, Mr. Bennett was chosen in 1865 to represent the Buffalo district in the State Senate, where he distinguished himself by devotion to the material interests of his constituents, giving special attention to the canal system, urging enlargement of the locks to admit boats of 600 tons, and pointing out the unfortunate results that have since followed, the inadequacy of the craft plying the Erie and Oswego canals. Jealousy, indifference, possibly worse, defeated his efforts, but that his services were appreciated at home was proven by his overwhelming election to the Forty-first Congress. Thoroughly convinced of the incapacity and illiberality of the New York Legislature in its dealings with the canal question, Mr. Bennett introduced and carried through the proper committees a bill transferring to the general government the Erie and Oswego canals, and imposing upon it the duty of enlarging and maintaining them free of tolls—the condition being that the State Legislature would accept the proposition. That august body declined, in consequence of which the through canals fell into a state of neglect and partial disuse, and even the plan of making them free at State expense has not had the effect of reviving their commerce. Meantime the Canadian ship canal is completed, and Buffalo sees a large portion of the Western wheat-handling trade carried past her very doors as the penalty of hide-bound selfishness at Albany—an injury which a later more liberal policy looking to the improvements of the canals will require years to remedy. This triumph comes to Mr. Bennett after a persistent struggle of seventeen years, during which time he incessantly fought the interested opponents of his pet measure abroad, and a short-sighted and shallow press at home, incapable of rising to a broad national and patriotic view of a subject so nearly affecting the commercial supremacy of the United States on this continent and the immediate business interests of Buffalo. He carried his fight not only into the halls of State and federal legislation but into the State conventions, both Republican and Democratic, meeting with repulse at every point, yet never despairing. Now, when the mischief is done and the damage from delay almost irremediable, he has the grim satisfaction of seeing his fiercest opponents and obstructionists flocking to his standard in a body.

The following remarkable letter was written by this indefatigable champion of the canals in the winter of 1885-86, and is well worthy of preservation as a portion of the history of this remarkable struggle:

"You will now allow me to bring to public notice, briefly, the action taken during the Forty-first Congress, in which I had the honor to represent this district. On the sixteenth of February I introduced a bill asking for an appropriation of fifteen million dollars, to be applied to the payment of the canal debt of the State of New York, and the prompt enlargement and improvement of the Erie and Oswego canals. This bill was discussed freely during the first session, and a new bill introduced and referred to the committee of commerce, of which I was a member. It was unanimously reported from this committee, also from the committee of appropriations. I then forwarded it to Mr. Alberger, a member of the State Legislature, asking for the passage of a joint resolution accepting the provisions of the bill. It was stopped there by him, without any apparent reason. I allowed the bill to remain quiet in the committee until after the adjournment, simply forwarding a copy of it to the chamber of commerce in New York, which, as you know, is a body composed of commercial men of high standing. I then addressed a letter to its chairman, the late William E. Dodge, asking for a hearing at this conference. He replied promptly, naming the days of their meetings, and expressing a desire to hear me at any time. I thereupon presented the measure, and my brief argument in support of it was received and a resolution passed, unanimously indorsing it, before they adjourned.

"With such indorsement as the two committees referred to above, composed of twenty-five men from all parts of the country, and the indorsement of the chamber of commerce of the city of New York, together with the convictions of the people of the country during the last seventeen years, of the importance of the measure, I believe our present representatives from this district can pass a bill calling for an amount amply sufficient to enlarge and improve the Erie canal to the full extent of the water to supply the same, having it expressed in the bill that if promptly passed during this session, so as to give the State of New York the summer to procure the necessary materials, that it shall be completed and ready for navigation on the opening of the spring of 1887."

THE WESTERN ELEVATING COMPANY.

A fair idea of the extent of the grain receipts at this port during the past seventeen years may be gathered from the subjoined statement of Secretary P. G. Cook, of the Western Elevating Company, to the canal committee of the General Assembly, February 25, 1885, to which are added the official figures for 1885 and 1886. Receipts for—

1870	32,208,039	1879	75,089,768
1871	61,319,313	1880	105,133,009
1872	58,703,666	1881	56,389,827
1873	65,498,955	1882	51,561,503
1874	55,665,198	1883	65,722,080
1875	52,833,451	1884	58,011,800
1876	44,207,121	1885	52,000,000
1877	61,822,292	1886	75,570,850
1878	78,828,443		

Concerning the facilities that exist here for handling this vast aggregate of grain, Mr. William Thurstone, in his "Commerce, Industries and Resources of Buffalo" (1883), says:

"With very few equals in the world as a grain port, its terminal facilities are very extensive and complete. Grain is received, transferred, stored and forwarded with greater dispatch than at any other port in this country. The river, for about a mile from its mouth, is lined with immense elevators and floaters, provided with all of the most improved appliances for handling cereals. The transfer of grain cargoes from vessels into storehouses and canal-boats, prior to 1843, was done by manual labor, being raised from the hold in tubs and bags. In that year Mr. Joseph Dart erected the first elevator ever built for storing and transferring grain, with steam power, and with a storage capacity of 55,000 bushels, and a transfer capacity of 15,000 bushels per day, near the mouth of Buffalo river. Now there are twenty-two elevators, ten transfer elevators and five floaters, thirty-seven in all, most of which are massive structures, costing in the aggregate about $6,000,000. Their combined storage capacity reaches 9,215,000 bushels, while their daily transfer capacity is 3,102,000 bushels. That is to say, the elevators of Buffalo are capable of receiving from lake vessels and transferring to canal-boats and cars, daily, 3,000,000 bushels of grain if called upon to do so. Much has been said and written against these Buffalo elevators, but the fact that they furnish such excellent facilities to carriers and shippers, insuring quick dispatch and freedom from costly delays, is an advantage that can be scarcely overestimated. These elevators are owned by private individuals, excepting that the Connecting Terminal Railroad owns one, and the New York, Lake Erie & Western Railroad one, and the New York Central and Hudson River Railroad two. Several of these elevators have machinery attached whereby 60,000 to 70,000 bushels of wet or damaged grain can be dried every twenty-four hours. The grain trade has steadily increased for years. The season's receipts for 1880 were the largest on record, aggregating by lake and Lake Shore & Michigan Southern Railroad 175,000,000 bushels ; last year, 101,122,705 bushels. The facilities for forwarding this vast amount of grain were as extensive as the terminal facilities. The capacity of the canal has never been fully tested, and the shipments of 1880, which were the largest ever reported, and reached 72,000,000 bushels, were forwarded with as little effort as the 36,000,000 bushels shipped in 1875. This fact is accounted for by the deepening and improvement of the canal so as to permit of the passage of boats with increased speed. The total of all articles carried from Buffalo in 1880 aggregated 2,286,922 tons, of the value of $59,539,048, and in 1883, 1,361,421 tons, valued at $35,866,304. The total freight received here was 553,846 tons in 1883. The canal and railway competition thus afforded always insures cheap transportation rates. The Central, Erie, Philadelphia and Lackawanna railroads give much attention to conveying grain, and each moves large quantities received by lake as well as its through shipments. Their tracks run directly into the elevators, so that there is no carting and no handling outside of the elevator. It is no uncommon thing to see a large lake vessel being unloaded and two canal-boats and two trains of freight cars being loaded at the same time."

Up to 1857 Buffalo boasted of but three elevators, and, there being no co-operation between their owners—no mutual agreement for the good of all—much confusion, inconvenience and loss ensued to all concerned. Warehouse receipts were of little value as collaterals; accommodations to parties having grained stored were obtainable only on unquestionable indorsement, and, in short, the honored axiom, " good as wheat," was of no weight at all. It was to remedy this state of affairs that the Western Elevating Company was organized in the year last named, and its benefits were so immediate, and have proved so great and permanent, that none save those

interested in the unreasonable increase of storage and freight rates have ever
questioned the usefulness or endeavored to obstruct the company's operations. As an evidence of the healthful effect of the pooling arrangement
upon the grain trade, there were but three elevators then in existence here,
all of which entered the combination, while there are now thirty-seven under
the control of the Western Elevating Company, as follows:

STORAGE ELEVATORS.	Nominal Capacity.	TRANSFER ELEVATORS.	Nominal Capacity.
* † Bennett....................	600,000	Chicago...................	....
† Brown....................	250,000	Western Transit...........	25,000
* † City....................	600,000	Fulton...................	25,000
* † C. J. Wells.............	350,000	Horton...................	....
* † Connecting Terminal R. R.	950,000	† Kellogg & McDougall......	75,000
† Erie Basin..............	200,000	Merchants...............	....
† Evans...................	250,000	Northwest................	15,000
* † Exchange...............	250,000	National Mills............	100,000
Lyon...................	100,000	† Schreck................	40,000
* † Marine................	150,000	Union...................	60,000
* † Niagara A.............	650,000	Total...................	340,000
* † Niagara B.............	1,200,000		
* † N. Y., L. E. & Western...	650,000	Capacity storage...........	8,625,000
† Richmond..............	250,000	Grand total	8,965,000
* Sternberg..............	150,000		
* † Sturges...............	300,000	FLOATING ELEVATORS.	
† Swiftsure............	175,000		
* † Tifft....................	350,000	Buffalo..................	....
† William Wells..........	200,000	Free Trade...............	....
* † Wheeler...............	200,000	Free Canal..	....
† Watson................	600,000	I. Y. Munn...............	....
* † Wilkeson	200,000	Marquette...............	....
Total...................	8,625,000	Niagara..'...............	....

* Have railroad connection.   † Running in 1886.

Elevating and storage rates have also steadily declined under this admir-
able system—thus: In 1869 the rate for elevating and five days' storage was
two cents per bushel; in 1885, three-fourths of one cent. It will be seen,
therefore, that the benefits secured by this company are not confined to its
own members, but are distributed with an even hand among its patrons,
and through them to the general public—to the consumers.

The company, as before intimated, is composed of the owners of all the
elevators in this port save two, newly erected. The officers are: C. A.
Bloomer, president; R. R. Buck, vice-president; P. G. Cook, jr., secretary
and treasurer. Office, No. 64 Pearl street.

President Bloomer is a very prominent business man and part proprietor
of the Exchange (Western and Canada railroad) elevator, 250,000 bushels
capacity, and a member of the Board of Trade and Merchants' Exchange.
Vice-President R. R. Buck is also a prominent and respected business man
and grain-handler ; while Secretary and Treasurer P. G. Cook, jr,, is, if we
may judge by his pamphlet on " The Elevators and the Canals," in refuta-
tion of groundless and mischievous charges against the former, an extraordinarily bright and well-versed man in all that concerns the interests which
he represents. The executive committee is composed of the following well-
known and responsible gentlemen: J. W. Whitney, G. F. Sowerby, E. T.
Evans, A. J. Wheeler, John Wilkeson, C. C. Ricker and R. R. Buck.

THE ERIE CANAL.

THIS superb and beneficent work, first opened for traffic throughout its entire length in 1825, has done more than all other agencies to build up the fortunes of Buffalo and of the West. It was first known as the Grand Canal, and the country owes an everlasting debt of gratitude to DeWitt Clinton, who more than any other one man—nay, than all other men—labored for its success and pushed it to completion. At the time of its inauguration the canal was 363 miles in length, 40 feet wide at the surface, 28 feet wide at bottom, four feet deep, and contained 83 locks capable of accommodating boats of 70 tons burden. The entire cost was $9,000,-000. The work of enlargement, to accommodate boats of 210 tons, was undertaken in 1835 and finished in 1865, at an additional cost of $32,000,000. Writing of the celebration at the opening in 1825, Hon. Cadwallader D. Colden said, prophetically : " When. these works are accomplished a water communication between the lakes and the Mississippi river and 40,000 or 50,000 miles of navigable streams beyond may be made without difficulty and at little expense. New York will have advantages greater than any city has ever had, and must forever enjoy them without a rival. The commerce of the Mediterranean is the support of many great cities, but New York will stand above all at the entrance of this extensive channel, and must be a greater emporium than ever called herself the mistress of commerce." The New York *Produce Exchange Weekly*, referring to the grain trade of the metropolis, says:

"The New York canals have not outlived their usefulness, whatever may be said to the contrary. The total quantity of flour, grain and meal, reduced to bushels of grain, received at New York during 1886, was 130,910,-062 bushels, showing an increase of 4,272,631 bushels, or 3.4 per cent. over the quantity received in 1885. Of this enormous quantity the New York canals delivered during the navigation season of 1886, May to November inclusive, 44,036,522 bushels, or 33.64 per cent., against 20,930,587 bushels during the navigation season of 1885, showing the remarkable increase of 14,105,935 bushels, or 47.13 per cent. Conditions were normal during 1886, a 25 cent tariff on grain from Chicago to New York having ruled throughout the season with very little deviation, which was not the case in 1885. The deliveries by rail during the five months of January, February, March,

4

Music Hall.—(See "Our Illustrations.")

April and December, 1886, equaled 36,531,886 bushels, and during the seven months of open canal navigation the deliveries by all the railroads were 48,209,284 bushels, including flour and meal. In other words, during the navigation season of 1886 all the railroads together delivered only 4.172,762 bushels more of grain, including flour and meal, than the canals did of grain alone. The total deliveries by rail during 1886 show a falling off of 8,227,370 bushels, or 8.85 per cent. compared with 1885, while, as shown above, the canal deliveries increased 14,105,935 bushels, or 47.13 per cent. over the previous season. The deliveries by river and coastwise during 1886 were small, forming only 1.63 per cent. of the total, and these show a decrease of 1,605,934 bushels, or about 43 per cent. as compared with 1885."

As this work goes to press the New York Senate has just passed a bill, now in the hands of the Assembly for concurrence, appropriating $550,000 for canal improvement. There is little doubt that the bill will become a law in time to enable the canal commissioners to again enlarge the locks and improve the Erie canal during the coming year sufficiently to admit of the passage of boats of 720 tons burden. At first, as before noted, the largest boats were of 80 tons; after the enlargement the standard was raised to 240 tons and freight rates reduced 50 per cent. A proportionate increase of capacity will unquestionably result in a similar reduction of freight charges and enable shippers to lay down grain in New York at about two cents per bushel, besides causing the use of steam as a motive power, thus shortening the voyage by increasing the speed. The appropriation referred to is in pursuance of a bill offered by the Canal Union, passed and approved December 28, 1886, which authorizes and directs the Superintendent of Public Works, before the opening of navigation in 1888, to cause to be lengthened one tier of eight or more locks east of Syracuse, and one tier of eight or more locks west of Syracuse on the Erie canal, * * * so as to most facilitate and improve the navigation of the canal. Said locks to be so lengthened and constructed as to be 220 feet long, and not less than 18 feet wide in the clear, and to conform to the length of the berme experimental lock, No. 50, on said Erie canal, and shall include such machinery and appliances as in the judgment of the Superintendent of Public Works shall render the locks most efficient. Said Superintendent of Public Works is also authorized to put machinery for facilitating the passage of boats in such locks of the Oswego canal as shall be selected, * * * and is also authorized and directed to improve the Champlain canal by deepening it at such points as he shall deem most important.

It is easily demonstrable that with the completion of the improvements referred to the capacity of the canal would be doubled at least.

At the first session of the Forty-ninth Congress (Jan. 5, 1886), Hon. John B. Weber introduced the following bill, which, in the hurry usually attendant upon the closing hours of Congress, failed to receive final consideration, and remains a legacy of incomplete legislation for action by the next Congress. The plan contemplated therein has much to commend it to the country at large:

A BILL for the permanent improvement of the Erie and Oswego canals, and to secure the freedom of the same to the commerce of the United States :

Be it enacted by the Senate and House of Representatives of the United States of America in Congress assembled :

That the Secretary of the Treasury be, and he is hereby, authorized and directed to issue and deliver to the State of New York, and to take the receipt of the Comptroller of said State therefor, coupon or registered bonds of the United States to the amount of five millions of dollars, in denominations of not less than one hundred dollars each, or so much thereof as may be necessary to make the permanent improvements upon the Erie and Oswego canals, in said State, hereinafter mentioned. Said bonds shall bear interest at the rate of 2½ per centum per annum, payable semi-annually, and shall, with the interest, be payable in coin. They shall be redeemable at the pleasure of the government at any time after ten years from their date, and due at the expiration of fifty years from their date.

SEC. 2.   That said bonds shall not be issued or delivered until the said State of New York shall, by act or joint resolution of its Legislature, have pledged itself that, after the delivery of said bonds, said canals shall be maintained by said State free to the commerce of the United States, and shall forever be free for the use of the United States Government from any toll or other charge whatever for any property or vessels of the United States Government or persons in its service passing through the same, and that in case at any time said canals shall cease to be free to the commerce of the United States, the said State will repay to the United States the said five millions of dollars, or so much thereof as may be paid to said State.

SEC. 3.   That said bonds shall be so issued and delivered to the State of New York to reimburse it for any and all expenditures it may make or may have made since January first, eighteen hundred and eighty-six, in improving the said canals by furnishing a depth of nine feet of water, excepting over culverts and aqueducts (over which the depth shall be eight feet), throughout their entire lengths, and by lengthening one tier of all their locks to double their present length, with the exception of those at Lockport; and that said bonds, or so many thereof as may be necessary, shall be so issued and delivered upon the completion of said improvement, and after said State shall have complied with the provisions of the second section of this act, upon presentation to the Secretary of the Treasury of a requisition of the governor of said State, accompanied by the certificate of its comptroller, State engineer, and superintendent of public works, certifying the completion of said improvement and the cost thereof.

On the following 23d of February the bill was favorably reported by the committee on railways and canals, of which Mr. Weber was chairman. The report was an able one, evincing thorough mastery of the subject and introducing such authorities in support of the object sought as Albert Fink, commissioner of transportation, Mr. Dodge, statistician to the Department of Agriculture, Consul-General Cramer, and Mr. Nimmo. The subjoined tables, prepared by the latter, show the balance of trade against the United States before tolls were cut down, and the balance in our favor since the low-tolls and no-tolls policy was adopted :

BALANCE OF TRADE AGAINST US FOR TEN YEARS, FROM 1866 TO 1875, UNDER HIGH TOLLS.

Years.	Exports.	Imports.	Excess of Imports over Exports.
1866	$348,859,522	$484,812,066	$ 85,952,544
1867	294,506,141	395,761,096	101.284,955
1868	281,952,899	357,436,440	75,483,541
1869	286,117,697	417,506,379	131,388,682
1870	392,771,768	435,958,408	43,186,640
1871	442,820,178	520,223,684	77,403,506
1872	444,177,586	626,595,077	182,417,491
1873	522,479,922	642,136,210	119,656,288
1874	586,283,040	567,406,342	....
1875	513,442,711	533,005,436	19,562,725
			836,306,372
			18,876,698
Balance against us in ten years			$817,429,674

There was an excess of exports over imports in 1874 of $18,876,698.

VALUE OF THE EXPORTS AND IMPORTS FOR TEN YEARS WITH LOW TOLLS.

Years.	Exports.	Imports.	Excess of Exports over Imports
1876	$540,384,671	$460,741,190	$ 79,643,481
1877	602,475,220	451,323,126	151,152,094
1878	694,865,766	437,051,532	257,814,234
1879	710,439.441	445,777,775	264,661,666
1880	835,638,658	667,954,746	167,683,912
1881	902,377,346	642,664,628	259,712,718
1882	750,542,257	724,639,574	25,902,683
1883	823,839,402	723,180,914	100,658,488
1884	740,513,609	667,697,693	72,815,916
1885	742,189,755	577,527,329	164,662,426
Total			$1,544,707,618

Balance in favor of this country, $1,544,707,618 under low tolls.

The reasons why New York State cannot well perform the work of enlargement at her own expense, and thus secure a sensible and beneficial reduction of transportation charges, are thus stated:

Several hundred miles of tributary canals have been grafted upon the trunk lines of the Erie, and every movement looking to the improvement of the main canals becomes complicated by arousing the jealousies of local interests connected with the lateral canals. All tolls were removed in 1882, and since the beginning of the season of 1883 the canals are free to the nation, while their care and maintenance fall upon the taxpayers of New York. This maintenance, embracing only absolutely necessary and ordinary repairs, amounts to about $800,000 annually, and until the canal debt of the State is extinguished about as much more is annually required to provide for that. For the present year the estimates of the comptroller of the State of New York require the levying of a tax for canal purposes of $1,702,102.30.

This burden the people of the State cannot reasonably be expected to add to by undertaking the enlargement, without which the canals are likely to fall into disuse or be abandoned to private corporations. Only eighteen of the sixty counties of the State border on the Erie and Oswego canals, and the hostile sentiment of the people off the line of the canals should not be permitted development by increase of burdens, lest this outlet of the great grain fields of the West and Northwest and this controller and regulator of the transportation interests of the country be strangled by the railroad monopolies of the land.

For the year ending December 31, 1885, there was delivered at New York of flour, grain, and meal (excepting beans and buckwheat), reduced to measure, 126,637,431 bushels, by the following routes:

Routes.	Bushels.	Per cent. of total by each route.
New York Central and Hudson River Railway.......	36,079,712	28.60
New York, Lake Erie and Western Railway.	24,979,551	19.73
Pennsylvania Railway............................	15,229,591	12.02
Delaware and Lackawanna Railway.................	5,718,428	4.52
West Shore and Buffalo Railway	10,001,299	7.90
Various routes..................................	959,959	.75
By river and coastwise...........................	3,738,304	2.75
By canal..	29,930,587	23.63
Total receipts	126,637,431	....

In a commercial sense these canals originally were largely local in character, but gradually and regularly they have been changing, and are now of national benefit and importance. In 1836 the Western States furnished but one-seventh of the total tonnage, while in 1882 seven-eighths of it came from the West, the proportion having vastly increased since that time.

January 5th and 6th last the House in Committee of the Whole and having under consideration Mr. Weber's bill for the permanent improvement of the Erie and Oswego canals, and to secure the freedom of the same to the commerce of the United States, that gentleman made a strong and convincing argument in its favor, dwelling upon the important factor which the freedom of the Erie and Oswego canals to the commerce of the country would form in providing cheap transportation for the products of the West to the seaboard. The provisions of the bill were fair to the nation and fair to the State of New York. The exhaustive report of the Committee on Railways and Canals was read in Mr. Weber's time, and consumed the greater part of the morning hour; and the committee rose without action.

Mr. Weber was followed in approving remarks by several Western members. Mr. Anderson, of Kansas, said: "As to the object to be attained by the proposed enlargement and improvement of the Erie canal as the great artery of lake commerce, in my judgment the State of Kansas has a greater direct interest in the attainment of that object than has the State of New York, for this simple reason: Every one knows that the farmer who raises wheat, or ships corn or hay in the form of pork or beef, always pays the freight to the final market. Now, the enlargement of this canal, enabling boats to carry double the cargoes they now carry, will necessarily have the effect of reducing the rate of freight upon grain at least 2 cents per bushel, and when the State of Kansas raises and ships 50,000,000 bushels of wheat, the farmers raising that wheat will receive for it $1,000,000 more in price than they now receive, simply because there will be a saving of $1,000,000 of freight upon the shipment. A similar reduction would occur on all kinds of traffic. And what is true of Kansas is true of Kentucky, of Ohio, of Indiana, of Missouri, of all the Northwestern States and of the Southern States. For this reason, sir, there has been no measure proposed at this session of Congress which seems to me to promise more direct practical and lasting benefit to the great farming interest of the country than the proposed enlargement of this canal, and for this reason I regard it as a national and not in the least as a State measure. But, Mr. Chairman, there is another reason why I advocate the bill, namely, the fact that the Erie canal stands to-day as the great check upon the rapacity of the railway companies in their freight charges. It would be worth a hundred million dollars to the New York Central, the Erie, the Pennsylvania, the Baltimore & Ohio, and the other trunk lines if, by any means, they could wipe out the Erie canal. And, just to the extent that this is true, it is true also that it is to the interest of the people of the whole nation, and especially of the farming classes, to take care that the Erie canal not only shall not be suffered to pass into disuse, not only that it shall not be kept at its present limited capacity, but shall speedily have that capacity enlarged and given the greatest efficiency. You will find in the near future that the control of freight charges must chiefly be effected by water-ways. Coming from the State which I in part represent, I shall advocate, not only this enlargement of the Erie canal, but also the construction of the Hennepin canal. Why? In order that we of the West may have a direct water-way to serve as the great controller of all the trunk lines, whether they pool or do not pool, whether you have an interstate commerce bill or not. In other words, the good God who made this world, who so constituted things that there is less friction in moving vast weights through water than there is in carrying them by any means on land, gave to us a principle of nature which is higher and more effective than any other which can be formulated in an interstate commerce bill or similar legislation of Congress."

Mr. Nelson, of Minnesota: " While we can do a great deal, Mr. Chairman, in the shape of legislation, I feel confident there is nothing so effective, and which will accomplish so much good for the whole country, as this matter of enlarging and extending the Erie canal. Coming, as I do, from the country at the headwaters of the Mississippi and St. Lawrence rivers, from a country which is one of the greatest cereal-producing sections of this Union, we have a vital interest in having our transportation facilities made as cheap, as fair, and as equitable as possible. And our people can conceive of no method so efficacious, so fully regulating this matter of the carrying trade of the Northwest to the seaboard, as enlarging and extending our canals. In the district I represent, sir, 20,000,000 bushels of wheat were raised last year, of which, besides what we used for home consumption, nearly all finds its way to the seaboard through the chain of the great lakes by way of the Erie canal. At least 12,000,000 bushels of the 20,000,000 raised in my district are thus shipped and exported. At the rate of 5 cents per bushel—the amount saved by transportation over this water route as against railroad transportation, if untrammeled—$600,000 would be saved annually to the farmers of my district. This water route is emphatically one of the greatest regulators of railroad rates."

Mr. Plumb: "In my opinion there has not been presented to this House a more important question than that which now engages its attention. It is, sir, nothing less than a question of public improvements upon a scale that has not hitherto received legislative favor for many years. It is a question that may years ago claimed the attention of the foremost thinkers and ablest statesmen in this land. It has been urged against improvements of this character being undertaken by the general government that they are altogether within one of the States, and that therefore they should not receive the encouragement and support of the Federal treasury, and some have gone so far as to declare such support unconstitutional, and yet it has been the constant practice to make just such improvements. It is not a question whether the improvement is wholly within a State or whether it extends through all of the States. The question is this, and this only: Is it for the benefit of the whole people of the country? The proposition is to improve the navigation between the metropolis on the sea-coast and the great inland metropolis, the City of Chicago; it is of the utmost importance to this country, and the small pittance that is asked in this bill can be given without any serious injury to any part and with decided advantage to the whole country. I hope, sir, when the time comes for a vote upon this bill it may receive the cordial support of this House, and become a law.

Mr. Brady : "Mr. Chairman—I cannot hope to add to the able and exhaustive remarks made upon the pending bill by the gentleman from New York (Mr. Weber), and by other members representing the East and the West; but I desire to heartily indorse the underlying principles of the measure. It is not difficult to understand the concern of the representatives of the great West and Northwest in the proper maintenance and improvement of the Erie and Oswego canals, for they are the vital arteries through which flow the products of their grain fields on the way to the seaboard. The marvelous progress of those sections, reflected as it is upon every part of this country, is primarily due to these works, and its further advancement hinges largely upon the continuance of the system and the ability to keep pace with the rapid forward strides of the transportation problem. The injustice which insists upon a free water-way for the nation to be provided by the State of New York can only result in the development of a desire and determination to cast off the burden, and the West may well view with grave apprehension the growth of this sentiment. But, sir, coming from the State of Virginia, a State some distance removed from the sections which may be considered particularly and locally interested, I can impartially stand upon ground far above the criticisms which will be leveled against those whose localities are especially interested. I stand here as a Virginian to advocate the principles of this bill, because I believe that my people desire their Representative to legislate for the whole country, and not to be restricted to the circumscribed lines of a Congressional district or a State. I am deeply impressed with the importance of a measure which in its scope assumes a character unquestionably national and far-reaching. In it is involved the prosperity of a great and growing section of this nation. It means to a certain extent the natural, irresistible regulation and control of interstate commerce without legislative enactments. It means wise assistance toward meeting the rapid, growing competition of the grain-fields of India and the East. It means a prudent help to continue the balance of trade in our favor. It means prosperity to the agricultural interests of the land, upon which our strength is founded. It means the advancement of the material wealth of the whole country, and therefore I welcome the pending measure with cordial sincerity as a step in the right direction, and hope that the seed sown here to-day may blossom and bear fruit in the interest and for the benefit of the American people."

The officers of the canal, located here, are: Ira Betts, assistant superintendent public works, Western division; George Chambers, section superintendent, office on canal, foot of Porter avenue; Charles G. Irish, collector of statistics; John W. Schlehr, John Siver, John F. Dean, John J. Coughlin, clerks; Wm. Shaughnessy, canal harbor master, office, No. 145 Erie street; inspectors, F. W. Warhus, Joseph Gates, Michael Lanning.

"THE GENESEE" HOTEL.

UTILIZING NIAGARA.

ONE OF THE MOST DARING AND COLOSSAL, YET PRACTICAL, OF MODERN ENTERPRISES.

FOR nearly a century it has been the dream of engineers to turn to useful account the vast and inexhaustible power afforded by the Niagara river in the vicinity of the falls, but hitherto every scheme proposed has been dismissed as impracticable upon sober and exhaustive investigation. It remained for the Niagara River Hydraulic Tunnel, Power and Sewer Co., organized and incorporated during the past year, to solve the knotty problem and set forth a practical plan whereby this object may be accomplished and a great manufacturing center established in near vicinity to, while not in any way detracting from, the sublime beauties of one of nature's greatest wonders.

The officers of the company are all prominent business men, as follows : President, Charles B. Gaskill, president of Cataract Milling Co., and president of the village of Niagara Falls; first vice-president, Henry S. Ware of Hardwicke & Ware, Buffalo, and International Hotel Co., Niagara Falls; second vice-president, Michael Ryan, merchant, and director of Cataract Bank ; treasurer, Francis R. Delano, president Cataract Bank and International Hotel Co.; secretary, Myron H. Kinsley, superintendent Niagara Falls Silver-plating and Manufacturing Works ; assistant secretary, George N. Miller, assistant superintendent of the same works; attorneys, Hon. W. Caryl Ely and James Frazer Gluck of Buffalo; engineer, Thomas Evershed, division engineer of New York State; trustees—Hon. Thomas V. Welch, Hon. Peter A. Porter, A. Augustus Porter and Hon. Benjamin Flagler.

From the prospectus, now before us, we learn that the object of the company is to utilize the enormous power of the Niagara river by constructing a subterranean tunnel from the water level below the falls, about 200 feet under the lofty bank of the river, extending through the rock to the upper river at a point about a mile above the falls, where a head of 120 feet is obtained. The tunnel is to extend thence parallel with the shore one and a-half miles at an average depth of 100 feet below the surface and at a distance of about 400 feet from the navigable waters of the river, with which it is to be connected by means of conduits or lateral tunnels.

It is known that in the same ratio that the country becomes settled and the forests are destroyed the water-power, dependent upon the precipitation of rain, diminishes, and steam has already largely supplanted water as a motor in many of the older States for that reason, thus increasing the cost of production and placing manufacturers at a disadvantage. It is unnecessary to say that this state of affairs can never affect the Niagara, with all of the great lakes for its sources of supply. The cost of constructing dams, the unreliability of the water-power, and the isolated location of many establishments on slender lines of railroads where rates are high, owing to a lack of competition, place manufacturers under great disadvantage with those who have the benefit of a steady power and abundant railroad and other shipping facilities. At Niagara nature has built an imperishable dam from the solid rock, which she maintains without cost to man, so that the manufacturer who avails himself of its power is assured that his mills can never stand idle for lack of water. There will, therefore, be nothing to interrupt the steady flow of yearly production at the minimum of cost. His means of bringing his products to the consumer are also of the best. The facilities for transportation afforded to the mills locating upon the sites of this company have no equal in the world. The mill sites are fixed upon the Niagara river at a point above the falls navigable for vessels. Hence, vessels passing through the great Western chain of lakes can come down the Niagara river with their loads of lumber, grain, coal, etc., and unload them on the wharves and docks of the mills and factories. Canal-boats can also receive and discharge freight at the mills, as the Niagara river connects with the Erie canal at Tonawanda, only seven miles distant. The tracks of the New York Central, West Shore, Erie, Grand Trunk, Rome, Watertown & Ogdensburg, Lehigh Valley, and Michigan Central railways adjoin and run parallel with the proposed tunnel and the entire plot of mill sites of the company, with provision for sidings to each mill site. The Delaware, Lackawanna & Western railroad has surveyed a route contiguous to the property of the company, and will undoubtedly lay its track soon. Freight rates to the seaboard and all points east and west are now made by the railroads from Niagara Falls and Suspension Bridge upon the basis of about one-half the through competitive rates from Chicago and other western points to the East. This is favorable to those locating here, and places the manufacturer in a position to compete successfully with manufacturers of any locality in the United States. Niagara Falls, then, offers to manufacturers unparalleled inducements in cheap, never-failing water-power, economy of production, competitive transportation and small cost for the moving of raw material and finished goods.

It is suggested, and the suggestion must eventually take practical shape, that Buffalo, Lockport, Rochester, and even more distant cities may be supplied with light and power to any extent by means of electricity generated here. Apparatus for the transmission of power by means of compressed air may also be utilized at this point at merely nominal cost.

Since the date of incorporation, March 31, 1886, the Niagara River Hydraulic Tunnel, Power and Sewer Co. has secured, surveyed and apportioned into mill sites sufficient land, fronting on the river and on the line of the projected tunnel, to accommodate 238 mills of 500 horse-power each (119,000 horse-power in all—the engineer's estimate of the tunnel's capacity), with ample streets and dockage, affording all necessary facilities for approach by rail or river. In a word, at ten per cent. for cost of construction, the power to be developed by this proposed tunnel far exceeds the combined available water-power in use at Holyoke, Lowell, Lawrence, Cohoes, Lewiston and Minneapolis. Based on the report of Engineer Thomas Evershed

(who is also division engineer of the State) the subjoined estimates are presented: Two hundred and thirty-eight mill sites, varying from 75 × 200 to
200 × 400 feet each, have been laid out, with streets 100 feet wide between
the rows of mill privileges, and with also a 100-foot reserve between the
rows of lots in the rear, for railway sidings, and to each site is allowed 500
horse-power, with conduit and cross tunnel, bringing the water within fifty
feet of each lot. Fifty or more of these lots can be made accessible for lake
and canal vessels.

Net cost of land, average of $3,000 per lot	$ 750,000
One tunnel	1,212,108
Twenty-four cross tunnels	448,430
Four shafts	38,700
Twelve raceways	329,927
Twelve bulkheads	12,200
Masonry and gates controlling sluices	27,500
Timber in cribs	45,000
Slope walls	90,000
Contingencies	46,135
Total cost	$3,000,000

To pay 5 per cent. on this amount to stockholders it is necessary that
only thirty privileges of 500 horse-power each be utilized. Fifteen thousand
horse-power at $10 each equals $150,000, or 5 per cent. on $3,000,000.

If 30 rentals will pay 5 per cent. upon the entire stock, it follows that
60 rentals will pay 10 per cent., 120 rentals 20 per cent. And when the 238
are used the yearly income of the company will equal 40 per cent. on the
capital stock.

The plan adopted for subscriptions to the capital stock is as follows:
There will be issued 30,000 shares of stock of $100 par value each, and no
payment or assessment of any kind is to be called for until the whole capital
stock is subscribed, which will insure the building and completion of the
tunnel and consequent development of the mill sites, insuring ample
earning capacity for the money subscribed. This assures the success of the
enterprise and is strictly fair to the subscribers.

In order to avoid any risk to stockholders, and prevent abuses, and to
render the stock fixed and valuable forever, it is made one of the conditions
of subscription, and so expressed on the face of each certificate, that no
bonds shall be issued nor mortgages given upon any rights, privileges, franchises or property of this company, except with the unanimous consent of
the stockholders. In other words, the stock shall represent and cover completely the property, real estate and franchises of this company.

The $200,000 capital stock of this company, authorized by its charter,
having already been subscribed in full, books for subscription to increase
the capital stock to the sum of $3,000,000, as also authorized by its charter,
are now open at the Cataract Bank, Niagara Falls, and the Manufacturers
and Traders Bank, Buffalo, N. Y.

The report of Thomas Evershed, Esq., C. E. and division engineer of
New York State, is herewith appended:

*To the President and Trustees of the "Niagara River Hydraulic Tunnel, Power and
Sewer Company," of Niagara Falls, N. Y.:*

GENTLEMEN—I would respectfully submit the following suggestions for your consideration of a plan for the construction of a town plat or arrangement of lots, streets,
mill-races, wharves and railroad tracks above ground on the bank of the Niagara river

above Port Day, in the town of Niagara, county of Niagara and State of New York, for the purpose of forming a town composed wholly of mills, factories and workshops, to be operated by the waters of Niagara river, by means of turbine wheels or other devices. And of a main and lateral tunnels below ground which shall serve as tail-races to the said mills, factories and workshops.

The town plat to be laid out between the said Niagara river and the tracks of the New York Central and Erie railroads.

It shall be laid out with streets running as near as may be at right angles to the course of the river and the New York Central railroad tracks.

Every other one of these streets shall be of such width as will allow of a raceway or conduit for the passage of the water from the river to supply the factories with power and to allow the usual traffic by teams, and also with proper sidewalks leading to the factories which shall front on these streets.

The intervening streets, which will be at the rear of the buildings, shall be of sufficient width to allow of tracks belonging to the different railroads and the necessary switches leading into the yards of the various industrial establishments, as well as teaming thereto.

The conduits or raceways shall be of such widths and depths as will furnish at all times the necessary quantity of water to supply the wheels located thereon, and they shall extend out into the river to a point at which the requisite depth is to be obtained.

Permanent embankments shall be made out into the river, economizing the material derived from the construction of the tunnels and raceways therefor.

These embankments shall be finished off at the outer end with crib work, running up and down the river in such a way as to form wharves for the landing of vessels navigating the river, and to protect the different raceways from floating ice.

The main tunnel from its mouth, which shall be at a point immediately north of the State reservation below the great falls to a point where the first mills can be erected above Port Day, I would recommend to be constructed with an area equivalent to a tolerably smooth tunnel of circular form of twenty-four (24) feet in diameter. Its mouth shall be located as low as high water below the falls will permit. It shall have a descent from a point half a mile above Port Day to its mouth of one in one hundred, or 52 and $\frac{80}{100}$ feet per mile.

Above Port Day the tunnel will gradually diminish in size, in accordance with the number of mills which have yet to empty their tail-waters into it, until at the upper end it will be of the same area as the cross tunnels which flow into it at that point.

The lateral or cross tunnels which shall receive the water from the different wheel-pits and discharge the same into the main tunnel, shall be of such size, and shall be located as shall best serve the requirements of the mills above them and the general ground plan of the town plat.

The bottom of these cross tunnels shall be so much above the main tunnel that they shall at all times be drained and accessible whenever the mills on that particular cross tunnel are not running.

The pits for the wheels shall be located in such a manner as to suit the particular requirements of the business to be carried on in the factory to which they belong, and shall conform to the general arrangement of the town plat.

The bottom of said pits shall be at such heights above the cross tunnels that work can be done in them at the same time the rest of the mills on that cross tunnel are in operation.

If the amount of water which will pass through a tunnel of twenty-four (24) feet in diameter, having a descent of one in one hundred, is used economically under heads ranging from one hundred and twenty-four feet to seventy-nine feet, through turbine wheels of the latest patterns, it will give a result equal to one hundred and nineteen thousand horse-power; or, in other words, is equal to two hundred and thirty-eight factories of five hundred horse-power each,

One has but to glance at this location, at the noble river on its front and the railroads in its rear, to see its perfect adaptability to the purpose here intended.

Here is a stream of which any one can say its surface height is always the same, and whose waters are of the purest quality.

Here will be no dams to break away, causing loss of life and devastating the country below.

Here no summer drought can cause a stoppage of wheels and busy hum of industry, to the loss of profit to the employer and of daily bread to the employed.

Here the manufacturer who erects his building may do it with a certainty that his work will go on uninterruptedly three hundred and sixty-five days in the year.

If the tunnel were to be begun to-day he could begin his workshop to-morrow, with the utmost faith that when both were completed he could start his machinery, and that if any stoppage occurred it would not be the fault of the ever-ready river, of the conduit which brought the water to his wheels, or of the tail-race which took it away, for they will be blasted out of the solid rock, and, like it, be imperishable.

Although for certain kinds of business, dependent on local custom for its support, steam may be the best, inasmuch as the fuel can be taken to the exact point at which the industry is to be carried on, yet for very many pursuits, where the materials used come from various sources and the articles manufactured are to be distributed all over the world, cheap water-power will always be sought for.

That cheap power this company will be able to give the manufacturer.

I have made out below a statement of the cost of running machinery by steam and water for one horse-power per year, as used in relatively large quantities, and as the latter power is leased in various localities in the Northern and Eastern States.

Mr. Cowles, of Rochester, gives the cost of running one horse-power by steam in that city at thirty-nine dollars per year.

Mr. Holly, of Lockport, gives, with coal at $4.00 per ton, the cost of running one horse-power at forty-six dollars per year.

Messrs. Poole & Hunt, of Baltimore, give the cost to be about six-tenths of a cent per hour with coal at $5.00 per ton, or forty-five dollars per year for one horse-power. And others about the same.

For rental of steam power in Boston $175.00 per year per horse-power is received. At Lowell the lowest is $100.00, with rooms. The Central Pacific Mill, with 1,000 horse-power, prefers to pay $60.00 per horse-power for water to using steam.*

The following prices are charged for water-power for one horse-power per year :

Paterson, N. J.	24 hours per day.		$37.50
Birmingham, Conn.	12 "	"	20.00
Mayanunk, Pa.	24 "	"	56.25
Dayton, O.	10 "	"	38.00
Wameset Dam	11¼ "	"	48.25
Lowell, Mass.	10 to 11¼ "	"	20.00
Lawrence, Mass.	10 to 11¼ "	"	20.00
Cohoes, N. Y.	10 to 11¼ "	"	20.00
Holyoke, Mass.	10 to 11¼ "	"	20.00
Lockport, N. Y.	24 "	"	16.66
Rochester, N. Y.	24 "	"	25.00

I would recommend that this company charge a price so low that it will be sure to prove an inducement to manufacturers to lease power.

I am of the opinion that ten dollars per year per horse-power, to be used twenty-four hours per diem, will effect this, and at the same time afford the capitalists holding the stock of the company ample returns for their money invested, notwithstanding the length of time which must elapse before the whole amount of power can be rented. This is only about one-quarter what is charged elsewhere, as shown above.

ESTIMATE OF COST.

One tunnel	$1,212,108
Twenty-four cross tunnels	448,430
Four shafts	38,700
Twelve raceways	329,927
Twelve bulkheads	12,200
Masonry and gates controlling sluices	27,500
Timber in cribs	45,000
Slope walls	90,000
Contingencies	46,135
Total	$2,250,000

Respectfully submitted.

THOMAS EVERSHED, C. E.

Rochester, July 1, 1886.

* From Samuel McElroy's pamphlet, in relation to water-power at Niagara Falls, read before the Western Society of Engineers, September 1, 1885.

OFFICE OF THE STATE ENGINEER AND SURVEYOR,
ALBANY, N. Y., July 19, 1886.

Chas. B. Gaskill, Esq., President " Niagara River Hydraulic Tunnel, Power and Sewer Co.," Niagara Falls, N. Y. :

SIR—I have examined the plans, computations and estimates forming part of the report to you of Thos. Evershed, Esq., upon the details of a method of utilizing a very extensive water-power at Niagara Falls by the construction of main and lateral tunnels which shall serve as tail-races to a large group of manufacturing establishments.

The general plan of the enterprise impresses me as the most comprehensive and economical scheme possible for using, on a grand scale, the almost unlimited hydraulic resources of Niagara.

These plans have been very intelligently elaborated, and the estimates for constructing the main and lateral tunnels and for the shafts, conduits, bulkheads and docks, are, in my opinion, amply sufficient to insure their completion at a rapid rate and in a thorough manner.

The advantages of the location are not overstated by Mr. Evershed, and may be briefly summarized to consist of an exhaustless supply of pure water, at a practically constant head, solid and durable rock, containing all the tunnels, shafts and conduits, and furnishing solid and imperishable foundations for all the structures and a nearly uniform surface of the proper elevation of the lands you have secured for the site of a manufacturing town to be developed by this enterprise.

Very respectfully yours,

ELNATHAN SWEET,
State Engineer and Surveyor.

BUFFALO GERMAN INSURANCE CO.'S BUILDING.

BARNES, HENGERER & CO.'S
GREAT IRON BLOCK.

DRY GOODS, CARPETS,
DRAPERIES AND SHOES,
Nos. 256 TO 268 MAIN STREET.

(See opposite page.)

REPRESENTATIVE HOUSES.

BUFFALO'S LEADING MERCANTILE, MANUFACTURING AND FINANCIAL CONCERNS.

' In the series of descriptive articles that follow we have endeavored to make concise and appropriate mention of every well-established, important and deserving mercantile, manufacturing and commercial house in Buffalo, feeling that so much of recognition is due to those whose industry, energy and capital are enlisted in building up the city's material interests and developing and maintaining her commercial supremacy. Only those establishments whose reputations are above suspicion have been mentioned, and if the list be incomplete it is not because of any bias on the part of editors or publishers.

With the utmost confidence we commend every business house named in these pages to the good-will and patronage of the entire country, East, West and South, as well as to our Canadian neighbors. Liberal, enterprising, of sterling personal and business character, this is the class of men upon whom the future growth of Buffalo and her influence upon the welfare of the country and the continent depend.

BARNES, HENGERER & CO.,

Importers, Jobbers and Retailers of Dry Goods, Notions, Carpets and Shoes— Nos. 256 to 268 Main St.

This great house succeeded the well-known firm of Barnes, Bancroft & Co., they in turn succeeding Barnes & Bancroft, and Sherman & Barnes, running back in a long and prosperous business career of over thirty years, making them, without exception, the oldest dry goods house in Western New York, and also the largest concern between New York and Chicago. The present firm name began in February, 1885, and is composed of Messrs. J. C. Barnes, William Hengerer, J. C. Nagel, C. O. Howard and J. K. Bancroft, the latter being a special partner, having retired from active business in the firm February 1, 1885. Mr. Barnes has been connected with the firm since 1850, Mr. Hengerer since 1861, Mr. Nagel since 1869, Mr. Howard since 1880, and Mr. J. K. Bancroft since 1871. Mr. W. G. Bancroft (partner with Mr. Barnes in the firm of Barnes & Bancroft, and later as Barnes, Bancroft & Co.) retired from business May, 1881, because of ill health, and died the following October. His brother, Mr. J. K. Bancroft, being a member of the firm, the old name was retained until the retirement of Mr. J. K. Bancroft, when it became the present firm, Barnes, Hengerer & Co., Mr. Hengerer having been a senior partner with Mr. Barnes since 1874.

The growth of this popular house has been wonderful—from a business of $200,000

5

to one of close on to $4,000,000 in Buffalo and $1,000,000 in Minneapolis, by their branch house there; which is, without doubt, the largest business by many hundreds of thousands west of New York and east of Chicago. The principles upon which this great house has built up its immense business have been to pay cash for all goods purchased, discounting every bill, large or small, and then selling upon small margins for cash, and at one price only to one and all. They employ, during different seasons of the year, from three hundred and fifty to four hundred persons in their different departments, retail, wholesale and manufacturing; over one hundred and fifty being employed in their cloak manufacturing department, which is a very important feature of their business, manufacturing over a quarter of a million dollars every year in cloaks and wraps of all kinds, jobbing large quantities in Pennsylvania, Ohio and Michigan, as well as our own State.

A partial description of the building in which this great business is transacted may be of interest to readers of this book. They occupy solely the immense building on Main street known as the "Great Iron Block," which is five stories high, entirely of iron, of magnificent proportions, and of great architectural beauty, 125 feet frontage on Main street, a depth of 235 feet to Pearl street, and a frontage on Pearl street of 145 feet. The first floor, which is one vast room, is used entirely for their large retail business. Some idea of the size of this immense floor can be obtained from the fact that seven times around it makes a mile. The basement, which is the same size as the retail floor, is used for the sale of oil-cloths, low-priced carpets, etc., and for the storage of the large reserve stock necessary in a business of this kind. The Main-street upper floors are used for the wholesale trade, which is very large, keeping from ten to twelve travelers constantly on the road. The Pearl-street building is used for their manufacturing business, which has been briefly outlined. No pains or expense have been considered in the fitting up of this model dry goods house for the comfort and convenience of their patrons—toilet and waiting-room for ladies, with female attendant; public drinking fountain; elevators, making access to wholesale departments easy and comfortable.

The members of this firm are courteous gentlemen of great affability of manner, with whom the transaction of business is a pleasure, which, taken with their great business sagacity and commercial integrity, is the secret of their wonderful success.

EXSTEIN & CO.,

Manufacturers and Jobbers of Men's Furnishing Goods—Nos. 104 and 106 Pearl St.

Among the variety of Buffalo manufacturing establishments there are comparatively few that transact a larger annual business than is done by Messrs. Exstein & Co. There is another feature of this business that has an important bearing on the general welfare of the city, and that is the amount of employment it furnishes to a very worthy class, and also the disbursement of a sum aggregating $50,000 a year for labor alone. This firm, which began business in this city in January, 1884, at No, 185 Washington street, is engaged in the manufacture of pants, overalls and shirts, and also as jobbers in gent's furnishing goods. The business increased rapidly, and now amounts to from $300,000 to $400,000 a year. In 1885 it was found necessary to secure more extensive quarters, when the firm removed to their present site at Nos. 104 and 106 Pearl street. Here a four-story building, 60 by 125 feet, is occupied, and a working force of seventy hands is required. The manufacturing facilities are excellent, and 75 machines, operated by a gas-engine, are run on the fourth floor of the building. Besides, a considerable quantity of work is done on the outside by women and girls who take it home. The trade of the house extends into Pennsylvania, Ohio, Michigan, Indiana, Illinois, Wisconsin and Minnesota, requiring the services of seven men on the road. The pay-roll amounts to $1,000 a week. The members of the firm are, J. Exstein, H. Waterman, I. Hyman and Max Weil, special. Mr. Exstein has resided in Buffalo for many years. He directs the manufacturing and has a general supervision of the entire business generally. Mr. Weil resides in New York, and is a member of the firms of Weil & Kohn, glove manufacturers, and the Crown Suspender Co. Mr. Exstein has always taken a lively interest in the city of Buffalo, and for a time filled the office of Park Commissioner.

This is a fair sample of the houses that have been largely instrumental in giving this city a status second to none in a good many lines.

JOHN B. MANNING,

Maltster and Importer of Canada Barley—Proprietor of Frontier Canada
Malt-house—Office, No. 59 Main St.

The malting of barley for brewing purposes is recognized as a leading American
industry, thanks to the immense German immigration that during the past half century
has flowed in and, to a great extent, revolutionized the bibulous tastes of our people by
the introduction of a less fiery beverage than that to which the fathers of the present
generation were accustomed. The port of Buffalo is especially well located for the
successful prosecution of this business for several reasons, prominent among which
may be mentioned her equable climate, permitting of a season some weeks longer in
duration than any other northern point, and her near vicinity to the famous barley-
growing regions of Western New York and Canada—regions producing heavier crops
and finer grades of this grain than can be found elsewhere in America. It is claimed,
and it is susceptible of proof, that Buffalo possesses ample facilities for the malting of
4,000,000 bushels of grain annually, which can be supplied to brewers all over the
country on the best possible terms, and, owing to the extraordinary advantages of the
city as a shipping point, either by lake, canal or rail, orders can be filled more promptly
and economically by Buffalo maltsters than by their rivals elsewhere.

It is not, however, of the malting interest in general that we set out to write, but
of the leading house here—perhaps the largest in the world—representing that interest,
viz., Mr. John B. Manning, whose name and whose large and extended trade are
familiar to every man at all conversant with this line of enterprise throughout the
States and the neighboring Dominion. Mr. Manning's malt-house, the "Frontier
Canada," is situated at Black Rock, foot of Auburn avenue, adjacent to the Grand
Trunk, Canada Southern and New York Central Railways and the Erie Canal, and near
the river. Side-tracks and elevators connect it with both canal and railways, and the
provision for the receipt and shipment of grain and malt is, beyond comparison, the
most complete of any in the country engaged similarly, there being also direct communication with the various railway lines traversing Canada and this State. This great
establishment, erected in 1873, is nine stories in height, 100 by 363 feet in area, contains
two steam elevators, has a storage capacity of 500,000 bushels, and an annual malting
capacity of nearly 1,000,000 bushels.

It is almost needless to say that the malt made in this house is invariably of the best quality, a favorite with brewers, and commands the highest ruling figures at all times. Mr. Manning is also a heavy importer of Canada barley—concededly the best grain for malting that can be procured. His business office is at No. 59 Main street, a location selected because of its contiguity and convenience to the various railways, the canal and river. He employs from eighty to ninety men in his malt-house, elevators and offices.

Mr. Manning came hither from Albany in 1856. Three years later he began business as a commission merchant and maltster, a calling to which he devoted himself with industry and assiduity, and thus founded upon a lasting basis his present great enterprise. He has also been successful socially, politically and as a public-spirited citizen, having succeeded Mr. Cleveland in the office of mayor, and filled the vice-president's and president's chairs of the Board of Trade.

GEORGE MUGRIDGE & SON,

Steam Bakery—Manufacturers of Choice Biscuits, Crackers, Cakes, Jumbles, etc.—Nos. 10, 12 and 14 Elk St.

It is always a matter of personal gratification to come in contact with the successful business man. This is particularly the case with the writer whose duty it is to chronicle the business affairs of a community, and more especially so when the aforesaid business man proves to be the true type of the perfect gentleman, in his counting-room as well as anywhere else. These observations are the outcome of impressions received in an interview with the house of Messrs. George Mugridge & Son. The result of a call there was prolific of a fund of interesting information in regard to one of the oldest and most successful of Buffalo's industrial interests.

Since 1841 this house has been engaged in the manufacture of that variety of indispensable as well as toothsome articles which the well-appointed steam bakery is constructed for. Its founder was the elder Mr. James Mugridge, a native of Ellsford, Kent, England, who arrived in New York with his family, including the head of the present firm, in 1831. He was then thirty-five years of age, and possessed of a capital largely made up of that indomitable energy and self-reliance which characterized the early settlers. He located in Utica in the fall of the same year, and finally came to this city in 1841. He began the business herein referred to on a very limited scale. The enterprise prospered from the start, and in 1850 its promotor retired from the business and was succeeded by Mr. Geo. Mugridge, the senior member of the present firm. January 1, 1863, Mr. James A. Mugridge was admitted a member of the house, when the present style was assumed. The business, under the careful management it always received, continued to expand until it has now reached proportions which its founder probably never anticipated. The buildings occupied, which front on Elk and Illinois streets, are of brick and specially designed for the business and include an area of 60 by 150 feet. It would be superfluous to enumerate the mechanical equipment in detail, as it includes all the latest and most improved inventions known to the trade. The daily output consumes 125 barrels of flour. An adequate idea can be formed of the different manipulations it receives when the one item of oyster crackers is turned out by the million each day. Take another item by way of illustration : In jumbles, 3,000 per minute are cut and placed in pans. The same magnificent scale of operations applies to the great variety of fancy cakes, biscuits, crackers, snaps, bread, rolls, etc. A working force of from sixty to seventy-five employees is constantly required, and the local trade alone necessitates a half-dozen wagons. The annual business is, in the aggregate, about a quarter million dollars, and extends to all the lake ports and through the States of New York, Pennsylvania, Ohio and Michigan. This requires the attention of several traveling representatives.

It is unnecessary to state that the uniform high standard of the goods of this house has always been maintained. Also, in their dealings with the trade, Messrs. Mugridge & Son invariably are the soul of liberality and high-mindedness. Both members give their personal attention to the business, and in every particular the house is and always has been a model one.

LEE, HOLLAND & CO.,

Manufacturers of Doors, Sash, Blinds, Shutters, Mouldings, etc.—Wholesale and Retail Dealers in Rough and Dressed Lumber of all Descriptions—Boxes, Nailed, Dovetailed or in Shooks—Corner Court and Wilkeson Sts.

A little more than thirty years ago Messrs. Eaton & Co. founded on a small scale the now great and celebrated door, sash and planing mill above illustrated. Since then several changes have occurred in the ownership—first, to Eaton, Brown & Co., then, in 1868, to Clarke, Holland & Co., and in 1881 to Lee, Holland & Co., who still own and operate the plant, which has grown in extent, value and volume of products until to-day it is one of the largest in the country, fronting 375 feet on Wilkeson street, 325 feet on Court street, with a depth of 65 feet on both streets, and a height of three and four stories. The machinery equipment is complete and costly, embracing every approved modern device for the rapid and economical working of wood, the dressing of lumber, the manufacture of finished building material, boxes. etc. A force of two hundred and fifty men is employed; the weekly pay-rolls average $2,500, and the average annual value of the output is about $450,000, most of which is manufactured to order for or sold to the trade in New York city, where a branch warehouse is maintained. It is scarcely necessary further to describe this splendid establishment, our engraving giving a much better idea of its appearance and extent than any words could do.

It will be noted that ample lumber yards and dry-kilns are attached, and that railroad tracks bound two sides of the premises, thus furnishing unsurpassed facilities for the delivery of raw material and the shipment of manufactured goods, the latter embracing full lines of pine and hardwood doors, solid and veneered, sash of all kinds, outside and inside blinds and shutters, mouldings, flooring, siding, ceiling, rough and dressed lumber for all purposes, boxes and packing-cases, in short, anything required in the line of mill work. The lounge and mattress works of Holland & Vilas, of which a detailed account will be found on another page, occupy a portion of these buildings.

The members of the firm are Messrs. James H. and Franklin Lee, Nelson Holland and Henry Montgomery. Mr. Henry Montgomery gives his undivided attention to the affairs of the house, here and in New York. Mr. Frank Lee is interested in lumbering at the West and in the dredging of the harbor and canals of Buffalo. Mr. Nelson Holland, one of the city's oldest and most conspicuous business men, is a member of the firms of Holland & Stuart and Holland & Vilas, and is a heavy lumber manufacturer at East Saginaw, Mich. In all, it is doubtful if any concern in the country commands a better array of personal character. energy, enterprise, business capacity and public spirit than are marshaled under the name and style of Lee, Holland & Co.

HOWARD H. BAKER & CO.,

Ship Chandlers, Riggers and Sailmakers—Dealers in Cordage, Wire Rigging and Rope, Steel and Iron Hoisting Tackle, Sails, etc.—Nos. 18, 20, 22, 24 and 26 Terrace.

Situated at the foot of lake navigation, controlling direct rail and water lines to the seaboard, the port of Buffalo is naturally and necessarily the headquarters and outfitting point of the shipping of our inland seas, and consequently the building and equipment of steam and sailing craft is a large and flourishing industry that rather increases than diminishes year by year, employing hundreds of industrious artisans turning out millions of dollars' worth of first-class work annually.

The most conspicuous Buffalo house engaged in the handling of cordage, wire rope, hoisting tackle, etc., and the making of sails, is the great ship-chandlery establishment of Howard H. Baker & Co., Nos. 18, 20, 22, 24 and 26 Terrace, occupying the entire triangular space lying between Commercial and Pearl streets and the Terrace, four stories and basement, one hundred feet front on the Terrace by seventy feet on Commercial and Pearl streets. The house was founded in 1830, by William S. Waters & Co., at the corner of Prime and Lloyd streets, removing in 1844 to the Union Steamboat Company's building, foot of Lloyd street. Kimberly & Waters in 1833 succeeded Wm. S. Waters & Co., and were in turn succeeded by Waters & Atwater in 1836, the latter firm changing to Atwater, Williams & Co. in 1841. In 1845 Williams, Howard & Co. became proprietors, and were succeeded in 1850 by Howard, Newman & Co., who retired to make room for Vosburgh & Baker. In 1883 the present firm, composed of Howard H. Baker and Thomas Warren, took charge, and have made the concern more successful in every way than ever before. Mr. Baker has been connected with it since 1854, while Mr. Warren has had a practical experience of twenty-five years in his calling.

This house employs about a dozen skillful riggers and sailmakers, the sailmaking department being known as D. Provoost's Sons; handle vast quantities of superior cordage, wire rigging and rope, steel and iron hoisting tackle, canvas, and everything required above decks in fitting out steam or sailing craft, large or small. They find their regular customers in all the lake ports and among the shipbuilders and owners of Buffalo, and do an annual business of $100,000. Their work, which can be found on all northern waters, speaks for itself.

Mr. Baker is an enterprising and prominent Buffalonian, a native of the county, and has resided here since 1847. He is a director of the Lake Erie Excursion Co., vice-president of the Young Men's Association, president of the City Club, and popular and respected in all the relations of life. Mr. Warren is a native of Canada, resides at Fort Erie, and attends strictly to business.

R. HUMPHREY,

Wholesale and Retail Dealer in Flour, Feed, Coal and Wood—Foot of Amherst St., Black Rock.

Mr. Humphrey established himself at the above location in 1882, and, with the assistance of Mr. A. W. Gilbert, who holds a silent partnership, invested capital to the amount of $23,000 in stock and facilities, which are first-class. A large and well-selected line of choice flour and breadstuffs, hay, grain and mill-feed, invite the attention of the trade, while he handles immense quantities of coal and wood. He offers the best in all lines on the most reasonable terms. Employing ten men in store and yards, and selling to the retail dealers of Buffalo, Tonawanda, and surrounding towns, his transactions average about $100,000 a year.

Mr. Humphrey is of Welsh nativity. He came to New York at the age of twenty, without capital, has farmed some and had the care of Mr. C. Gilbert's horses for twelve years.

DAVID TUCKER & CO.

Photographic Supplies, Picture Frames, Mouldings, Stereoscopes, Albums,
etc.—Nos. 410 and 412 Main St.

Philo Allen founded this house in 1850—more than thirty-six years ago—since
which time it has been conducted by several successive proprietors, coming into the
hands of the present firm, composed of David Tucker and Stephen B. Butts, in 1868.
Mr. Tucker has had an experience of many years in the handling of photographic
supplies and kindred goods, and is an expert in all that concerns the art and its requirements. Mr. Butts was formerly engaged with Philo Allen as clerk, and has always
been in this business, joining Mr. Tucker when he entered, and has mastered all of its
details so thoroughly that he is now justly considered an authority on the subject of
advanced photography, its history and its needs.

The firm occupy three commodious floors at the above number, each 25 by 100 feet,
elegantly fitted up in every department and stocked with an exhibit of photographic
goods of all kinds, American and imported, such as perhaps no house west of New
York can show, embracing full lines of photographic apparatus, materials, cameras,
plates, chemicals—in short, anything and everything relating to the art, together with
an endless assortment of rosewood, walnut, velvet, gilt and fancy frames and mouldings. This grand depot of supplies can fit out a complete photographic studio down to
the most insignificant item, ready for business, within twenty-four hours. Everything
handled by the house is guaranteed as represented, while its reputation for promptitude
and reliability is established and secure.

LOUIS A. LENHARD & CO.,

Produce Commission Merchants and Wholesale Dealers in Butter, Eggs,
Cheese, Poultry, Fruits, Vegetables, etc.— No. 602 Washington St., opposite Washington Market.

The above enterprising house was established in 1880, and has proved a very successful one, doing already an average annual business of $50,000, extending throughout
Western New York and Pennsylvania, as well as the city. The firm, composed of
Louis a Lenhard and J. J. Zimmer, occupy one floor at the above number, 22 by 80 feet,
and carry fine stocks of fall goods in their line, embracing dairy, orchard and farm products, poultry, etc., and make specialties of butter, eggs and cheese, of which they
handle large quantities on commission. Both partners are experienced commission
men, and their house is enjoying great prosperity.

THE RICHMOND ELEVATOR. (See opposite page.)

THE RICHMOND ELEVATOR.

Mrs. Mary E. Richmond, Proprietress—Buffalo River, Opposite Foot of Main St.

Any account of the business history of Buffalo would be incomplete that should neglect special mention of the Richmond Elevator, which, standing opposite the foot of Main street, has for nearly twenty-two years exerted a beneficent influence upon the commerce and contributed to the glory of the city.

This fine elevator was built by the noted Richmonds, Dean and J. M., in 1865, and has always been a valuable and desirable property. Dean Richmond died in 1866, and in 1880 his widow purchased the interest of J. M. Richmond, thus becoming sole owner. James McCredie. Esq., No. 236 Main street, is attorney and agent for the Dean Richmond estate. Mr. George Emslie, who entered the service of the Richmonds at the opening of the elevator in 1865, as assistant superintendent, has for more than ten years filled the post of superintendent, while his son, Mr. Henry P. Emslie, is foreman, having under his direction about one hundred men.

The Richmond Elevator, eligibly located with reference to lake and canal navigation and railroad communication, occupies premises about four hundred feet square, fronting on Buffalo river and the Blackwell canal. The building itself is 125 by 125 feet, with a height of 125 feet, and is fitted up in the best manner throughout, the largest dry-kiln in the United States, with a capacity of 15,000 bushels per day, forming a portion of the equipment. The storage capacity is about 300,000 bushels, or 6,000,000 per annum.

Like the other elevators here, the Richmond is a member of the Western Elevator Company, more extended notice of which will be found under the proper heading elsewhere.

DENTON & COTTIER,

Sole Agents for Steinway & Sons' Pianos—Music Publishers—Importers of All Kinds of Musical Merchandise—No. 269 Main St.

Most refined people are more or less musical; consequently, the more intelligent and refined the community, the more inclined is it to musical pursuits. Hence Buffalo, while making no noisy pretensions to extraordinary musical culture, is, nevertheless, as the home of a well-to-do, educated people, really a musical center of no small merit, and its people liberal patrons of all that tends to encourage and elevate the art. Consequently, the vocation of the dealer in music, musical goods. etc., takes high rank here, and is generously supported by the public at large, and more especially by those whose social and pecuniary position is such as to require and justify the necessary outlay.

The oldest and most conspicuous musical emporium here—the one that has contributed most to develop the musical taste of the Buffalo public—is that of Denton & Cottier, No. 269 Main street, established by James D. Sheppard in 1827. The style became Sheppard, Cottier & Co. in 1863, Cottier & Denton in 1867, and, by the association of the last named junior partner with the widow of the former senior in 1888, the present firm of Denton & Cottier was formed. It is needless to speak at length of the experience of Mr. Denton, who has been a partner in the house for nearly twenty-three years, and now has the active management. He is known, personally or by reputation, to nearly everybody in Western New York, and popular with all. The house does a prosperous business of from $75,000 to $100,000 a year, and handles one of the largest, most complete and finest line of musical goods of any establishment between New York and Chicago, requiring for salesrooms and storage purposes the entire four-story and basement building. 20 by 100 feet, in which it is domiciled. The stock embraces a great variety of superior pianos, comprising fine selections of the justly celebrated Steinway & Sons, Steck, Mathuschek, Fisher and others, together with Wilcox & White and Schoninger organs, etc. The firm are also direct importers of every description of musical merchandise and instruments, and publishers of sheet music, in which latter specialty the house enjoys an enviable celebrity.

Mr. Denton is an Englishman, formerly a successful teacher of music, a church organist of note, and a past master of Erie lodge No. 161, F. and A. M.

ROOT & KEATING,

Tanners of Hemlock Sole Leather—Office and Warehouse, Nos. 14 to 24 Wells St., Buffalo ; Tanneries, Port Allegany, Pa., and Olean, N. Y.

The manufacture of leather, one of the most important and indispensable of industries, is well represented in Buffalo by the splendid house of Root & Keating, whose great warehouse, illustrated by the accompanying cut, forms an attractive feature of the city in the vicinity of the Union depot. This fine building fronts 127 feet on Wells street, with a depth of 134 feet, and is five stories high, furnishing ample storage room for all the leather made at the firm's vast tanneries at Olean, N. Y., and Port Allegany, Pa., the former of 600 and the latter of 700 sides daily capacity.

Messrs. Root & Keating give exclusive attention to the manufacture of superior hemlock sole leather, and have every desirable facility, as above indicated, for placing upon the market vast quantities of the highest grades of this material, the demand for which increases from year to year as its excellent quality becomes more widely known. Their tanneries, as before stated, are among the largest in the world. They are also among the best arranged, supplied with improved machinery and every available modern device for the rapid and effective manipulation of hides, and conveniently situated with reference to the hemlock forests of New York and Pennsylvania as well as to the lines of transportation. The firm find ready demand in American and European markets for every pound of sole leather they can produce, their goods, by reason of careful and skillful workmanship, commanding the confidence of consumers and the highest prices wherver offered. Some two hundred men are employed in all, and the value of the output ranges up into the millions.

The members of the firm, Messrs. Francis H. Root and Robert Keating, are experienced, able and popular business men, famous throughout Northern and Western New York. The industry under consideration was founded in 1864 by Jewett & Keating, passing into the hands of the present firm in 1876. Mr. Root was formerly of the house of Jewett & Root, who began the manufacture of stoves in Buffalo fifty years ago. Mr. Keating was of the same firm until 1864, when the firm of Jewett & Keating was formed. Both members give their exclusive attention to the firm's present interests, and have built up their sole leather manufacture from small beginnings to its now commanding position among the largest and most valuable business enterprises on the continent. Both are earnest, energetic, enterprising and public-spirited men, and are adding largely to Buffalo's commercial prestige as well as to their private fortunes.

CLARK & ALLEN,

Wholesale and Retail Dealers in Wall Papers, Paper Hangings, Art and Mural Decorations, Window Shades and Fixtures, etc.— No. 570 Main St.

Interior decoration is no longer a mere trade that may be pursued successfully by any one who can obtain a paper-hanger's outfit, but an art hardly second to that of the fresco painter, whose labors it supplements and sometimes even supplants. Thanks to this art, the palaces of the rich and the cottages of the poor alike are rendered more luxurious, more beautiful and more homelike than ever before, while skill and invention are more than ever stimulated to new and pleasing combinations of patterns, colors and effects.

"There is always room at the top" in every calling, and, acting upon this truism, Messrs. Thomas S. Clark and William S. Allen, recognized masters of the art, in 1885 entered into a copartnership and opened the now popular and well-patronized establishment at No. 570 Main street, and achieved an immediate and remarkable success. Their establishment occupies two floors of the handsome building indicated, each 18 by 105 feet, and is stocked with superb lines of choice goods pertaining to interior ornamentation, embracing all the favorite varieties of wall papers, art and mural decorations, including the famous Lincrusta-Walton for hangings, wainscoting, dadoes, friezes, borders, ceilings, etc., plastic relief for hand decorating, plain and fancy room mouldings, chair rails, etc. Carrying complete new stocks of novel and standard designs in hangings, and employing a corps of competent workmen, the house is prepared to make contracts at comparatively low rates for paper-hanging in all its branches, fresco and plain painting, tinting and decorating, producing novel and artistic effects and doing first-class work. They also make to order any desired style of window-shade. No pains or expense is spared to please, and Messrs. Clark & Allen have fairly earned their remarkable success.

BUFFALO ACADEMY OF DESIGN AND ART SCHOOL.

E. Henri Kelly, Principal—Southeast Corner Main and Mohawk Sts.

The object of this most beneficent and successful institution is to place ample means of theoretical and practical instruction within reach of all who desire to advance themselves in draughting and the practical construction of buildings. It is organized and conducted upon broad and comprehensive principles, such as will afford the student rare scope and opportunity for perfecting himself in the higher mechanics, and gives him a kind and degree of training unattainable in any of the mere technical schools or workshops where only theory is taught upon the one hand and practice on the other. An experienced, practical designer, draughtsman and builder has practical direction of the school—a gentleman who possesses not only the knowledge required, but the ability and tact which enable him to impart it to others. The branches taught —beginning at the foundation and systematically grounding the pupil in the fundamental principles upon which to rear a substantial superstructure—are : The arts of designing, mechanical draughting, architectural draughting, surveying and civil engineering, mathematics, geometry and philosophy, commercial law, pencil drawing, crayon drawing, India ink drawing, water-color drawing, etching and stipple drawing.

Not only are draughting and construction taught theoretically, but the pupil is rapidly advanced to the mechanical or building department, where tools, materials, etc., are furnished free, and he not only draughts the plan but constructs a miniature building in all its parts, thus gaining practical as well as theoretical knowledge of the mechanic arts. Designs for every description of buildings and bridges are furnished, and approved principles of construction taught by precept and practice.

The school is a valuable auxiliary to the building trades especially, and is largely availed of by those who, either with or without previous training, desire to perfect themselves as first-class mechanics. The course comprises four terms of three months each, night sessions also being held.

Prof. E. Henri Kelly originated and founded this school, the first session beginning September 1, 1882, and has received a great deal of encouragement, both moral and material, at the hands of the classes it is designed to benefit. Mr. W. D. Phelps is professor of mathematics and geometry. Mr. Kelly, during his ten years of experience as a teacher, has instructed some 5,600 pupils, any of whom will testify to the benefits received. The academy occupies an entire floor of the large building southeast corner of Main and Mohawk streets, 30 feet front by 80 feet deep, has a fine attendance, and is steadily growing in popularity and usefulness.

One of the visible results of the Buffalo Academy of Design is the introduction of veneered brick architecture, already much in vogue east, and of which the residence of Dr. S. W. Wetmore, No. 176 Franklin street, is a fine example. The plan of construction, which, it is claimed, saves ten to fifteen per cent. of the cost of building and renders the house fifty per cent. dryer and warmer, is to erect a balloon frame, to which one course of bricks is anchored with nails. This style of building is sure to become popular on its merits.

GEO. W. TIFFT, SONS & CO.,

Manufacturers of Steam Engines and Boilers, Propeller Wheels, Mill Gearing, Architectural Castings, etc.—Repair Work a Specialty—Office, No. 35 Washington St.

For nearly half a century Buffalo has been celebrated for the character and extent of her manufactures in iron and steel, and more particularly in the departments of engines, boilers, mill machinery, architectural iron work, and kindred lines of products. It is safe to say that in the building up of the superb reputation of the city in this direction no rival establishment has done more, if so much, as the famous old house of Geo. W. Tifft, Sons & Co., founded in 1842 as the Buffalo Steam Engine Works. Since then many changes have occurred in the *personnel* of the firm, but the ancient and honored style adopted in 1857 has been retained, while the same splendid business management and mechanical skill have marked its entire career. At present the firm is composed of Mr. Charles L. Whiting, the general manager, who has had charge since 1865, Mrs. C. C. F. Gay and Mrs. George D. Plimpton, both of whom entered the house on the demise of Mr. John V. Tifft, some two or three years ago.

The works front on Washington street, from No. 15 to No. 35, cover four acres of ground, and embrace three three-story buildings, containing a machine shop of 18,000 square feet, two large foundries, two boiler shops, a pattern shop, and a separate one and three-story fire-proof warehouse devoted to the storage of patterns, of which an immense and extremely valuable stock is carried, comprising most of those originated by or used in the works during the past forty-five years, and presenting an almost complete exhibit of its productions since the first casting was made by the original owners.

A complete equipment of modern improved machinery and appliances forms a valuable and indispensable portion of the plant, which is the most extensive of the kind in Buffalo, if not in the entire State. A force of 250 to 275 skilled mechanics and laborers find steady and remunerative employment in the various departments, and from $90,000 to $100,000 is annually disbursed in wages alone.

The leading specialties of the establishment are the manufacture of engines and boilers of all kinds, marine and stationary, mill gearings, and superior architectural castings, for which they have unsurpassed facilities and a heavy trade extending throughout New York, Pennsylvania, Ohio, and to all portions of Canada and the

Northwest, where their work is held in the highest repute for style, workmanship, durability and all excellent qualities.

Mr. Geo. W. Tifft, a stockholder in the original company, and for more than twenty-five years head of the firm of Geo. W. Tifft, Sons & Co., laid down the burden of an honored life some years ago. He was universally respected and regarded as one of Buffalo's most valuable citizens, contributing of his time, labor and means to place and keep her in her present proud position as Queen of the Lakes. He was an acute, far-seeing and public-spirited business man, to whom the city is largely indebted for her material and moral growth.

Mr. Whiting, Mrs. Gay and Mrs. Plimpton are also the proprietors of the Tifft Furniture Company, and largely interested in all that tends to the welfare and prosperity of Buffalo.

Of the fine work done by the architectural department of Geo. W. Tifft, Sons & Co. we have space here only to particularize the iron work—stairways, etc.—of the new Buffalo Library building and Music Hall, German Insurance building, Becker's new store, Masonic Temple, Elmira, and the Lockport Court-house, all fine artistic work, unsurpassed by the most celebrated iron founders and architects of this country or of Europe.

THE MANUFACTURERS AND TRADERS BANK,

Pascal P. Pratt, President; Francis H. Root, Vice-President; James H. Madison, Cashier; Harry T. Ramsdell, Assistant Cashier—Capital, $900,-000; Resources, $4,346,762.60—Southwest Corner Main and Seneca Sts.

The Manufacturers and Traders is one of those powerful and influential financial corporations of which New York boasts so many, organized and operated under wise State laws which, while extending proper encouragement and protection to the investors of capital in this most necessary branch of enterprise, yet hold the banker to a strict accountability to his depositors and public opinion.

The Manufacturers and Traders' Bank of Buffalo was chartered March 24, 1856—nearly thirty-one years ago—with $200,000 capital; Henry Martin, president; Pascal P. Pratt, vice-president; D. F. Frazell, cashier, and the following board of directors: Pascal P. Pratt, Francis H. Root, William H. Glenny, jr., Bronson C. Rumsey, Guilford R. Wilson, Myron P. Bush, Sidney Shepard, A. H. Anderson, Jason Sexton, George Truscott, S. V. R. Watson and Wells D. Walbridge. In 1859 the capital was increased to $500,000, and in 1870 to $900,000, at which figure it has ever since remained. The bank has been removed several times. First established at No. 2 Swan street, the first change was to the Harvey block, No. 273 Main street, in December, 1856; the second to No. 22 West Seneca street, in 1861, and the third and last to the spacious fire-proof iron building, southwest corner of Main and Seneca streets, in April, 1880.

This bank, established especially for the accommodation of manufacturers, merchants and others engaged in active business, has carried out its original plan to the letter, its vast capital, careful and conservative management and the well-established personal and mercantile character of its founders and promoters enabling it to extend moral and financial aid to its patrons and the general public in time of need, and uphold and foster the material interests of the city in the most effective manner. Prudence and economy have characterized its entire career, and it commands the entire confidence of business circles at home and abroad. The subjoined quarterly statement for December 11, 1886, gives in condensed form the condition of this leading institution at the present time: Resources—Loans and discounts, $3,814,612.10; overdrafts, $532.60; due from banks, $525,502.94; real estate, $41,541.75; bonds and mortgages, $42,671.35; United States bonds, $67,500; specie, $75,745.28; currency, $110,500; cash items, $2,081.12; total, $4,680,687.26. Liabilities—capital, $900,000; undivided profits, $144,-903.75; due depositors, $3,464,109.71; due banks, $171,673.80; total, $4,680,687.26. The officers of the Manufacturers and Traders Bank are: President, Pascal P. Pratt; vice-president, Francis H. Root; cashier, James H. Madison; assistant cashier, Harry T. Ramsdell. Of these Mr. Pratt was first vice-president and Mr. Root one of the original board of directors. Mr. Madison has been cashier since July, 1869. Directors—Pascal P. Pratt, Francis H. Root, James H. Madison, Sherman S. Jewett, Bronson C. Rumsey, Gibson T. Williams, William H. Glenny, Richard Bullymore, John D. Hill, Franklin D. Locke, John L. Williams, Nelson Holland and Robert L. Fryer.

This institution does a regular legitimate banking business in deposits, loans, collections, exchange, etc., receives accounts of banks, bankers, manufacturers, merchants and others on the most favorable terms, remits collections at lowest rates, and renders satisfaction to all customers.

HATCH & JENKS.

Buffalo Coffee, Spice and Drug Mills—Importers and Jobbers of Teas, Coffees and Spices—Manufacturers of Pure Spices, Baking Powder, Flavoring Extracts, etc.—Nos. 155 and 157 Washington St.

The demand for pure drugs, spices, coffees, etc. —demoralized by the civil war and the reckless speculative methods consequent thereto, which led to adulterations and misrepresentations of the grossest kinds in the name of legitimate business —has revived under the fostering care of a small but resolute class of upright importers and manufacturers, and once more it is possible, with care and discrimination, to obtain genuine Mocha and Java, genuine imported spices, and drugs that have not been tampered with by the deft fingers of the "manipulator." It is still, necessary, however, to look well to the name of the manufacturer and avoid counterfeit labels when purchasing ground goods of any kind.

A Buffalo firm that has contributed much to this end, and which, in consequence, has earned for itself an enviable reputation with the trade and consumers, is that of Hatch & Jenks, Nos. 155 and 157 Washington street, whose finely-equipped mills, forty-five feet, and four stories high, comprise one of the most valuable plants of the kind in the country. Messrs. Hatch & Jenks are heavy importers and jobbers of fine teas, coffees and spices, and, having the advantage of steam power and a complete line of modern improved machinery, they put upon the market large quantities of roasted coffees, ground spices, etc., conveniently packed for the trade in such a manner as to retain their aroma and strength indefinitely. They also grind drugs to order for the trade, and guarantee satisfaction in all cases. They give special attention, besides, to the handling of pure teas of their own importation, of which they carry at all times an extensive and carefully selected stock, comprising all the favorite brands of Chinese and Japanese growths. Catering only to the highest class of trade, the house handles no inferior goods. The Buffalo Coffee, Spice and Drug Mills were erected in 1849 by Messrs. Bradford & Chase, and for many years enjoyed a fame co-extensive with the Union, changing hands several times. In April, 1881, Messrs. Hatch & Jenks, importers of teas, coffees and spices, purchased these mills with the view of extending their operations, which they have succeeded beyond their anticipations in doing, their average sales for several years exceeding $150,000. They employ five travelers and fourteen operatives, and are flourishing as they deserve. They are also manufacturers on a large scale of chemically pure baking powders and flavoring extracts, and will fill all orders promptly and satisfactorily. Such a house is a credit to any city.

SPENCER HOUSE,

Cor. Washington and South Division Sts.—George Sperber, Proprietor.

This popular hotel was first opened in 1860. Since 1881 the present proprietor, Mr. George Sperber, has been in charge, and the house has been entirely refitted and refurnished. It is a very popular resort for the theatrical profession, and every week the representation among that fraternity is as large as that of any other in the city. They have every inducement in the way of first-class fare and accommodations. Mr. Sperber has had an extended experience in the business. He was four years at Delmonico's in New York, and has resided in Buffalo over three years. He was a member of the Sixth Bavarian infantry three years, is a Mason and also a member of the order of United Friends. Mr. Sperber has been a great traveler, having visited every country of Europe. He thoroughly understands catering to the traveling public, and has made the Spencer House a popular resort.

W. H. GLENNY, SONS & CO.

Importers and Jobbers of Crockery, China and Glass, Kerosene Chandeliers, Lamps and Trimmings, Clocks, Plated and Sterling Silverware, Gas Fixtures, etc.—Nos. 253 to 257 Main, and 260 and 262 Washington St.

One of the most attractive of Buffalo's mercantile establishments is that of Messrs. W. H. Glenny, Sons & Co., Nos. 253 to 257 Main street, of which great thoroughfare its superb iron and glass front is an ornament that at once arrests the attention and excites the admiration of the sojourner in the city. This fine five-story edifice, fronting fifty-five feet on Main, extends through, two hundred feet, to Washington street, and is in all respects one of the most elegant and convenient business structures in America. It is, however, the beautiful and useful contents that attract the visitor and leads him or her on from department to department until the entire display has been looked upon with pleasure and approval.

It would be vain to attempt, within the limits of a notice of this kind, a detailed description of all the fine and handsome objects of ornament and utility carried by Messrs. W. H. Glenny, Sons & Co. Suffice it to say that it embraces full lines of imported and American household goods for the trade—plain and ornamental china, glass, crockery, chandeliers, gas fixtures, lamps of all kinds, with trimmings for same, clocks in every conceivable design, sterling silver and plated ware, and a variety of goods too numerous to even name here. The house also makes a specialty of a full line of domestic housekeeping goods of medium grade and low prices, enabling their trade to supply consumers with anything required, suitable for people in every station and of every degree of means.

As before remarked, this is one of the largest establishments in the country. The founder of the house, Mr. W. H. Glenny. came hither from the north of Ireland in 1836. He was of Scotch descent, and partook largely of the thrift and virtues of that people. His first employment here was as clerk in A. W. Wilgus' bookstore. In 1840 he embarked in business for himself as proprietor of a small crockery store. The growth of the business obliged him from time to time to enlarge his quarters until, in 1877, he was obliged, for the proper accommodation of the stock, to erect the block now occupied by the firm, which consists of Wm. H., Bryant B. and John C. Glenny and Irwin R. Brayton, who, upon the death of W. H. Glenny, sr., succeeded him in business.

Some idea of the operations of the house may be gleaned from the fact that, in addition to the building already noticed, the firm has a six-story warehouse, 65 by 125 feet in area, at No. 45 Pearl street, stocked at all times from cellar to roof with goods of all grades in their line, exclusively for the wholesale trade.

Messrs. W. H. Glenny, Sons & Co. maintain a broad territorial connection with the trade in general, extending all over New York, Pennsylvania, Ohio, and throughout the West and Northwest. The firm is one of the most liberal and obliging in existence, and offers rare inducements to buyers. The office of the house is at No. 251 Main street.

GERHARD LANG'S PARK BREWERY.

Office, Corner Best and Jefferson Sts.; Depots: Boston, Baltimore and
Washington.

This now celebrated brewery, among the largest in Western New York and enjoying
a national reputation for the superior quality of its product, was founded in the year
1845 by Mr. Philip Born, to whom Mr. Jacob Webner succeeded, Mr. Lang buying out
the latter in 1863.   Under the present administration the property has grown to
extraordinary proportions and immense value, the malt-houses and brewery buildings
occupying an entire block, bounded by Jefferson, Best, Berlin and Dodge streets, and
the architectural character of the improvements are of the handsomest and most substantial description, as will be seen by reference to our engraving.   The establishment
employs in all one hundred and ten men, and the average annual output is not less
than 100,000 barrels of the finest quality of lager beer, a favorite brand at home and
sold largely throughout the Atlantic States, as far south as Virginia, requiring the
maintenance of depots at Boston, Baltimore and Washington, the New York and
Philadelphia markets being supplied by direct shipments from Buffalo in refrigerator
cars.   All the malt required in the brewing operations is made on the premises from
selected Canada barley, and is of the highest grade.   The brewery itself is equipped
from vault floors to roof in the most complete and perfect manner with every improved
modern appliance, including several immense ice machines, and additional facilities and
conveniences are added, from time to time, as required.   The leading specialty is
Bohemian larger beer for export and home consumption, and it is safe to say that no
finer article is made either in this country or in Europe.
   Mr. Gerhard Lang, the head of this great brewing and malting industry, is a
native of Germany, and emigrated to this country in 1848, when but fourteen years old.
He learned the trade of butcher, which he successfully pursued until his marriage.
in 1867, when he took possession of Born's brewery at the corner of Genesee and
Jefferson streets.   Industrious, energetic and enterprising, it was not long ere he had
built up a business too extensive for his facilities.   Looking about him in search of
elbow-room, he secured the ground he now occupies, and has continued to prosper and
add to his trade and manufacturing capacity from year to year until now, although he
owns an entire square where his brewery stands, he has been compelled to extend his
malting facilities by the purchase or erection of buildings in other portions of the city,
and turns out about 250,000 bushels of this product per annum.
   Mr. Edwin G. S. Miller, Mr. Lang's genial and popular son-in-law and partner, has
for the past two or three years assumed an active part in the business management of
these several enterprises, and has sole charge of all actual operations in brewery
and malt-houses.   The effect of this infusion of young blood is seen in the many
improvements, rapid advance and redoubled activity that has recently characterized
every department.
   Mr. William Simon, the intelligent and skillful superintendent of the brewery, has
been in the same employ for the past six or seven years, and is one of the most capable
and progressive men in the business.
   "Good wine needs no bush."   Lang's Bohemian larger beer speaks for itself, and
every competent judge of the amber beverage pronounces the same verdict in regard
to it—nothing better can be made from malt and hops.

NIAGARA ELEVATING COMPANY.

George F. Sowerby, Manager and Cashier; George S. Wride, General Foreman—Ohio St., Foot of Chicago; Office, Room 44 Board of Trade.

Oliver Evans invented the grain elevator in 1780, but it was not until 1842 that it was diverted from its original employment in the mill to the transferring of grain in bulk from vessel to warehouse and from warehouse to canal-boat and railroad car ; and to Buffalo belongs the credit both of that long forward stride and the erection of the first combined steam elevator and grain warehouse. Mr. Joseph Dart, who originated this innovation, referred to it in 1865 as follows : " My experiment, from the very first working, was a decided and acknowleged success. Within a month after I started, a leading forwarder, who had confidently predicted that shippers could not afford to pay the charges of elevating by steam, came to me and offered double rates for accommodation, but my bins were all full. The great saving of time by the use of the elevator was immediately seen. To give an instance that occurs to my mind, the schooner John B. Skinner came into port, with four thousand bushels of wheat, early in the afternoon, and was discharged, received ballast of salt, and left the same evening ; made her trip to Milan, Ohio, brought down a second cargo and discharged it ; and on her return to Milan, went out in company with vessels which came in with her on the first trip down, and which had but just succeeded in getting rid of their freight in the old way." Of course the handling of grain at this port immediately received a fresh impetus, and the erection of mammoth elevators became the order of the day. It is, in fact, to the grain elevator, combined with her geographical, lake and railroad transportation advantages, that Buffalo owes her remarkable development and extraordinary prosperity during the past forty-five years.

The most capacious and complete elevator ever built here by private capital was that of the Niagara Elevating Co., erected at Ohio and Chicago streets in 1868, with a storage capacity of 650,000 bushels, and facilities in the way of machinery, etc., for the transfer of 96,000 bushels per day. Three years later Mr. Thomas Clark purchased the plant, and continued to operate it with unvarying success until in 1881–82 he built Elevator B (the old one being since known as Elevator A), of 1,400,000 bushels capacity, both together having facilities for the storage of 2,000,000 bushels. Mr. Clark continued at the head of this immense business on his own account until his death in September, 1882, when it again passed into the hands of the Niagara Elevating Co., of which Mr. George F. Sowerby became manager and cashier, and Mr. George S. Wride general foreman of elevators.

About fifty men are employed, and seven hundred dollars per week is paid in wages. We have already referred to the capacity of these monster elevators, which are located at the foot of Chicago street, occupying the ground between Ohio street and the City

6

canal, with the advantage of side tracks and every convenience for the forwarding of grain.

Manager Sowerby came to Buffalo from Wyoming county, N. Y., in 1883, entering the service of the Niagara Elevating Co. as general manager and cashier, still retaining his present responsible position by dint of unflagging industry and business ability. He has charge of the office, room 44, Board of Trade. Foreman Wride, who personally directs operations at the elevators, is a native of Sodus, Wayne county, N. Y., came to Buffalo in 1883, and has acceptably fulfilled the duties of his present position ever since, having full control of the elevators and employees.

F. A. KENNEDY CO.,

Manufacturers of Fine Biscuit—Factories, Cambridgeport, Mass., and Chicago, Ill.—Office and Warehouse, No. 15 East Swan St., Buffalo—Manager, F. P. Hazen.

Mr. Kennedy established his wonderfully successful venture in 1839, at Cambridgeport, Mass. More recently, a splendid branch factory was erected at Chicago, and, the demand justifying the movement here, in the spring of 1886, warerooms and a wholesale agency were opened at No. 15 East Swan street, Buffalo, under the management of Mr. F. P. Hazen, who had a previous experience of ten years in the company's service at other points. The F. A. Kennedy Co., as at present organized, is officered as follows : F. A. Kennedy, president ; J. W. Hazen, secretary and treasurer at Cambridgeport; H. J. Evans, secretary and treasurer at Chicago.

The Buffalo agency is handsomely fitted up, occupying the storeroom and basement above named, 30 feet front by 100 feet deep, and carries full stocks of the Kennedy Company's unequaled goods, embracing the justly celebrated " Champion," " Cream," " Butter," " Zephyrs," " Fancy Graham," " Cold Water," " Oswego," " Columbia," " Vanilla Cream," " Illinois Butter," "Rockaway " and " Cream " wafers, many of which are packed in one and two-pound packages, handsomely labeled for family trade, and carried by all leading grocers. It is scarcely necessary to write a word of praise of these goods, they are so widely and favorably known.

The Buffalo agency already has a large and growing trade with grocers and others in this State, Pennsylvania and Ohio.

POWERS, BROWN & CO.,

Miners and Shippers of Reynoldsville Gas and Steam Coal and Coke—Coal and Iron Exchange.

Of the leading corporations that have played a prominent part in making Buffalo a great coal market, that of Powers, Brown & Co. ranks with the foremost. For this reason, and also from the extent of their operations, the company is entitled to more than a passing notice. Their mines, which include the Soldier Run, Sprague, Hamilton and Pleasant Valley, are located at Reynoldsville, Pa., the center of a vast bituminous region. The mines have a daily capacity of 2000 tons, and are supplemented by sixty-two coke ovens. Their average annual output is from 300,000 to 400,000 tons of coal and coke. This is distributed throughout this State, the New England States and Canada. About 500 tons goes to New York city daily. The working force required to operate the mines and coke ovens is about 600 men, and the monthly pay-roll ranges from $17,000 to $20,000.

This company was established in 1865, and first transacted business in Buffalo at No. 7 Main street, where it continued until 1885. The company was incorporated in 1879, with the present officers, as follows : J. Craig Smith, president ; Geo. H. Lewis, vice-president; Andrew Cant, secretary and treasurer. The capital of the company is $450,000, from which it can be readily inferred that unlimited facilities for carrying on the business are possessed. The company's general offices in the Coal and Iron Exchange are handsome and commodious, and the business at this end is under the immediate direction of Mr. Cant. It goes without saying that he is the right man in the right place.

CORNELL LEAD CO.,

Manufacturers of White Lead, Lead Pipe, Sheet and Bar Lead—A. P. Thompson, President; S. Douglas Cornell, Vice-President; Henry Spayth, Treasurer; Sheldon Thompson, Secretary—Office and Works, corner Delaware Ave. and Virginia St.

The general public have a very imperfect idea of the important part lead performs in the mechanic arts and domestic economy. Though classed as one of the base metals, dull and unattractive in appearance, destitute of glitter and musical ring, and of comparatively small money value, it is nevertheless a fact that the strictly useful trades, commerce and some of the finer arts could much better dispense with gold and silver than with our humble, unpretentious, yet ever useful and faithful friend in the blue gray coat, who, in one form or another, protects our homes from the elements, carries water to every room, stops the leaks in all the gas-pipes, secures the glass in the sky-lights, forms a component part of the glass itself, smiles at us from the pictures on the walls, and meets and serves us at every step of our daily lives.

Everybody knows that lead is dug from the bowels of the earth, that it is purified by fire, and that it is cast into bars called pigs, in which form it is simple commercial galena; but comparatively few are conversant with the processes by which it is prepared for final use by the painter, the plumber, the glass-worker, the builder, the sportsman and the soldier. As at present we have only to deal with the subject as related to the useful trades, we shall omit further reference to the manufacture of sporting and ordnance stores, and confine our attention to a description of what we saw on a recent visit to the Cornell Lead Company's works, corner of Delaware avenue and Virginia streets, this city, where about two acres of valuable land is devoted to the production of white lead, lead pipe, sheet and bar lead. The buildings comprise one of four stories, 40 by 60 feet; one of four stories, 25 by 80 feet; one of four stories, 20 by 60 feet; a one-story corroding-house, 60 by 200 feet, and a large and commodious laboratory and office. The plant is one of the most complete in existence, embracing a costly equipment of the latest improved machinery and an 80-horse power steam engine and boiler. From thirty to sixty men are employed, and the capacity in all departments aggregates 3,000 tons per annum; five tons of the best white lead and an equal weight of lead pipe and bar lead every working day the year round. S. G. Cornell's hydraulic process for the production of lead pipe, the most effective ever discovered, is in use here, turning out vast quantities of pipe which for uniformity, density, strength and freedom from flaws, is unrivaled. It is the manufacture of white lead, however, which, involving extraordinary skill, care, time and patience, possesses greatest interest for the visitor. With the unsurpassed facilities at hand, each process is as carefully studied as though the company were making but 100 pounds per day. Every step is directed toward securing the utmost purity of product, and every possible precaution is taken to preserve it from anything calculated to deleteriously affect it, the company having a standing offer of twenty dollars per ounce for all adulterations and impurities found in their goods. This explains why only the best results are obtained, and why the "Cornell" brand commands such decided preference among practical painters and dealers in white lead.

The material employed is the ordinary pig lead of commerce, which is received in heavy consignments of eighty and one hundred-pound bars, direct from the mining districts of the West and Southwest. It is removed from the cars to the casting-house, where, with the aid of an ingenious casting machine, it is formed into circular "buckles," five inches in diameter and one fourth of an inch in thickness. After cooling, these "buckles" are conveyed to the corroding-house, where they are placed separately in small earthen jars or pots, with cup-shaped bottoms, each containing about a half pint of acetic acid. When filled, the jars are ranged in tiers, one above another, the bottom tier resting upon a heavy dressing of tan-bark, spread upon the ground, and each tier being covered with a plank floor dressed in like manner with tan-bark, upon which rests the next tier, course after course succeeding, until the roof is reached, when the whole mass is allowed to remain undisturbed for about ninety days, during which time the acetic acid acts upon the lead, evolving carbonic acid gas, thus reducing the metal to carbonate of lead. The carbonate is then carefully removed and dumped into a screen specially designed to separate the converted from the unconverted lead, the latter passing into a conveyer which carries it back to the yard, while the crude carbonate goes into a hopper, and thence between powerful rolls to be crushed and pulverized. From the rolls it is elevated to another screen, where any uncrushed particles that remain are separated and again returned to the rolls for further pulverization. The finely reduced carbonate is then passed through another screen corresponding to the bolting screen of a flour mill, provided with an automatic attachment supplying the proper quantity of water, and is made ready for the water mills, of which there are several, each provided with a run of the finest French burrs. After leaving the mills the carbonate is, of course, about as smooth and fine as repeated and minute trituration can make it; still, lest some coarse particles may possibly remain, it is subjected to the further and final test of the "floating" apparatus, where mechanical agitation separates the last vestige of grit, which returns to be reground, and the mass goes into the settling vats, and the water drawn off until the snowy lead is reduced to the consistency of paste. Thence it is removed to the drying kilns, and afterward ground in oil or packed for shipment in the dry state.

The Cornell Lead Company, at this time the only house of the kind in Buffalo, and one of the most extensive in the United States, was founded in 1852, by Messrs. S. G. Cornell and G. T. Williams, under the style of the Niagara White Lead Co. In 1859 they bought out the old firm of Thompson & Co. In 1861 S. G. Cornell & Son became sole proprietors, and in 1867 the Cornell Lead Co. was organized ; S. G. Cornell, president ; A. P. Thompson, vice-president ; S. Douglas Cornell, secretary, The present officers are named at the head of this article. They are all able, experienced, industrious and enterprising gentlemen.

MERCHANTS BANK OF BUFFALO.

W. H. Walker, President; James R. Smith, Vice-President; F. W. Fiske, Cashier; William H. D. Barr, Assistant Cashier—Chartered 1881—Capital Stock, $300,000—No. 208 Main St.

As will be seen by reference to the statistical portion of this work, the banks of Buffalo command a vast aggregate of capital and do a very large business in loans, discounts, collections and deposits. One of the soundest and most reliable of these institutions is the Merchants Bank of Buffalo, Nos. 206 and 208 Main street, which, though only chartered in 1881, is already in the front rank as regards character, solidity, usefulness and public confidence—a result referable to the excellent management that from the beginning has marked its course and the superb directory and list of officers who have controlled its affairs. So well, indeed, have the officers performed their functions, that but one change has occurred since the original organization, Mr. W. H. Walker, the prominent shoe and rubber merchant, succeeding Mr. A. P. Wright in the presidency. With the advantages referred to, and a cash capital of $300,000, it is not, after all, surprising that the Merchants has proved a successful and profitable venture, as is shown by the following exhibit, condensed from the official statement of December 11, 1886 : Resources—Loans and discounts, $1,311,448.22; overdrafts, $130.77; bond and mortgage, $4,354.20 ; United States bonds, $1,000.00; real estate, $24,465.97; due from banks, $177,810 56; currency, $66,955.00; specie, $41,219.18; cash items, $19,371.79; total, $1,646,755.69. Liabilities—Capital, $300,000.00; profits, $65,152.48; due banks and bankers, $53,495.61; due depositors, $1,228,107.60 ; total, $1,646,755.69. The average surplus of the bank has been, for five years past, $60,000 ; earnings, $140,000; dividends, $81,000; average deposits, $1,200,000. The list of depositors is quite large, among the best classes of the community, and is constantly increasing in numbers, while the deposits grow day by day perceptibly.

The officers' names will be found in the caption of this notice. The board of directors is composed as follows : W. H. Walker, president and wholesale shoe dealer ; James R. Smith, vice-president and wholesale lumber merchant ; Alfred P. Wright, ex-president and commission dealer in grain and stocks ; John B. Manning, maltster; William H. Gratwick, lumber dealer ; Robert B. Adam, of Adam, Meldrum & Anderson ; J. F. Schoellkopf, miller and tanner; George Urban, jr., miller ; George W. Miller, largely interested in the Buffalo Car Manufacturing Company, Scoville's Car-Wheel Company, and the Buffalo Cast-Iron Pipe Company ; Daniel O'Day, president of National Transit Company; and Daniel N. Lockwood, a leading attorney.

THE CRANDALL HOUSE.

Asa B. Crandall, Proprietor, East Buffalo Stock Yards.

Mention of the Stock Yards and the live stock interest would be incomplete without a reference to the hotel accommodations for the men engaged in the business. For many years Mr. Asa B. Crandall has been, to drovers and stock dealers, one of the best-known citizens of East Buffalo, in his capacity of hotel proprietor. He first took charge of the Stock Exchange Hotel in 1877, and soon established a popularity which is peculiarly the birthright of the born hotel man. In October, 1881, he became proprietor of the hotel which now bears his name. It is a very commodious and well-appointed house, and is run in strictly first-class style. It has accommodations for 170 guests, which have frequently been taxed to the utmost. The interior was re-furnished and decorated last spring at an outlay of $8,000, and additional accommodations are contemplated. Mr. Crandall is a New Yorker by birth, and has been in the hotel business all his life. The Crandall House is looked upon as a regular headquarters for stock men while in Buffalo. The rates are $1.50 per day, and it is no exaggeration to say that it is not surpassed by any at the same price in the country. The dining-room is where the patrons get in their work, as many as 350 dinners having been served on the same day. Mr. Crandall is ably seconded by his amiable wife, who equally understands and supervises the direction of affairs.

THE SCOTT SIGN CO.

T. B. Schwarz, Albert Hutter, Proprietors—No. 348 Main St.

This is an age of progress, and the art of sign-painting progresses with the times. Not that all sign-painters are artists; far from it; but the sign-painter who is an artist is necessarily a progressive one, an original genius as well as a skillful handler of the palette, brush and maulstick, and is never content to criticize his own or any other man's work with the mediocre ultimatum, "That'll do." With him the instinct of excellence is strong, and not until he has done his very best in the way of design, proportion, color and effect, is he satisfied to lay down his implements, wash his hands, deliver his work and collect his money.

Such men as this compose the famous Scott Sign Company, successors to the celebrated Frank B. Scott, whose reputation extended throughout the North and West, he having carried on the business here for nearly fifty years, and attained a most enviable eminence therein. The members of the present company, Messrs. T. B. Schwarz and Albert Hutter, are young, enterprising, public-spirited, capable and extraordinarily skillful in their vocation, both trained from boyhood to the highest class of sign-painting, theoretical and practical, and associated for the express purpose of revolutionizing the art so far as Buffalo is concerned. That they have made great strides in this direction is attested by the hundreds of samples of their skill which already adorn the city's business houses, among them, and especially worthy of mention, being the signs of Down the jeweler, the Globe clothing-house, Bliss Bros., photographers. Sippel & Son, tailors, the Wheeler & Wilson Sewing Machine Co., E. N. Yerxa's grocery house, and others—signs that are true works of art, beautiful in proportion and design, appropriate and attractive.

The Scott Sign Co. occupy the entire fourth floor of No. 348 Main street, 25 by 65 feet, employ a large force of competent workmen, superintend all work themselves, are prompt, earnest and reliable and very popular.

PRINTING ROOM of
COSACK & COMPANY
LITHOGRAPHERS & PUBLISHERS
The largest and most complete Press Room in the
United States: Daily capacity over 200,000 sheets.

(See opposite page.)

COSACK & COMPANY.

Herman Cosack, H. T. Koerner, Charles E. Hayes—Lithographers and Publishers—Nos. 90 to 100 Lakeview Ave., Buffalo—Branches in New York, Chicago, Philadelphia, Boston, Cincinnati, St. Louis, Hartford, Pittsburg and Toronto.

The art of lithography becomes daily of greater excellence and utility to the world. Its field of usefulness is practically unlimited, and it has become an important factor in the cluster of manufactures that have developed in the United States during the past fifty years. The aggregate capital invested in the United States is nearly twenty million of dollars, and the number of hands directly employed over twenty-five thousand. The rare skill of its designers, artists and craftsmen have easily placed lithography in the very front rank of artistic usefulness, and at the same time brought the cost within the reach of the merchant and the manufacturer. Each year witnesses new developments and discoveries in the art, and the establishment of colossal new houses devoted to its pursuit. Buffalo has long been noted for the number and high rank of its lithographers. Cosack & Company have contributed principally to extend her fame abroad through the land, and have marked the progressive steps of the art in achievements which have placed them among the first three establishments in the United States. Proof of the commanding position long held by them was supplied by the special authorization given them by the Centennial commissioners in entrusting them with the lithographic reproduction of the most important exhibits of the Centennial Exposition—a tribute to the glory of lithography and a lasting monument to the ability and skill of this firm. Originally founded in a modest way by Mr. Cosack, April 4, 1864, the house has earned its title to distinction by the energy, enterprise, skill and liberality that has ever characterized its operations. Mr. Cosack's first establishment was located on Main street; in 1867 removed to 251 to 257 Washington street, in what was then well known as the "Commercial Advertiser" building; in 1880 to 204 to 210 Exchange street, from where, by the operations of the West Shore road, they were obliged to remove to temporary quarters, corner Swan and Ellicott streets. In 1885 they finally removed to the present splendid building, erected by them specially for the business, on Lakeview avenue. Several changes had occurred previously in the firm by the admission, withdrawal and death of partners, and the present firm of H. Cosack, H. T. Koerner and Charles E. Hayes was organized in August, 1881. Messrs. Cosack and Koerner are practical lithographers of commanding talent and skill, and personally superintend the operations within the establishment, while Mr. Hayes has charge of the business department and supervises the various branches of the company in New York, Chicago, Philadelphia, Boston, Cincinnati, St. Louis, Hartford, Pittsburg and Toronto. The firm's building, erected in the center of an immense open square, 103 by 318 feet, has a frontage of 70 feet on Lakeview avenue and a depth of 300 feet, two stories high in front and three in the rear. The general offices and private offices of Messrs. Cosack and Hayes occupy the ground floor front, while Mr. Koerner's office, which commands a full view of the lithographing and press-rooms and the artists' rooms, occupy the second story front, commanding a fine prospect of Lake Erie, Niagara river and the picturesque and historical Canada shore. We copy the following well-written description from the Buffalo *Commercial Advertiser* :

" The press-room on the ground floor, opening immediately from the main offices, is the largest press-room in the United States, measuring 70 by 200 feet and 40 feet high, without a single post, partition, belt, shaft or pulley to obstruct the view or to impede the movements of the employees. The roof is supported by fourteen trusses of immense strength resting on brick and stone abutments. To the right of the room are the large stop-cylinder Hoe presses, on solid foundations placed in one line, occupying a length of 147 feet. At the end of these are the paper-cutters, bronzing machines, stone planers, ink mills, etc. Immediately in the rear of the presses are 14,000 feet of drawer racks for printed paper, with a capacity of over 200,000 sheets—a day's run. In a line with the racks is placed all the stones, selected and arranged according to size, three by six inches to 34 by 48 inches, numbering in all over 4,000. On the left-hand side of the press-room are the hand presses of the provers and transferrers. In a straight line back of these are the stone grinders and the shipping department. As we leave the press-room two large doors give entrance to the drying-room, 70 by 70 and 40 feet high, filled with high drying-racks. From here a magnificent view of the lake, the Niagara river and the new proposed park are obtained. All of the rooms, offices, press-room and drying-rooms are located on one floor, making up the total length of the building. One flight of stairs down from the drying-room brings us to the bindery and paper stock rooms, also 70 by 70 feet. A little door to the left, through the intersecting wall, dividing the press-room from the drying-room, explains the absence of all belts, shafting, counter-shafting, pulleys, etc., with their complement of oil, grease, dust and danger from the press-room. Here, running from the level of the bindery floor to the offices, underneath the entire press-room, is a tunnel, 200 feet long, 18 by 11 feet, in which all of the shafting, etc., and all of the driving machinery of the establishment is placed, thus effectually doing away with the greatest obstacle printing rooms of all classes are subjected to. This is at once the most novel and useful feature of this model establishment. Immediately below the bindery floor, on a level with Fourth street, is the engine and boiler room, coal pit and general storage-room of the company. Two boilers of 75 and 50 horse-power respectively, with Andrew Ritter's smoke consumer attached, furnish the power for a large 75-horse-power Tifft engine, which runs the works, and a 30-horse-power Rice's automatic engine for the Weston incandescent electric light dynamo, by which the entire plant is lighted."

From 175 to 220 persons are employed in this great lithographic establishment, including artists, pressmen, transferrers, feeders and assistants in all departments. Wages to the amount of $1,800 per week are disbursed, and the firm's output averages $300,000 a year. The leading specialty is fine color work, for which the house is justly famous. Cosack & Company are a credit to Buffalo, and perform their full share in spreading abroad the fame of the " Queen City of the Lakes."

W. H. WALKER,

Wholesale Boots, Shoes and Rubbers—Nos. 210 and 212 Main St.

The wholesale trade of Buffalo in boots, shoes, rubbers and kindred goods is very large, and grows with a healthy and permanent growth that must be very gratifying to the business community at large, as well as to those directly engaged in it. In the introductory chapters of this work will be found the statistics of this, with those of other branches of commerce, and it must be acknowledged, by even the most indifferent, that they present a pleasing exhibit.

Of the leaders in this branch of enterprise few, if any, have of late years exercised a more powerful or beneficent influence than the gentleman whose name heads this notice. For more than thirty years previous to 1876 he was of the celebrated firm of O. P. Ramsdell & Co., where he acquired a thorough knowledge, theoretical and practical, of the boot, shoe and rubber business. Withdrawing in the year named, he established his present colossal house, Nos. 210 and 212 Main street, where he has achieved, in ten years, a success and reputation that most men would be proud to have earned in a life-time.

Mr. Walker's regular customers are found all over Western New York, Northern Pennsylvania, Ohio, Indiana, Michigan, other Western States, and the Dominion of Canada. In his specialties of men's, women's, boys', misses' and children's boots, shoes and rubbers, no house, East or West, can offer better inducements as regards styles, workmanship, materials or prices, nor in the careful filling of orders, promptitude and liberality. His goods are from the most reliable manufacturers, and a bill of lading from W. H. Walker is tantamount to a guarantee. As to the volume of his sales little need be said—in fact, no better evidence of the confidence in which he is held, or the condition of his business, could be adduced than the simple statement that for several years past his annual transactions have averaged $700,000.

His store and warehouse are among the most commodious and convenient on the continent,—the former 37 by 80 feet, five stories and basement ; the latter located in the rear, 60 by 60 feet and six stories, and devoted almost exclusively to rubber goods. An immense and extremely valuable stock is carried at all seasons, and buyers will always find here a varied and carefully selected assortment from which to choose. Several elevators, operated by silent Otto gas engines, facilitate communication between the numerous floors of both buildings, and, with excellent light and ventilation, add much to the comfort and pleasure of a tour through the premises.

Mr. Walker employs, in all, twenty men, seven of whom travel for the house, while the remainder are utilized as bookkeepers, clerks, salesmen and porters.

Mr. Walker also stands very high as a citizen and in mercantile and financial circles. He is president of the Merchants' Bank of Buffalo, and enjoys the unbounded confidence and respect of all classes.

On the first day of January, 1887, Mr. Walker admitted as partners Edward C. Walker and William A. Joyce, and the style of the firm is now, Wm. H. Walker & Co. These gentlemen have been with Mr. Walker for many years, and this advancement is a just recognition of their faithfulness and ability.

BUFFALO CEMENT COMPANY (Limited),

Manufacturers of Hydraulic Cement.—Lewis J. Bennett, President; Andrew Spalding, Vice-President; William W. Pierce, Secretary and Treasurer—Office, No. 110 Franklin St.; Works, Buffalo Plains.

Among other important lines of manufacture for which Buffalo has secured a leading position for unsurpassed excellence may be mentioned that of cement. A representative of this work was fortunate in paying a visit to the works of the Buffalo Cement Company (Limited), which are located in the suburban portion of the city out Main street known as Buffalo Plains. With the able assistance of the president of the company, Mr. Lewis J. Bennett, a complete tour of inspection was made of the works and surrounding premises. The result completely demonstrated the fact that this company is manufacturing an article of cement which is equal in every respect to the imported article known as the world's standard — Portland cement. This company owns 220 acres of land, containing valuable deposits of stone particularly adapted, with the special methods of treatment employed by this company, for the production of the best quality of cement. Mr. Bennett is an accomplished geologist, as well as a mechanical expert, and has given the subject years of the closest investigation and study. The result will be briefly sketched.

The Buffalo Cement Company (Limited) was incorporated March 7, 1877, with a capital of $100,000. New works were erected on a large scale. There are twelve kilns, with a capacity of 1,200 barrels per day. The mill is 50 by 60 feet, and, included with a warehouse, 130 by 50 feet. Adjoining, on the west side, is another warehouse, 162 by 49 feet, and adjoining on the east is another warehouse, 182 by 36 feet. A new warehouse, 200 by 51 feet, will occupy a position parallel with the track of the Erie railroad, which reaches the works. The disintegrating mills are worthy of mention. This mill is Mr. Bennett's patent, and is different from any other in the world. It readily reduces the hardest quality of stone after coming from the kilns, and which formerly could not be utilized. This, when ground, makes the best quality of cement, equal in every respect to the Portland article. Tests were taken of cement, which showed the following results: A briquette, one inch square, twenty-one days old, showed a tensile strength of 300 pounds; another, thirty-nine days old, broke at 316 pounds, while the average at one year, without being mixed, was about 600 pounds, pure cement. The crushing strength is ten times the above. In 1878 Mr. Bennett made over 1,000 tests of all the different cements, a record of which is on file. It was found that the cement of this company would carry sands with the Portland. The Sewer Commision of this city tested over 26,000 barrels used in sewer construction, with the most satisfactory results.

The product of the works for the year 1886 aggregated 225,000 barrels. From 125 to 150 men are employed, and the pay-roll averages $6,000 a month. The total storage capacity will be 50,000 barrels. Mr. Bennett is a native of Fultonville, Montgomery county, this State, and has been a resident of Buffalo for twenty years. In the course of his investigations Mr. Bennett has secured numerous fine fossils and geological specimens. Many of these have been secured by the Smithsonian Institute. He also has complete specimens of the geological formations to a depth of 500 feet, secured with a diamond drill at the works.

THIRD NATIONAL BANK OF BUFFALO,

Charles A. Sweet, President; John D. Hill, Vice-President; Nathaniel Rochester, Cashier; William H. Stebbins, Assistant Cashier—Capital Stock, $250,000; Surplus Fund, $65,000; Average Deposits, $1,500,000—S. E. Corner Main and Swan Sts.

The Third National Bank of Buffalo, a recognized leading financial institution, was organized and chartered February 14, 1865, and has therefore been in existence nearly twenty-two years, during which time it has performed its full duty toward its customers and the public and contributed in a marked degree to the progress of the city and the development of its material interests.

That wisdom as well as liberality characterize the operations of this bank under its present administration is abundantly shown by the last quarterly statement, as follows : Assets— Loans, $1,218,656.18 ; United States bonds, $225,000 ; real estate and B.M., $62,186.46 ; premium paid, $27,500 ; due from banks, $290,292; cash, $160,957.93; total, $1,984,792.57. Liabilities —Capital, $250,000; profits, $12,554.65; surplus, $65,000; dividends unpaid, $30; circulation, $45,000; deposits, $1,612,207.92 ; total, $1,984,792.57.

The board of directors is composed of a selected list of prominent business and professional men, representative of their respective classes, as follows : Pascal P. Pratt, of Pratt & Letchworth, manufacturers of malleable iron, etc.; Emanual Levi, capitalist ; Hon. L. L. Lewis, judge of Supreme Court ; John Satterfield, Charles G. Curtis and John N. Scatcherd, merchants ; Robert Keating, of Root & Keating, wholesale leather ; John D. Hill, physician, and Charles A. Sweet, president of the bank. The officers are experienced and capable gentlemen, urbane and obliging, and popular with the business community. The Third National Bank building is a handsome and substantial four-story and basement structure, centrally situated and eligibly adapted to the banking business, fronting 40 feet on Main street and 176 feet on Swan, well provided with fire and burglar-proof vaults, and the banking-room remodeled, refitted and doubled in floor space during the past summer. The Third National is an eminently safe, flourishing and reliable institution which embarks in no questionable ventures, its management having long ago learned the value of the word " no " when properly used.

BUFFALO CITY FLOUR MILLS.

Harvey & Henry, Proprietors—Manufacturers of Highest Grades Roller Process Flours for Bakers and Family Use—Dealers in Grain, Mill Feed, etc. —Nos. 91 to 107 Chicago St.—Up-town Office, No. 227 Washington St.

Nothing more nearly affects the health and happiness of mankind than the bread they eat, and, as good bread is impossible without good flour, it is safe to say that the miller is more closely identified with the source of human enjoyment than any other of all the thousands who contribute thereto. Buffalo has long enjoyed peculiar and important advantages as a milling center—first as the metropolis of the former great Western New York wheat region, and later as the grand entrepot and point of transhipment of Western grain to the Atlantic seaboard —and it is safe to say that, though she cannot now boast of such immense mills as are found in Minnesota and some other newer States, nevertheless Buffalo ingenuity, enterprise and capital have done as much or more to bring the art of flour-making to its present stage of perfection than has ever been contributed by any other milling city on this continent.

There are still, however, several very large and valuable flouring mills here, turning out vast quantities of superior flour, and one of the most prominent of these is the Buffalo City Flour Mills, corner of Chicago and Miami streets, a substantial four-story brick building, 115 by 125 feet square, comprising two entirely separate and distinct mills under one roof—one devoted to the reduction of winter wheat, the other to hard spring wheat. The best obtainable grades of grain only are used, and as a result the flour produced is absolutely unexcelled in all desirable qualities and immeasurably popular with all competent judges who have given them a fair trial. Of course these flours are made by the latest improved patent roller process—a system which of late years has completely revolutionized the whole art of milling.

These mills were erected by Mr. H. J. Harvey in 1867, Mr. F. J. Henry securing a partnership in 1874. The equipment embraces a powerful steam engine, seven run of gradual reduction stones, a full complement of improved roller process machinery, and all the appliances necessary to a complete flouring plant, the capacity being about six hundred barrels per day. The firm also have ample storage facilities, and usually carry from 100,000 to 125,000 bushels of wheat. The firm also have the requisite machinery for the manufacture of the best grades of middlings, mixed feed, wheat screenings, etc., deal extensively in corn-meal, oat-meal, oil-meal and grain, and make quite a feature of their trade in dry feed, selling largely to city and country trade.

Mr. H. J. Harvey is a native of this State and a member of several prominent Buffalo business houses—Harvey Bros., Smith, Falke & Co., the Niagara Baking Co., Harvey & Dake, etc. Mr. F. J. Henry is of French birth, but has resided here since 1858. In all, the concern does an annual business of $2,200,000, and is truly one of Buffalo's great industries.

JOHN R. POTTER,

:Photographer—No. 323 Main St., Opposite the Churches.

None of the arts come nearer to our homes and affections than does photography. By its means the poorest as well as the wealthiest are enabled to preserve the pictured semblance of their loved ones, and adorn their walls with faithful reproductions of the masters' best efforts.

Photographers, however, are of several classes, ranging from the true artist of talent, attainments and experience, whose heart is in his work, down to the veriest botch, and those who would obtain satisfying results must perforce exercise judgment and discrimination ere sitting for portraits.

One of the most accomplished and skillful members of the profession of whom we have any knowledge is Mr. John R. Potter, whose fine studio and gallery of art occupy the third and fourth floors of the handsome building No. 323 Main street. These rooms are 25 by 80 feet in dimensions, beautifully lighted, and fitted up in the completest and most attractive manner—the operating apartment and studio with all the latest improved and most effective apparatus and appliances, the gallery elegantly furnished and attractive with a display of rare gems of photography which attest the taste and skill exercised in their production and arrangement.

Mr. Potter has devoted more than twenty-three years of his life to mastering his art in all its details, constantly experimenting and conscientiously striving for the highest excellence He is a native of East Aurora, N. Y., where he also maintains a flourishing branch establishment, opened three years ago. His headquarters here was founded in 1874 at No. 305 Main street, whence he removed first to No. 256 Main street, and last year to his present desirable location. He is a popular gentleman, studious and attentive, and in every way a successful and prosperous man.

F. W. CAULKINS,

Architect and Superintendent—Room 68, Chapin Block.

Much of the credit for Buffalo's rapid advancement as a city of late years is due to her architects, many of whom occupy prominent places in the front rank of the profession. One of the most conspicuous of these is Mr. F. W. Caulkins, whose handsome office, a little hive of bustling yet studious industry of itself, occupies room 68, Chapin block. Mr. C. is a successful man in the best sense, for his success has conferred and continues to confer substantial and lasting benefits upon the community with which he has cast his lot. A polite and kindly gentleman, an active and enterprising business man, and an architect of the highest class, he has achieved a personal popularity and professional eminence such as any man might well be proud of.

Mr. Caulkins was born in Hartford, Conn., removing when a youth to Toledo, Ohio, where he studied architecture from 1865 to 1871, when he took charge of Charles Coots' office at Rochester, N. Y. Thence he went to Knoxville, Tenn., where he managed A. C. Bruce's architectural business for a while, returning to Mr. Coots, with whom he remained until 1875, when he became connected with Mr. M. E. Beebe of this city. In 1878 he opened an office for himself at Main and Swan streets. Four years later he removed to Minneapolis, Minn., and October 14, 1885, returned to Buffalo and established his present office.

Of the work he has done here and elsewhere the following list, while but a partial one, exhibits most of the most artistic, imposing and costly : Buffalo—Residences for George Francis, North street and corner Franklin and Allen streets ; Mr. Lynes and F. W. Caulkins, Franklin street; Dr. J. B. Coakley, Dr. A C. Hoxsie and James G. Forsyth, and remodeling residence for Mrs. George C. Whiting, Delaware avenue ; residences for Nelson Holland and Porter Hickox, Bryant street ; for Mrs. I. S. Bennett, Frank C. Porter and Mrs. McNevin, on the Circle ; for James H. Smith, Ferry street ; E. B. Smith, Linwood avenue ; remodeling residence for same, Linwood avenue and Perry street ; fifteen frame houses on Fourteenth street ; Chapin block, Swan and Pearl streets ; Austin's fire-proof building, Franklin and Eagle streets ; remodeling Calvary Presbyterian church, Delaware avenue ; Prospect Avenue Baptist church, Prospect avenue and Georgia street ; remodeling Church of the Messiah, Main street ; St. Louis Catholic school-house, Edward street ; malt-house of W. W. Sloan, Hydraulic ; Marine bank, Main street ; extension of Barnes, Hengerer & Co.. Main street ; store for Louis Bergtold, Genesee and Ellicott streets ; store for William F. Garbe, Seneca street. Elsewhere—Citizens' bank, Minneapolis, Minn.: county jail, Eau Claire, Wis.; store for Budge & Eshleman, Grant Forks, Dak.; residence for T. B. Casey, Minneapolis, Minn. ; State bank, water-works and pump house and store for George P. Smith, Tonawanda, N. Y.; opera-house, Olean, N. Y.; house for G. T. Rogers, Binghamton, N. Y. ; bank at Cattaraugus, N. Y. ; residence for Grant Warren, Fort Erie.

Mr. Caulkins adds thorough training to the highest order of talent, is well and ably assisted by a competent office force, and is in all respects capable and reliable.

BANK OF ATTICA.

G. Barrett Rich, President; F. L. Danforth, Cashier; J. W. Smith, Assistant Cashier — Corner Pearl and Seneca Sts.

This is a State bank, and the oldest bank in Erie county, established in the village of Attica in 1836, and removing to Buffalo in 1842, transacting business in Spaulding's Exchange until 1860, when it removed to the large and handsome iron building now occupied, corner of Pearl and Seneca streets. The capital stock, originally $160,000, was, in June, 1856, increased to $200,000, and in October of the same year to $250,000, with $80,000 surplus. The original board of directors, all long since dead, was as follows: Gaius B. Rich, A. J. Rich (son of G. B. Rich), John S. Ganson, Horace White and Hamilton White. From these G. B. Rich was selected for president, and A. J. Rich for vice-president. Broken health forced President Rich into retirement in 1852, whereupon he was succeeded by his son, A. J. Rich. Mr. G. Barrett Rich, who now presides over the destinies of the Bank of Attica, is a grandson of the founder, three generations of the same family having held that responsible post.

This noble old bank, during its career of half a century, has seen all of its local contemporaries disappear from the scene of action, followed by many of more recent date, yet it has never failed to meet its liabilities, dollar for dollar, and is to-day stronger, richer and more influential than ever. Always liberal to its customers, public-spirited and enterprising in its management and policy, sound conservatism and caution have nevertheless characterized every act of the directory and officers, and it would be difficult indeed to name a fiduciary trust that enjoys a larger share of public confidence than is lavished upon the Bank of Attica. The officers are named in our caption. The following named gentlemen compose the present board of directors: E. G. Spaulding, F. L. Danforth, P. P. Pratt, G. Barrett Rich, George S. Hazard.

The Bank of Attica does a legitimate banking business in all that the word implies, including the payment of interest on deposits, loans, discounts, collections, etc., and has regular correspondents at all the leading monetary centers. The subjoined official report exhibits its financial condition at the date of publication, December 11, 1886—a most satisfactory showing: Resources—Loans and discounts, $816,787.91; overdrafts, $528.88; due from banks, $138,996.76; United States bonds, $1,000.00; specie, $20,590.79; currency, $34,769.00; checks for exchanges, $6,741.25; current expenses, $7,119.01; total, $1,026,533.60. Liabilities—Capital stock, $250,000.00; profits, $82,307.28; due depositors, $687,544.26; due banks, $6,682.06; total, $1,026,533.60.

O. A. TAFT,

Artist Photographer—No. 272 Main St., near Swan.

Mr. Taft is a rarely accomplished and successful photographer, who for twenty-eight years has devoted his native talent and energy to the uninterrupted study and pursuit of his profession in all of its higher branches, the result being the achievement of a reputation second to that of no artist legitimately engaged in photography west of New York city. Mr. Taft was born in Vermont, and has had practical experience in his vocation in three States, thus acquiring a knowledge of men and women and their tastes which enables him to give a degree of satisfaction in pose, style and general effect seldom attained by photographers as a class.

Mr. Taft has resided and labored at his profession in Buffalo since 1881. In 1882 he first occupied his present location, where he has the third and fourth floors and employs a capable force of assistants, his parlors and operating rooms being models of neatness and convenience. He has a large and steadily increasing circle of desirable patrons in the city and surrounding country, and may be fairly classed as a successful business man as well as artist. His specialties embrace all the higher grades of portrait photography, bromide enlargements, crayon portraits, and the most perfect and beautiful work in all branches. A visit to his gallery and studio will well repay lovers of art and admirers of the beautiful, whether they desire to sit for their own counterfeit presentments or merely to profitably and pleasantly while away an hour or two of leisure time.

The view of Main street from the windows is enlivening, and persons out shopping find this a delightful lounge, where they can rest as they examine the works of art. Teachers and others find it a pleasant way of passing an hour or two of their leisure time.

M. B. SHANTZ & CO.,

Manufacturers and Importers of Fine Buttons—Nos. 14 to 24 Wells St., Buffalo—J. Y. Shantz & Son, King St., Berlin, Ont.; M. B. Shantz & Co., No. 107 Grand St., New York ; No. 56 Summer St., Boston.

Good clothes—with buttons on them— distinguish the civ- ilized and enlight- ened being from the barbarian, and the loss of a button may and frequently does set the wheels of progress to spinning backward at a ter- rific rate,threatening to plunge the car in-

BUFFALO.   BERLIN.

to primeval darkness or chaos—as witness the conduct and language of *pater familias* on discovering that the wife of his bosom has gone forth to her orisons leaving his last clean shirt minus the all-important collar-button, while missing suspender and waist- band buttons have cost the recording angel oceans of tears in expunging pardonable profanity.

But we set out to say something about the manufacture of these useful and orna- mental appurtenances to masculine and feminine apparel, and to give our readers some account of the firm of M. B. Shantz & Co., the leading button manufacturers of this continent.

In 1870 Messrs. J. Y. Shantz and E. Vogelsang formed a partnership and erected works at Berlin, Ontario, Mr. Vogelsang having brought the art with him from Germany. They prospered and added to their facilities from time to time until 1876, when Mr. Vogelsang retired, and the firm of J. Y. Shantz & Sons was organized. In 1884 the Buffalo branch was opened by Mr. M. B. Shantz, the senior member and one of the sons, D. B. Shantz, remaining in charge of the original works at Berlin, comprising three neat two-story factory buildings, respectively 40 by 130, 40 by 60 and 30 by 40 feet, illustrated above. We also present an engraving of the building, one floor, 125 by 180 feet, of which is occupied by the Buffalo house.

The machinery employed is of the best, much of it invented by the members of the firm, and all of it constructed especially for their use. At Berlin 300 operatives find steady work ; at Buffalo, 125 to 150. A large percentage of the finer work is imported in the rough from the Berlin house, and finished here. The leading specialties embrace every description of ivory and pearl buttons, fine buttons for clothing and for the use of merchant tailors, with whom the " Shantz " brand of these goods is extremely popular.

The house has a vast and fast-growing trade all over the United States and the Canadian provinces, and is known as a most liberal and progressive one.

CLINTON BIDWELL,

New York and Pennsylvania Agent of the Du Pont Gunpowder Works of Wilmington, Del.—Office, No. 14 West Swan St.

Gunpowder is an agent of civilization, without which much of the progress of the past few centuries would have been impossible. Putting aside its employment in war —which, by the way, consumes but a small proportion of the total—gunpowder is indispensable in quarrying and mining operations, the removal of obstructions to navigation, the construction of tunnels, canals and internal improvements of every description, for fireworks, for field sports, and for many other purposes that will readily occur to the intelligent reader.

The oldest and most extensive gunpowder works in the United States are those of the Du Pont family, on Brandywine creek, near Wilmington, Del. These works were founded by Eleuthere Irenee Du Pont, a native of Paris, who also founded the

American branch of that family. He was a son of a prominent French gentleman, Du Pont de Nemours, and a student under Lavoisier, superintendent of the royal saltpetre depots and powder factories. The French revolution caused the Du Ponts to emigrate in the winter of 1779–80, arriving at Newport, R. I., January 1st of the latter year. At that time the manufacture of gunpowder in this country was in its infancy and the product very poor, while that imported from England was but little better. This suggested to Irenee Du Pont the feasibility of constructing works and regularly embarking in the business of supplying the market with superior grades of gunpowder for all purposes, an idea which he carried into effect in 1802 by the erection of the original plant on the Brandywine. The energetic emigrant died of cholera in 1831, at Philadelphia, his works being at that time the largest and most famous on the western hemisphere. Since then the immense business has been ably managed by his sons and grandsons, who retain the old firm name. The works are now the largest of their kind in the world. In addition to the buildings devoted to the manufacture and storage of gunpowder, they embrace a saltpetre refinery with laboratory attached, charcoal houses, machine shops, carpenter and blacksmith shops, planing and saw mills. The firm owns over two thousand acres of land, that stretch for three miles along both sides of the Brandywine, and on which are located three woolen mills, a cotton mill, flour mill, etc., giving employment to upward of five hundred operatives. There are good roads, substantial bridges, mostly of stone, and in fact no money has been spared to make the estate a model one in every respect. The high reputation permanently maintained by Du Pont's powder is due to the care bestowed upon its manufacture, and to the constant personal supervision maintained over all the processes and character of materials. The quantity of saltpetre and nitrate of soda annually consumed here is enormous, amounting to over eight million pounds, imported mostly from India and South America. The firm take especial pains to have a thoroughly pure and reliable quality of saltpetre used in their powder, and consequently have devised the most rigid tests. All descriptions of powder for military or naval purposes are made at the works, such as hexagonal, prismatic, cannon, musket, rifle, mortar and pistol. In this connection it may be noted that the firm supplied all the powder used in recent experiments with heavy cannon, including those made with the Haskell multicharge gun. It also manufactures diamond grain, eagle, chokebore, and the various grades of canister and rifle powder, as well as shipping, blasting, mining and fuse powder. The firm owns a large depot at San Francisco for the requirements of the Pacific States, and have agencies throughout South and Central America and elsewhere.

For eighty-four years these works have maintained their supremacy in this country, both for extent and quality of products, proving a powerful and faithful ally of the government in all of its wars, and a just source of pride as well as wealth to the descendents of Du Pont Nemours & Co.

Mr. Clinton Bidwell is agent for the company at this point, controlling its interests in Western New York and Pennsylvania. His office is at No. 14 West Swan street; magazine—a substantial one-story structure, 25 by 40·feet square—some distance in the country. He carries an immense stock of gunpowder of all grades for all purposes, and will fill orders promptly and in the best manner.

ADAM HAUCK,

Dealer in General Hardware, Stoves and House-furnishing Goods, Bird Cages, Lamps and Plated Ware—Nos. 505 and 507 Main St.

Mr. Hauck established himself in his present business as long ago as 1854, and the famous " Model Hardware and Stove Store " is a Main street landmark known to almost every old citizen of Buffalo. In 1868 he admitted a partner in the person of a Mr. Garono, but the latter retired in 1880, and Mr. Hauck has never cared to associate himself in business with any one else. He occupies a substantial three-story brick building, 25 by 80 feet, carries a stock valued at $12,000 to $15,000, and does an annual business of $35,000 to $40,000 in general hardware, stoves, house-furnishing goods, bird-cages, lamps, plated ware, etc., his leading specialties being McGee's ranges and parlor stoves —a line of superior goods for which he has a steady sale.

Mr. Hauck came to New York from Germany in 1840, went into business at Eton Corners in 1854, and two or three years later removed to Buffalo, where he has since resided. Last summer, accompanied by his estimable better-half, he revisited the scenes of his youth in the Fatherland, but returned better satisfied than ever with his home in the free New World.

HOLLAND & VILAS,

Manufacturers of Lounges and Mattresses—Nelson Holland, Freeman M. Vilas—No. 270 Court St.

Among the varied industries represented on a large scale which have combined of late years to give the City of Buffalo a national reputation may be mentioned the manufacture of lounges and mattresses. This city has the credit of having one of the largest establishments of this kind in the country. At the same time, for a variety of styles in lounges and artistic finish, it acknowledges no superior. The one referred to is that of Messrs. Holland & Vilas, successors during the past year to the late H. J. Comstock. The business was established by the latter in 1872, the premises occupying three floors of the mammoth block of Lee, Holland & Co., having a frontage on Court street of 1,000 feet. Being possessed of an extended experience and the very best of facilities for conducting the business, it expanded rapidly. Mr. Comstock's death occurred October 4, 1885, and on March 15, 1886, the present firm was organized. Of the individual members, Mr. Holland is one of Buffalo's leading business men, being a member of the firm of Holland & Stewart, wholesale lumber, and of Lee, Holland & Co. Mr. Vilas comes from Plattsburg, N. Y., where he was vice-president of the Vilas National Bank, and is an enterprising and accomplished business man. The active management of the business in all its details devolves on him, and the showing since he has been in charge demonstrates that he is the right man in the right place.

A working force of seventy-five skilled artisans is employed, and over 150 different styles of lounges are manufactured. They include everything known to the trade in lounges, and new designs are being originated constantly. In the mattress department complete lines in wool, cotton, curled hair, moss and husk are manufactured, also on a large scale and of unsurpassed excellence. An adequate idea of the extent of the business of Messrs. Holland & Vilas can be had from the fact that during the past year it amounted to a quarter million dollars. The item of wages alone is $50,000 a year. Several traveling men are constantly on the road, and the trade of this house extends throughout the different sections of the United States. Its future is certainly most flattering.

ENSIGN BENNETT,

General Manager for the Buffalo Coal Co., Northwestern Coal and Iron Co., and Fairmount Coal and Iron Co.—Offices, Coal and Iron Exchange Building.

The importance of Buffalo as a distributing point for the bituminous coal trade cannot be overestimated. The position which this city now occupies has been reached by the unsurpassed shipping facilities afforded by the different railway lines tapping the coal fields of Northwestern Pennsylvania, and which converge to this point. A much better idea can be obtained from a personal inspection of the numerous coal docks here of the magnitude of the trade than an array of figures presents. They are among the most extensive in the country, as the coal shipments from this port form an important factor in its lake commerce.

Mr. Ensign Bennett is the general manager for three companies whose operations are very extensive. His offices are located in the building referred to, and he is a fair type of the urbane and gentlemanly representatives of one of Buffalo's leading interests. A few interesting figures are presented which will show the extent of the business done by the companies referred to. The Buffalo Coal Company owns 16,000 acres in McKean County, Pa., and has a capital of $1,000,000. Its operations are confined to coal and lumber. The annual output has been 80,000 tons of coal and 200,000 feet of lumber. About 100 men have been employed, and the pay roll averages $7,000 per month. Mr. G. Clinton Gardner of New York is the president. It has been in operation since 1880, and the trade is principally in this State. The Fairmount Coal and Iron Co., with a capital of $1,500,000, owns 4,800 acres in Clarion county, Pa., and 600 acres in Jefferson county, and turns out annually 145,000 tons of coal and 10,000 tons of coke. The pay roll for the 175 hands averages about $10,500 a month. Col. B. K. Jamison of Philadelphia is the president, and the trade is distributed in Pennsylvania, New York and Canada. The Northwestern Coal and Iron Co. completes the list. G. Clinton Gardner is the president, and the company's property consists of 660 acres in Venango county and 1,400 acres in Clarion county, Pa. The annual production is 125,000 to 175,000 tons of coal and 7,000 tons of coke. The number of employes is 110, who earn $7,000 a month. The capital of this company is $1,000,000, and the trade goes to Canada and this State and Pennsylvania.

It can be seen that these companies have ample capital and facilities to handle a large volume of trade. In the hands of Mr. Bennett their interests are ably looked after, and a large proportion of the business done is chiefly due to his adaptability for the important office which he fills.

HARVEY BROTHERS,

Flour, Grain and Seed Merchants—No. 221 Washington St.

This famous old house, founded by Harvey & Allen in 1858, not only has the advantage of great age and long experience, but of an established reputation for enterprise, probity and reliability as high as that of any similar concern in the United States. The present firm, composed of Horace J. and John H. Harvey, was formed in 1865, and is a recognized power and authority in the flour and grain trade. Mr. Horace J. Harvey, the senior partner, is interested in several outside business ventures, among them Smith, Falke & Co., bakers, and Harvey & Dake, Niagara Baking Co. Both are natives of Washington county, connected with this house for twenty-seven years or more, and both members of the Board of Trade.

The leading specialties of the house comprise the finest grades of winter and hard spring wheat roller process flour, selected grain, and seeds of all kinds, in which latter they are the heaviest dealers in the State. They also handle great quantities of superior bird seed, which they pack for the convenience of the trade and supply in quantities to suit.

Messrs. Harvey Brothers occupy all of the large four-story building No. 227 Washington street, 25 by 125 feet. They do an immense business in the specialties above enumerated, averaging over $2,000,000 per annum, and extending throughout Western New York. The bulk of their sales, however, are made to retailers and consumers in the city and surrounding towns—one of the best possible proofs of the character of the house and its goods. All the flour handled by this firm is from the renowned Buffalo City Flour Mills of Harvey & Henry, noticed more at length elsewhere in this work.

7

BUFFALO GLOVE AND WHIP MANUFACTORY.

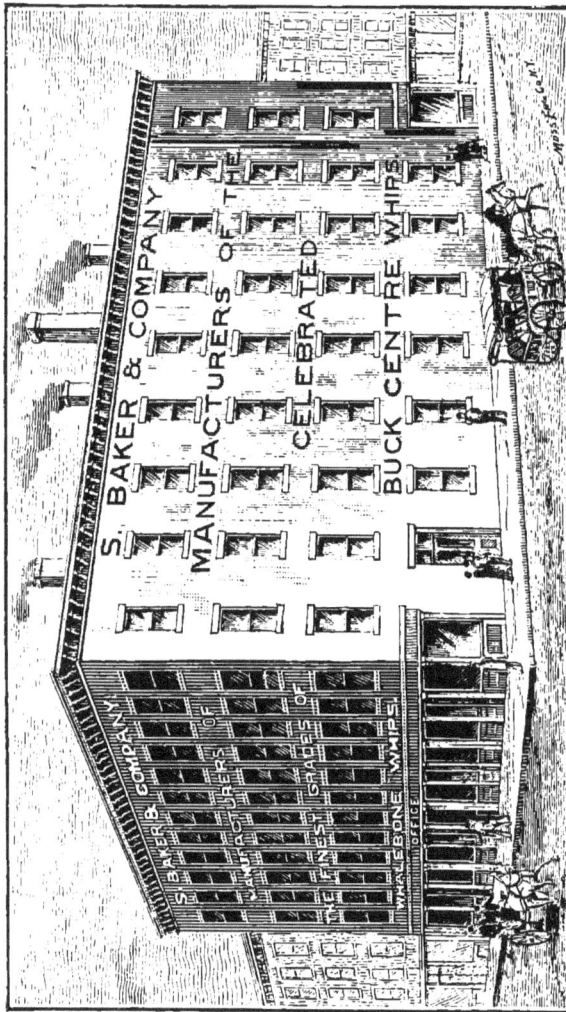

(See opposite page.)

S. BAKER & CO., NOS. 18 TO 26 TERRACE.

BUFFALO GLOVE AND WHIP MANUFACTORY.

S. Baker & Co., Proprietors.—Factory, Nos. 18 to 26 Terrace; Office, Nos. 112 and 114 Commercial St.; Warerooms, Nos. 13 and 15 Pearl St.

One of the industries upon which Buffalo may justifiably pride herself is the manufacture of whips and gloves upon a large scale, and one of the most conspicuous establishments of the kind in the United States is that of Messrs. S. Baker & Co.—the Buffalo Glove and Whip Manufactory—Nos. 18 to 26 Terrace square. The house occupies for manufacturing and storage purposes in all six floors, viz. : one 70 by 100 feet, three 25 by 40 feet, and one 35 by 60 feet, with basement of like dimensions. Sixty-five operatives and eight travelers are employed, and the capacity, which is taxed to the utmost by orders from the trade, is 100 dozen whips per diem and 13,000 dozen of gloves a year, valued at about $125,000, the goods going to all portions of the United States and Canada. This is said to be, and probably is, the only concern of the kind in this country that is never compelled to close down for "dull times," running a full force from the first of January to the last of December every year, while others suspend from February until June. This fact alone speaks volumes for the character of Messrs. Baker & Co.'s products, for it is certain that merit alone can command such a continuous run of orders.

Mr. Baker, the head of the firm, is of English birth, and was reared to the business, his father having been a glove manufacturer before him. Mr. Henry H. McMartin, the junior member, is a native of this State and has always been connected with this trade. Both are enterprising, liberal men, and it is pleasant to know that they are successful and prosperous, the demand for their goods steadily increasing, and their personal and business popularity growing year by year.

IRLBACKER & DAVIS,

Plumbers, Gas and Steamfitters—Nos. 529 to 531 Main and 504 to 508 Washington St.

Messrs. Irlbacker & Davis are the leading representatives of their special industry in Buffalo, and conduct the largest and most famous plumbing, steam and gasfitting establishment in the State, outside of New York city, occupying a substantial and conveniently arranged building four stories in height on Main and three on Washington, 200 feet deep, fronting 37 feet on the former and 58 feet on the latter street, and employing an average of over 80 skilled workmen in all departments, together with a full complement of all necessary machinery, special tools, etc. Their weekly pay-roll alone foots up about $1,300, and most of the larger and more intricate contracts for first-class work in their line awarded in this city and vicinity are given them, for the excellent reason that their facilities and resources are known to be entirely adequate to any demand that may be made upon them.

The house was established by the present proprietors in 1861—more than twenty-five years ago—with small capital besides their skill and industry. At this time the actual investment represents $100,000, and in recent years their transactions have aggregated about $200,000 per annum. Mr. Irlbacker has resided in Buffalo since 1844. Mr. Davis was born and reared here. They are half owners of the brass foundry and machine shop of Fries & Co., No. 508 Washington street, and hold half the stock of the Kast Copper and Sheet-Iron Co., corner Washington and Scott streets, and are, besides, reckoned among the liberal, progressive and public-spirited citizens of Buffalo, fully alive to the city's interests and quick to perceive and encourage every movement looking to her material development.

FRONTIER ELEVATOR CO.

John C. Graves, President; Gustav Fleischmann, Vice-President; Edward N. Cook, Treasurer; J. H. Prescott, Jr., Secretary—Elevator, cor. Hatch Slip and City Ship Canal ; Office, Room 32, Board of Trade.

The Frontier Elevator Company was organized early in 1886, with a cash capital of $400,000, and at once proceeded to the erection of its splendid new elevator at the intersection of Hatch slip and the city ship canal. It is built upon an entirely novel and original plan, combining great capacity with economy of space and power, and is of the following dimensions : Building exclusive of engine-house, 72 by 267 feet lineal measurement; height of transfer or machinery department, 111 feet; height of marine towers, 127 feet; height of elevator above storage warehouse, 77 feet; number of bins, 126, each 8 by 18 feet square and 52 feet deep. The engine-house at the east side is of brick, one story in height, 26½ by 132 feet, the equipment comprising one elevating engine, one engine and windlass for handling cars, and a small Rice patent engine to run the dynamo for lighting the entire establishment on the Edison incandescent system. The large engine is of the Hamilton-Corliss pattern, 500 horse power. The buildings are roofed with iron, and every precaution has been taken to avoid danger from fire. The company design erecting another building of the same dimensions as the present storage house on the west side of the engine-house, which will also be covered with corrugated iron, iron-roofed and substantial. The Chase system of low bins prevails, as elevators of this kind are considered much safer than the old style, and insurance rates are about one-third lower. Spouts above and below the bins are also dispensed with, thus still further reducing the risk.

The location of the Frontier Elevator is especially advantageous for the unloading of lake vessels and the loading of cars, the ship canal on one side and railroad tracks on the other providing all desirable shipping facilities. Steam shovels do the work of unloading with extraordinary rapidity, and if necessary the elevator can handle 15,000 bushels per hour or 360,000 bushels per day. About 100 men are employed, the company having commenced receiving October 11th last. They are doing a large and steadily increasing business, and confidently expect to run to the limit of their capacity hereafter.

The Frontier Elevator Company is composed of A 1 business men. President Graves is a lawyer by profession, formerly Clerk of the Superior Court, and at present a park commissioner and trustee of the Buffalo City cemetery. Vice-President Fleischmann and Treasurer Cook are of the firm of F. N. Cook & Co., prominent and successful distillers.

WALBRIDGE & CO.

Wholesale Hardware, House-Furnishing Goods, etc.—Nos. 317, 319 and 321 Washington St.

This is one of Buffalo's most extensive, reputable and influential business houses, representative in its *personnel*, in the volume of its b u s i n e s s transactions, and in the high character and public spirit that have ever marked its career. It was founded by Charles E. Walbridge and George A. Bell, February 1, 1869, and up to January 1, 1885, was conducted under the name and style of Charles E. Walbridge, when the change to Walbridge & Co. was made. The firm is composed of Charles E. Walbridge and Harry Walbridge, general partners, and George A. Bell, of Brooklyn, N. Y., special partner. The location, Nos. 317, 319 and 321 Washington street, n o r t h e a s t c o r n e r o f South Division, is one of the best in the city for the purpose, convenient to the business center, the hotels, railroad stations and wharves. The building occupied is a handsome and substantial five-story brick with basement, fronting 70 feet on Washington and 130 feet on South Division street, the interior specially arranged for the accommodation of the business to which it is devoted, which embraces wholesale and retail departments in hardware, implements and house-furnishing goods. A force of ninety men, including book-keepers, clerks, salesmen, mechanics and porters, is required to carry on the local operations of the house, besides competent and successful travelers scattered throughout New York, Pennsylvania, Ohio, Indiana, Illinois, Michigan, Wisconsin, and other Western States.

January 1, 1886, Walbridge & Co. purchased the entire hardware stock and goodwill of Pratt & Co., which house retired from the trade at that time after an honorable and prosperous career of half a century. Many of Pratt & Co.'s force of trained house and traveling salesmen also passed into the employ of Walbridge & Co., who control most of the trade built up by the old house during a long series of years, and are constantly adding thereto.

Messrs. Walbridge & Co. possess every facility for the prompt and satisfactory shipment of orders for the hardware trade, their stock comprising full assortments of all goods pertaining thereto—light and heavy hardware, iron, steel, house-furnishing and builders' hardware and trimmings, including bronze locks, knobs, escutcheons, hinges, etc., in late and artistic patterns from the most celebrated manufacturers, and an endless variety of tools for the use of wood and iron-workers. One large department is devoted exclusively to shop and foundry supplies, and here will be found complete stocks of nuts, bolts, rivets, sheet-brass, emery—in short, any and every item required for this class of trade. Particular attention is given to the retail trade in the goods above referred to, and parties in want of anything in the hardware or tool line, from a tack to an engine lathe, will find it here.

Herewith is presented an illustration of the new reservoir vase, for lawn and cemetery adornment, of which Walbridge & Co. make a specialty. They are made in a variety of styles and sizes, ranging from 20 to 55 inches, and in price from $10 to $34. These vases are made with a reservoir to hold water. The moisture is drawn up into the earth by capillary attraction. The soil does not get caked and hard as in vases where water is poured on the top of the earth. Reservoir vases only need watering once in ten to fifteen days, making them invaluable for cemetery use. Catalogue and price-list mailed on application.

BUREAU OF ILLUSTRATION. BUFFALO, N.Y.

H. H. LITTLE,

Architect—Office, Room 114 White Building.

Mr. Little has resided and prosecuted his vocation in Buffalo for many years, and is deservedly popular, not only with property-owners, contractors, builders and others directly interested in improvements, but with the business community and general public. His office, room No. 114 White fire-proof building, Nos. 292 to 298 Main street, is one of the most centrally situated, pleasant and best-equipped in the city, readily accessible by elevator, and in all respects desirable. A competent corps of practical architects, draughtsmen, etc., is regularly employed, and it is a busy place.

Mr. Little's specialties, to which he devotes his attention almost exclusively, embrace all classes of public buildings and fine residences, in the designing and construction of which he has no superior. In addition to the numerous business blocks, hotels, etc., that owe their beauty and fine proportions to his skill, Mr. L. has erected, in this city, some of the handsomest residences that adorn its fashionable thoroughfares, among others, those of W. W. Sloan, Delaware avenue ; Dr. H. L. Foster, Wadsworth avenue ; W. C. Fisher, Main street ; John Thompson, Linwood avenue, etc. In the fall of 1885 he was appointed superintendent of construction of the new post-office, and under his direction the work progressed more rapidly than ever before.

Mr. Little is a member of the City Council, and a courteous, obliging and liberal gentleman.

Booth & Riester, Manufacturers of Ecclesiastic and Domestic Art Stained Glass—No. 29 Pearl St., Nos. 23 and 25 Terrace, Up-stairs.

The art of glass staining for architectural purposes is a very old one, the credit for the discovery of which is due to the mediæval monks of Southern Europe. Many of the most elaborate and beautiful examples of this art now extant are found in the windows of ancient cathedrals and churches scattered all over the continent, some of which are hardly rivaled in our own day, notwithstanding the vast strides since achieved in mechanics and the multiplied appliances evoked by three centuries of unprecedented progress. Yet we advance, and the modern glass-stainer and artist in stained glass are gradually attaining a degree of perfection, each in his own specialty, that promises a complete elucidation, eventually, of the long-lost secrets of the craft and results that will eclipse the grandest conceptions and most magnificent achievements of the old masters.

It is conceded that Buffalo holds a high position among the art centers of the New World, though the arts most patronized here are those which combine the useful with the beautiful. Among these is the art of glass-staining as applied to ecclesiastical and general architecture—the beautifying by its means of the temples of worship, the places of amusement the halls of assembly, the public buildings and private residences of the people. While it is true that the city boasts but one considerable art industrial establishment of this kind, it is also a fact that in point of extent and the fame of its productions it is justly a source of pride and gratification to her inhabitants. We refer to the renowned Buffalo Stained Glass Works, founded on a small scale in 1845 by the late William G. Miller, who was succeeded, in 1864, by Messrs. Booth & Riester. The works at present occupy commodious rooms at No. 29 Pearl street and over Nos. 23 and 25 Terrace, having three floors 60 by 60 feet square, where twenty skilled artists and operatives are employed and an immense amount of intricate and costly work is done, the demands upon them steadily increasing and a corresponding augmentation of facilities and growth of output resulting, so that it is impossible to form a conjecture, from one year's transactions, what will be the volume of business for the next.

Mr. Booth, the senior partner, is of English birth, coming to this country in 1849. A practical and accomplished art glazier, connected with the trade since early manhood, he devotes his undivided attention to this branch of the business. Mr. Riester, the junior, is a native of France, where he received his early training in the studios and workshops of the most celebrated teachers. He came to Buffalo in 1852, and has devoted his whole mature life to the pursuit of this art.

The firm of Booth & Riester is famous throughout the length and breadth of the land for the taste, skill, beauty and durability of their work, thousands of examples of which are to be seen all over the Eastern, Western, Northern and Southern States, British America and the Sandwich Islands, as well as in most of the churches, public buildings, theaters, libraries, hotels and stylish private houses of this city. Among the latest fine specimens of their handicraft in this vicinity may be mentioned a beautiful memorial window in the Oleau Baptist church, the illuminated windows of St. James Protestant Episcopal church, this city, the English Lutheran church, Canton, O., the Presbyterian church, Gowanda, N. Y., a Catholic church at Gallitzin, Pa., and the new Polish church of Buffalo.

That the firm is a prosperous and flourishing one and a credit to the city goes without saying. That it has done and is doing much to spread abroad the fame of, and attract trade and population to, Buffalo, is equally certain.

BUSH & HOWARD,

Manufacturers of Hemlock Sole Leather—No. 105 Main St.

This representative old house, founded by Messrs. Myron P. Bush and George Howard in 1843, occupies a most influential position in relation to the leather trade of the country at large. Mr. Bush passed to the reward of a well-spent life in September of 1885, and was followed to his rest by his old and faithful associate last summer. Since Mr. Howard's death the firm has been reorganized, the present members being Messrs. George R. Howard and James H. Smith, who for some years were active partners in the establishment under the former *regime*. The name and style, location of tannery, office and warehouse, and approved methods of business are retained ; honest goods and reasonable figures will prevail as of yore, and there is every reason to predict for the concern under its new auspices as large if not larger prosperity than attended its previous long and honorable career. The office and warehouse at No. 105 Main street occupy a substantial four-story brick building, 50 by 150 feet, providing ample storage and counting-house facilities, while the yards and appurtenances cover several acres of valuable land on both sides of Chicago and Scott streets.

The single specialty of the house is the manufacture of superior hemlock slaughter sole leather, of which it produces and markets from 75,000 to 80,000 sides per annum, valued at $300,000 to $400,000, finding ready sale for the same all over this country, principally in the West, where this grade of sole leather is popular by reason of its uniform quality and durability. Such establishments as that of Bush & Howard are an honor to any community, potent for good, and always active in upholding those enterprises which promise benefit to the business and social interests with which they are identified.

AMIDON & WHITE,

Manufacturers of Bit-Braces, Gold, Silver, Nickel and Copper-Platers—Nos. 135 and 137 Main St., 10, 12 and 14 Quay St.

Of the entire catalogue of smaller tools none are more indispensable for the use of the mechanic than a reliable and effective bit-brace that can be employed indifferently with a variety of boring and drilling implements. The American inventor has performed wonders during the past quarter century in devising new or simplifying and improving old tools, but it is doubtful if any expenditure of time, labor and ingenuity in this direction has been productive of more universally acceptable results than have attended the efforts of Mr. Charles H. Amidon, of Buffalo, a practical and exceedingly skillful mechanic and machinist, who has for many years devoted his time and inventive talent to perfecting the bit-brace in its various forms, and to the devising and erection of special machinery for its manufacture. Having succeeded in the application of mechanical principles to practical results, Mr. Amidon, in October, 1883, formed a business partnership with Mr. Ansley D. White, formerly connected with the Merchants Bank, and the new firm of Amidon & White at once secured and occupied as a factory the commodious building No. 135 and 137 Main street, two floors of which, 35 by 150 feet, were fitted up expressly for their use with a complete plant of the latest improved and costly machinery. At present the firm employs from forty to fifty hands, pays $300 to $350 per week in wages, and puts upon the market nearly $100,000 worth of goods per annum, an output that meets with prompt sale, and is being constantly augmented. The trade of the house is general all over this continent, mechanics everywhere who have tested the bit-braces and other goods manufactured by Messrs. Amidon & White always giving them the preference when replenishing their outfits. The line of braces made by the firm comprises a variety of improved forms specially adapted to the requirements of workers in wood and metal. Amidon's patent globe-jawed brace is entirely new, and is confessedly the most complete and perfect brace ever made ; is simple, substantial, and quickly operated ; holds the largest shank bits, down to the smallest drills, of any and every shaped shank—round, square or tapering (any degree of taper)—and each shape receives the same even, tremendous "screw-lever-and-wedge" grip. When in use for bits the jaws are left with the largest opening up and the bit is dropped into the bottom of the socket, which is accurately centered. When required for drills, the proper slot in the jaws is turned up ; and, if the drill is long enough, it may be dropped into the bottom; if not, it can be put in as far as desired, and held just as firmly as otherwise. This is the only brace in existence that takes both bits and drills with the same jaws. No other brace in the market will take any and every size, shape and taper of shank of bits or drills. There never was a brace that held with such remarkable strength, nor any which distributed the pressure equally to all sides of any shank, as the globe-jaws roll in any direction, to fit any form. There can be no brace made to operate easier or with less effort in tightening. It is what every mechanic has long needed; as, with it, small drills can be used to great advantage. It also makes a very convenient hand-vise, and can be used for screwing in picture-nails, etc. It is handsomely made and full nickel-plated, with steel sweep, lignumvitæ head and cocobolo handle.

Of the other bit-braces, etc., manufactured by this house, and of which Mr. Amidon is the inventor, we have space only for brief mention of the wonderful corner brace, herewith illustrated, the only practical tool for boring in corners and close to walls, and is indispensable to carpenters, bell-hangers and plumbers. Amidon's Barker improved bit-brace is universally recognized as a first-class brace for ordinary use, and their new "Eclipse" ratchet brace, of which we present an engraving, is the simplest to operate and most durable of the kind ever made, besides being the handsomest tool in the market. This firm also manufacture a novel drill and lathe chuck involving the same principle as the globe-jawed brace, the only thing of the kind on the market. The patent corner breast-drill, constructed on the same principle of the corner brace, promises to supersede all older devices for the same purpose.

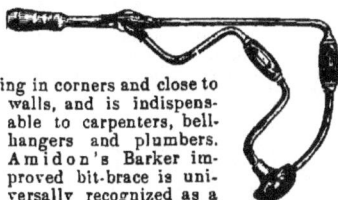

In addition, the firm are extensively engaged in gold, silver and nickel-plating, and are prepared to do all work in that line to order in the best style.

The trade will find it to their interest and profit to correspond with and obtain the illustrated circulars and catalogues of this house.

J. H. ROSS,

Manufacturer of "Buffalo" Quick Lime and State Land Plaster—Manufacturers' Agent for Akron Star Brand Cement and "Best" Ohio Sewer Pipe —Wholesale and Retail Dealer in Imported Portland Cements, Calcined Plaster, Ohio White Lime, Plastering Hair, Marble Dust, Fire Brick, Fire Clay, Soapstone Finish, etc.— Office, No. 141 Erie St.; Cement Warehouse, River St., Erie Basin Elevator; Quick Lime Warehouse, No. 213 Perry St.

Building operations and city improvements consume vast and constantly increasing quantities of the above materials, and it would surprise even many of those connected with the trades to see the figures in detail.

Among the largest dealers here is Mr. J. H. Ross, whose office at No. 141 Erie street is well-known and the resort of many of the leading builders and others in search of the goods of which he makes specialties. He has large warehouse facilities and carries immense stocks, carefully selected with reference to the wants of this market. His cement warehouse is connected with the Erie Basin elevator, and has a slip to the lake as well as a railroad switch communicating with every line that enters the city, thus securing ample shipping facilities to and from all points. His quick lime warehouse, No. 213 Perry street, is a large two-story frame building, 50 by 150 feet, provided with private switch and all requisite facilities for receiving and shipping merchandise.

Mr. Ross's business, established in 1879, is large and steadily growing in volume, and territorially covers this State, Ohio, Pennsylvania, Indiana and Michigan. Everything he handles is of the best, his prices are reasonable, delivery prompt, and every attention given to orders. Personally, Mr. R. is a pleasant, active and popular gentleman, respected by all who know him.

JAMES MOONEY,

Real Estate and Insurance Agent—Room No. 20 Arcade Building.

The popular and successful gentleman whose name heads this notice is not alone in his faith in Buffalo's magnificent future, nor in his belief that as a point for real estate investment she stands in the front rank of American cities. Mr. Mooney, however, is not content, like so many dreamers, to sit down with folded hands and await events, but is up and doing, early and late, in well-directed and intelligent efforts to bring about a realization of his hopes, laboring zealously, faithfully and untiringly for the development and aggrandizement of his adopted home. His office, in room No. 20 Arcade building, is one of the most elaborately and elegantly fitted up in the city, roomy, well lighted and convenient, and a favorite resort for those who seek buyers and sellers of property and insurance in reputable and responsible companies, of which he represents some of the best, including the American Central of St. Louis, the United States Fire of New York, the Reading Fire of Reading, and the Pennsylvania of Pittsburg—all old, famous and reliable.

In the specialty of real estate Mr. Mooney does a larger business than any of his local competitors, handling hundreds of thousands of dollars' worth annually, principally in and around Buffalo, though he accepts commissions for the purchase and sale of city property, farming lands, etc., in all portions of the country, doing a legitimate business in all its branches, buying and selling in the capacity of broker and on his own personal account. He also manages estates, collects rents, pays taxes, and in other ways looks after the property of non-resident owners and others who, for any reason, desire relief from the annoyance and burden of personally managing their property.

Mr. Mooney is a conspicuous citizen and thorough business man, public-spirited and popular, a gentleman of affable manners, culture and refinement, and has been president of the Buffalo Real Estate and Brokers' Board since its organization in 1883. He is of Irish birth, but has resided here since 1850. He was for two years president of the National Land League—1882–83—and still takes an active interest in the local branch, though he holds no office. He is, in all respects, a worthy gentleman of high personal and business character, and deserves the prosperity he enjoys.

RUMRILL & RUPP,

Builders and Contractors—No. 1 Arcade Building.

Of the hundreds of builders and contractors who have so ably seconded the architects in constructing the thousands of imposing public edifices and beautiful homes that adorn Buffalo and surrounding cities, probably none are more deserving of credit than the firm above named, composed of Henry Rumrill and Charles A. Rupp, founded in 1839 by the present senior member, Mr. Rupp being admitted in 1876.

Messrs. Rumrill & Rupp have a handsome office in Room 1, Arcade building, corner of Main and Clinton streets, where one or the other of the partners will always be found in business hours, ready and willing to inspect plans, make estimates, and discuss business with those who contemplate building. They do a very extensive business in the city and all over Northern and Western New York, amounting to about $100,000 a year. Among the more prominent of the buildings erected by them in the past may be mentioned The Genesee hotel, the Fitch Institute, the German Evangelical church, the Buffalo High School, the State Normal School, Becker's building (Palace of Trade), the Glenny building (Main near Seneca street), the Richmond block (Seneca and Ellicott streets), the New York State Reformatory at Elmira, and many others, the list running up into the hundreds. In each and every instance the firm have given complete satisfaction, and every contract ever awarded them has been executed to the letter, and in the best, most skillful and substantial manner, their specialty being mason work, in which they excel.

Mr. Rumrill is a Vermonter by birth, coming to Buffalo in 1836—over half a century ago—where he has steadily pursued his chosen vocation ever since. Mr. Rupp was born here, and has been in the building line for more than twenty years. Skillful, conscientious and successful in business, he is, besides, a popular citizen. He has represented the Eleventh ward in the Board of Aldermen for two years, and is a director of the Times Company and of the Delaware Avenue cemetery.

Such a firm of substantial, energetic, public-spirited men is an honor to the city, which is not slow to recognize their worth and their claims upon public support.

T. J. MAHONEY,

Real Estate and Insurance Agent—Notary Public and Commissioner of Deeds—No. 9 Niagara St.

There is no more inviting field for real estate operations than the city of Buffalo presents at the present time. The scale on which public improvements are being conducted, with the vast outlying territory constantly being laid out and within reach of the improvement extensions referred to in the way of the finest paved and drained streets, water, gas and electric light facilities, augmented by one of the most rapidly increasing populations in the world, all combine to give real estate investments a stability, with assurance of rapidly enhancing values, which would be hard to duplicate. Mr. T. J. Mahoney, No. 9 Niagara street, occupies a prominent position among the real-estate agents of the city. The business was established in 1881, and has grown to be one of extensive proportions. The facilities which Mr. Mahoney possesses are unsurpassed for buying, selling and renting real estate; rents are collected, taxes paid, loans on real estate effected, tax and title searches furnished, and a general insurance business done. The fire companies which Mr. Mahoney represents are the Royal of Liverpool, Commercial Union of London, Phœnix of London, Westchester of New York, Orient of Hartford, Phœnix of Brooklyn, Western of Toronto, Kings County of Brooklyn, Prescott of Boston, and Exchange Fire of New York.

There are probably few men in this city better qualified for the business than Mr. Mahoney. His long and creditable political career as a city official in different departments gave him an experience few men are fortunate enough to possess. He has held the offices of City Comptroller, Assessor and Auditor, besides having been cashier in the City Treasurer's office. At present he is a director, treasurer and member of the executive committee of the Lake View Brewing Co. Personally Mr. Mahoney is a very courteous, accommodating gentleman to come in contact with. In business he is prompt and reliable.

CO-OPERATIVE STOVE CO.,

J. H. Ludwig, President; W. Richardson, Vice-President; Michael Doll, Secretary and Treasurer; Thomas Norton, Superintendent and Manager—Manufacturers of Ranges, Cook and Heating Stoves—Iron Castings Made to Order—Particular Attention to Pattern Work—Office and Works, Corner Amherst and Tonawanda Sts., Black Rock.

The Buffalo Co-operative Stove Company was organized in 1854, under the manufacturing laws of the State of New York, with a capital stock of $75,000, of which about $50,000 have been paid in. Its business is managed by the following board of directors: John H. Ludwig, Wm. Richardson, Michael Doll, Edward Kener, Wm. Baynes, Adam Wick, Ignatz Scheisel, Jacob Shoemaker, most of whom are practical, and all are known as successful business men.

The superintendent and manager, Thomas Norton, a skillful, experienced and industrious moulder, removed to Troy more than forty years ago, securing employment with, Fuller, Warren & Co., where he remained as journeyman and foreman for 26 years. Theirs was then the leading American stove works, and during one season of Mr. Norton's administration as foreman manufactured one thirty-fifth of all the goods of this kind produced in the United States. He accepted the superintendency of the Co-operative Stove Company's works in January, 1886, and has been successful in introducing system and economy and securing the best results in every department.

The company's premises at the corner of Amherst and Tonawanda streets, Black Rock, embrace five acres of ground. The buildings consist of the ware-rooms, mounting and finishing shops and salesrooms under one roof, four stories in height, 80 feet front and 60 feet deep; foundry, 80 by 160 feet; cleaning and grinding, engine and boiler rooms, 60 by 80 feet. Eighty men are employed; about $1,000 a week is disbursed in wages, and the sales for the past year aggregated $125,000, mostly to Western points, the surrounding country and Pennsylvania.

It is scarcely necessary to say that the goods are the very best that carefully selected material and superior workmanship can produce.

BALL BROS. GLASS MANUFACTURING CO.

Manufacturers of Fruit Jars, Green and Amber Glass Bottles, etc.—Nos. 10 to 32 Porter St.

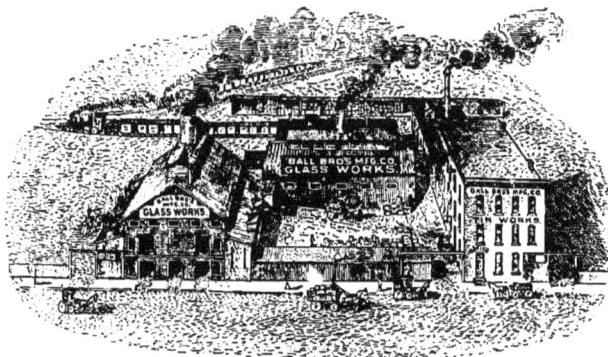

It will be a gratifying thing, and one the citizens of Buffalo may well be proud of, when the exhibit of this city's manufacturing interests appears in the present work. Almost every line is represented, and the returns show that the results are most satisfactory. In glassware the business is represented by the Ball Bros. Glass Manufacturing Co. It is the only establishment engaged in the manufacture of glass in Buffalo, and the lines they work on are fruit jars and green and amber bottles. Besides, a large business is done in the manufacture of tin cans, galvanized iron tanks, and specialties in stamped tinware. The business was started in 1879, the style of the firm being Ball Brothers. The works are at Nos. 10 to 32 Porter street, and are well equiped in every respect. They extend from a frontage of 212 feet on Porter street 265 feet deep to Heacock street. A working force of 150 hands is employed, and the weekly outlay for wages amounts to $1,000. When we consider the extent of the fruit-raising interest of Western New York and the vast quantity which is put up by the numerous canning industries, it can be seen at a glance that the demand for the products of this company is very large. The bottling business also takes large quantities of glassware, for which the local demand is large. The annual business of the company amounts to $210,000. Its officers are F. C. Ball, president ; E. B. Ball, vice-president, and George A. Ball, treasurer. They are all first-class business men, and have already achieved a grand success.

JOHN WENDELL & SON,

Proprietors of Wendell's Star Laundry and Custom Shirt Factory—No. 350 Washington St.

Of remarkable developments in business of late, the growth of the laundry industry is one of the most interesting. The heathen Chinese demonstrated what was in it, and the popular antipathy against the almond-eyed Celestial soon opened the way for native enterprise. Among the several establishments now doing a business of large proportions in this city may be mentioned Wendell's Star Laundry and custom shirt factory. It is located at No. 350 Washington street, opposite the City Club, and was started in 1881 by Messrs. John Wendell & Son. They do an annual business of $15,000, and employ on an average thirty hands. A very fine line of custom work in shirts is done, and the facilities for doing first-class laundrying cannot be surpassed. The head of the firm was formerly with W. B. Sirret & Co. for a number of years, and is an A1 business man. The junior member was formerly in the gents' furnishing goods trade, and is also a first-class man for the position. A branch is carried on at No. 63 South Division street. Mr. John Wendell is a native of Germany, and came to Buffalo in 1849. He has had a long and successful business career, and is one of Buffalo's most respected citizens.

THE EXCHANGE ELEVATOR

And United States Bonded Warehouse—Greene & Bloomer, Proprietors—
Erie Basin, bet. Peacock and Palmer's Slips.

Not one of Buffalo's forty-five elevators is more eligibly located or better equipped
for the handling of grain, either by rail or water, than the splendid Exchange,
situated on the Erie basin and flanked by the Palmer and Peacock slips, provided with
side tracks communicating with the New York Central & Hudson River, Grand Trunk,
Michigan Central, West Shore and all Eastern and Western railroads entering Buffalo.
The storage capacity of the Exchange is 275,000 bushels, and the elevating facilities,
comprising the latest improved and most effective machinery, provide for the
elevating from vessels and transferring to canal-boats and cars of 75,000 bushels
per day. This elevator is also a regularly constituted United States bonded warehouse
and a recognized convenience and necessity to importers, who find here every facility,
official and otherwise, for the handling of Canadian grain.

The Exchange elevator was erected in 1862 by Messrs. Wm, Rankin, Alfred Ely and
Ashley H. Ball, and after passing through various hands Mr. Bloomer succeeded to the
Stewart interest in 1881, the firm thereupon becoming Greene & Bloomer, the latter
president of the Western Elevating Co. since May, 1885. Mr. Bloomer is a native of
Cayuga county, N. Y., born in 1818, and one of Buffalo's most respected citizens. He
is a practical millwright, and more than thirty-five years ago was superintendent and
manager for the late Stephen Whitney of New York, having under his charge fourteen
large flouring mills located at Oswego, Rochester and Black Rock. Mr. B., though well
along in years, yet retains much of his former activity and vivacity, and is as full of
enterprise and spirit as most men of forty. He has performed his full share in the

building up of Buffalo's commerce, and is as much interested in all that promises further developments thereof as ever.

The Messrs. Greene are also public-spirited and prominent business men, sons of the late Wm. H. Greene, Esq., who died in April, 1882. The latter was a native of Boston, a graduate of Dartmouth, who studied law and was admitted to the bar at Skaneateles, N. Y., removing to Buffalo in 1837. He rose to eminence as a counselor, practiced here for more than forty-six years, and was a noble citizen as well as conspicuous business man. He was an active member and friend of the Young Men's Association, an officer of the Buffalo Historical Society, and a trustee of the State Normal School. He died universally respected and lamented. The sons partake of the father's lofty qualities, and rank with Buffalo's best men.

BUFFALO CLOAK MANUFACTURING CO.,

Manufacturers of All Kinds of Cloaks—No. 38 West Seneca St.

The growing importance of Buffalo as a manufacturing center has attracted attention from all directions within the past few years. The extent and variety of the different lines represented demonstrates the fact that the time is not far distant when this city will acknowledge few superiors in any of them. The Buffalo Cloak Manufacturing Co. is one of the leading concerns whose operations are of sufficient importance to merit notice. The business was established in 1878 by Mr. M. Block. His operations were on a comparatively limited scale at the start, but have expanded rapidly under judicious management. From a trade of $15,000 the first year the business has grown to $150,000, the latter being the figures for the past year. The entire attention of Mr. Block is devoted to the manufacture of cloaks. The very best talent is employed in designing and the selection of late styles. This is a feature of the utmost importance, and is very successfully disposed of by the talent employed for this specific purpose.

The facilities possessed by this firm are unsurpassed. A splendid five-story building is occupied, and every department is complete in itself. From 75 to 100 hands are employed, representing an outlay of $500 a week for wages alone. Mr. Block is a gentleman whose knowledge of the business and experience insures the permanent success of the enterprise. It has been almost entirely due to his efforts that it has developed so rapidly, and this is a fair criterion of what will be done in the future.

JOHN A. BELL,

Real Estate and Insurance Agent and Coal Dealer—No. 30 East Eagle St., near Washington.

No city in the Union offers better inducements for real estate investments than does Buffalo, or more wide-awake, enterprising and public-spirited real estate agents. Prominent among these is Mr. John A. Bell, who, though established in business at his present location, No. 30 East Eagle street, less than three years, has already achieved extraordinary success, both in the handling and insurance of property, his transactions for account of buyers and sellers reaching a very large figure during the past twelve-month particularly, with prospects of a marked increase in the future. He gives special attention to the care of estates and property of non-residents, the collection of rents, payment of taxes, the purchase and sale of houses, lots and lands, and, possessing unusual facilities, renders unvarying satisfaction to his patrons. When required, he also executes bonds and mortgages, furnishes tax and title searches and negotiates loans, and, in brief, renders any service usually expected of a general real estate agent, promptly and on reasonable terms.

In his capacity as an insurance agent, Mr. Bell represents some of the soundest and most reliable companies, and will take pleasure in placing insurance that insures, in fire, accident, plate glass, fidelity and steam boiler associations, as follows: Royal Fire of Liverpool, Buffalo Fire, Manufacturers' Fire and Marine of Boston, Insurance Company of North America, and Pennsylvania Fire of Philadelphia, Lloyd's Plate Glass Insurance Co., of New York, and the Accident Insurance Co. of North America, Montreal. All losses equitably adjusted and promptly paid.

Mr. Bell is also a dealer in coal on a considerable scale, and fills all orders with fidelity and dispatch. He is a native of St. Lawrence county; has resided here since 1870, and was bookkeeper for the Singer Manufacturing Co.

NATIONAL AND GLOBE FLOUR MILLS.

Thornton & Chester, Proprietors—Office, No. 212 Eric St.

Buffalo's trade in breadstuffs is large, and continues to increase from year to year. Its extent is set forth at length in the statistical portion of this work, and those who either feared or hoped that this port had reached the point of decadence in the matter of grain and flour will be agreeably or disagreeably surprised (as the case may be) by the exhibit. Whether the proposed extension of grain storage facilities shall be realized or not, it is evident that the Queen of the Lakes holds her own most satisfactorily in this particular, assertions to the contrary notwithstanding. Milling, too, is prosperous here, and hundreds of thousands of barrels of Buffalo high-grade flour is annually shipped East, besides what is required for local consumption.

One of the largest flouring plants east of the Mississippi, having a capacity of 200,000 barrels per annum, valued at about $1,000,000, is the National and Globe Mills, herewith illustrated, owned by Messrs. Thornton & Chester. The plant is remarkably complete in all departments, but it would be impossible to give a detailed description of the interior, and we therefore pass it by with the simple statement that in point of equipment for every process, from cleaning the grain to the packing of the flour, everything required in each process is as perfect as the modern millwright can devise or money procure.

The special brands upon which Thornton & Chester base their claims to superiority are " Thornton & Chester's Best Patent" and the "Globe Mill." These brands are universal favorites wherever introduced, as is proven by their popularity throughout New England, where none but the best can find a market, as well as at home, where many families decline to purchase any other flour.

These mills were originally erected at Black Rock, but becoming cramped for space the owners removed their plant to the present location, since which time the enterprise has prospered exceedingly.

The firm is composed of, first, Mr. Thomas Thornton, who has been with the mill ever since its establishment in 1848—nearly forty years; he is a member of the Board of Trade and a respected and public-spirited citizen; second, Mrs. Mary P. Chester, relict of Thomas Chester, a former member of the firm and one of its founders; third, Mr. J. F. Chard, a native of Buffalo, and member of the Board of Trade, an active, enterprising man and good citizen. The trade can find no better firm to entrust their orders to.

A. A. ENGLE,

Proprietor of Schreck Elevator and Feed Mill—Nos. 366 and 368 Ohio St.

The grain trade of Buffalo has always been the particular feature of prominence to which this city has pointed with pride. When it is considered that a large proportion of the grain product of the West is transferred from the lake craft to the canal at this port, it can be seen at a glance that the elevator facilities required are necessarily of great magnitude. Mr. A. A. Engle is prominently identified with the business. He is the proprietor of a fine elevator on Ohio street, which has a capacity of 100,000 bushels, built in 1881. The feed mill, which was erected in 1880, is a three-story building, and turns out a large quantity of ground and crushed feed for stock. His specialties include corn, corn-meal, cracked corn, corn and oats (chopped) and ground oats. He also grinds anything in the feed line that may be needed.

Mr. Engle came to this city from Hazelton, Pa., in 1879, and his annual business amounts to $200,000. He is a member of the Board of Trade, and one of the live, active representatives of this important interest.

HEINZ & MUNSCHAUER,

Manufacturers of Refrigerators, Water Coolers, Filters, Baths, Coal Hods, Coal Vases, Bird Cages, Children's Sleighs, etc.—Corner Randall and Superior Sts.

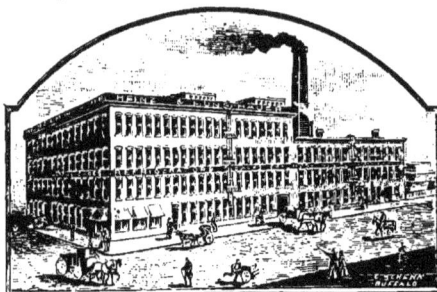

The large and handsome three and four-story factory illustrated herewith was built by its present occupants in 1884 and is of brick throughout, fronting 102 feet on Superior street and 250 feet on Randall, with a convenient lumber yard, 55 by 125 feet, lying on both sides of Randall street. The entire establishment is a hive of industry from basement to roof, employing 130 workmen in the various departments and a complete, novel and costly equipment of machinery, much of which was specially designed and constructed for these works. The productions of the firm cover a wide range, embracing complete lines of refrigerators and ice-chests for hotel and domestic use, water-coolers of approved styles and improved construction, filters, baths, coal hods, coal vases, children's sleighs, and the finest, most tasteful and varied line of bird cages of all kinds, sizes, grades and prices manufactured by any establishment in the United States.

This great manufacturing house was founded in 1865 by Messrs. Gesellgen, Heinz & Co., who established themselves in a small way on Mechanic street. The firm became Heinz, Fisher & Munschauer in 1868, and in 1873 removed to Hanover street, the style becoming Heinz, Pierce & Munschauer, Mr. Pierce retiring in 1878, since which time Messrs. Heinz & Munschauer have conducted the business without change of firm or other mutation save the erection of the new factory and a triplication of the volume of their transactions, reaching every city and town in the Eastern, Western and Northern States and the Canadas.

Both members of the firm are interested as partners in the flourishing Niagara Stamping and Tool Co., whose works are across the street. Mr. Heinz is a practical workman in the goods made by the firm. He is a German by birth, and came to Buffalo in 1850. Mr. Munschauer was born here, served in the Union navy in the war of the rebellion, and has been in his present line of business for the past nineteen years.

FRANK L. GEORGER,

Wholesale and Retail Paints, Oils, Varnishes, Artists' Materials, Painters' Supplies and Pure Mixed Paints—No. 246 Washington St., Opposite Post Office.

The manufacture and use of paints of all kinds for exterior and interior use is steadily growing, and it is no longer customary, as formerly, for each member of the craft to mix and grind his pigments and oils, since he can save time and money by purchasing them ready for use, or nearly so, from those who make a business of this specialty. One of the most skillful and successful men in this branch of the trade is Mr. Frank L. Georger, of No. 246 Washington street, opposite the post office, who, besides being a prosperous business man, is a pleasant and obliging gentleman. The trade will find it to their advantage to call and inspect his large and valuable stock, which embraces everything required for house, steamboat and sign painting and for artists' use, including complete lines of Cornell's and Pittsburg white lead, Devoe's tinted leads, pure linseed oil, varnishes and shellacs, spirits turpentine, naphtha, gasoline, sperm, lard and lubricating oils, illuminating oil, dry colors, colors in oil and distemper, colors in japan, tube colors, glues, kalsomine, whiting, putty, window glass, polished plate glass, brushes, sandpaper, and painters and artists' supplies generally. Mr. Georger has been established for several years, and is making a fine reputation with the trade.

McDONNELL & SONS,

Quarry Owners and Manufacturers of Monumental Statuary and Artistic Memorials and Building Work—Works and Quarries at Quincy, Mass.; Branch Office and Yards, Nos. 858 and 860 Main St., Buffalo.

One of the best examples ever presented of what may be accomplished by pluck, industry and square methods is found in the career of the above firm. Patrick McDonnell, a wide-awake young Irishman, came to America at the age of 17 with a sovereign in his pocket, found his way to the town of Quincy, Mass., and entered the service of Thomas Drake, stonecutter, as an apprentice. When his time was out he steadily wrought as a journeyman for his former master, until he had accumulated a small capital, when he purchased a partnership in the business and became in his turn an employer. A few years later he found himself sole proprietor of a flourishing granite works, and has had the satisfaction of seeing it expand into one of the most extensive, valuable and profitable plants of the kind in the United States. His two sons, Thomas H. and J. Q., he carefully trained to the same vocation, and at this time their quarries in all cover thirty acres of the best granite ground in Massachusetts, fifteen acres of which belong to the father and fifteen to the sons. Besides the quarries the equipment of steam engines, drills and other appropriate machinery for operating them is very complete and effective, and some of it, specially constructed for the use of the firm, quite costly, yet necessary, since McDonnell & Sons, in addition to their monument interests, do more in finished and building granite than any other Quincy house. One of their derricks alone is capable of removing a *hundred-ton* block at a single lift, and 30,000 feet of lumber is annually consumed in boxing goods for shipment. Some 150 hands are employed, and it takes $6,000 a month to pay for labor at the quarries and yards. A strong force of blacksmiths is required to keep the tools in order.

The very noticeable advance in public and private taste, developed during the past few years in Buffalo, induced the firm to open a branch office and works at Nos. 858 and 860 Main street, in August of 1884, and it is safe to say that the venture has proved a successful one. The premises are 50 feet front by 100 feet deep, and are stocked with a splendid exhibit of fine monumental work, the office itself, with its beautiful and elaborate polished Quincy granite front, being the handsomest in the United States—a recognized work of art that attracts the attention of every passer-by and excites admiring comment from all. Our cut gives a fair notion of its appearance.

Among the more conspicuous examples of McDonnell & Sons' work in this vicinity may be mentioned the magnificent canopy at Forest Lawn cemetery, which cost $20,000, the Michael monument, and others of greater or less note.

The C. W. Mackey family monument at the Franklin (Pa.) cemetery is a superb work, completed last September. The Franklin *News* says of it: "This monument—the work of McDonnell & Sons—stands conspicuous among the elegant works in that beautiful spot, for the harmony of its proportions and the elegance of its workmanship. It is of Quincy granite, polished throughout above the bottom base, its surface having that perfect and flinty glaze which only Quincy granite takes on. The base is 6 feet feet square; the die is 3 feet at its base and 3 feet 7 inches high, and is capped with an artistic design that greatly adds to the completeness of the work; the solid shaft is about 15 feet in length, and the entire height of the monument to the pyramidal apex about 28 feet."

The Seventy-seventh Regiment monument at Saratoga, the Shoemaker monument, Spring Grove cemetery, Cincinnati, and hundreds of other striking specimens of their handiwork on a large scale, might also be referred to did space permit.

The house was established in 1857. The elder Mr. McDonnell has retired from active business, Mr. Thomas H. McDonnell directing operations at Quincy, while John Q. has charge of the Buffalo branch. A magnificent line of fine monuments and headstones, from novel and original designs, are constantly kept in stock, and challenge the visitor's admiration.

8

BUFFALO'S LEADING CLOTHING ESTABLISHMENT.

(See Opposite Page.)

ALTMAN & CO.,

Manufacturers, Jobbers and Retailers of Men's, Boys' and Youths' Clothing and Furnishing Goods—Nos. 68, 70 and 72 Seneca St., Corner of Ellicott.

This house, established in 1854, is the most extensive of the kind in Buffalo. It occupies an immense five-story building with basement, 72 feet front by 120 feet deep, employs 1,500 cutters, clerks, salesmen and operatives the year round, and transacts an annual business exceeding $1,000,000. The members of the firm are Isaac, Julius and Henry Altman and D. Rosenau. The Altman brothers were born in Rochester, came to Buffalo in 1857, and have devoted their entire lives, since leaving school, to this branch of trade. Mr. Rosenau is of German birth, emigrated to this city in 1859, and has ever since been engaged in the manufacture and sale of clothing. It will thus be seen that all of the partners are experienced and successful men, and when it is added that by dint of industry and enterprise they have extended their trade to every State and Territory, East, West and South, the reader will readily perceive that they possess ability and energy in no small degree.

Messrs. Altman & Co. are heavy importers and jobbers of every description of cloths, cassimeres and tailors' trimmings, wholesale manufacturers and retailers of men's, boys' and youths' clothing suitable for all seasons and latitudes. They have extraordinary facilities in every department, having capable, wide-awake buyers in all the leading European and American markets who promptly avail themselves of every favorable opportunity to purchase and forward the latest novelties as well as standard goods, which the house here is enabled to offer the trade at the earliest possible moment, either uncut or made up in latest styles. The stock of superior suitings, dress goods, trimmings, etc., is always kept very full and of the best selections, while the trade in ready-made clothing will find here everything desirable, from the finest to the coarsest, at the lowest possible prices and made in the best manner.

B. F. GENTSCH & SONS,

Manufacturers of French and German Mustards—Pickle Packers—Wholesale Dealers in Cider, White Wine and Cider Vinegars, Chow Chow, Mixed Pickles, etc.—Nos. 329 and 331 Broadway, 232 and 234 Walnut St.

Whether it be an evidence of refinement or a mere perversion of taste, it is, nevertheless, a fact that the civilized palate craves stimulants in the form of condiments and acids, as is proven by the immense consumption of mustard, pepper, vinegar, etc., by the most advanced nations as compared with barbarous peoples. In any event, the average mortal has a hankering, more or less strong, for the things mentioned, and would seriously object to being deprived of them altogether; consequently, the manufacturer of vinegar, pickles, mustard, ketchup, and other sharpeners of the appetite, is in no immediate danger of bankruptcy and the almshouse, provided his goods are pure, sound and wholesome.

The most prominent house in Buffalo devoted to this branch of industry is that of B. F. Gentsch & Sons, Nos. 329 and 331 Broadway and 232 and 234 Walnut street, founded in 1847 by C. R. Mennig. Mr. Gentsch, senior, purchased the plant, in connection with his brother, in 1859, and thus continued and enlarged its operations and facilities until January 1, 1885, when his two sons were admitted. Two buildings are required to accommodate the manufacturing, storage and shipping requirements—the one at Nos. 329 and 331 Broadway being two stories in front and three in the rear, 52 feet front by 100 feet deep; the other, at Nos. 232 and 234 Walnut street, two stories in front and three stories in rear, 30 feet front by 112 feet deep. The equipment of machinery and appliances is complete in every department. Seven workmen and boys are employed, and the output averages in value $40,000 a year, embracing full lines of superior French and German mustards, pickles, cider, white wine and cider vinegar, chow chow, mixed pickles, and other varieties of appetizers and condiments, all of which are popular with the trade and the public of Buffalo and vicinity.

Mr. B. F. Gentsch was born in Saxony in 1835, and landed in Buffalo with a capital of $4 in 1854. Industry, economy and thrift did for him what they have done for many others, and he is a prosperous, genial and popular citizen. He was elected to the General Assembly in 1879, served creditably, and abandoned politics at the end of his term. He was a volunteer fireman, and is a member of the Exempts. The eldest son is 26, the youngest 23, and all are quiet, pushing young business men.

The merchant tailoring interest of Buffalo is on a plane with what might be looked for in a city that is rapidly assuming metropolitan proportions. Among the firms engaged in the business that have contributed toward elevating the tastes of the gentlemen of Buffalo to a proper appreciation of what constitutes the correct thing in wearing apparel, may be mentioned the firm of Laird & Co. Mr. S. E. Laird is an artist, as the term is applied to proper outfitting in the best styles of suitings. Having been engaged in the business since he was a boy, and prior to going into business on his own account having been associated with several of the best establishments in the country, it is not overdrawing the situation to say that he is thoroughly posted in the different branches of custom tailoring. To secure the best results in shapes requires a keen judgment as to effect. This is where so many would-be representatives of the merchant tailoring business are found deficient, because they adhere too much to the contour of the figure and lose sight of the important fact that "the apparel oft proclaims the man." Mr. Laird's business has developed to large proportions, running from $20,000 to $25,000 a year. His display of goods is always complete and comprises the finest importations. Prices are reasonable and perfect satisfaction is guaranteed in all cases.

BLISS BROTHERS,

Artistic Portrait and View Photographers—No. 368 Main St., Corner Eagle.

Twenty-eight years ago H. L. Bliss established himself here in the business of photography, and in the course of time, by close application to his art in all its branches, made for himself a reputation wide as the continent. Last spring, full of years and honors, Mr. Bliss retired, leaving to his sons, A. C. and H. L. Bliss, the splendid business he had created with their assistance and the task of conferring upon their names additional luster by achieving fresh triumphs in their chosen calling. That they will succeed admits of no question. Trained under the eye of a master, in the most exacting school of the art, these young men are fully capable of meeting every demand upon their practical skill and technical knowledge, and of prosecuting investigation and experiment and making new discoveries in the inexhaustible field of endeavor which it presents.

Their gallery and operating rooms occupy the entire fourth floor of the handsome building No. 368 Main street, southwest corner of Eagle, splendidly lighted, elegantly fitted up, and provided with all the latest and best photographic apparatus and appliances for the making of portraits in the best and most life-like style. This, however, is the smallest portion of their business, their great specialty being the taking of views and landscapes and photographs of machinery and manufactured goods, in which they have no rivals. Some of their interior work—photographic views of leading business house interiors—are the very acme of perfection and beauty, notably the "Palace of Trade" interior, taken by electric light, with all the startling effects of that kind of illumination brought out with dazzling brilliancy. Their studio and gallery form a perfect exhibition of fine views, prominent among which are many of Buffalo's most noted buildings, the fine bridges of the Erie, New York Central, Lake Shore and other railroads. Their photographs of machinery of all kinds are also of the highest order.

HALL & SONS,

Manufacturers of Fire Brick and Pressed and Common Building Brick, and Dealers in Architectural Terra Cotta, Fire Clay, Kaolin, etc.—Office, Room 58 Chapin Block.

The utilization of fire-clay has proved one of the most useful of discoveries, since from its heat-resisting, element-defying properties, when properly prepared, it has made possible many mechanical and scientific processes that without its aid could never have been attempted, and not a few of the ordinary industrial appliances of our time—the crucible, the retort, fire-proof furnace lining, etc.—would have been unknown. It is not, therefore, too much to say, that fire-clay and its products are indispensable factors in the prosecution of those arts and industries that form the crowning glory of the nineteenth century.

One of the most conspicuous houses in the world engaged in the mining and manipulation of fire clay is that of Hall & Sons, who, in 1881, succeeded to A. Hall & Sons, established at Perth Amboy, N. J., in 1846. Mr. Edward J. Hall is now at the head of the Buffalo business, with principal works at Black Rock and main office in room 58 Chapin block, this city, where he will be found during business hours, prepared to exhibit samples and take orders for the products of his establishment.

The works at Black Rock embrace some four acres of land, upon which have been erected two commodious brick buildings respectively 50 by 180 and 50 by 120 feet in area, two extensive kilns, and a large shed for storage purposes. A complete plant of all requisite machinery also forms an important portion of the outfit, which is one of the most valuable of the kind in existence, employing about thirty men and putting on the market $50,000 worth of finished goods per annum, embracing every description, size, shape and grade of fire brick, and including all kinds of tile, retort settings, etc., for gas works; charcoal furnace linings and boshes; glass works furnace brick; stove brick, for 200 different stoves; eighty sizes of square tile, from 4 inches to 4 feet in length; fifteen kinds of locomotive brick; Strong's and Dodge's patent grate settings; all ordinary grate settings; Johnson's patent furnace doors; blocks for door arches and jambs; fire brick grates; feed pots, etc., for burning wet tan bark; lime kiln arches, piers and linings; twelve-inch tile for bakers' ovens, etc., etc. All furnace bricks are pressed on the edges to secure uniform thickness. Blocks from twelve to twenty-four inches in length are made to order, as are odd shapes—a specialty of this house. With forty years' experience, unlimited supplies of best quality New Jersey and Pennsylvania fireclay, and complete facilities, the firm can manufacture any desired shape in the best manner and at short notice.

Hall & Sons are also agents for the renowned Perth Amboy terra cotta works at Perth Amboy, N. J., and are prepared to fill orders for every description of work in that line. Illustrated catalogues furnished on application. Fire-clay, fire mortar, ground brick, fire sand, kaolin, etc., furnished by the barrel, ton or cargo.

MARSDEN DAVEY,

Surveyor and Engineer—Room 11 Austin Building, Franklin cor. Eagle Sts.

For more than twenty-one years Mr. Davey has been established here in his profession, and has attained an eminence to which few can pretend. His first important work here was the surveying and laying out of Forest Lawn Cemetery at the instance of the trustees, by whom he was appointed engineer of that lovely city of the dead, a position which he held for a period of fourteen years. He next surveyed the driving park, and afterward the city park and State Asylum grounds, and has since done much local surveying for the city, for associations and for individuals. He was also chief engineer of the Buffalo Creek railroad for ten years, and has held the same position with the Street Railroad Company for fourteen years last past. He was also chief engineer for the Buffalo division of the Lehigh Valley railroad, and a member of the board of directors of the same road. It will thus be seen that Mr. Davey is a civil engineer of rare attainments and ability, and one whose services are in request in works where a high order of skill is indispensable. He is prepared to attend calls at home or from a distance, and to render satisfaction in every instance.

THE PITTS AGRICULTURAL WORKS.

M. A. Brayley, President; Carleton Sprague, Vice-President; Thomas Sully, Secretary and Treasurer—Manufacturers of Buffalo Pitts Threshing Machinery, Portable, Traction and Straw-Burning Engines, etc.—Established 1851; Incorporated 1877.

Of all the industries, past and present, that have combined to render the " Queen City of the Lakes" famous throughout christendom, probably no single one has contributed so much to that result as the Pitts Agricultural Works. Established on a small scale in 1851—thirty-six years ago—by John A. Pitts, the inventor of the apron thresher, which then and for many years after was operated by horse-power exclusively, these works have developed gradually, but certainly, advanced in facilities and volume of products, as well as in improvements on their threshers and the devising of means for the application of steam power as a motor for agricultural machinery, until they now occupy a leading position and stand a head and shoulders above all competitors.

Mr. John A. Pitts died July 1, 1859, and was succeeded by his son, Mr. John B. Pitts, and his son-in-law, Mr. James Brayley, under the style of Brayley & Pitts. These gentlemen conducted the works with marked success, extending their trade, enlarging their plant and adding improvements to their machines, until 1877, when the concern was incorporated as the Pitts Agricultural Works; capital, $300,000. The new company at once started out upon a career of brilliant triumphs that rapidly spread its reputation abroad, and was already introducing its machinery in foreign lands, when, in July, 1879, the entire establishment, with all of its valuable plant of machinery, patterns, tools and appurtenances, was burned to the ground.

Almost before the ruins had begun to cool the work of reconstruction began, and in an astonishingly brief space of time the works were rebuilt, better than ever and more perfectly equipped for the prosecution of operations in all departments, so that on February 1, 1880, they were in full operation again. As they now stand they cover four acres of ground and include one of the most extensive plants, embracing foundry, blacksmith, machine, wood-working, engine and paint shops, controlled by any similar company in the country. It would be difficult to state the full capacity of the works or the value of their annual output. Suffice it to say that, in addition to the vast plant of improved machinery, they furnish steady employment for over 300 mechanics of various kinds, and have turned out, in a single year, 800 threshers and 300 engines, which were shipped to dealers and farmers upon orders. The trade of the house extends wherever the march of improvement has invaded or progress has planted its banner, and the Pitts engine and thresher are heard all over the United States, in South America, in Australia, in Mexico, in Italy, Spain and Africa. Especially are they popular among the boundless wheat fields of the Northwest—in Dakota, Washington Territory, Oregon and California. Oliver Dalrymple, the renowned Dakota wheat-grower, owns and operates some forty-two of the Pitts threshers, and his estimate of them is contained in a note to the manufacturers of January 13, 1886, in which he says : "The ten large California threshers that I purchased from you this season, as well as the threshing engines, did good work and gave me satisfaction."

The Pitts Agricultural Works build a variety of traction engines of the highest grade. They also build several patterns of portable and semi-portable engines for farm work, light saw and grist milling, etc. In all of these engines the leading idea has been economy of fuel and space, combined with great power, and it would appear that the problem has been satisfactorily solved. These engines are constructed as desired to burn coal, wood or straw, or coal and wood, wood and straw, or all together, by simply changing grates. They generate steam rapidly, furnish all the power required, and are safe, cheap, strong and handsome.

We have not space here for a detailed description of either the engines or the threshers manufactured by this company We may safely say, however, that they are unapproachable for simplicity, durability, neatness, capacity for good work, and cheapness. Large farmers and the trade should send to the company here for illustrated catalogues containing full information concerning these wonderfully effective and successful machines, which are doing so much to develop the new Northwest and the vast grain regions of this and other continents.

LAKE VIEW BREWING COMPANY.

George Sandrock, President; John Bachert, Vice-President; Henry W. Brendel, Secretary; Timothy J. Mahoney, Treasurer—Brewers of Sparkling, Delicious, Healthy Lager Beer—Lake View and Porter Aves.

The above-named great brewing and malting company was chartered under the laws of New York June 24, 1885, and is, consequently, now in the second year of a remarkably successful career. The authorized capital is $150,000, in shares of fifty dollars each, and the board of directors is composed of Messrs. George Sandrock, Alois Schaefer, Henry W. Brendel, Timothy J. Mahoney, John Basher, James Boland, William Drennen, George Irr and Frank C. Longnecker. The officers are named above.

The Lake View Brewing Company's plant, illustrated herewith, is a very valuable one, embracing, with malt-house, brewery, yards, etc., three-quarters of an acre of ground, desirably located, convenient to the canals, and commanding a superb view of lake, river and Canada shore. The malt-house is three and a-half stories in height, the brewery two and a-half stories, with immense cellars, and all of the handsomest and most substantial description, erected expressly for the purpose from the designs and plans of a competent architect, and first occupied by the original proprietor, Alois Schaefer, in October, 1881. The capacity of the establishment is 20,000 barrels per annum, the leading specialty being their own celebrated " Sparkling Lager." Twenty men are regularly employed, $200 per week is disbursed in wages, and the value of the annual output is stated at $150,000, all of which is eagerly sought by and sold to local dealers and the trade of Northern and Western New York and Pennsylvania.

The *personnel* of the company is of the best, all active and responsible business men.

GEORGE ELSHEIMER,

The Modern Sign Painter—Signs, Store Shades, Banners, Show Cards, Flags—No. 360 Main St.

In none of the useful arts has there been greater progress of late years than in sign painting, which is no longer a mere mechanical trade but has advanced to the rank of an art. One of the most accomplished and progressive designers and painters of artistic signs with whom we have ever come in contact is Mr. George Elsheimer, whose studio and workshop are located at No. 360 Main street, Kremlin block. His handiwork may be seen all over the city, and stamps him a master of his calling. Signs, of course, are his leading specialty, but he gives strict attention to all orders in his line, embracing banners, flags, store shades, show cards, and every description of fine lettering and color work. He is very popular with the mercantile community particularly, and his services in constant request by those who require the best possible work. His orders are chiefly from the Buffalo public, but he does many fine and tasteful jobs for parties at a distance, his fame having extended throughout this entire region.

Mr. E. is a native of this city, has had fifteen years' experience, and is thoroughly up in sign and decorative painting. Those who secure his services can rely upon first-class work and no shirking of details.

AMERICAN PALACE STEAM LAUNDRY.

SKINNER & GODFREY, Proprietors. (See opposite page.)

AMERICAN PALACE STEAM LAUNDRY.

H. J. Skinner and L. W. Godfrey, the Wonderful New Process Steam Launderers—Works, Nos. 238 to 254 Fargo Ave.; General Office, No. 306 Main St.

If there is a more extensive laundry in existence than the American Palace of Buffalo, the writer of this, with a wide experience and accurate knowledge of leading cities, has failed to discover it; at any rate there is not one more prosperous, famous, or more deservedly popular. It was established in 1882 by its present proprietors, Messrs. Skinner & Godfrey, who had for some five years owned and operated the American Steam Laundry of Bradford, Pa.—an institution which they continue to conduct on the same liberal principles that distinguish their management of the principal establishment here, and which at this time requires a fine two-story brick building 132 feet front and 200 feet deep for its accommodation. Besides nearly 100 skilled operatives, a valuable plant of novel and improved special machinery—invented and patented by the members of the firm—vastly increases the capacity of the works for doing large quantities of laundry work of every description at the shortest notice and in the best possible style, without injury to fabrics or loss of goods—an exasperating incident of patronizing some laundries conducted on the slam-bang, slipshod, hit-or-miss plan of guesswork and irresponsibility. Among the machinery upon which the firm pride themselves may be mentioned seven washers of their own invention, each designed for a distinct class of work, and which they perform perfectly, and known as the "New Process," "Wheel Washer" and "Stem-Winder," besides four others of standard make and approved model, together with a variety of ironing, starching, collar-and-cuff-turning and dampening machines. A neat, twenty-five-horse-power engine operates all of these and some other machines and an elevator for conveying operatives and work between the floors. The mechanical appliances alone are valued at $20,000. In point of fact, the purifying, starching and ironing of linen has by this firm been reduced to a science, both as regards dispatch and perfection, and they find their reward in the immense patronage bestowed upon them by the hotels, sleeping-car, dining-car and steamboat companies and thousands of private families of Buffalo and surrounding cities and towns within a radius of 100 miles. As an indication of their local patronage it may be stated here that they require two telephones—732 A and 732—and seven delivery wagons for the accommodation of city customers alone. While they give careful attention to every description of laundry work, their specialties are fine shirts, collars, cuffs, lace curtains and fluting. The firm do an average business of $75,000 a year, and are constantly increasing it.

Mr. Skinner is a native of Attica, N. Y., born in 1831. He has served nine years as first and second lieutenant of the 61st and 67th N. G. S. N. Y., going to Gettysburg in 1863 with his regiment, but arriving too late to participate in the perils and glory of that historic field. He still exhibits with some pardonable pride commissions signed by Washington Hunt and E. D. Morgan. He also served two years in the Dunkirk City Council. From 1872 to 1876 he engaged in railroad building in Texas, where he was very successful until overtaken by disease and disaster. He is a Mason, Odd Fellow and Son of Temperance.

Mr. Godfrey was born in 1339, in Wyoming county. He entered the service of the Erie as an engine-wiper, rose to the rank of conductor, served eleven years in that capacity on that road and one year on the Union Pacific. He then built the first shuttered house in Saunders county, Nebraska, farmed there for fours years, then came to Bradford, Pa., and joined Mr. Skinner in the laundry business. He is an Odd Fellow.

The citizens of Buffalo and strangers within the city's gates may be fairly congratulated upon having in the American Palace Steam Laundry such ample and excellent facilities for procuring the best possible work in that line. Guests of hotels, families in the city and suburbs, and all others who appreciate the luxury of clean and well-prepared linen, either for wear or for their beds, the workmanlike and skillful laundrying of laces of every description, promptitude, neatness and moderate charges, will find it to their interest in all ways to patronize Messrs. Skinner & Godfrey.

TROY LAUNDRY.

Mrs. Kate Fogarty, Proprietress—Hand Work Exclusively—Nos. 36 and 38 East Eagle St., Near Washington.

The success achieved by the energetic, thoroughgoing proprietress of the above-named popular laundry shows what may be accomplished by a wide-awake woman when she is in earnest. Mrs. Fogarty came to this country from Stockport, Lancashire, England, when but five years old. Her parents, poor, but industrious and respectable people, were unable to provide for their daughter further than to give her a plain common school education and a good example, and while still quite young she sought and obtained employment in one of Troy's great laundries, where she soon became noted for intelligence and capacity, and was elected President of the Troy Collar Laundry Union, which office she retained for five years, taking an active part in the strike of 1874. She then came to Buffalo, where she has remained ever since, attending strictly to her business, and gradually gaining the confidence and patronage of the public, and particularly of that class who recognize and appreciate first-class laundry work.

At present Mrs. Fogarty occupies the entire three-story building, 46 by 60 feet, Nos. 36 and 38 East Eagle street, between Washington and Ellicott streets, where she employs some twenty-seven skillful laundresses, pays the best wages in the city for that kind of work, and does an annual business of nearly $20,000. No machinery whatever is used in the establishment, and consequently garments are done up in superior style and without injury. The specialty, of course, to which greatest attention is given, is the laundrying of gentlemen's shirts, collars and cuffs, both for the trade and for individual customers, though every description of men's washing is done to order in the best manner and at short notice.

The Troy Laundry was established by Misses Malony (now Mrs. Fogarty) and Carll in 1871, the former succeeding in 1875. Mrs. Fogarty has made the reputation of the laundry, and well deserves the prosperity that has attended her efforts.

WILLIAM SCOTT,

Florist and Plant-Grower—Plants, Cut Flowers, Bulbs and Florists' Supplies —Decorations for Weddings, Parties, etc., a Specialty—Green-houses Corner Main and Balcom Sts.; Store, No. 498 Main St.

The love of flowers is almost universal—an instinct implanted by an all-wise Creator for the softening of our hearts and the opening of our spiritual eyes to the beauties of the world He has given us for a temporal habitation. Flowers are the very poetry of nature—the language whereby our tenderest sentiments are most fittingly expressed ; hence no wedding or obsequies—those occasions which call out our deepest emotions, of joy on the one hand, of grief on the other,—is complete without them. The cultivation of flowers is one of the most delightful of employments, and he who engages in it confers upon others, whose avocations prevent their doing so, much of the pleasure which he himself enjoys.

We are led into these reflections upon recurring to a recent visit and stroll through the superb flower-gardens and conservatories of Mr. William Scott, at Main and

Balcom streets. The grounds embrace an acre and a half, one-half of which is covered with tasteful one-story buildings, roofed with glass, and provided with every necessary appliance, including apparatus for heating by steam during the cold months. The whole place is a bower of beauty—the outdoor garden a wilderness of bloom and greenery, while the conservatory and hot-houses present a veritable scene from the "Arabian Nights"—a treasure-house of rare, curious and gorgeous tropical and semi-tropical plants and blossoms. It would be difficult to name any ornamental member of the vegetable kingdom worthy of a place and capable of cultivation in garden or conservatory that may not be found here.

Mr. Scott's tastefully-arranged and popular floral bazar at No. 498 Main street is Buffalo headquarters for cut flowers, floral designs of every description and for all occasions, where at all times will be found ample supplies of flowering and ornamental plants for parlor, window and terrace.

Mr. Scott came from Hampshire, England, to Buffalo in 1870, at the age of 26. Born and bred in one of the largest and most carefully-kept gardens in the South of England, with an inherited love for flowers, he naturally turned his attention to the calling in which he has accomplished so much. Without capital or influential friends he went to work, with the result we have seen. His garden and improvements are easily worth $20,000, and he sells annually-increasing quantities of flowers, shrubs, bulbs, florists' supplies, etc., his business for last year reaching $11,000.

CHARLES RICHARDSON,

Wholesale Fruits and Produce Commission—Nos. 58 and 60 West Market St.—Established 1876.

The splendid establishment and flourishing business of Mr. Charles Richardson, Nos. 58 and 60 West Market street, are a fitting monument to his energy, industry, strict attention to the wants of the public and upright dealing. Mr. Richardson, a native of Birmingham, England, has resided here nearly or quite twenty years, fourteen of which have been devoted to building up, from a small beginning in Washington market, the most extensive wholesale fruit and produce house in the city. His example is well worthy of emulation by the thousands of listless and shiftless young men who complain of chronic penury and lack of employment, and who might—however, they wouldn't take advice if we were never so generous with it.

As intimated, Mr. Richardson's business is the most extensive of the kind in Buffalo, aggregating over $200,000 for the past year and still growing. He commenced a few doors from his present location in 1876, two years later occupying No. 58 West Market street. Enlarging his operations as his trade increased, he afterward took No. 60 adjoining, and now requires the full capacity of the two stores, which together make a frontage of about 50 feet by 100 feet deep. His facilities for the receipt and handling of all kinds of fruits and produce generally are unsurpassed. He is by far the largest receiver in the fruit and produce business here, and seems to have the faculty of disposing of vast quantities. He employs good men, and runs his business with thorough system. Each and every salesman seems fully to understand his position or branch of the business. Mr. R. handles largely in car lots foreign and domestic fruits and vegetables in their season, and is also a large receiver of eggs, butter, game and poultry, this department being handled exclusively by itself and by one salesman.

Mr. Richardson employs from ten to twelve men the season through, and has an excellent trade both local and with adjoining towns. Well known in his line of business, east, west, north and south, he enjoys an excellent reputation and is worthy of all respect as a thorough practical business man.

W. H. SMITH & CO.,

Proprietors Cutler's Patent Pocket Inhaler and Carbolate of Iodine Inhalant, for Catarrh, Bronchitis, Asthma, Hoarseness and All Diseases of the Throat and Lungs—No. 410 Michigan St.

Diseases of the lungs, throat and air passages are so common among Americans as to have long ceased to be a matter of wonder, and it is a rare circumstance, more especially in this latitude, to find a man or woman unaffected by any of these complaints. Two or three hundred years of constant failure to cure this class of troubles by loading the stomach with nasty compounds, cod liver oil and tar, finally led to experiments with treatment by inhalations, the natural and rational method of reaching the afflicted organs, and further research developed the fact that all infectious diseases are spread by parasites (bacteria) so minute as for a long time to have escaped detection even by the microscope. Putting these facts together, Mr. W. H. Cutler, a well-known Buffalo lawyer, set himself to the task of finding the best remedy for the diseases referred to, and the best preventive of contagion, and later to devising the best, surest and most convenient means of administering the medicine. The results we have in Cutler's Carbolate of Iodine Inhalant and Cutler's Pocket Inhaler, manufactured by Messrs. W. H. Smith & Co., No. 410 Michigan street, Buffalo.

Full instructions are given to show the manner of charging the inhaler, full directions accompanying each instrument.

It is confidently claimed—and the claim is substantiated by the indorsement of many eminent physicians as well as thousands of testimonials from those who have been relieved and cured—that carbolate of iodine, as administered through Cutler's pocket inhaler, will positively cure any curable case of catarrh, bronchitis, hay fever, sore throat and hoarseness, asthma, and bad breath produced by those causes, and will invariably prevent the transmission of infectious diseases, such as small-pox, yellow fever, cholera, etc. Of those who have publicly testified to these facts and the incalculable value of Mr. Cutler's invention, we are permitted to mention Dr. W. Kempster, physician and surgeon to the State lunatic asylum at Auburn; Dr. R. H. Bakewell, health officer of Trinidad; W. D. Blain, M. D., Chicago; Lafayette Bingham, M. D., Corning, N. Y.; Dr. William R. Ford, deceased, Albany, N. Y.; William F. Channing, M. D., Providence, R. I.; A. F. Worthington & Co., druggists, Cincinnati, O.; Dr. Andrew Nest, New Albany, Ind.; Dr. J. A. Nattrass, Springfield, Mo.; Dr. J. R. McCarty, Ridgeway, Ont., and hundreds of other prominent people at a distance, besides such conspicuous Buffalonians as Dr. George Hadley, late professor of chemistry and pharmacy in the University of Buffalo; H. T. Appleby, pharmaceutist and chemist; Dr. L. P. Dayton, Hon. Nelson K. Hopkins, Hon. D. N. Lockwood, Rev. Dr. H. Muller, Rev. Mrs. S. M. Paddock, W. L. G. Smith, deceased; F. Kendall, and many others. After careful examination of Cutler's inhaler, Prof. Hadley wrote:

The material of which it is constructed, viz., filtering paper, which is pure vegetable fibre, readily absorbs all liquids, and is at the same time least affected by chemical re-agents of all organic substances. It is especially more enduring and unchangeable than nitrogenous bodies of animal origin, such as hair, wool, silk, sponge, etc.

1st. The paper tubes insure in every instrument the same definite and constant supply of air, which no accident can either lessen or cut off. No filling with loose cotton, sponge, etc., can possibly secure the same supply of air in different instruments, or even in the same instrument, when the fluid it contains varies in quantity.

2d. With a given liquid, the temperature remaining constant, the quantity of vapor exhaled is exactly proportioned to the surface presented to the air; every instrument will therefore yield the same amount of vapor, when charged with the same volatile body.

3d. If necessary for substances of different volatility or medicinal activity, the proportion of vapor may be regulated by changing the length of the bundle of tubes, or by varying the diameter of the tubelets.

4th. In my opinion, medicines for inhalation should not be mixed for purposes of dilution with inert substances of different volatility from themselves, for the reason that the amount of vapor evolved from such mixture will vary with the progress of the inhalation, in an increasing or diminishing ratio, according to the volatility of the diluent; whereas, if but a single substance, with a constant boiling point, and consequently uniform rate of evaporation, is employed, as long as the paper tubes are tolerably well saturated, the evaporation will take place at an equal rate during the whole progress of inhalation.

On the whole, this inhaler seems to me to accomplish its purposes by novel, yet by the most simple and effectual means, to be philosophical in conception, and well carried out in the execution.   GEORGE HADLEY.

It supersedes all other inhaling tubes and contrivances. It is equally adapted to the mouth and the nostrils. No steam required—no blowing necessary. The great obstacle to successful treatment by inhalants, that the bottles and apparatus are complicated and inconvenient, is by this curious little instrument entirely overcome. Made of deodorized hard rubber, it may be carried in the pocket as handily as a pen-knife or a buttonhook. No danger of breaking or spilling; always ready, and may be used with the same ease and facility as a cigarette, or a lady's smelling bottle.

The superior advantages claimed for it are:

1st. Its cheapness, simplicity and durability.
2d. It admits of the use of all volatile fluids, even the most concentrated.
3d. It has a certain and unchanging area of exhaling surface.
4th. A definite supply of air which is in no danger of being varied.
5th. It insures an equal rate of evaporation during inhalation.
6th. It is as efficient in the hands of a novice as the adept—a child may use it.

DE LANEY FORGE AND IRON COMPANY.

C. A. De Laney, John Slote, James Howard — Manufacturers of Light and Heavy Forgings, Car Axles and Hammered Shapes of Every Description from Wrought Iron or Siemens-Martin Steel—No. 300 Perry St.

Established in 1850—thirty-six years ago—the De Laney Forge and Iron Company is still in the front rank of Buffalo's industrial enterprises, a mammoth manufacturing concern, with few peers on the continent, either in extent, variety or excellence of its peculiar products. These embrace many specialties, among them forged and finished iron and steel work, marine and stationary engines, railroad engines and car forgings, Siemens-Martin and Bessemer steel forgings, oil engine cranks, oil tool forgings, and the best quality of hammered car axles. A detailed description of these great works would perhaps weary the reader, but we cannot forbear passing mention of the fact that the equipment of machinery is vast and complete, embracing everything desirable, from the smallest drill up to the tremendous steam hammers, and one immense lathe, seventy feet long, capable of finishing the largest and heaviest shafts.

The De Laney Forge and Iron Works are constantly under the personal supervision of practical men, and nothing is permitted to leave the establishment until thoroughly tested and approved. The shipping facilities, both by rail and water, are excellent.

JOHN ERNEWEIN,

Manufacturer of Center Tables in All Styles—Nos. 223, 225 and 227 Mortimer St., corner Matthews.

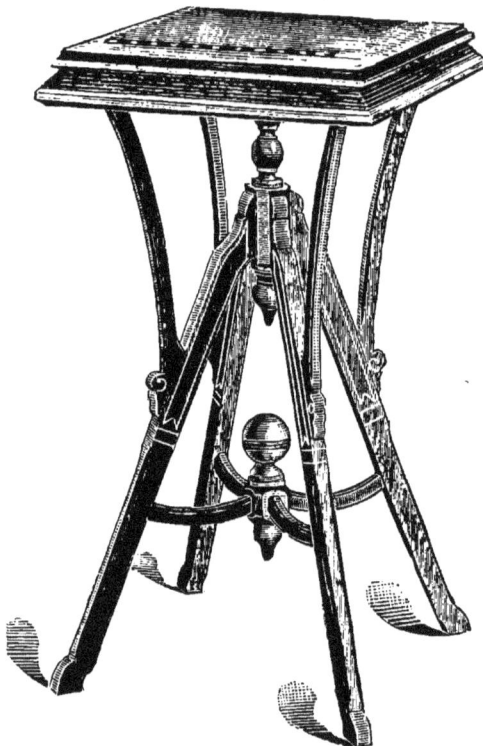

This now prosperous concern was established by Ernewein & Ritter in 1879, Mr. Ritter dying the same year. The factory occupies a commodious three-story brick building, 40 by 75 feet, to which is attached a convenient two-story warehouse, 23 by 40 feet, and yards 88 by 125 feet, where ample stocks of fine lumber are stored and seasoned. Some forty workmen find steady employment in the shops, and, with the assistance of a fine plant of late improved machinery, turn out about $50,000 worth of goods per annum, for which a ready market is found all over the United States.

The house makes a specialty of the manufacture of fine and medium marble-top and plain center-tables from original designs, many of which are exceedingly rich and attractive. None but the best selected material is used, and the workmanship and finish of all these goods is equal to any we have ever seen, while the prices are remarkably low for this grade of work.

Mr. Ernewein was born at Eden, this county, coming to Buffalo nearly thirty-four years ago. He has been in the cabinet-making business since his fifteenth year, and has a thorough practical knowledge of all its details. Himself an industrious, enterprising man, who enjoys the confidence of all who know him, he has the active aid of three fine sons in his establishment, one of whom, John H., jr., has charge of the machinery department, a most capable man for the place. Mr. E.'s trade grows steadily year by year, in territory and volume, and his prospects are excellent indeed, his goods being popular wherever introduced.

J. G. HAFFA'S SONS,

Importing Tailors—No. 14 West Eagle St.

Among the merchant tailors who left an enduring reputation for the superiority of the work turned out in this city, was the late J. G. Haffa, whose death occurred during the past year. He was among the pioneers in the business, and established a reputation that will undoubtedly be handed down through his sons for years to come. The elder Mr. Haffa took a deep pride in being proficient in his calling, and counted among his intimate friends the leading citizens of Buffalo. He was, for a number of years, located at No. 325 Washington street. On March 1, 1886, his sons, George J. and Elias, formed a partnership, the style of the new firm assumed being J. G. Haffa's Sons, for two years previous to which Mr. G. J. Haffa was with his father as partner. They removed to the present location, No. 14 West Eagle street, at that time, and fitted up what is probably the finest establishment of the kind between New York and Chicago.

Both gentlemen have had the benefit of a thorough practical training in the business, under the senior Mr. Haffa. They also studied the fine points of the business during a period spent in New York city especially for that purpose, under one of the leading metropolitan artists. Being thus successfully qualified for the profession, they started in under the most favorable auspices in this city. Their establishment is stocked with a splendid assortment of the finest imported woolens, and it goes without saying that their work is artistic in the strict sense of the word. Both the Messrs. Haffa are courteous, painstaking gentlemen, and their success is assured.

METZ, BARK & MEYER,

Successors to Weller, Brown & Mesmer—Manufacturers of Interior Hardwood Finish and Fine Furniture—Office and Factory, Nos. 292 to 308 Elm St.

This is one of those old-established industries, rightly regarded as pioneers, which aided in laying broad and deep the foundations of Buffalo's present greatness. It was founded in 1836 by Messrs. Hersee and Zimmerman, passing through various hands until 1884, when the present firm took possession.

Mr. Metz is a native of Buffalo, born in 1839, and has always resided here. He is an enterprising, thorough-going, devoted business man, who has never worried his brains over public display or office. He looks after the finances and commercial concerns of the house.

Mr. Bark was born in Sweden in 1851. He is a graduate of the Berlin high school, architectural department; emigrated to Buffalo in 1867, and entered the employ of Weller, Brown & Mesmer, under Mr. Meyer, then superintendent, as designer, in which work he soon distinguished himself, becoming first a stockholder, and later (in 1880), a member of the firm. He has made artistic designing as applied to the mechanic arts his life study, and probably there does not exist a more thorough master of his art, besides which he is a superior business man.

Mr. Meyer emigrated to Buffalo from Hanover, Germany, in 1866. Already a finished mechanic, he for several years devoted his time to mastering the methods in vogue among American artisans. For eight months in 1870 he labored as a journeyman for Weller, Brown & Mesmer, when, in recognition of his superior executive capacity, knowledge and skill, he was made superintendent of the works. Ten years later, in 1880, he also, with Mr. Bark, was taken into the firm as a partner, retaining his interest on the accession of the present house.

Metz, Bark & Meyer are renowned all over this country, and even in Europe, Mexico and South America, for the beauty, appropriateness, elegance, originality and finish of their interior hardwood decorations and general work, than which nothing finer or more sumptuous is produced anywhere ; nor, indeed, does the house recognize many equals in this specialty, particularly in the ornamentation of churches, masonic and other halls, hotels, banks, private residences, palace and dining-cars and elsewhere, demanding the exercise of trained artistic taste combined with a high degree of mechanical merit.

The works are illustrated above. They cover a space of 180 by 180 feet in area, with handsome and substantial three and four-story buildings. The equipment of modern machinery is complete and costly, much of it built expressly for the firm. From 160 to 180 skilled mechanics are employed, and last year's output exceeded $250,000 in value—a figure which will be largely increased from year to year.

WILLIAMSVILLE QUICK LIME CO.,

Dealers in Quick Lime, Cement, Stucco, etc.—Sole Proprietors of the Celebrated Young's and Fogelsonger's Quarries—Office, Cor. Broadway and Elm St.

Buffalo is noted for the superiority of the lime-stone products which are manufactured in the immediate vicinity. As a distributing point for quick-lime, cement, stucco, etc., she is unsurpassed ; the volume of material is large, and among the important items that go to swell the rapidly-increasing returns each year. The leading establishment in the business is the Williamsville Quick-Lime Co. It is composed of W. Fogelsonger & Son and J. S. and F. H. Youngs. It was organized in 1871, and the office and warehouses at the corner of Elm street and Broadway are very extensive. At Williamsville, a very old suburb of the city, ten miles distant, the company owns and operates a valuable body of quarry land to the extent of twenty acres. Six kilns are almost constantly in full blast, and the product in quick lime and cut and building stone is distributed throughout the western part of the State and Pennsylvania. The annual business of the company amounts to $90,000, and the number of employes is thirty-five.

Of the members of the firm, Mr. W. Fogelsonger is a native of the Keystone State, but has resided in Erie county since the days of the early pioneers. His son Henry is a native of this county, and has resided in Buffalo during the past eleven years. Mr. J. S. Youngs is a native of Erie county, and has resided in Buffalo since 1872. He is a civil engineer, and served a term as city engineer during 1880–81. At present he is sanitary engineer of the city, and also chief engineer of the Buffalo & Williamsville railroad. Mr. F. H. Youngs resides at the works, and is engaged in farming The elder J. B. Youngs, father of thè present member of the firm, was one of the oldest and best-known citizens of Erie county. He was born in what is now the town of Lancaster, June 26, 1812, and always resided in this county. His occupation was that of a farmer and manufacturer of lime. He was a great friend of workingmen, and took a deep interest in the welfare of the poor. Politically Mr. Youngs was always an active and consistent Republican. Among other offices held by him was that of Assemblyman and Supervisor. He was also one of the members of the original Board of Commissioners for the erection of the City and County Hall. His death occurred May 30, 1886, lamented by a wide circle of friends.

TIFFT FURNITURE CO.,

Manufacturers and Dealers in Fine and Medium Furniture of All Kinds—Nos. 477 and 479 Washington St.

The furniture trade of Buffalo is very extensive, permeating not only the northern and western half of New York, but even penetrating to many of the Western and Southern States. Prominent among the furniture manufacturers of this city, and, in fact, one of its leading establishments, is the renowned Tifft Furniture Company, founded in 1871 by the late Geo. W. Tifft, who also originated the famous firm of Geo. W. Tifft, Sons & Co., whose steam engine and boiler works is still one of Buffalo's most noted and prosperous concerns, and is conducted by the same firm composing the Tifft Furniture Company, the individual members of which are Mr. C. L. Whiting, Mrs. M. A. Plimpton and Mrs. S. A. Gay. Mr. George D. Plimpton has the management of the furniture house, while Mr. Whiting directs the affairs of the boiler and machine works, the latter named industry being described in another part of this work.

The Tifft Furniture Company occupy a fine five-story building, Nos. 477 and 479 Washington street, corner of Mohawk, 32 feet front by 115 feet deep. The firm's goods embrace a long line of household furniture for parlor, dining-room, bed-room and hall, in all grades for which there is any considerable demand, and suitable for all classes and conditions of people, from the humble laborer to the merchant prince.

In furniture styles are ever changing, so that what is most popular and costly this year may be relegated to the garret next, to make way for the newest fashion in form or material. Just now the craze is for richly stained cherry and antique oak, which some years ago gave place to chestnut, ash, oak and walnut. In these beautiful materials the Tifft Furniture Company presents many novel and attractive original designs, and are having a great run upon their best patterns in every line.

Old-established, reliable and fully up with the times, this is a house that deserves well at the hands of the trade and of consumers.

CLARK'S BUSINESS COLLEGE.

C. U. Johnson, President and Proprietor—Coal and Iron Exchange, Washington St., between Seneca and Swan.

Among the best business schools of this kind that have ever come under our observation is Clark's Business College, which occupies one entire upper floor of the Coal and Iron Exchange building, Washington street, adjoining the postoffice. Above we present a view of the Exchange, one of the handsomest, largest and most massive buildings in Buffalo. Mr. C. U. Johnson is president, while Mr. John C. Ryan is secretary. The course of study, from which all mere ornaments have been eliminated, is of the most practical kind, embracing penmanship, double entry book-keeping, commercial arithmetic, actual business practice, rapid calculations, commercial law, business correspondence, the drawing of every description of commercial papers, orthography, etc. A common school education is all the preparation needed. Each student receives separate instructions, and from four to six months' study will fit any young man of average capacity and application for active business. Clark's progressive book-keeping, practical and common-sense at every step, is the system taught. The course of training includes actual mercantile and commercial transactions between Erie and Buffalo, thus imparting the soundest kind of business training by the best possible method—practice. The faculty is a remarkably strong and able one in every department, selected for individual attainments and capability of conveying to youthful minds the knowledge they have themselves acquired by long and arduous experience. The course differs from that of most business colleges, in that it is thoroughly progressive and modern, and when the pupil completes the curriculum he knows enough to take charge of a set of double-entry books and is fitted for any position that is open to him. The student, upon entering the actual business course, starts in as a retail merchant, doing business with the different business offices, and with students in the other college. This teaches him neatness, commercial customs, and impresses upon him the great necessity of giving special attention to details. He is accordingly more painstaking with his business papers, as they go into the hands of strangers, and he becomes acquainted through correspondence with those engaged in business, desiring to do by them as he would be done by. There are eight separate offices in the actual business exchange, consisting of two banks, merchandise emporium, postoffice, insurance office, railroad office, commission office and real estate, supplied with all the conveniences usually found in first-class business houses, and under the supervision of the teacher students become familiar with the usages and customs of such places, besides being required to keep a regular set of double-entry books, as used in each office.

Mr Johnson does not guarantee situations to graduates, though he renders them such assistance as is legitimate and proper. Business men frequently apply to him for competent accountants, and in this way many of his most faithful and capable male and female students are provided for. Students may enter at any time. Life scholarships, entitling the holders to tuition until they graduate, are sold for $50. Reviews— additional instructions—are given graduates at any time. Board may be had at from three dollars per week up.

The night school continues throughout the year, the same as the day session, and students receive every advantage that can be given them. This school is intended for those who are engaged during the day, and not only are all the branches taught that the business course includes, but any of the common English branches may be taken, either separately or all together. It is the best place for young and middle-aged men and women to get a start in life, if they are unable to attend the day session.

9

McCLURE, BLOESER & EGGERT.

Manufacturers of Boys', Youths', Ladies', Misses' and Children's Fine Shoes— No. 370 Ellicott St., Opposite Washington Market.

For a new house the above named has been remarkably successful in the face of eager and determined competition. Its doors were first opened in November, 1883, and in a career of three years it has already built up a business of more than $5,000 a month, occupies a handsome three-story building, 24 feet front by 140 feet deep, employs 50 operatives and four travelers, and has extended its trade into every State north of Mason and Dixon's line and west of New York. The factory equipment is first-class, embracing all the modern machinery of approved makes and practical value, and the specialties turned out comprise all the fashionable and popular styles of fine and medium ladies', misses', children's, boys' and youths' footwear, all of the best material and workmanship and superior finish and appearance.

The members of the firm are thoroughly practical men, experienced in their business, capable and industrious. All were formerly employes of W. H. Walker, the famous Main-street wholesale shoe merchant.

Mr. McClure, a native of this county, who has personal supervision of the factory, was reared to the shoe trade, his father having pursued it for many years, and he himself having been the junior member of Taylor & McClure, retail shoe dealers of this city. Mr. J. Bloeser, born in Erie, Pa., attends to buying stock, and also travels for the house at times. He was formerly a retail shoe merchant at Erie, Pa. Mr. E. B. Eggert has charge of the office and books, and this is his first business venture. He was born at Eggertsville, this county.

As an indication of the firm's resources, we may here state that they are now manufacturing eighty-five distinct styles of shoes and slippers, none of which are for men. Such push and enterprise cannot. but reap a rich reward in both money and reputation.

GEORGE D. WIGHTMAN,

Designer and Engraver on Wood — No. 60 Pearl St., near Seneca.

The wedded arts of designing and engraving on wood are progressive in their nature, and, as a general thing, it is safe to conclude that, other things being equal, the individual who has the longest and most varied practical experience in either or both of these pursuits is the most skillful and most capable of producing the best effects. Buffalo has long enjoyed a high reputation for the excellent work turned out by her artists in these specialties, and it is safe to say that much of the credit therefor is due to the gentleman whose name appears above. Mr. Wightman is of English birth, born in London, and established himself here, in the old Exchange building on Main street, as long ago as 1847. Later he removed to the Arcade building, then, after a few years, to Brown's building, and last, in 1866, to his present convenient quarters at No. 60 Pearl street.

Mr. Wightman is a remarkably skillful artist, naturally talented, whose fine taste and superior workmanship are known and recognized at home and abroad. His specialties cover a wide range, and embrace the drawing and engraving of portraits, landscapes, buildings, machinery, etc., and fine catalogue work of all kinds. The writer of this recently had occasion to visit Mr. Wightman's studio, and speaks from personal observation when he pronounces the work there exhibited equal to any he has ever seen.

CENTRAL COAL CO. (Limited), Incorporated.

Z. B. Lewis, President; J. W. Haywood, Vice-President and General Manager; J. F. Everhart, Secretary and Treasurer; H. I. Cook, Superintendent at Yard George H. Clarke, Assistant Superintendent, in Charge of Marine Department—Miners and Shippers of Hard and Soft Coal —Office, Second Floor Third National Bank, Corner Main and Swan. Sts., and No. 300 Main St.

This successful and flourishing coal company, which, within little more than a year from its inception, extended its trade to all available points throughout the States and Canada, was established in a modest and unpretentious way at No. 7 West Seneca street, October 12, 1885, by Messrs. J. W. Hayward and H. I. Cook, and removed to its present eligible quarters over the Third National Bank, southeast corner Main and Swan streets, in April of 1886. The growth of the Central's trade and the development of its influence have far exceeded the most sanguine expectations of its founders, and placed it upon an equality with the oldest and most powerful of its competitors. The need of more workers and more capital became so pressing, in order to meet the demands of their business, that Messrs. Z. B. Lewis, J. F. Everhart and George H. Clarke were induced to join them, and the "Central Coal Company, Limited" was incorporated in September of the same year.

Their local and shipping business is phenomenal, and the company is very popular with consumers, handling the best grades of coal, both hard and soft, from its own mines, for manufacturing and domestic purposes, heating and steam generating.

The *personnel* of the company is of the highest order. Mr. J. W. Hayward, who, with Mr. H. I. Cook, originated and established it, was, for a dozen or more years, traveler for various coal mining and shipping firms, at a later period conducting on his own account an extensive business at Oneida, N. Y., with a branch at Jackson, Mich. Having outgrown the markets afforded by these places, he came to Buffalo, where he found ample scope for his abilities and enterprise. His personal and business worth are known and recognized by the trade generally.

Mr. H. I. Cook was formerly for five years Buffalo ticket agent of the New York Central Railroad Company, previous to which time he was engaged in railroad construction, having been prominently identified with the building of the famous Cazenovia tunnel, some thirteen or fourteen years ago. Resigning his ticket agency, he devoted several years to traveling and prospecting in the West, the South and Canada, finally joining Mr. Hayward in establishing the Central Coal Company. He has charge as superintendent of coal delivery at the company's coal trestles on Van Rensselaer street, near Exchange, East Buffalo, and has won golden opinions on all hands for promptitude, fair dealing and politeness.

President Z. B. Lewis, of Niagara Falls, Ont., was unanimously chosen to that position at the first election of officers on reorganization of the company. He is a native of Wentworth, Township of Saltfleet, Canada, and is widely and favorably known throughout the western portion of the Dominion for his enterprising spirit and business sagacity. For ten years previous to his present venture he was a prominent wholesale and retail coal dealer, saw and planing mill and bakery proprietor. He fills his present position with dignity and to the credit and satisfaction of his company.

J. F. Everhart, A. M., M. D., secretary and treasurer, is a native of Philadelphia, and came to Buffalo three years ago to prosecute certain literary labors upon which he had been engaged for a decade. He was induced to connect himself with the coal trade as offering a better field than he could elsewhere find for the practical study of coal geology, a science that had for the twenty years previous possessed great charms for him, and it is safe to say that in his specialty—the fixing of the analytical and economic value of the various grades of anthracite and bituminous coals—he has no equal in Western New York. On accepting the position of secretary and treasurer he was appointed, with President Lewis, a commission to proceed to the Pennsylvania anthracite region and select a line of fuel that would succeed in this market in competition with that carried by the established coal kings as the standard. The result has fully vindicated the wisdom of the choice made.

Captain George H. Clarke, who manages the marine interests of the company, is an old-time lake shipper, more recently connected with marine insurance and the coal trade. He also entered the Central Coal Company at its reorganization, and his great experience and wide acquaintance, in connection with his personal popularity and high character, render him one of its most valuable members. He is a well-preserved and remarkably active man for his years, cheery and wide-awake.

CROCKER'S BUFFALO FERTILIZER AND CHEMICAL WORKS.

Smith & Becker, Trustees—Manufacturers of Ammoniated Bone Superphosphate and Ground Bones—Office, No. 60 Pearl St. ; Works, Babcock St., East Buffalo.

Few intelligent farmers in the Eastern and Middle States are ignorant of the merits of Crocker's Buffalo Fertilizers, which during the past twelve years have become more famous than any similar products ever were before. These fertilizers are prepared under the personal supervision of an eminent chemist, are uniform in quality and constituents, and unquestionably the purest and best commercial fertilizers on the market. They are five in number, each specially designed for a certain class of grains, plants, vegetables or fruits, as follows : " Buffalo Ammoniated Bone Super-phosphate," " Buffalo Potato, Hop and Tobacco Phosphate," " Buffalo Vegetable Bone Super-phosphate" (for vegetables, root crops, berries, grape-vines, lawns, etc), "Buffalo Queen City Phosphate," and " Crocker's Buffalo [No. 2] Super-phosphate." In addition, these works manufacture a superior article of pure ground bones, strictly genuine, particularly recommended for grass lands. These fertilizers are especially rich in plant feeding constituents, as phosphoric acid, ammonia, potash and nitrogen, and furnish the best possible substitutes for the natural elements of the soil, withdrawn by long-continued and severe cropping.

Messrs. James R. Smith and Emil A. Becker manage the Buffalo Fertilizer Works as trustees. Mr. Becker, of German birth, has resided here since 1870, nearly twelve years of which time have been devoted to his present pursuit. He is a member of the Board of Trade. Mr. Smith is a native of Buffalo, a trustee of the Board of Trade, vice-president of the Merchants' National and director of several other banks.

The works, established by L. L. Crocker in 1874, cover about eleven and a-half acres of land, five and a-half acres of which are enclosed and covered with buildings connected by switches with the several railroads. The best and latest improved machinery and from 80 to 100 men are employed, turning out an immense quantity of superior fertilizers per annum. The house annually publishes a handsome pamphlet full of information on the subject of fertilizers, which will be mailed free to all who desire it.

FORBUSH & BROWN,

**Wholesale Boot and Shoe Manufacturers—Nos. 103 and 105 Main St.,
Cor. Scott.**

Among the varied industrial resources of Buffalo which have been exhaustively
treated in the pages of this work, reference will be found to what is done in boots and
shoes. The house of Messrs. Forbush & Brown is the oldest and most extensive
establishment of the kind in Buffalo, and, probably, in Western New York. It was
established in 1853, and has kept even pace in expanding with the growth and development of this city from a village to a city of a quarter million inhabitants. At present
a very commodious building is occupied at Nos. 103 and 105 Main street, corner of Scott.
It is four stories high, 60 by 130 feet, amply equipped throughout with all the necessary
modern mechanical facilities. The annual business of the house amounts to $200,000,
and a working force in the factory of from 250 to 300 skilled artisans is employed. The
pay-roll amounts to about $1,200 per week, and is continuous the year around. A
specialty is made of genuine Buffalo hand-made boots and shoes, which have attained
a splendid reputation throughout the country. The trade extends through the Western and Southwestern States, and is efficiently taken care of by an able and active
corps of traveling salesmen. It is not going out of the way to remark that each successive season finds this house at the front with a superior line of the most approved
styles, which in shape and finish are second to none from any boot and shoe manufacturing center in the land. They come from an old reliable house, whose aim has always
been to supply the trade with goods that must invariably establish close and
confidential relations between the dealer and consumer.

Of the individual members of the firm Mr. N. Brown retired in 1883. The business
has been since continued under the old style by the present proprietor, Mr. Jonathan C.
Forbush. Although about sixty years of age, Mr. Forbush is as active as ever, and
gives his personal supervision to the affairs of the business, particularly the manufacturing department. He is a native of Grafton, Mass., and came to this city in 1853,
when the present business was begun. As a successful and prominent citizen, with a
long and honorable career, his worth has been duly recognized.

STAR MACHINE CO.,

**Manufacturers of Star Portable Forges, Blacksmiths' Hand Blowers, Wood-
Working Machinery, Self-Oiling Loose Pulleys, etc.—Office, Nos. 198 and
200 Terrace.**

Among the flourishing
concerns of this kind here,
one of the most conspicuous
is the Star Machine Co., Nos.
198 and 200 Terrace, of
which Hon. Arthur W.
Hickman is president, and
Mr. Charles Hamelman sec-
retary and treasurer. We
present above a fine view
of the works, which are 32
by 107 feet, four stories and
basement. The capital of
the company, which was
organized April 24, 1886, is
$50,000, and it is calculated
that the output for the first
year will reach a value of
$40,000 to $50,000. The leading specialties embrace a
splendid line of improved
wood-working machinery,
including, among others, C.
Hamelman's improved pat-
ent "Star Planer and
Matcher," "Star Band Saw," "Star Pony Planer," and "Star Self-Oiling Loose Pulley."

The "Star Forge," and "Star Blacksmith's Hand Blower," are Mr. Hamelman's own
inventions, and have been vastly improved since first brought out. These forges are

made in styles adapted to the uses of boiler-makers, iron bridge builders, architectural iron workers, boiler repairers, quarrymen, miners, machinists, tinsmiths, copper. iiths, plumbers, gasfitters, manufacturing jewelers, gun and locksmiths, and workers in metals generally. No. 4, illustrated herewith, is the medium size, weighing only 110 pounds, and has an open hood. No. 5, with simple dash at back, weighs 100 pounds, while No. 6, with closed hood, weighs 120 pounds. The Blacksmith's Hand Blower, operated by a combination of the wheel and lever, occupies only four square feet of floor space, and is readily attachable to any stationary hearth.

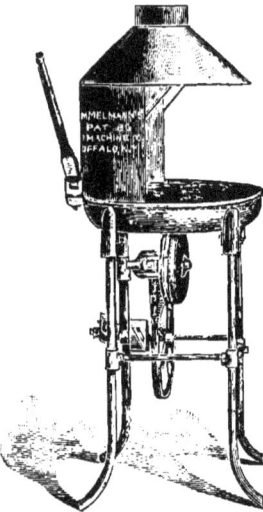

It will produce, with very little labor, all the blast required by any blacksmith's fire. The principle upon which this forge and blower works is as simple as it is effective, its principal points of superiority over all others being: It has fewer working parts than any other made, consequently there is less friction to overcome in working it. By reason of its simplicity it will never get out of order. There is only one large wheel in its construction. This is driven by the rack, which is moved up and down in the guides attached to the legs of the machine, and which engages with the pinion on the clutch hanging on the same shaft (which is stationary) as the band-wheel. The shaft is so arranged that any wear of the pinion and rack can be taken up by means of set-screws. The rack receives its motion from the lever, which is hung on a swivel, thereby enabling the worker to move about on a considerable radius while working. The ease with which the machinery can be started is surprising, and is owing both to the principle and simplicity of its construction.

The clutch has fewer pieces than any other, and is so constructed that there is practically no wear.

Steel shafting is used, and best Babbitt for journals. These forges and blowers are guaranteed to be easier working, more durable and of stronger blast than any other. They are for sale by all leading hardware and machinery dealers throughout the country.

BUFFALO REGISTER WORKS.

O. F. Swift, Proprietor—Manufacturer of Registers, Ventilators, Refrigerator Trimmings, Locks, Knobs, etc.—Nos. 432 to 438 Niagara St.

The careful observer, in looking over the range of this city's manufacturing resources, cannot avoid being impressed with the fact that of late years it has become widely diversified. Numerous auxiliary lines have sprung up in specialties for which there is a widespread demand. An illustration can be found in such an establishment as the Buffalo Register Works. The business was started in July, 1884, by Mr. O. F. Swift, at Nos. 10 and 12 Perry street. Owing to the rapid expansion, additional facilities were required, and in May, 1886, the present commodious premises at Nos. 432 to 438 Niagara street were secured. Here an area of 40 by 80 feet, including three well-appointed floors, are occupied, and the goods manufactured include such articles as the vertical wheel warm-air registers, ventilators, borders, frames, refrigerator trimmings, locks, knobs, etc. With the advantages of the best machinery and other equally important features, this firm is able to successfully compete with any in the country. When required, special locks and hardware trimmings are made to order.

Mr. Swift is a man of wide experience in the practical management of the business. He was formerly proprietor of the Empire State Manufacturing Company, and in all that pertains to hardware specialties he is an undisputed authority. A working force of from twenty to twenty-five skilled artisans is constantly employed, and the trade extends to all parts of the country. Mr. Swift also, for a period of fifteen years, was extensively engaged in logging and the wholesale lumber business in Wisconsin. All his ventures have proved successful, and his present enterprise, from indications, will be no exception.

L. B. CROCKER,

Supe atendeut Live Stock Department New York Central & Hudson River Railroad—Office, Stock-Yards, East Buffalo.

Among its army of officials and employes the New York Central & Hudson River Railroad Company has no more faithful, industrious, energetic, or capable man than Mr. L. B. Crocker, superintendent of its live-stock department at Buffalo. Mr. Crocker was born in 1856 in this city, and from boyhood has been connected with the handling of live stock in transit, his father and grandfather having preceded him in his present position, which he has held since 1874, previously for a year acting as yard superintendent at Buffalo, Toledo, Detroit and Joliet. At each he instituted reforms and improvements that have resulted in a vast access of business and the establishment of a perfect system, and all are in a condition of prosperity never before known. The yards at East Buffalo, under his immediate supervision, present a model of neatness, cleanliness, good order, exactitude and facility in the transaction of business such as can be found nowhere else. Every drover who has visited these yards during the present administration will testify to the uniform courtesy, promptitude, liberality and strict honesty that characterize every transaction in which Mr. Crocker is concerned. As a consequence he is a universal favorite with shippers and their employes on every line converging here that carries live stock.

As before intimated, Mr. Crocker is the third of the name and family who has filled the position. His late grandfather, Mr. Leonard Crocker, came to Buffalo from Argyle, Vt., early in 1856, and purchased a farm on the lake shore, now called the Tifft farm, and was soon afterward appointed superintendent of the stock yards on their inauguration. The yards were transferred to the New York Central & Hudson River Railroad in 1865, and Mr. Crocker continued in charge, and to his energy and enterprise is largely due the development of the business during its earlier years. Generous and public-spirited, he was popular with and respected by all who knew him. He was drowned on the lake shore in the memorable storm of January 2, 1870.

Mr. Lemuel L. Crocker, son of the last-named, succeeded him in the superintendency of the yards, and infused much of his own energy and high character into the conduct of the business. There seemed no limit to his enterprise and liberality, not only toward shippers of stock, but toward individuals and business ventures in need of aid. He was born at White Hall, N. Y., November 23, 1828, and died in this city March 27, 1885. He was the founder of the now celebrated Buffalo Chemical and Fertilizer Co.

O'BRIAN & SONS,

Merchant Tailors—Nos. 100 and 208 East Seneca St.

"An honest man is the noblest work of God," we are informed by the poet ; but his honesty will hardly gain him the *entree* to the best society unless he is well dressed ; in fact, self-respect, respect for others, and a proper regard for their respect are best manifested by due attention to outward appearances, and particularly in the matter of dress. Though the tailor does not make the man, he may, and usually does, when given opportunity, make the man look as well as his physical imperfections will permit. We are not now speaking of ready-made clothing dealers—whose shabbily-made hand-me-downs sometimes turn a really handsome man into a scare-crow—but of tailors, artists in cloth, who, after a rigid apprenticeship on the bench, with the tape, and with the shears, have devoted years to mastering all the mysteries of the craft—styles, cutting, fit, the proper selection of goods, and study of the popular taste. Such are Messrs. O'Brian & Sons, whose two elegant merchant tailoring establishments, Nos. 100 and 208 East Seneca street, are almost as well known and a good deal more popular with the well-dressed men of Buffalo and adjacent territory as the Union Depot.

Mr. Thomas O'Brian, sr., established himself in the tailoring business here in his native city in 1855, nearly thirty-two years ago, and has a reputation equal to that of any of his rivals, however pretentious—an honest reputation, fairly earned and modestly enjoyed. The sons, John M. and Thomas J. R., were bred to the same calling, and are artist tailors in the best sense. They were admitted as partners in 1880.

The headquarters of the firm are at No. 100 East Seneca street, where they occupy a handsome four-story building, 25 feet front and 100 feet deep. The branch house is at No. 208 same street, one floor sufficing for the wants of the house at that point. They employ, in all, from 25 to 30 hands, skilled tailors exclusively, and do from $80,000 to $90,000 worth of first-class work annually, their specialty being fine custom work, which they deliver promptly at moderate prices, fit and style guaranteed. O'Brian & Sons have the best run of profitable tailoring in Buffalo.

JOHN C. POST,

Importer and Dealer in Paints, Oils, Glass, Artists' Materials, Brushes, Porcelain, Brass and Papier-Mache Plaques, Canvases, Crayon Paper, etc.—No. 20 East Swan St., Corner Washington.

This old and famous house was established by Charles H. Coleman in 1836, Mr. John C. Post, a native of Holland, succeeding to the proprietorship in the eventful year of 1861. It has always been a leading and prosperous concern, but of late years has added more than ever before to its high reputation for punctuality, reliability and responsibility, as as well as to the extent and character of its operations—a result largely due, no doubt, to the assistance rendered by Mr. Post's five wide-awake and energetic sons, John H., Henry, James, William and Peter, all natives of Buffalo and eminent among her rising young business men. Mr. Post's business premises comprise a commodious four-story-and-basement building, 22 by 60 feet, but which his trade, especially in window and polished plate glass, has outgrown, and in the spring he will occupy the fine store No. 16 Swan street with the finest, largest and most valuable stock of these goods, French and American glass, ever shown in Buffalo. It may be remarked here that this is a recognized specialty of the house, which handles more window and plate glass than any city rival, and has supplied hundreds of the finest public edifices and private residences on contract. Mr. Post is a direct importer, which gives him decided advantages in this department.

Returning to the paint and oil department, the house is the largest handler of these goods in this market, carrying at all times a vast and varied stock of all descriptions of paints, dry and in oil, white lead, colors, Windsor & Newton's and F. W. Devoe & Co.'s oil and water colors, Lacroix's China colors, etc., together with a full line of flitters and colors for lustre and Kensington painting, brushes of all kinds, canvases for oil painting and crayon paper mounted to order, porcelain, brass and papier-mache plaques, and innumerable other items pertaining to the trade.

Mr. Post came to Buffalo in 1837 with nothing but a good character and two strong hands. He is a self-made man, and decidedly a good job.

J. H. ULLENBRUCH & CO.,

Scientific Opticians, Importers of and Dealers in Spectacles, Eye-Glasses, Optical, Mathematical and Scientific Instruments and Apparatus—No. 274 Main St.

Mr. J. M. Ollendorff established the above-named concern in 1877, and was succeeded by the present proprietors, Messrs. J. H. Ullenbruch and Albert Landsberg, in 1882. The store and salesroom occupies the ground floor of the large four-story brick building No. 274 Main street, 22 by 100 feet in area, and is a most elegant and well conducted place of business. The stock embraces full lines of fine optical goods of all kinds, of which the firm are importers, together with a rare assortment of mathematical instruments, thermometers, barometers, opera, marine, field and spy-glasses, telescopes, microscopes, artificial eyes, etc. A specialty is made of the scientific testing and fitting of eyes with superior glasses. In addition, a general and very choice stock of fine jewelry and fancy goods is offered the public on reasonable terms, and the firm are gradually extending their trade to neighboring States.

Mr. Ullenbruch came to this country from Germany in 1867 and settled at Detroit, where he remained in the employ of L. Black & Co., opticians, until he came here to succeed Mr. Ollendorff. He is an experienced and skillful optician, and both he and Mr. Landsberg are polite, capable and accommodating gentlemen.

HENRY E. SMITH,

Shipper of Anthracite and Bituminous Coal—Office, No. 23 West Swan St., Chapin Block.

Buffalo is one of the largest inland coal markets in the world—a consequence of her superb shipping facilities by rail and water to all Western, Northwestern and Canadian points. The Coal Exchange is an institution of the city scarcely second in importance to the Board of Trade ; tens of millions are invested in the trade, and everything combines to prove that coal, its receipt, storage and shipment, form a most conspicuous interest of the city.

The gentleman whose name heads this item has ample yards and docks, the former on Louisiana street near Perry, the latter on the Blackwell Canal—one of the biggest of Buffalo's numerous big docks. He also has control of fine storage facilities and transfer pockets at the Tifft farm, enabling him to load both vessels and cars in the shortest possible time. Mr. Smith's specialties embrace choice grades of hard and soft coal from the anthracite and bituminous regions of Pennsylvania, and he is prepared to supply the trade in large or small quantities, on as favorable terms as any honest dealer can afford.

Mr. Smith's pleasant and commodious offices are located at No. 23 West Swan street, Chapin block, where the trade will always be welcome.

THE BUFFALO TRICYCLE COMPANY.

F. C. Atherton, J. M. Fisher—Manufacturers of Improved Tricycles—No. 640 Linwood Ave.

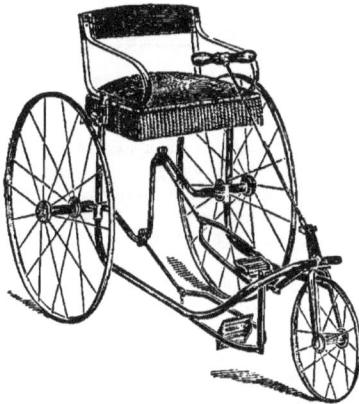

The tricycle herewith illustrated emphatically speaks for itself. It is a strictly Buffalo machine, first-class in material, workmanship and finish, and embraces several novel improvements not found in others. They have been thoroughly tested and approved, sell rapidly, and are desirable vehicles, both for the trade and those who use them. The new movement —is a walking motion—is graceful and easy, imparts greater power and speed with less exertion, and cannot fail to commend the machine to ladies and girls. They are made in the best manner, with improved steel wheels, steel axles, iron frames, and adjustable plush seats, and are the handsomest, easiest propelled and fastest running tricycle known.

This machine was patented and introduced in 1885, and the second season (1886) saw six times as many sold as the first, while the indications are that the same rate of increase will continue for the approaching season. Mr. Atherton opened the factory on a small scale in 1885, and January 1, 1886, finding the business too heavy for him alone, admitted Mr. Fisher, since which time the Buffalo tricycle has been introduced and become popular all over the United States.

Mr. Atherton is an Ohio man, and invented the new tricycle while in the employ of the United States Express Company in this city. With a patent in his pocket he commenced manufacturing for the city trade, succeeded, and is now, with Mr. Fisher's assistance, building up a large and profitable business. There is no question about the merits of the machine. Two new sizes are to be added for this year's trade; these will be 36 and 42 inches, for adults.

BINGHAM & TAYLOR.

The Clinton Iron Works—Manufacturers of Railroad and General Castings, Extension Service and Valve Shut-off Boxes for Gas and Water—No. 157 Church St.

In the department of heavy iron-work the city of Buffalo has the best of facilities for manufacturing, which are not surpassed by any rival. The advantages of an abundant cheap fuel from the Pennsylvania coal fields and cheap transportation by rail and water, both for receiving the raw material and reaching disputed territory, are utilized to the fullest extent. In the manufacture of railroad and general castings the firm of Bingham & Taylor take a leading position. Their establishment is located on the corner of Church and Jackson streets, and the business was originally begun in 1849. The style of the firm at that time was Eddy & Bingham. Their facilities possessed for everything required in castings for railroad purposes are unsurpassed, and for years this branch of the business has largely entered into the vast development of the different railway systems. The firm as it is now constituted consists of Charles F. Bingham and William P. Taylor. Mr. Bingham has been associated with the business for a great many years, and is an experienced man in every particular when this line is referred to. Mr. Taylor became a member of the firm two years ago, and prior to that time was general manager of the Canada Southern railroad. His prominent connection with the railroad business proves a very important factor in securing the favorable consideration of railroad officials for that branch of work. Mr. Taylor also takes an active interest in politics, and is at present a member of the Democratic county committee. The capital of the firm is $100,000, and from 75 to 90 hands are employed, the pay-roll averaging $1,000 a week. The manufacture of extension service and valve shut-off boxes for water and gas is also a prominent feature of the business. This firm has a well-established reputation for the general superiority in all classes of work turned out. In this they have aided in giving a prestige to the manufacturers of Buffalo which is now pretty generally acknowledged abroad.

BUFFALO STORAGE AND CARTING CO.

W.° P. Taylor, Proprietor; T. J. Avery, R. G. Martin, Managers; F. J. Abel, Cashier—Nos. 350, 352, 354 and 356 Seneca St., and 165, 167, 169 and 171 Myrtle Ave.

We herewith present a view of the Buffalo Storage and Carting Company's great warehouse, fronting on Seneca street and Myrtle avenue. This immense six-story brick and iron edifice, 80 by 180 feet, has three acres of floorage—a capacity equal, perhaps, to any demand that may ever be made upon it—and was erected during the past year at great cost, especially for the convenience of owners of household goods, merchandise, etc., who, having no immediate use therefor, are desirous of storing the same where it will be safe and properly taken care of at a reasonable rental. In the construction of this warehouse 1,000,000 bricks, 200 cords of stone and 300 tons of iron were consumed, and it is phenomenally strong at every point, fireproof and secure, as is proved by the fact that insurance rates on goods stored therein are lower than are obtained for any other storage warehouse in Buffalo.

In the basement are located the stables and shelter for the wagons of the company, there being 130 hardwood stalls, besides three box-stalls for sick animals, and room for the 50 two-horse vehicles employed by the company. Under the Seneca street sidewalk is situated the fine fifty-horse-power boiler and powerful Westinghouse engine for running the elevators, one of which is of ten tons capacity, and will carry a loaded wagon to any of the upper floors. The same engine furnishes power for the feed-cutters, while the warehouse, piped throughout, is heated by steam from the boiler. The first, or ground floor, is securely calked like a vessel's bottom, thus preventing the rising of unpleasant odors from the stables and engine-room. All feed, being stored on the sixth floor, is delivered in the basement by means of chutes. On the ground floor, opening on the street, are the offices and wagon scales, the elevator platform, and, on the Myrtle-avenue front, a fine, large, comfortable room used as a place of assembly and shelter for the employes. A double row of heavy iron pillars extend the length of this floor, supporting the one above, which in turn is provided with powerful iron girders and structural supports from the Central Bridge Company's works. The second, third and fourth floors are devoted to general storage purposes, while the fifth floor, divided into compartments, is used exclusively for household goods. The sixth floor is reserved for the company's own use, and here are stored the wagons, stages, feed, etc., of both the Storage and Carting and Buffalo Stage Companies. An abundant supply of water is provided at both ends, and on every floor.

Mr. W. P. Taylor, the proprietor, is also president of the Buffalo Storage Company, and a member of the firm Bingham & Taylor, proprietors of the Clinton Iron Works. He is a wide-awake, energetic, pushing business man of great capacity, and very popular with the citizens of Buffalo.

The carting and storage business of this city was organized twenty years ago under the name of the Lake Shore Transfer Co., and was succeeded by the present company three or four years ago. The facilities are unsurpassed for handling and storing furniture and baggage, carriages, sleighs, machinery, flour, salt, groceries, general merchandise, seeds, etc. Experienced packers, large moving vans and careful watchmen (themselves in turn watched by the American Watchman's Time Detector) are employed, itemized receipts issued, and goods received from and forwarded to all points. The system, in short, is complete, and the most perfect safeguards provided against loss or damage.

CHARLES J. HEINOLD,

**Wholesale Grocer, Wine and Liquor Dealer—Nos. 269, 271 and 273
Broadway, corner Bennett St.**

Mr. Heinold is a native of Wurtemburg, Germany, born in 1847. He came to Buffalo in 1854, began at the bottom of the ladder, working as a boy for his board and clothes, advanced step by step from errand boy to book-keeper, saved his money, and finally established himself as a retail grocer at Pine and North Division streets, on a cash capital of $140, in 1867. He was polite and liberal to his customers, worked hard, economized, pushed his trade, added to his facilities from time to time, and at last opened as a wholesale merchant in groceries, wines and liquors, his sales now aggregating about $125,000 a year. At present he occupies the three commodious stores Nos 269, 271 and 273 Broadway, corner Bennett street, each 20 feet front by 80 feet deep, and carries an immense and carefully selected stock of superior goods, embracing staple and fancy groceries, grocers' sundries, flour, provisions, fine foreign and domestic wines, liquors and cordials, all of which he offers to the trade on the most reasonable terms.

Mr. Heinold takes no active part in politics; has served eleven years in the 74th N. Y. S. N. G., attends closely to his own business, is a good citizen and a prosperous man.

CHARLES KUHN & CO.,

**Importers and Wholesale Dealers in Musical Goods of Every Description—
Agents for Sohmer, New England, and Christie & Son Pianos—Organs
of Popular Makes—Nos. 525 and 527 Main St.**

Very few residences of people in even moderately comfortable circumstances are destitute of pianos, and it is not unusual to find in the same house—sometimes in the same parlor—both piano and organ. It is a question whether any non-professional can become a first-rate performer on both instruments, but where there are several daughters of differing tastes, and *pater familias* can afford the expense, it is not unreasonable to expect that he will provide the means whereby all may cultivate whatever of musical talent they may possess.

Buffalo, notwithstanding her devotion to manufactures and commerce, is rapidly gaining an enviable distinction as a city of homes, refinements and art, not the least of her claims to merit being based upon the encouragement given musical culture, professional and private. As a consequence, the trade in music and musical merchandise is in a flourishing condition and grows steadily in importance. One of the leading houses here in this line is that of Charles Kuhn & Co., Nos. 525 and 527 Main street, established in 1860 by Messrs.

Charles Kuhn and G. H. Riegelmann, at No. 517 Main street, and removed to the present convenient and commodious stand in 1881. The firm occupy two floors, each 30 by 100 feet, of a handsome four-story building, where they carry an immense stock of all standard musical goods, including a variety of pianos, organs, etc., of the most celebrated makes, among them the favorite "Sohmer" piano (illustrated above), "New England," and "Christie & Son" pianos, and a variety of organs of celebrated makes and in many styles. The house also publishes music on a liberal scale, some of which—notably several of Mr. Riegelmann's own compositions ("Evening Bells," "Dreaming of the Past," etc.) have achieved great popularity. As importers and jobbers of instruments and musical merchandise of every description, this firm enjoy extraordinary advantages and are prepared to supply the trade on the best possible terms.

With a very large and constantly growing trade in the city and throughout the tributary territory, Messrs. Charles Kuhn & Co. have established branches at Tonawanda and Lancaster for the convenience of musical people in those cities. The house has passed the experimental stage, and is a fixed and prosperous venture, doing a business of $40,000 to $50,000 a year.

Mr. Kuhn is a native of the city, has been interested in the handling of musical goods since early manhood, and is himself a master, having, for six years, conducted the musical exercises and taught the pupils of Canisius College. Mr. Riegelmann, as previously stated, is a successful composer. Born in Berlin, Canada, he came to Buffalo in 1868, and has always been identified with the melodious art.

BUFFALO ARTIFICIAL LIMB CO.

George W. Hall, Manager—No. 9 West Eagle St.

Expert mechanical skill is one of the most remarkable of human attainments. It is the creator of every indication of material progress, and in numerous instances is displayed genius of a very high order. Among those in this city entitled to honorable mention in this connection Mr. George W. Hall merits such recognition for a variety of reasons. Were a committee of disinterested, competent citizens appointed to determine what product of mechanical skill had been the means of alleviating the greatest amount of human suffering and inconvenience, there is not the shadow of a doubt but that the palm would be awarded to artificial limbs.

During the past twenty-six years Mr. Hall has been engaged in the manufacture of artificial limbs in this city. It is the only establishment of the kind in Buffalo, but such has been the degree of proficiency attained by Mr. Hall that it is known from one extreme of the country to the other. In the course of the extended experience which this gentleman has had in the business, there is an important fact worth considering. As a mechanical expert in the work he is undoubtedly without an equal in the United States. This is more particularly the case in the making of substitutes for the natural members, and in this connection there is a feature which has had an important part in bringing out Mr. Hall's talents in this direction, and that is, for the past thirty years Mr. Hall has had to use an artificial leg himself. The idea occurred to him that the clumsy substitute in vogue then could be improved upon, when he started in the business, and ever since then there has always been a double incentive to strive for excellence. Every improved feature that he could devise was sure not only to redound to his pecuniary advantage, but his personal comfort as well. So successful has Mr. Hall been in his work that nobody would detect from his walk that he wore an artificial limb.

Since the war Mr. Hall has furnished hundreds of limbs to soldiers on the government account by order of the Surgeon-General of the United States army. Apparatus is also provided for resections of the arm, fore-arm, and unjoined fractures. Feet are applied for disarticulation at the knee and ankle, and in the whole range of malformations of the limbs, requiring the best apparatus, or to aid surgical operations, the best results are obtained. The wood is the best grained and seasoned weeping willow, obtained from the banks of the Schuylkill river.

Personally Mr. Hall is one of the most whole-souled, genial, kindly-tempered gentlemen to be met in a day's travel.

GOODYEAR RUBBER COMPANY.

F. M. Shepard, President; J. A. Minott, Secretary; E. A. Rockwood, Manager — Nos. 240 Main and 9 West Seneca St. — Manufacturers of and Dealers in Rubber Goods of Every Description.

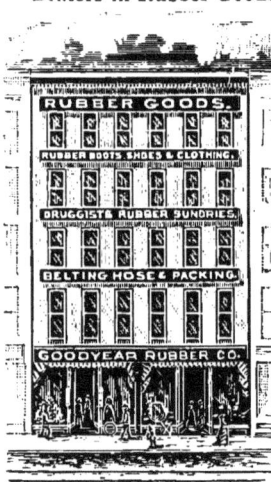

The vast development of the trade in rubber goods is one of the commercial wonders of the age, and owes its primary impetus to the genius, industry and determination of one man more than to all others combined —to Charles Goodyear, who in 1834 began the series of investigations and experiments which resulted five years later in the discovery of the vulcanizing process, which at once rendered practicable the employment of rubber for the multitude of uses to which it has since been applied. Many improvements have since been made in methods and apparatus, but the process is still essentially the same, and is universally known as the "Goodyear process." The Goodyear Rubber Company, the largest in existence, is the result of a consolidation of several wealthy corporations, and perpetuates in its name and products the fame of the great inventor. The principal offices are at No. 487 Broadway, New York, with branches at 57 Maiden Lane, New York, and in Washington City, Chicago, Milwaukee, St. Paul, Minneapolis, St. Louis, Kansas City, San Francisco, Boston, Montreal and Buffalo—the house here being under the personal management and direction of Mr. E. A. Rockwood, who from 1855 to 1871 was connected with some of the largest New York importers, the last five years as buyer for Lee, Bliss & Co. During his fifteen years' control of the Goodyear Rubber Company's Buffalo interests he has proved himself the right man in the right place, and possesses, as he well deserves, the unlimited confidence of his principals.

The Goodyear Rubber Company is incorporated under the laws of New York with a paid-up capital of $1,000,000, and stands a head and shoulders above all competitors in character, variety and extent of manufactures, its products comprising every conceivable article of use and ornament made of this material. Its factories are located at Harlem, N. Y.; Middletown, Conn.; Bristol, R. I.; Elizabeth and Lambertville, N. J. Their boot and shoe factory at Harlem is the only concern of the kind in the world that rejects shoddy and old rubber. Not an ounce of any other material save pure Para rubber is employed; consequently the "Goodyear" stamp is an incontestible guarantee of superiority, both in workmanship and material.

The Goodyear Rubber Company is also the sole general agency for the National Rubber Company for all its manufactures other than boots and shoes—one of the leading American rubber companies. It is also the general agency for Western New York for the celebrated "Red Jacket" fire hose of the Boston Woven Hose Company, whose products in this line are too well known to need commendation.

The Goodyear Rubber Company fills all orders from its Buffalo store at manufacturers' prices, without any extra freight charges, doing a heavy business in both wholesale and retail departments, but giving special attention to the former, supplying many

of the principal jobbers all over the country. Besides a magnificent and almost limitless stock of rubber boots and shoes an immense line of goods for every conceivable purpose is carried for the trade, embracing, among other items, rubber belting of all widths and weights, packing, hose, light and heavy clothing, druggists' sundries, air cushions, pillows, beds, water beds, urinals, stopples, tubing, nursing bottles, aprons, rubber bands, mats, rubber drill and other carriage goods, enameled oilcloth, oiled clothing, etc., horse clothing, firemen's clothing, gloves, spittoons, door mats, rubber cement, etc. In the hose department will be found a variety of approved hose-reels and brass goods for hose. The National "Anchor" hose is confessedly the best made, stands 700 pounds pressure to the square inch, and gives perfect satisfaction under all conditions. As a proof of its popularity we may state that over 50,000 feet of ¾-inch 3-ply Anchor hose is annually retailed to consumers here in Buffalo.

The house here embraces two branches—the wholesale department, No. 9 West Seneca street, 40 by 60 feet, five floors, and the retail department, No. 240 Main street, two floors, 20 by 100 feet, thus forming an L. A stock valued at $100,000 is carried at all seasons, and the average annual sales reach $500,000. The territory covered comprises, besides the city and vicinity, all of Western New York, Ohio, Pennsylvania and Michigan.

This is headquarters for the finest line of syringes, combs, rubber bands and other choice goods in this material.

NIAGARA BAKING COMPANY,

Manufacturers of Best Buffalo Crackers, Biscuits, Cakes, Snaps, Pastry Bread, Rolls, etc. — Steam Bakery — Office and Salesrooms, Nos. 23 and 25 Ellicott St., near Seneca.

In no branch of manufactures is the concentration of skill and capital and the division of labor more marked or fraught with better results than in the production of farinaceous food, under which head comes every description of bakers' goods—crackers, cake and pastry. Of the many prominent houses engaged in this branch of enterprise we know of none that have, within the past few years, achieved a greater degree of well-earned success than the Niagara Baking Company, whose extensive works, equipped with steam power and all requisite improvements in machinery and appliances, is located in the handsome three-story brick building Nos. 23 and 25 Ellicott street, between Seneca and Swan, with a frontage of 44 feet and a depth of 100 feet. Every variety of superior bakers' goods is turned out here in immense quantities and popular styles, embracing full lines of plain and fancy crackers, biscuits, cakes, snaps, jumbles, pastry, etc. The company enjoy special advantages for procuring the highest grades of flour, the senior partner being one of the most prominent millers in the Eastern States.

The Niagara Baking Company was organized in 1881 by Messrs. H. J. Harvey and M. W. Dake, the former a member of Harvey Bros., flour and grain merchants, and of Harvey & Henry, proprietors of the Buffalo City Mills. He is also connected with Smith, Falke & Co., wholesale bakers, Michigan and North Division streets. Mr. M. W. Dake came hither from Livingston county in 1883, and was formerly a hardware merchant at Nunda, N. Y. The Niagara Baking Company has a capacity of 100 barrels of flour daily. Only the best selected materials are used, and all goods are guaranteed of the finest quality. Sixty-five trained operatives are employed, and four traveling salesmen are constantly on the road securing orders from old and new patrons in the trade, all over the country, principally in New York, Pennsylvania and Ohio. The transactions of the house increase steadily, and last year footed up about $200,000.

THE STAFFORD,

D. G. West & Co., Proprietors—Corner Washington and Carroll Sts.

This is one of the leading hotels of Buffalo. It was originally the Bonney House, and has always been a popular resort for the traveling public. In 1884 Messrs. Stafford & Co. became the proprietors, and the name was changed. Shortly afterward the present proprietors, Messrs. D. G. West & Co., took charge of the hotel. An outlay of several thousand dollars made a complete transformation throughout. The house was entirely refurnished in a style equal to any in tho city, and in the matter of interior decoration a very high class of artistic work was performed. The proprietors are Messrs. D. G. West and D. W. Burt. Mr. West has the active direction of the affairs pertaining to the management. He is one of the best hotel men in the country, having had years of experience in the business. A long residence in the oil country, in the hotel business at Bradford and other points, has made Mr. West acquainted with the entire traveling public of Western Pennsylvania This class invariably make The Stafford their headquarters while in Buffalo. In every respect The Stafford is a strictly first-class hotel. The cuisine is unsurpassed, and has secured for the house a degree of popularity that is peculiarly its own. There are ninety-three rooms in the house, single and *en suite*, which render it sufficiently commodious for a large patronage.

H. G. WHITE,

House, Sign, Ship and Fresco Painter—No. 83 Main St.

Probably no Buffalo artisan is more widely and favorably known than Mr. H. G. White, who, for more than fifty years has occupied a leading position among Buffalo painters, a large proportion of the most elaborate and artistic house, sign and fresco work done here during the past half-century having been designed by him and executed under his direction, while many of the handsomest steam and sailing craft that during the same period have ridden the waters of the great lakes owed their tasteful painting and decoration to the same trained eye and master hand. It is scarcely necessary to enlarge upon the taste and skill that have always distinguished Mr. White ; the innumerable examples of both found in the private residences, public buildings, hotels and churches of Buffalo sufficiently attest these merits, while the volume of his business proves the hold he has upon the confidence and patronage of the property-owning and building public. He employs from twenty-five to one hundred painters and artists, dependent upon the season, pays an average of $500 per week in wages, and does an annual business of $40.000 to $50,000.

Mr. White was born at Burlington, Vt., June 8, 1814; came to Buffalo July 4, 1836, and has made his home and conducted business here ever since—for the past thirty-three years occupying the same location, No. 83 Main street. He is a well-preserved, genial and active man to this day, with the suns and snows of seventy-two years upon his head, and bids fair to survive many younger men yet.

THE REBSTOCK STOVE CO. (Limited).

Manufacturers and Wholesale and Retail Dealers in Hardware, Stoves and Ranges, Furnaces, House Furnishing Goods, Agricultural Implements, etc.—Nos. 564 and 566 Washington St.

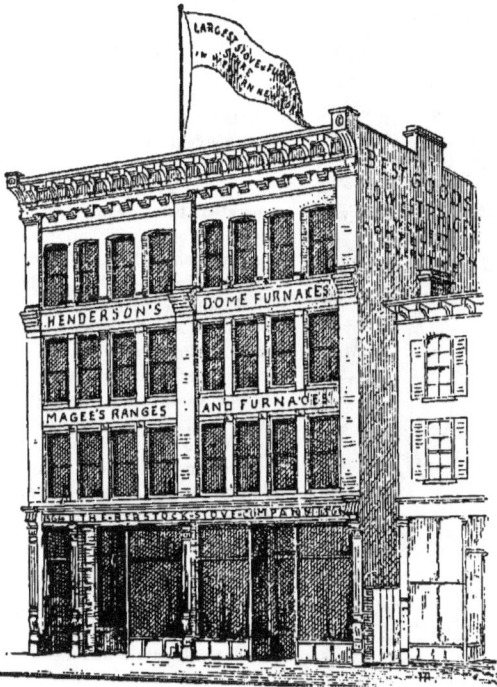

This fine house was established by Mr. J. E. Rebstock in 1880, the present company organizing and succeeding to the business July 10, 1885, with J. E. Rebstock, president, Geo. F. Mings, treasurer, and J. H. Rebstock, secretary; capital stock, $20,000. The company's building is a commodious one, 43 by 95 feet, four stories and basement, and is thoroughly equipped in every department for the transaction of a large and growing business such as is being built up by the energetic gentlemen above named, embracing a number of specialties, including hardware of all kinds, full lines of superior stoves and ranges, house furnishing goods, agricultural implements, and a thousand other items coming under the general heads we have designated. They also deal heavily in furnaces for public and private buildings, and control the celebrated " Royal " and " Magee " furnaces and " Magee " ranges in this market. Employing more than thirty skilled workmen, most of whom devote their whole time and attention to the setting and repairing of furnaces and ranges, the company are enabled to render unvarying satisfaction to their patrons.

President Rebstock and his brother the secretary are natives of Buffalo, as is Treasurer Mings. The first named has been in the same line of business for eighteen years, and in 1885 was owner of the *Christian Advocate.* Mr. Mings, who came into this firm nearly two years ago, is an active young man, and was formerly in the livery business with his father. Mr. J. H. Rebstock has been connected with the stove and hardware trade for ten years. All are industrious, liberal and worthy men, and have excellent business prospects, individually and collectively.

Mr. J. E. Rebstock last autumn purchased a large tract of land—ninety-two acres—at Black Rock, where he purposes to erect an extensive foundry during the present year. Other parties, among them a Troy stove manufacturing company, will be interested with him in this enterprise, which will employ about 200 mechanics and be one of the leading industries of this section.

10

THE STEWART HEATER CO.

David P. Stewart and George A. Otis—Patentees and Manufacturers of Feed Water Heaters, Single and Double Plunger Boiler Feed Pumps, Tube Cleaners, Flue Blowers, etc.—Nos. 37 and 39 Clinton St.

The above-named flourishing company commenced operations on Mechanic street in January, 1888, but was forced by heavy increase of orders to remove in July, 1884, to Nos. 37 and 39 Clinton street, where two well-lighted and convenient floors, each 30 by 100 feet, are occupied, and an excellent plant of appropriate machinery is operated by a competent force of skilled workmen. The members of the company, Messrs. David P. Stewart and George A. Otis, are both practical and experienced steam engineers and are the inventors and patentees of the devices manufactured in their works, comprising Stewart's patent feed water heater (illustrated herewith), single and double plunger boiler feed pumps, " Engineers' Favorite" steam boiler tube cleaner, " Red Jacket" steam boiler flue blower, and the Otis tubular heater.

All of the Stewart Heater Company's machines and devices are enthusiastically indorsed by practical engineers wherever tested. It would be impossible in the limits of a notice of this kind to illustrate and describe all of these inventions, but those interested will be supplied with all desired information, descriptive and illustrated circulars and catalogues on application by mail or in person. Over 100 of this company's feed water heaters are in use in Buffalo's leading mills and factories, and may be inspected at any time in operation.

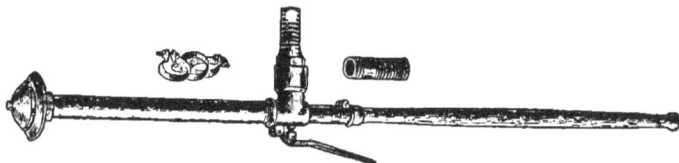

THE BUFFALO CHEMICAL WORKS.

Albert M. Kalbfleisch, President; Franklin H. Kalbfleisch, Vice-President;
Theo. V. Fowler, Secretary and Treasurer—Manufacturing Chemists—
Works, Abbott Road and Buffalo Creek; Office, No. 255 Washington St.,
Coal and Iron Exchange.

The Buffalo Chemical Works, of which we herewith present a bird's-eye view, are
among the finest of the kind in the United States, covering with appurtenances a tract
of ten acres at the crossing of the Abbott road and Buffalo creek. Eight acres of the
ground are devoted to the company's brick buildings, thirteen in number, one and two
stories in height, provided with a superb equipment of machinery, chemical apparatus,
etc., including two new platinum stills of large capacity, manufactured by Johnson,
Matthey & Co., of London, and the finest ever imported. In addition to the shipping
facilities afforded by the Buffalo creek, which extends along one entire front of the
property, and by which they are directly connected with the Erie canal, they have
switches and tracks from the Buffalo Creek railroad, bringing them into direct connection with every railroad entering Buffalo. When these works were first erected—
some fourteen or fifteen years ago—they were completely isolated, but are now surrounded by many large manufacturing establishments, and by various railroad tracks,
thus rendering the plant and its location among the most desirable and valuable in the
vicinity of this city.

The Buffalo Chemical Works Company was organized and chartered in 1883, with a
cash capital of $300,000, and the venture has proved remarkably successful, both as a
business venture and for the influence it has exerted upon all of those interests related to
chemistry as a productive industry. Messrs. Albert M. and F. H. Kalbfleisch, respectively president and vice-president, reside in New York, where they own and operate
extensive works of the same kind. Mr. Theo. V. Fowler, secretary and treasurer, has
the general management, assisted by a competent corps of practical chemists and
about one hundred skilled workmen and laborers. The specialties comprise a superior
line of acids, embracing high grade sulphuric, nitric, muriatic, acetic, mixed acids for
explosives, etc., together with best qualities alum, ammonia, tin crystals, glauber salts,
salsoda, bi-carbonate and sulphate soda for glass manufacturers, etc., for which they
have a ready demand in all the markets of the United States and Canada. In fact, they
have not been able hitherto to meet the growing request for their acids, but expect,
with the increase of their plant and the aid of the new stills referred to, to be able in
the future to fill all orders as fast as received.

The works turn out immense quantities of products, as may be inferred from the fact that the company maintain a large number of tank cars, constructed especially for their use. Their supplies of material come from widely distributed sources—the brimstone from Sicily, the alum clay from France, the nitrate of soda from Chili, etc.

Mr. Fowler, the manager, is an expert manufacturing chemist, a perfect man of business, and an accomplished gentleman. He came hither from New York and took charge of the works at their inception, and is devoted to his calling and the interests of his company.

A. NEUPERT & CO.,

Importers and Jobbers of Paper Hangings, Window Shades and Fixtures, Floor Oil Cloths, Room and Picture Mouldings, Mats, Mattings, etc.— Palace of Trade Building, Nos. 464 and 466 Main and 271 and 273 Pearl St.

This splendid establishment, founded about the year 1868 by Messrs Robinson & Korzelius, passed into the hands of the present proprietors in 1876, since which time it has flourished as never before, enlarging its sphere of operations and gaining thousands of new patrons at home and abroad, while retaining the confidence and custom of the old ones.

The Young Men's Association building, a portion of which was so long occupied by them, having been remodeled for other purposes, on the first of November last Messrs. Neupert & Co. removed to their present quarters, the north half of the superb Palace of Trade building, Nos. 464 and 466 Main street, 22 feet front by 235 feet deep to Pearl street, of which they occupy the first floor and basement. The arrangements for the transaction of a large and growing business are very complete. each department being separated from all others and a perfect bazar in itself, the polite and attentive proprietors, seconded by skillful and obliging salesmen, giving personal and prompt attention to all customers and visitors.

The stock, always full and fresh, embraces all standard goods and imported and domestic novelties in artistic and plain paper hangings, bronzes, embossed and solid gilts, borders and friezes, ceiling decorations, window shades and fixtures of every kind and price, floor oil cloths, gold and silver gilt room and picture mouldings, imported and American mats and mattings, and, in short, everything in the line of house decorations for which there is any demand. Having unusual advantages in the way of special arrangements with home and foreign manufacturers, this house is at all times enabled to supply the trade with the latest styles and patterns promptly and at the lowest prices.

Messrs. Neupert & Co. have a large and rapidly increasing trade at home, as well as throughout this and adjoining States, their last year's sales aggregating over $200,000. They employ an average of thirty men in all departments, four of whom are regularly on the road in New York, Pennsylvania, Ohio, Michigan and Canada, surely and steadily extending their connection into new territory year by year.

Mr. A. Neupert, the senior member and financier of the firm, is of German birth, has resided in Buffalo for more than thirty-five years, and has been in this house since its organization, previous to which he was for some years a member of R. W. Bell & Co., and one of its originators. Mr. P. Metzen, jr., was born in Buffalo; formerly in the dry goods trade, but has had sixteen or seventeen years' experience in paper hangings and kindred goods. He has charge of the interior decorations department. Mr. J. C. Lutz looks after the wholesale department. He also is a native Buffalonian, formerly in the book and dry goods line. For the past eighteen or nineteen years he has been handling the same line of goods in which he is now interested. This is a reliable and liberal house, and deserves the marked success that has attended its efforts to gratify a cultivated taste and make Buffalo a metropolitan market for art decorations.

ROSEDALE FLORAL HALL.

Mrs. J. Hale, Florist and Dealer in Birds, Cages, Seeds, Gold Fish, Aquaria, Globes, etc.—No. 174 Pearl St., near Niagara.

Mrs. Hale, formerly a successful and popular market gardener, possessed of natural artistic taste and a love of the beautiful, established herself as a florist in 1871, at the corner of Eagle and Washington streets. For two years previously she had been cultivating flowers on a liberal scale at her four large green-houses at the western end of West Seneca, near the lake shore, and was therefore well prepared with ample stocks upon which to draw. With a wide acquaintance among the best people of the city, great skill and aptitude and remarkable business talent and tact, Mrs. Hale necessarily prospered—so much so that in 1880 she removed to more commodious quarters at No. 4 North Division, and later, her good fortune continuing, in 1883 she again removed, this time to the handsome and elegantly arranged storeroom No. 174 Pearl street, which she still occupies. Her green-houses, four in number, are each 20 by 100 feet, built, heated, ventilated and conducted upon scientific principles and filled with a wilderness of the rarest, sweetest and most popular plants, buds and blossoms, from which her customers are supplied with all the latest designs of floral decorations and tributes for presents, parties, weddings, funerals, and all occasions to which flowers are appropriate, together with cut flowers, potted plants, Cape flowers, natural grasses, pampas plumes, immortelles, pressed ferns, autumn leaves, and all novelties in floral favors. A large and varied assortment of baskets, new styles in terra cotta ware, flower seeds, etc., form a portion of her stock, while she makes a leading specialty of canary birds and gold fish, and cages, globes and food for the same, doing in all a business of about $15,000 a year.

Mrs. Hale was born in Buffalo, manages her own business, and is an ardent student and admirer of flowers and birds. She is ably seconded in her efforts to please and benefit the public by her two polite and enegetic sons, George D. and F. S., the former of whom, a floral artist of high repute, has charge of the salesroom and designing department, while the latter, an educated florticulturist, manages the green-houses.

F. H. C. MEY,

Manufacturer of Mey's Patent Grain Dryer and Cooler; also, of Improved Detachable and Semi-Detachable Chain Belting for the Transmission of Power in Mills, Elevators, etc., and Elevator Buckets—Nos. 64 to 68 Columbia St.

Mr. F. H. C. Mey, the inventor and patentee of the grain dryer and chain belting that bear his name, is an ingenious mechanic and devoted student of the arts relating to mechanics. He is a native of Erfurt, Prussia, and came to Buffalo in 1854. Ten years later he constructed and patented his first grain dryer, and for the past twenty-two years has been constantly improving upon the original idea, until now it stands unrivaled for simplicity, capacity and effectiveness. The above cut conveys a very clear idea of the dryer, which is constructed upon the principle of subjecting the grain to heat and motion, and is composed of a series of lengthwise-vibrating sheet-iron pans six to eight inches deep and provided with perforated covers. The grain or other substance to be dried is deposited upon the top pan by means of elevator No. 1, and then, by the vibration of the pans, passes from one to the other until it reaches the bottom, heated air being forced into the pans and into contact with the grain, malt, etc., by means of a fan, at a pressure of one to five ounces per square inch, and, when dry, is carried by elevator No. 2 to the cooler, and from there to place of storáge or shipment.

MEY'S CHAIN BELTING

FOR

Elevating, Driving and Conveying Purposes.

The above cut illustrates Mr. Mey's improved detachable and semi-detachable chain belting, patented 1876, for driving machinery, elevating and conveying malt, grain, brewers' grains, sawdust, tan-bark, coal, coke, stone, clay, phosphates, chemicals, fertilizers, and other heavy substances requiring great power for their movement, for which purposes it is unequaled.

Mr. Mey is also the inventor and manufacturer of a variety of mill and elevator appliances, including elevator boots, Buffalo Champion elevator buckets, conveyors, etc., for descriptions of which we have not space in these pages. Illustrated catalogues will be mailed to all interested parti-s who apply.

Mr. Mey's devices are unreservedly indorsed by the officers of the Buffalo Board of Trade and by most of the leading elevator men, millers, maltsters, coal dealers, brick manufacturers, insurance agents, etc., of this city.

VOSBURGH, WHITING & CO.,

Wholesale Booksellers and Stationers—Importers of Albums and Fancy Goods—No. 304 Main St.

Vosburgh, Whiting & Co. is the only wholesale book and stationery firm in Buffalo, and, having exclusive control of the market tributary to this city, do a very heavy business with the retail trade, local and country. They occupy the entire four-story business building at No. 304 Main street, which with basement, 20 feet front and 90 feet deep, is none too large for their requirements. They carry an immense stock of all goods in their line, embracing all standard library and educational works—history, travels, philosophy, science, poetry and romance, together with heavy lines of blank books for all purposes, scrap books, toy books, etc., and an infinite variety of stationery of all kinds for business and correspondence, fancy *papeteries,* office supplies, etc., all of the most careful selections, best grades and latest styles. The firm also import direct every description of novelties in photograph, autograph and souvenir albums, of which they make a specialty, and are prepared to offer as fine goods at as reasonable prices as can be obtained in New York city. Their travelers cover all of Western New York and Pennsylvania, and the house is building up a large and flourishing trade, their sales for the past year aggregating about $150,000.

Messrs. John L. Vosburgh, DuMonte A. Whiting and Willis P. Whiting compose the firm. All are young men of great industry and capacity, and all from Rochester, N. Y., where Messrs. Vosburgh and W. P. Whiting gained their practical knowledge of the business, both having traveled for Rochester's leading book and stationery house.

GEORGE M. KYLE,

Wholesale Manufacturer of Dress, Upholstery and Drapery Trimmings— Works, Cor. Washington and Clinton Sts.; Office, Room 46 Arcade Building.

A moment's reflection will convince any one that the above business—the manufacture of trimmings—must aggregate a vast amount annually, whether measured by quantity or value, and that it is, in fact, a very important industry. Mr. George M. Kyle, formerly book-keeper for H. J. Comstock, lounge manufacturer (now Holland & Vilas), was the first to recognize in Buffalo an advantageous site for the establishment of a modern trimmings factory, and, seizing the opportunity presented by the retirement of Frederick Hiages and his son William, who, for twenty years, had struggled under difficulties in the same line, purchased, remodeled and refitted the plant at Washington and Clinton streets, in the Arcade building, in 1886, and has already made a pronounced success of the new venture, employing a competent force of skilled operatives, and supplying the trade of Buffalo and vicinity with the best and most elegant goods in his line, sales for the first year reaching $10,000 in value, with prospects of a rapid increase.

Mr. Kyle's office is in room 46, Arcade building, convenient and inviting. His sales-rooms adjoin, and buyers of trimmings of any description, for dresses, cloaks, upholstery, etc., fringes, tassels and kindred goods, will find what they want here in every grade. A specialty is made of making goods to order, and duplicates of any desired pattern are made at short notice and satisfaction guaranteed.

THE ACADEMY OF MUSIC.

Meech Bros., Proprietors—Nos. 245 to 249 Main St.

The Academy of Music is Buffalo's dramatic temple *par excellence*. It was originally erected about the year 1855 by Henry T. Meech, father of the present owners, who died in 1870 after a managerial career of half a century—a career full of event and of interest, during which he became the intimate associate of most of the celebrities of his time, including the elder Booth, Forrest and scores of the greater lights of tragedy and comedy. On his decease he was succeeded by his sons, Henry L. and John H., both natives of Albany, born in a theatrical atmosphere and literally bred to dramatic management, both in the office and on the stage. The Meech Brothers have had long and valuable experience in their vocation, and have brought out several of the most successful and popular ornaments of the American stage—among them Joe Emmett, as a reminder and souvenir of which each carries a magnificent gold chronometer presented by "Unser Fritz" as a mark of gratitude and regard, he having made the first appearance of his remarkable career under their management in 1869.

As before stated, the elder Meech built this theatre, naming it the Metropolitan. He also built the Rochester opera-house in 1868. On the accession of the sons in 1870 the name was changed to the Academy of Music, under which it became one of the most famous places of amusement in this country, outgrowing its capacity and accommodations. Consequently, in 1882, the entire establishment was remodeled, the entrance brought around from Washington to Main street, the stage and auditorium reconstructed throughout, and everything that good taste, artistic and mechanical skill, backed by ample resources, could do was done to render the Academy commodious, attractive and comfortable. The building, three stories on Main and four on Washington, is 200 feet deep, 51 feet front on the former and 70 feet front on the latter street, and is an architectural ornament to the city. The property belongs to the brothers, who are noted for public spirit and enterprise, popular with the people at home, and well-known and popular among the theatrical profession from San Francisco to London.

The best attractions on the road, embracing both the legimate drama and opera, are regularly presented on the boards of the Academy, and the most eminent actors and singers appear here when they visit Buffalo.

SIBLEY & HOLMWOOD,

The Buffalo Steam Confectionery Works—Manufacturers of Staple and
Special Confectionery—Southwest corner Seneca and Wells Sts.

The city of Buffalo, among
its varied and numerous industries, boasts one of the
m o s t extensive manufactories of confectionery in the
United States—that of Sibley
& Holmwood, whose elegant
four-story b r i c k building,
fronting 50 feet on Seneca
with a depth of 100 feet on
Wells street, is herewith
illustrated. The concern was
founded by the present proprietors in 1873, at No. 133
Seneca street, removing to No.
111 Seneca street in 1876, and
to the present location, erected specially for the purpose,
in 1880. The house has been
a prosperous one from the
start, Mr. Frank Sibley having had many years' experience as a traveler for leading
confectioners, and Mr. James
Holmwood being thoroughly
conversant with the business
for six or seven years previous to the formation of the
firm.

The firm of Sibley & Holmwood employ from 175 to 200
operatives in all departments,
besides the finest and most
complete equipment of ma-
chinery suitable for the business to be found in Western
New York, turning out some
$300,000 worth of goods an-
nually. They make a spe-
cialty of penny goods, and
probably produce and sell more of them than any other house in the United States,
finding eager customers all over the East, West, North and South as far as Baltimore.

That the house is in a flourishing condition is evidenced by the fact that in order to
keep up with their orders they have been compelled to lease two great upper floors of
the adjoining building, each 35 by 100 feet, for manufacturing and storage purposes.

GUS. E. KURTZ,

Fashionable Tailor—No. 10 East Eagle St.

Mr. Kurtz came to Buffalo from New York, of which latter city he is a native, in
1881, and established himself at his present location in 1885, having been for a year
previous at No. 193 Seneca street. He has a very handsome store, occupying the ground
floor of the large four-story building at No. 10 East Eagle street, 25 feet front and 40
feet deep. He employs a full force of skillful operative tailors, and does a large business with the fashionable people of Buffalo and some Western cities.

Mr. Kurtz has a thorough practical knowledge of custom tailoring in all its details,
is an energetic, enterprising and industrious gentleman, and gives his large and growing
circle of patrons entire satisfaction in quality, style and prices.

THE DEMPSTER ENGINE WORKS,

Manufacturers of and Dealers in Engines, Boilers and Machinery—Nos. 34, 36, 38 and 40 Washington St.

This leading industrial establishment was founded by Mr. Robert Dempster in 1855, and has had several changes of style, under each of which its reputation has become more and more generally known, and its status as a representative house more firmly fixed. The leading specialty is the Dempster vertical engine and boiler combined, made in four sizes from three to four, six and ten-horse power. They are constructed on the old plan of durability—the boilers of wrought iron and steel plate (no cast iron used); three-horse power can be run at a cost of two cents per hour, and occupies only 24 by 42 inches of floor space. The highest grade of scientific and mechanical skill have been lavished upon its perfection. This engine requires no more attention than an ordinary heating stove, is strong, safe and compact, and remarkably cheap—half of former price. The subjoined table gives dimensions and capacity of the Dempster vertical engines and boilers :

Number.	Horse Power.	Diameter of Cylinder.	Length of Stroke.	Diameter and Face of Fly Wheel.	Diameter and Face of Pulley.	Revolutions per Minute.	Diameter of Boiler.	Height of Boiler.	Diameter of Fire Box.	Number of Flues.	Length of Flues.	Diameter of Flues.	Weight.	Price F. O. B. Cars Here.
1	3	4	4	16 × 4	10 × 4	200	20	48	16	20	15	2	900	$225 00
2	4	4	6	20 × 4	12 × 4	175	24	60	18	30	24	2	1500	300 00
3	6	5	6	20 × 4	14 × 4	160	28	60	20	36	28	2	1700	350 00
4	0	7	8	36 × 6	18 × 6	150	34	60	24	44	34	2	2400	525 00

Parties in want of economical and serviceable engines will do well to address the Dempster Engine Works, Nos. 34 to 40 Washington street, Buffalo, N. Y. The works are very complete in all departments, employ a fine line of improved modern machinery and many first-class workmen, and are prepared to fill all orders promptly and in the best manner. The past history of the house is the best guarantee of its future.

CITY AND TIFFT ELEVATORS.

N. Y. C. & H. R. Railroad Co., Proprietors; J. W. Whitney, Manager—City Elevator, foot of Michigan St.; Tifft Elevator, foot of Chicago St.

These two superb elevators are among the most conspicuous in this port. The City elevator was erected by the New York Central & Hudson River Railroad Company in 1866, and has storage capacity for 550,000 bushels of grain. The Tifft elevator, built in 1867 by the late George W. Tifft, and purchased by the railroad company in 1873, is of 270,000 bushels capacity. Both together are capable of handling, in first-class style, 25,000,000 bushels annually, and, being located directly upon the Buffalo river and railroad tracks, have every requisite for the receipt and shipment of grain. Our engravings give a better idea of the appearance and extent of these great elevators than could be conveyed by any amount of descriptive writing. Constructed with special reference to the handling of bulk grain, its transfer from lake vessels to railroad cars, and provided with the latest improved and most powerful machinery, both for elevating purposes and the handling of cars, nothing desirable has been neglected in their equipment.

Mr. J. W. Whitney, the manager, is a member of the grain commission firm of Whitney & Gibson, rooms 14 and 15 Board of Trade, and a resident of Rochester. He is a thorough business man of great capacity and large experience, and conducts the affairs of the City and Tifft elevators to the satisfaction of shippers and railroad company alike. The Central Railroad Company is to be congratulated upon securing the services of so competent and popular a manager, whose best efforts are given to the service of its patrons.

THE BRUNSWICK-BALKE-COLLENDER CO.,

Manufacturers of Billiard and Pool Tables, Bar Fixtures and Bowling Alley Outfits—Buffalo Office, Nos. 587 and 589 Main St.

The Buffalo branch office of the Brunswick-Balke-Collender Co. was opened in June, 1881, for the successful handling of the business in this city and surrounding territory. The magnitude of the operations of this company can be inferred from the fact that branch offices are maintained in all the leading cities. There are thirty of these, including two in Canada, and at each a complete stock is carried. For a long time the rivalry between the J. M. Brunswick & Balke Company and the H. W. Collender Company was sharp. They were the acknowledged leaders in the manufacture of billiard tables, and each left nothing undone to bring out some new or novel feature. The stimulus which this rivalry gave to a proper cultivation of the gentlemanly game of billiards is well known. The best talent in the country was brought to the front in tournaments and exhibitions, until it seemed as if the possibilities of the game were unlimited. The consolidation of these two great establishments resulted in advantages to both and the trade as well. It enlarged the scope of the new company's operations and at the same time largely reduced expenses, which, as a matter of course, was immediately felt by the trade. The manufacturing establishments of the consolidated company, at New York, Chicago and Cincinnati, are ample for all requirements of the trade, which extends into several foreign countries. Mr. A. G. Frankenstein is the Buffalo agent of the company, and has been very successful in that capacity. He was formerly bookkeeper for the Jost Brewing Co., and is a first-class business man. He personally looks after the trade of the house, and does it very effectively.

THE MANSION HOUSE.

Wesley Crouch & Co., Proprietors—Exchange St., from Main to Washington.

The traveler of experience usually judges the cities he visits by their hotels. This fact is so generally recognized that public-spirited citizens tacitly and with one accord yield to the principal and representative hotels everywhere a large proportion of their support in acknowledgment of the influence they exert in attracting and detaining strangers from a distance—tourists for business or pleasure—and impressing them favorably with local resources. The old-established and popular Mansion House—Buffalo's historical and favorite hostelry of eighty-one years standing—has always occupied a position in the front rank of inland hotels, not only because of the good cheer dispensed within its hospitable walls, but because of its location and convenience to the manufacturing and wholesale districts, the railroad depots, the canal, elevators and wharves.

The present Mansion House site was originally occupied in 1795 by William Johnson, the famous British-Indian interpreter, who erected there a log-house. In 1806 John Crow opened a frontier tavern on the same spot, there being but ten houses in the village, and in 1809 a Mr. Landon occupied the same location with Landon's tavern, which was used also as a court-house, and was the principal public house of entertainment. The house fell a prey to the torch when the gentle British and savages burned the village in 1813. The house was subsequently rebuilt, and occupied by Mr. Burton, who, in 1825-26, gave it the name which has ever since clung to it. Mr. Burton was succeeded by Philip Dorsheimer, and he in regular line by others. The house was reconstructed in 1843, and again in 1846, and enlarged and improved from time to time until the present commodious and elegant hotel resulted, a six-story, substantial brick building, 100 feet front on Main street by 200 feet on Exchange, completely remodeled about four years ago and refitted and refurnished in the best manner throughout, with 150 large, well-lighted and well-ventilated sleeping-rooms, parlors, reading-rooms, office, baggage-room, bath-rooms, and all desirable appurtenances, capable of comfortably accommodating 200 guests. The house stands clear of other buildings; all hall and cross walls are of brick; roof of iron; heated by steam; lighted by incandescent electric lamps throughout; provided with fire-escapes, and the safest caravansery in Buffalo. Electric bells and a fine passenger elevator contribute to the comfort, ease and security of patrons. The furniture, furnishings, decorations, etc., are all that could be desired, the service first class, the table equal to any in the country, the beds luxurious, clean, broad and inviting, the proprietors and clerks polite and obliging, and, to crown all, the bills moderate. A skilled painter and paper-hanger is regularly employed the year round, and nothing is permitted to suffer from neglect.

Since Messrs. Wesley Crouch & Co. took charge of the Mansion House, a year and a half ago, the patronage has more than doubled—the best possible testimony to the efficiency and acceptability of their management. A curiosity of the establishment, exhibited with pride to visitors, is a receipted bill of a guest, paid Jan. 29, 1840—forty-seven years old—which is framed and hangs in the office.

J. M. VAN NORMAN,

Photographic Parlors and Studio—No. 359 Main St.

A more interesting place than a photograph gallery, for any person who is an admirer of the beautiful in art, would be difficult to find. Especially is this the case where there is such a fine collection of portraits as the studio of J. M. Van Norman's contains. Here is an illustration of what enterprise combined with the necessary business qualifications can accomplish. A little over two years ago this gentleman located at Murdock's old stand, No. 359 Main street. He immediately effected a complete transformation in the establishment, and it is now conceded to be one of the best equipped galleries in the country. The cabinet work executed by Mr. Van Norman is unsurpassed in finish. Since his first bid for the patronage of citizens of Buffalo and vicinity this gentleman has been accorded remarkable success. This is due to the fine artistic taste exhibited in posing, and that happy combination of light and shade which secures the best results. During an experience of twenty-one years in the business Mr. Van Norman has always personally attended to finishing all work intrusted to his hands. Then again, his prices are an important factor in diverting patronage from the older establishments. For, instance, cabinets, single face, are but $4 a dozen, while at other places the price ranges up to $8 on work which in no particular can claim superiority. In grouping Mr. Van Norman shows his ability to great advantage. The writer was shown a group of twenty-two young ladies, students at St. Margaret's school, which was in the true artistic sense a gem. In accessories Mr. Van Norman's studio equals any other in the city. Here are a few of them, by way of illustration : Seavey's rustic cottage, rustic window, Seavey's well, boats, summer house, Mexican hammock, grove, swing, large and small rocks, Seavey's rustic stile and steps, interior steps, balustrade, bridge, elegant new rustic seats, circular seats with tree, new rustic fences with gates, cutter with horse and dog, fine phæton, gas-lamp and rocks for winter, brass instruments, musket, caps, high hats, straw hats, fans, parasols, guitar, banjo, violin, fife, music stand; also any kind of back-ground desired—snow scenes, summer scenes, interior and plain grounds.

Mr. Van Norman is a native of Titusville, Pa. He is certainly entitled to great credit for the unsurpassed facilities afforded this city in photography.

MILLER, GREINER & CO.,

Wholesale Grocers and Produce Dealers—Nos. 341, 343, 345 and 347 Washington St.

The wholesale grocery trade of Buffalo is among her leading business interests, and the house of Miller, Greiner & Co. is one of the most prominent representatives of that interest. The house was founded by Mr. A. D. A. Miller, who began business at Commercial and Canal streets in 1834, removing to the foot of Main street in 1849. In 1852 the style was changed, on the admission of Mr. John Greiner, to A. D. A. Miller & Co. Later Messrs. Albert C. Miller and Charles Greiner became members of the firm, and the concern was removed to the present location, where they occupied a splendid four-story brick building, 70 by 175 feet, in 1875, since which time they have rapidly developed their trade, the transactions now reaching $1,000,000 to $1,500,000 per annum, and extending all over New York, Pennsylvania and Ohio.

Mr. A. D. A. Miller is a native of Switzerland, coming to Buffalo in 1834. Mr. John Greiner came here from Alsace in 1836, and has been in the grocery business since 1840. Both of these gentlemen were for many years members of the Board of Trade. Messrs. Charles Greiner and A. C. Miller are natives of Buffalo, the former a brother of Mr. John Greiner. He has been in the trade since 1854 and is a director of the Erie County Savings Bank. Mr. A. C. Miller is a son of A. D. A. Miller, and as before stated has had a business experience of more than twenty-one years.

Messrs. Miller, Greiner & Co. are strictly wholesale dealers in groceries and produce, embracing full lines of sugars, coffees, teas, syrups, molasses, dried, smoked, salt and pickled fish, soaps, candles, grocers' drugs and sundries, spices, fancy and shelf goods, manufactured tobacco and cigars, flavoring extracts, baking powders, whisky, woodenware, cordage, dried and green fruits, and, in short, everything required by the trade, all of the best grades and sold at lowest market quotations. The retail dealer who replenishes his stock without inspecting the goods and prices of this firm will probably make a mistake, as no more liberal or accommodating house, or larger or better assortment of goods can be found between the Atlantic and Pacific.

QUEEN CITY SHIRT CO.,

Manufacturers of Gentlemen's White Shirts—Nos. 44 to 48 Exchange St.

Among the more prominent wholesale manufacturers of shirts, the Queen City Shirt Company of Buffalo stands conspicuous. This now flourishing concern was established on a modest scale in November of 1881, occupying one floor at Mohawk and Main streets. Later, in order to secure increased space and facilities, the factory was removed to the Wright block, No. 563 Main street, where, occupying nearly three entire floors, employing a large force of hands, and turning out immense quantities of superior goods, the company remained for two years and a-half. Again finding themselves cramped for room, they on January 1, 1886, took possession of their present convenient and commodious premises—three floors, 50 by 105 feet each, of the fine building Nos. 44 to 48 Exchange street. Five hundred hands are employed, and it is estimated that from $200,000 to $250,000 worth of finished goods will be put upon the market per annum. The specialties of this most extensive house of the kind outside of New York and Troy embrace all popular grades of gentlemen's fine and medium white unlaundried shirts. The firm consume an average of twenty cases of best cotton goods per week. All machinery employed is run by steam, and the factory runs steadily and with a full force of operatives during ten months of each year, the slack time being

June and parts of November and December. A stock of eight to ten thousand dozen of shirts is carried, subject to orders at all seasons. Three experienced salesmen are constantly on the road, and orders pour in steadily from year's end to year's end from all portions of the East, West and South.

The proprietors are Messrs George P. Raymond, C. S. Guild and M. Nellany. Mr. Raymond has charge of the finances, and is general manager of the manufacturing department; Mr. Guild has charge of the sales and agents, and Mr. Nellany is a silent partner, but lends his advice in matters of importance.

Mr. S. N. Peck is foreman of the principal factory here. Extensive branches are maintained at East Buffalo, Tonawanda and Lockport.

G. ELIAS & BRO.,

Manufacturers and Wholesale Dealers in 'Hard and Soft Timber and Lumber—General Office, No. 22 West Swan St. ; Yards on Ganson St.

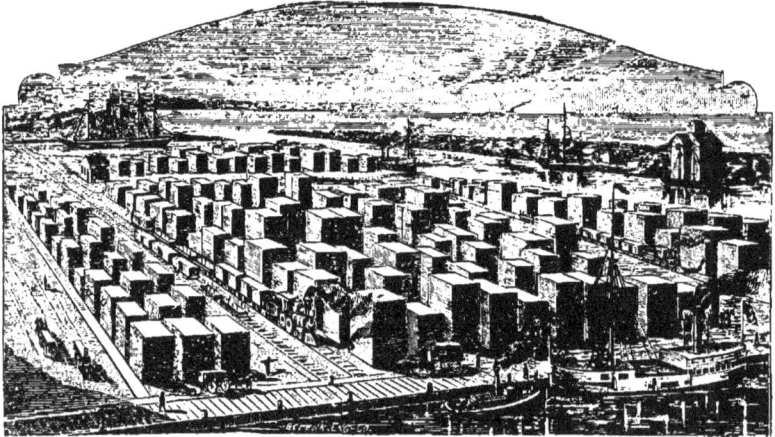

The lumber trade is one of Buffalo's leading industries, owing both to the convenience of her location to the pine and hardwood regions, which are easily and expeditiously reached by rail and lake, and to the numerous outlets by rail and canal leading east, west, north and south. The energy, enterprise and public spirit manifested by the owners of the various establishments here, devoted to this branch of business, has long been a subject of comment, and as an example of the spirit displayed in the development of the lumber trade the brilliant career of G. Elias & Bro., No. 22 West Swan street, supplies an excellent illustration. Since 1875, when this now prominent firm was established, their business has steadily expanded territorially and in the volume of sales until at this writing it extends from Oregon on the west to Liverpool and Glasgow on the east. Their experience and skill in the manufacture and sale of this product, with their thorough knowledge of every possible detail of the business, reinforced by their wonderful sources of supply—owning and operating five mills of their own in Pennsylvania, Ohio and Kentucky, sawing millions of feet annually in order to keep pace with the demand—with their vast trade constantly increasing, shows that even the full measure of prosperity so far vouchsafed the house will be surpassed in its future business operations.

G. Elias & Bro.'s docks and yard, located on Ganson street, extend over several acres of ground, and are admirably located with reference to the receipt and shipment as well as storage of lumber and timber, both by rail and water. The firm carry immense stocks of hardwood and pine in all grades and of every description, employ a large force of men, and make a specialty of sawing to order pine, hemlock and oak bill stuff for the trade, and with the possession of unexcelled facilities are prepared to fill orders, large or small, carefully and promptly, a fact that will be cheerfully attested by all old and new patrons, whose name and number is legion, both at home and abroad, their sales averaging three-quarters of a million dollars annually.

DR. E. S. BURNHAM, OPTICIAN,

No. 390 Main St.

None save those who have lost it can fully appreciate the value of good eyesight, nor can any one outside the profession measure the difficulties that lie in the way of successful treatment of diseases of the eye and even partial restoration of impaired sight. Diseases of the organs of vision, too, are on the increase., as may be seen by the constantly augmenting number of those who, for one reason or another, are compelled to resort to the use of glasses at an age when the eyes of our fathers and grandfathers were at their best—it being nothing unusual to meet very young children so afflicted. The causes are doubtless to be found in the altered modes of life that now obtain—late hours, strong artificial lights, too close application to study, etc.; whatever they are, the fact remains that we are fast becoming a purblind people, and the only remedies at hand are an abandonment of our social and reading habits or resort to the optician—for medical and surgical science offer us but temporary relief at least, and skillfully fitted glasses present the only practicable hope for those whose eyes exhibit symptoms of deterioration.

Of the numerous eminent professional gentlemen residing in Buffalo few have a wider, more enviable or better deserved reputation in their several pursuits than has Prof. E. S. Burnham, the well-known and successful optician at No. 390 Main street. Dr. Burnham is a native of Vermont, but has made his home and practiced his profession here for the past six years or so, building up a first-class fame, more particularly for his success in fitting every description of weak and diseased eyes with spectacles and eye-glasses—a branch of his art of which he makes a specialty and in which he has no superior, as is attested by the fact that much of his best patronage comes from the Eastern States, while he has a constantly growing *clientele* all over the Union. Prof. Burnham carries a superb assortment of gold and other frames, and the largest and most varied stock of axis pebble and Paris-white crystal glasses ever brought to Buffalo, which he fits upon actual examination of the eyes, risking no haphazard guess as to suitability in any case. He makes a leading specialty of preparing glasses for sufferers from myopia, presbyopia, hypermetropia, dispiopia and astigmatism, and his success in the treatment of these affections is the best guarantee of his scientific and professional knowledge. Parties troubled with difficulties of vision, arising from whatever cause, will find Prof. Burnham prepared to afford them relief and render the most satisfactory aid possible from a thorough knowledge of the subject and practically unlimited mechanical and scientific resources.

E. GALLAGHER,

Forwarding and Commission Merchant—No. 61 Pearl St.

Of the old-established and well-known forwarders and commission merchants of Buffalo, Mr. E. Gallagher, No. 61 Pearl street, is one of the most conspicuous. Mr. G. first embarked in canal forwarding in 1860 as a member of the firm of Joseph Carley & Co., composed of Messrs. Joseph Carley, James Jamison, William Foot (now deceased), and Mr. Gallagher. Two years later Mr. Foot retired, and the late Gilbert Candee succeeded to the vacancy. After three years more Mr. Carley withdrew, the style becoming E. Gallagher & Co., S. A. Gillespie being admitted. This firm was dissolved at the end of three years, Mr. Gallagher conducting the business on his individual account until 1867, when the firm of Lothridge, Gallagher & Co., composed of A. L. Lothridge, E. Gallagher and the late Jeff. Collins of Troy, was organized. This firm was dissolved by the death of Mr. Collins in the autumn of 1881. The following spring saw the formation of the firm of Gallagher, Bissell & Co., composed of E. Gallagher, A. A. Bissell and James Mulhall, jr. This firm also was dissolved, in 1884, and since that time Mr. Gallagher has had no partner. He does a very extensive business in the forwarding of freights—grain, lumber, coal, iron, stone, oil, etc.—from the various lake ports to Troy, Albany, New York, Philadelphia, Baltimore, and all intermediate points, is agent for a considerable fleet of canal craft, gives through rates when desired, and makes a point of handling all freights promptly and satisfactorily to shippers. His agents and consignees are as follows: David Taylor, No. 14 South street, New York; F. O. Potter, West Troy and Albany; A. N. Pomeroy, Utica.

C. P. CHURCHILL'S SONS,

Wholesale and Retail Grocers—No. 120 East Seneca St.

The grocery trade is one of the few branches of business in which every man, woman and child in the world is directly interested, for it caters to the wants of all alike—the rich, the poor, the old, the young, of all conditions, colors and sizes, without reference to religious belief or political bias. The grocer, and more especially the wholesale grocer, is the missionary of home comfort, the apostle of good cheer, and above all men should be honest, just and liberal, for upon him depends the health and happiness of a vast constituency. And, happily for us all, the wholesale grocer is usually an upright and faithful servant of the public.

Probably the oldest wholesale house of this kind now in existence here is that of C. P. Churchill's Sons, No. 120 East Seneca street, founded by Mr. C. P. Churchill in 1840, the first stand being at Main and Ellicott square. Later he removed to Main and Court streets, then to Main and Mohawk, and in 1870 to the present location. There have also been several changes in the style, which was first C. P. Churchill, then Churchill & Parker, then Churchill & Co., then C. P. Churchill again, from 1878 to 1879; then C. P. Churchill & Sons, and finally, in 1885, on the death of the senior member, the firm as it now stands succeeded. In all the years of its existence, nearly half a century, the house has maintained a first-class reputation for fair and liberal dealing, and has prospered accordingly, the annual sales now reaching about $100,000. The premises now occupy three floors and basement, 25 by 80 feet, and the stock, as well selected as any ever brought to this market, comprises full lines of staple and fancy groceries—sugars, coffees, teas, house-keeping goods, provisions, flour, molasses, syrups, imported and American luxuries, canned and shelf goods—in short, everything usually found in an establishment of the kind, of the best quality, fresh, pure and wholesome.

C. P. Churchill's Sons are prepared to make lowest quotations to the trade for all goods in their line, making specialties of foreign and domestic green and dried fruits, teas, coffees and spices, butter and cheese of highest grades, and canned goods of all kinds.

The Churchills come of revolutionary New England stock, their great-grandfather having fallen in that great struggle. Their grandfather was also a soldier, taking part in the war of 1812. At the age of twenty-two their father embarked in business here. At that time Buffalo numbered but about 6,500 inhabitants. During his forty-eight years of active business life it has grown to over 200,000 inhabitants. He also had the satisfaction of seeing the unpretentious retail business of long ago expand and flourish until to-day the wholesale department as well as the retail is something to be proud of.

JOHN C. DUNHAM,

Manufacturer of Fine Shirts to Order—Proprietor of Dunham's Steam Laundry—Nos. 60 and 62 Niagara St.

A neat-fitting, well-made fine shirt, perfectly laundried, is the supreme requisite of a gentleman's toilet, the lack of which cannot be compensated. The art of shirt-making has taken wonderful strides of late years, and all who wish—and who does not?—may indulge in elegant linen at very small outlay. Ready-made shirts are sold for a song everywhere, and do very well for those whose means are limited, or whose tastes are easily gratified; but the better and more particular class are not so easily satisfied, and require shirts made to measure that minister to the wearer's comfort, and can be depended upon not to go to pieces in the hands of the laundress. The experienced and tasty shirt manufacturer, therefore, has plenty of liberal support and a steady trade, let the times be what they may. Such an one is Mr. John C. Dunham, Nos. 60 and 62 Niagara street, who learned the trade in his father's large factory at Troy. Coming here in 1872, he was with the well-known old house of S. N. Lawrence & Son for five years, establishing himself on his own account in 1877. In October, 1880, he admitted a partner, the firm being Dunham & Shepherd; in March, 1882, Mr. Shephard withdrew, since which time Mr. Dunham has conducted the business alone and with remarkable success. He has removed several times, but now has a very desirable location, occupying two floors, 47 by 100 feet, running a first-class laundry in connection with his shirt factory, employing some fourteen hands, and doing an annual business of over $12,000 —the laundry being a very popular one in and around the city, and the shirt trade extending all over the United States. A flourishing branch is maintained at No. 78 East Eagle street.

BICKFORD & FRANCIS,

Manufacturers of the Celebrated "B. C. and D." Brand Strictly Short-Lap Pure Oak-Tanned Leather Belting and Hose, the Very Best Produced—Nos. 53 and 55 Exchange St.

With the development of the country and the establishment of new manufacturing enterprises the demand for all classes of machinery and equipments is constantly augmenting, and with experience owners of industrial plants learn that in the purchase of supplies, as in other matters, the best is the cheapest and always makes the best returns for the outlay. The march of improvement, too, is not confined to any one particular path, but ramifies every avenue of effort, so that a forward step in one direction is invariably but the precusor of a like stride in another. Thus it is that in milling and other industries employing steam the crude and feeble and uncertain engine of an earlier date is superseded by new forms and appliances that economize fuel, time and labor, and supply vastly enhanced power at even less expenditure of space and fuel. The same rule holds true in the transmission of power, and the broad, strong and reliable belt, constructed upon correct principles and capable of withstanding almost any strain, has replaced the crooked, unsafe and exasperating devices with which our progenitors were forced to be content.

Yet there are belts and belts. While most of those now made are excellent both in material and workmanship, it is nevertheless a fact that some of them are immeasurably superior to others. Take, for example, the two pieces illustrated herewith. The first is the old style, square-cornered lap in general use; the corners on both sides give way first, the dirt and oil find their way between the rivets, causing a grinding effect, and in a short time the belt requires a new splice. On the opposite side of the page is shown a joint of the "B. C. & D." belting of Messrs. Bickford & Francis, Nos. 53 and 55 Exchange street, this city. The superiority of this lap must be evident to the most superficial observer. Speaking of these belts Messrs. Bickford & Francis say in a recent circular:

"We are aware of the prices offered by various makers of oak-tanned belting, and we can furnish grades to meet any competition; but it is not economy to be governed entirely by price in purchasing belt. The best is the cheapest. We can make from 30 per cent. to 40 per cent. more belting from a given lot of leather, where price is the consideration, than where it is of the first importance to make a perfect belt, and yet both will look equally well to most men, but in buying the 'B. C. & D.' brand you avoid the loss of time and vexation caused by inferior quality. Our belts are made from the center of the heaviest and best selected pure oak-tanned hides, and we cut and stretch our leather in narrower strips than other makers, thus making more waste, which does not show in the manufactured belt, but becomes very apparent when put into use. If you want our belting call for it, and don't be put off by accepting an inferior article.

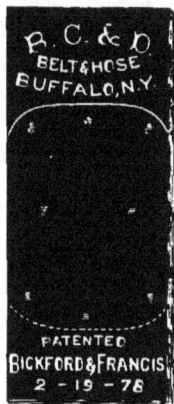

11

Any dealer can get it for you if you insist upon having it. You can, however, order direct from factory, and all orders will have prompt attention and shipment. We make a specialty of large driving belts and can furnish promptly all kinds of single and double belting from one-half inch to 64 inches wide. We would like your order for a trial of our belt in the hardest place you have—then if we suit you in price and quality we would like your trade. We challenge any manufacturer in the world to produce belting superior to our 'B. C. & D.' brand belt."

This house was founded by Bickford & Curtiss in 1846, and has always ranked high in the trade, doing a business at this time of some $250,000 per annum, covering a vast territory from ocean to ocean and from the lakes to the Mississippi.

Mr. R. H. Bickford, still taking an active part in the business, has been connected with it forty years. Mr. William C. Francis, the junior partner, was one of the founders of the Francis Axe Co. of Buffalo, and is still interested in a similar concern near Buffalo. Both are liberal, energetic, enterprising gentlemen and worthy citizens, who have contributed much to bring Buffalo up to her present proud mercantile and manufacturing position.

W. C. TIFFANY,

Wholesale and Retail Dealer in Picture Frames, Mirrors, Mouldings, Brackets, etc., etc.—Nos. 233, 235 and 237 Seneca St.

Much of the beauty of our homes, hotels, places of public resort, etc., is referable to the pictures and mirrors that adorn the walls, and which in their turn are set off to more or less advantage as good or bad taste is exercised in the selection of frames. In our time there is no reason why every production of the painters', engravers' or photographers' art should not be appropriately mounted, since the manufacture of frames has attained a perfection never before dreamed of, and every city of any pretensions has one or more establishments devoted in whole or in part to the sale and fitting of these goods.

Buffalo's leading picture and mirror frame house is that of W. C. Tiffany, Nos. 233, 235 and 237 Seneca street, established in 1872, occupying a three-story brick building, 66 feet front by 80 feet deep, and doing an annual business of $30,000 to $40,000, supplying the trade and many retail buyers of Buffalo and Western New York as well as adjacent portions of Canada.

In addition to his fine taste in such matters, Mr. Tiffany has had many years of practical experience in supplying these goods, and is remarkably successful in executing commissions for rare goods in his line. His stock of frames and mouldings is always the largest in the city, and embraces all styles from the richest to the plainest.

SCHLEE & STEPHAN,

Proprietors of North Buffalo Box and Heading Works—Nos. 2084, 2086 and 2088 Niagara St.

This house was established in 1878 by Ternier & Schlee, to whom the present firm soon after succeeded. They have premises 80 by 100 feet, on which is a convenient and well-appointed two-and-a-half story factory, 40 by 60 feet, employing some twenty-five hands and turning out from $15,000 to $20,000 worth of finished boxes and heading per annum, for which they find ready sale in Buffalo and vicinity, their goods being popular with consumers. Mr. George Schlee is a native of Buffalo, aged 33, and has had long experience in his present business. Mr. Herman Stephan was born in Germany in 1844, came to Buffalo in 1854, and has been a journeyman cooper and teamster; saved his earnings, and was enabled to purchase an interest with Mr. Schlee. Both are industrious, worthy men, and church members.

D. E. MORGAN & SON,

Exclusive Jobbers and Dealers in Carpets, Drapery and Upholstery Goods, Oil Cloths, Mattings, Feathers, etc.—No. 259 Main St.

Messrs. D. E. Morgan & Son, whose elegant and beautifully appointed establishment is an ornament to Buffalo's principal business thoroughfare, are the only exclusive dealers in the line of goods above enumerated west of New York, and are the most famous merchants in their specialties in the United States, with perhaps one or two exceptions. This business house fronts 25 feet on both Main and Washington streets, extending 200 feet from thoroughfare to thoroughfare, and is five stories in height, every floor presenting a complete magazine of fine goods, and representing every department of the carpet, drapery and upholstery goods trade.

The firm as at present constituted, composed of Messrs. D. E. and W. K. Morgan, commenced operations in 1881 at No. 331 Main street, removing to the much superior and more commodious store in the early part of 1886, at the same time more than doubling their storage and salesroom capacity and extending their business facilities in every direction. So attractive and inviting, indeed, is this house, that it enjoys not only most of the trade of discriminating people hereabouts but has vast numbers of regular and transient customers from adjacent portions of New York, Pennsylvania, Ohio and Canada, doing, besides, a liberal and growing jobbing trade with the merchants of surrounding cities and towns, the annual sales ranging from $200,000 to $250,000, and the operations in all departments giving steady employment to some fifty persons, male and female.

It would be impossible, within the limits of a brief sketch like this, to enumerate and describe even a portion of the vast, varied and magnificent stock carried at all seasons. Suffice it to say that everything new, tasteful and useful in carpets, draperies, upholstery goods, oil cloths, matting, etc., can be found here in infinite variety, quantity, quality, style and price.

The elder Mr. Morgan is one of Buffalo's substantial citizens, and has been engaged in merchandising here for a quarter of a century. He was formerly a member of the famous houses of Sherman, Barnes & Co. and Chester, Morgan & Arend, and is the oldest carpet man in Buffalo. He is also a prominent Freemason, and a liberal, public-spirited man.

R. CALLAHAN,

Livery Stable—Light Carriage Factory—General Repairing and Horseshoeing—No. 36 Niagara St., near Pearl.

Of manufactures having direct reference to local wants, none are of greater importance to the citizens of Buffalo than the building of light business and pleasure vehicles. Among the most successful and popular of those engaged in this industry is Mr. R. Callahan, whose handsome establishment at No. 36 Niagara street is one of the most complete and best-appointed in the city. Mr. Callahan has been connected with the carriage-making and livery business for nearly thirty-one years, first establishing himself at No. 262 Washington street, between North and South Division. He removed to his present convenient location in 1879, and has enjoyed a large and steadily increasing patronage from that time up to the present, occupying the entire building indicated, four stories in height, 27 feet front by 115 feet deep. The upper floors contain the wood-working, painting and storage departments; the blacksmith shop is in the basement, and the ground floor is devoted to the purposes of a livery stable, where a fine line of buggies, carriages, sleighs and harness horses are constantly kept for the accommodation of the public.

Mr. Callahan employs only the most skillful men in his shops, and is prepared to execute promptly, skillfully and satisfactorily all orders with which he is favored for the making and repairing of buggies, carriages, business wagons and light vehicles generally. Himself a practical carriage-maker, he can guarantee all work from his shops, and those who have once patronized him have no hesitation in commending him to others. Special attention is given to scientific horseshoeing, for the excellence of which work Mr. Callahan is justly famous. He carries a fine assortment of all vehicles in his line, and can offer advantageous terms to both buyers and those who merely wish to hire.

Mr. C. is a native of Buffalo, has lived here always, and is justly popular as a business man and citizen. His present quarters are growing too small for him, and he proposes, in the near future, to secure ground and build a great factory and stable better suited to the growing needs of his trade.

CYRUS K. PORTER & SON,

Architects—Room No. 20 American Block.

The science of architecture is one of the most useful of those pursuits that tend to elevate public taste and at the same time minister to the comfort, enjoyments and happiness of the individual by providing for his healthful shelter and convenience. The master of this art must needs be a student, not only of books but of physics, not only of mathematics but of men; and happy indeed is he if even then he does not sometimes fail to reap the just reward of his conscientious toil. Usually, however, with the architect as in other professions, the best proof of merit is the measure of success that has crowned his efforts; and, judged by this standard, the attainments and deserts of Mr. Cyrus K. Porter, of this city, are of the highest order. Mr. Porter has had an active experience of the most valuable kind, extending over a period of forty years, and is fairly entitled to the name of Nestor of the profession in this section of the country. He settled in Buffalo in 1865, having been born in Onondaga county, N. Y. Three years ago he associated with himself his son, Mr. Jesse R. Porter, who for the previous ten years had devoted himself to the technical, theoretical and practical mastery of architecture in his father's office. Thoroughly conversant with his profession, and abreast of the times in which he lives, with a laudable ambition to excel, there can be no more question of the younger Mr. Porter's future than there is of his father's distinguished past and present.

With their ripe experience, their vast accumulation of original designs, their valuable selected library of the choicest architectural works, and an established reputation, they are now in a position to prepare designs and superintend the erection of buildings of every class, public or private, from the humblest cottage to the most gorgeous palace.

Especial attention will be given to the erection of churches, a branch of the profession to which the senior member of the firm has devoted a life-time of active service. All orders will receive prompt attention. Preliminary sketches are always sent for the approval of patrons at a distance, previous to making completed drawings.

The elder Mr. Porter is president of the Buffalo Society of Architects.

G. & J. SCHAEFER,

Watchmakers and Jewelers—No. 402 William St.

Among the leading firms doing business out on William street, in that remarkably busy section east of Jefferson street, are Messrs. G. & J. Schaefer. They have a jewelry establishment that is a credit to that part of the city. There is a large volume of business done out on this part of William street, and this firm is coming in for a good share of it. The business was established in the year 1881 by Charles H. Pfeiffer, who continued it until July, 1886, when the present firm came in. They increased the stock and added additional lines, thereby making the assortment equal to all demands from the trade in this section of the city. A full line of jewelry, including watches, clocks, silverware, etc., is carried, and a specialty is made of repairing. An idea can be formed of the rapid growth of the business when it is stated that it reaches as high as $25,000 a year. As good bargains can be secured here as elsewhere in this market. Both members of the firm are enterprising young men, and will succeed.

BUFFALO HAT MANUFACTURING CO.

Wholesale and Retail Manufacturers of Hats and Caps—Factories, Newark, N. J., and No. 77[Seneca St., Buffalo.

Neat and becoming headgear is as necessary to the male biped's comfort and respectable appearance as any other item of dress. The Buffalo Hat Manufacturing Company, No. 77 East Seneca street, is doing yeoman service to the public, and there is no excuse for high or low, rich or poor, old or young, wearing shabby hats, when all tastes and all purses can be suited from the immense stock exhibited upon the shelves of this house, or made by the shopful of practical hatters employed upon the premises. Messrs. M. H. Mark and H. Guggenheimer, the affable and enterprising proprietors, established this house in 1885, and have already made of it a marked and substantial success. Having the advantage of two factories, here and at Newark, N. J., the firm are always prepared with the latest styles as soon as brought out, and are enabled to sell on a closer margin than most of their competitors. They make a specialty of medium goods, but carry a heavy stock of the finer grades. Besides their large and growing local custom they sell extensively to the trade in this and adjoining States, and offer the most liberal inducements to that class of buyers.

Mr. Mark is a native of Greenville, S. C.; has always been in the hat trade, and came to Buffalo in 1834. Mr. Guggenheimer, born in New York city, was formerly in the cloth trade ; came to Buffalo and entered the hat business in 1835.

It must not be supposed, because of the low prices asked for the goods of the Buffalo Hat Co., that they are of inferior grade, or produced by cheap labor. On the contrary, they employ Union workmen only, and every hat they sell bears the Union label. They can make a new fine silk hat to order in four hours.]

THE PEOPLE'S PRESS.

Matthews, Northrup & Co., Art Printing Works—J. N. Matthews, President ; William P. Northrup, General Manager ; George E. Matthews, Treasurer ; Henry Matthews, Superintendent of Printing ; Henry Straub, Superintendent of Binding ; Charles E. Austin, Assistant Treasurer—Nos. 177 to 183 Washington St. and 36 to 48 Exchange St. ,

This concern, which has attained a reputation extending all over the country, was founded in 1878 by Mr. J. N. Matthews, editor and proprietor of the *Buffalo Express.* After he had disposed of his interest in the *Commercial Advertiser*, where for many years the firm of Matthews & Warren had been famous for fine printing, he associated with himself his brother, Mr. Henry Matthews, who for many years had been superintendent in the *Commercial Advertiser* printing office ; his son, Mr. George E. Matthews, and Mr. J. C. Bryant, and under the firm name of Matthews Bros. & Bryant they commenced the printing business, using the top story over Nos. 177 and 179 Washington street, down to No. 42 Exchange street. At the same time Mr. Matthews formed a co-partnership with Mr. William P. Northrup to carry on the map engraving business, which had been founded by Mr. Northrup's uncle, Mr. E. R. Jewett, the inventor of the relief line process. The firm also furnished wood engravings, and the business of engraving was carried on under the firm name of William P. Northrup & Co.

As a bindery is a necessary adjunct to a printing office, arrangements were made with Mr. Henry Straub, who for many years had been known as among the best binders in this part of the country, to occupy the third floor and conduct his bindery there. The business was carried on in this way for three years, the firm of Matthews Bros. & Bryant extending their reputation as printers, and the name of William P. Northrup & Co. becoming well known in connection with map engraving, especially for railroads.

It was found that there were difficulties in carrying on the divided business, and the firm of William P. Northrup & Co. was consolidated with that of Matthews Bros. & Bryant, the new firm being known as Matthews, Northrup & Co. At the same time Mr. George E. Matthews became a partner in the bindery with Mr. Straub, and that business was carried on under the firm name of Henry Straub & Co. In 1883 Mr. J. C. Bryant retired from the firm, his interest being divided among the remaining partners. No further change was made until the beginning of the current year, when a further consolidation was made, the bindery owned by Henry Straub & Co. being annexed, Mr. Straub becoming a partner with Matthews, Northrup and Co. At the same time Mr. Charles E. Austin, who had been in charge of the counting-room ever since the establishment of the business, was admitted as a partner. The management of so extensive a business, and with so many diverse interests, necessarily approaches closely to that of a stock company, and therefore the departments of the various partners have been distinguished by the designation usually employed in such companies. Mr. J. N. Matthews acts as president, Mr. William P. Northrup as general manager, Mr. George E. Matthews as treasurer, Mr. Henry Matthews as superintendent of printing, Mr. Henry Straub as superintendent of binding, Mr. Charles E. Austin as assistant treasurer.

During the eight years of growth thus described the capital invested in the business has increased four-fold, and the amount of work done over eight-fold. The premises now occupied by the concern and the *Buffalo Express*, which is under a kindred management, occupy more than an acre of floor space, and employ over 200 people. Their facilities are such that they make the claim to be the most complete concern in the trade, justifying it by the statement that every requisite to a first-class work, except the raw materials, is furnished on their own premises, it being the only concern in which every kind of engravings, including photo-engraving by two processes, engraving upon wood, metal and relief-line engraving, are all furnished.

The general estimation in which the productions of this house is held is well shown by the following quotation from the *Art Age*, the recognized organ of advanced printing in this country:

"Printing is more than a trade. Of late it has sunk to deplorable depths, and the process of redemption is slow. But as long as such firms as Messrs. Matthews, Northrup & Co., Messrs. Livermore & Knight, Messrs. Theodore L. De Vinne & Co., the Bullard Printing House, Mr. M. R. Walter and a few others show by example and good work that it requires brain, skill and scholarship, honesty, the art instinct, and dignity to rise above the level of unscrupulous performance, with money-getting as the first purpose, and creditable achievement as the last, it is probable that the trade as a profession will continue to rise in general esteem, and the total quantity of meritorious work, in proportion to all the printing done, greatly increase."

The productions of this firm are widely spread, their customers being gathered from every part of the country, and some of their work being exported.

BUFFALO PRINTING INK WORKS.

F. L. Hurlbutt, President; George E. Matthews, Treasurer; C. R. Wilber, Secretary; R. E. Pollock, Superintendent—Printing and Lithographic Inks and Varnishes—Nos. 11 and 13 Dayton St.

The printer or lithographer who attempts fine work with inferior ink will find himself, to use an expressive Westernism, "left," for the thing cannot be done; and no matter how skillful, tasteful or appropriate the typography or lithographic design, poor inks will ruin the effect as surely as the most elaborate botchwork in any other of the steps that lead to its completion.

While most competent printers and lithographers are good enough judges of colors and effects, comparatively few are sufficiently informed to pass upon the comparative merits of the inks offered by different manufacturers, and they are therefore dependent to a great degree upon the integrity and good faith of those from whom they buy; consequently it is of the first importance that their orders should be placed with those manufacturers who have character and reputation to maintain as well as skill and experience in their business, and self-interest as an additional incentive. Such a house is the Buffalo Printing Ink Works, whose officers are named above. This company was organized December 1, 1884, Mr. Pollock, the present active and efficient manager, being admitted and appointed to his post of responsibility just one year later. He has had the advantage of many years' experience as a practical ink manufacturer, and has entire personal supervision of the works, assisted in each department by careful and skillful foremen. Mr. Hurlbutt, the president, acts in the capacity of general salesman. He also is an experienced man, having traveled for years for some of the most prominent concerns of the kind in the United States. Mr. George E. Matthews, the treasurer, is also a member of the firm of Matthews, Northrup & Co., art printers, engravers, lithographers and binders, *Express* building, Washington and Exchange streets. It is not difficult to infer that a desire to experiment in improvements upon the inks used by his firm may have had its influence in inducing Mr. M. to enter the Buffalo Printing Ink Co. Mr. C. R. Wilber, secretary, is a well-known and energetic business man, formerly in the wholesale watch trade, and later in Government employ. All in all the company is composed of the best possible material—of men who have the capital, stamina and brains to push it to a conspicuous success, and that they will do so admits of no reasonable question.

The works were originally located at Washington and Scott streets, but soon outgrew the accommodations, and on the first of last May were removed to Nos. 11 and 13 Dayton street, where they have a commodious five-story building, 45 by 90 feet, fitted up with every facility and convenience for the prosecution of a large and growing manufacturing business, the plant being complete in all respects as regards machinery and appliances.

The firm manufacture all grades of printers' and lithographers' inks and varnishes, making a specialty of the finer grades, immense quantities of which they supply to the trade at home and abroad, even shipping extensively to foreign countries. Wherever used these splendid inks have given unqualified satisfaction, and the demand grows at a most gratifying rate. Last year's sales footed up some $70,000, and there can be no question that they will go far beyond that total for the present year. This work is printed with ink manufactured by this house.

DAVID BELL,

Iron Shipbuilder and Manufacturer of Steam Engines, Locomotives, etc.—
Norton, Water and Evans Sts.

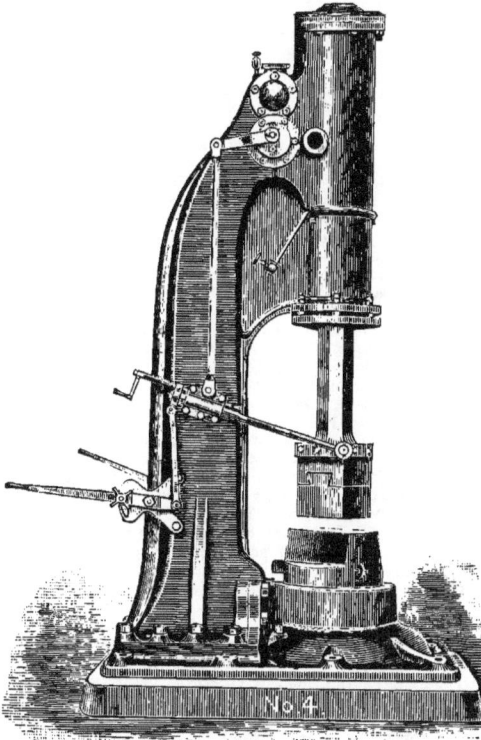

Mr. David Bell, the representative manufacturer on the shores of the great lakes, is emphatically a self-made man. He was born in Amesfield, Dumfriesshire, Scotland, on December 7, 1817. When seventeen he was duly apprenticed to learn the millwright trade. It was not long before he had a practical knowledge of the trade, and he afterward visited England, acquiring new ideas and additional skill and experience. Eventually he decided to go to America. A brother of his had also some time before gone to St. John, New Brunswick; and so in the spring of 1841 he sailed for New York. Mr. Bell was first employed in the South Boston Steam Engine Works, in 1841, at the rate of $1.50 per day, and during the fall of the same year he paid a visit to his brother in St. John, N. B., and worked in the machine shops there for about a year, when, better prospects opening before him in the West, he returned to the States in 1842, and came direct to Buffalo, where he was at once engaged by the Buffalo Steam Engine Works, but soon after went to Cleveland and worked a short time in the Cuyahoga Steam Works, subsequently returning to Buffalo, where he was employed in the building of the propeller " Hercules," the first screw steamer that ever successfully plied on the lakes. Mr. Bell left the employment of the Buffalo Steam Engine Works in 1845, and formed a copartnership with Mr. William McNish, under the firm name of Bell & McNish; and it was from this time onward that Mr. Bell demonstrated his great abilities both as a practical business man and a skillful engine-builder. The firm had but a small capital, but what they lacked in that way they made up in grit and practical knowledge of their trade; and so, after erecting a small shop, on what is now the site of Mr. Bell's great foundry, they sought business. It came very slowly—Buffalo at that time had barely a population of 25,000, and the trade returns show that the Erie canal tolls were then only about $400,000 per annum, so that it bore no comparison to the metropolitan Buffalo of to-day. However, the young firm of Bell & McNish did not lose heart; they were hopeful and persevering, faithfully performed such small foundry jobs as they got, and gradually worked their way into a paying patronage, one of their first undertakings being the building of a steam engine for the " Dart " elevator, the first one ever built either in Buffalo or anywhere else, so that Mr. Bell was the first man to build an elevator engine. This was a good advertisement for the firm, as the engine gave great satisfaction, and they built successively the engines for the elevators

"Seymour and Wells," "Evans," "Sterling," "Bugbee," and others. In addition to
engines for elevators, the firm also constructed marine engines for a number of the
powerful passenger steamers being placed on Lake Erie about this time. They were
also the first to build and develop the possibilities of the handy tug engine, which
enables these useful craft to pull a tonnage immensely disproportionate to their
displacement. It was in 1850 that the copartnership was dissolved, Mr. Bell continuing
the business alone until 1854, when he rented his shop, and sold his machinery, tools,
etc., to the Buffalo Steam Engine Company, and became the superintendent of the
works at a salary of $2,500 per annum, taking the place of a man who had once offered
Mr. Bell $1.25 for his services. The company not having sufficient capital to carry on
the business, Mr. Bell resigned his position, and taking advantage of this brief period of
leisure, paid a visit to his native land, returning to Buffalo in 1855, when he again took
possession of his old shop, and started anew to build up a trade in his line of business.
Fire soon after destroyed his shop and tools, and, unfortunately for him, just after a
heavy policy of insurance had expired. Before even the bricks in the ruins had cooled
he was superintending their relaying, and erected the spacious and specially constructed
building on the triangular plot bounded by Norton, Water and Evans streets, and which
as Bell's foundry and machine shop is to-day one of the best known and most flourishing
industrial establishments in the city. Among other noteworthy achievements of his
was the building of the steam-tug and canal-boat fleet which made such a triumphant
voyage over the Erie canal at the time steam was first successfully brought into use to
propel boats. It was in 1858, and Mr. Bell, as the recognized commodore of the little
fleet, took it down to Rochester, where Governor King and a distinguished party
embarked, and were brought triumphantly up to Buffalo, where the guests were received
enthusiastically. The impromptu commodore of the peaceful canal-boat fleet felt a
genuine pride in the grand display of his adopted city, which demonstrated the great
feeling of satisfaction that the problem of steam navigation on the canals had first been
solved by a tug built by a Buffalonian. In 1861 Mr. Bell began to build the first iron
propeller ever launched on the great lakes. It was 720 tons burden, and was constructed
for Messrs. J. C. & E. T. Evans; many croakers doubted the success of this great
innovation in marine architecture, but Mr. Bell was from the start fully assured of the
wonderful benefits that must accrue from the use of iron; and he was right. The new
propeller was a perfect success, and more were ordered. The war of the rebellion broke
out about this time in all its fury, and Mr. Bell was one of the first to render material
aid to the Federal cause. His handsome, swift and powerful tug-boats were about
this time making a great stir in the world. The Government gladly purchased
several of them, and it was a tug he had built that was engaged in towing the old
"Constitution" at the time she was scuttled off Newport News. He likewise built the
tug that was used as a transport on the James river and around Norfolk, and it was this
historic tug that carried the information to President Lincoln and members of his
cabinet at Fortress Monroe, that resulted in the eventual destruction of the Confederate
ram "Merrimac," in Norfolk harbor. In another field of enterprise, equally broad and
grand, has Mr. Bell been successful. In 1865 he began to build locomotives. He
created additional shop facilities, put in new and improved machinery, and energetically
went to work, his first locomotive appearing in due season, for the Erie & Pittsburgh
railroad. As a deserved compliment to the builder, it was named the "David Bell." It
was the first locomotive ever built in Buffalo, and its trial trip up to Dunkirk was the
occasion for a great celebration by the citizens of Buffalo of such an auspicious event.
Mr. Bell was one of the movers and organizers of the Mechanics' Institute, which was
first formed in 1865, and duly incorporated in 1869, Mr. Bell being unanimously elected
the first president, while he was also one of the incorporators. It was largely owing to
Mr. Bell that this organization held the first International Exhibition in Buffalo, in
1869, and which proved such a grand success. He worked hard and infused his
associates with much of his own zeal and energy, and the results bore abundant
evidence to his sound judgment and great executive abilities. The receipts were over
$18,000, and after all expenses were paid there remained a balance of $4,500 on hand.
He was re-elected to the presidency for the succeeding year. Mr. Bell has also served
as president of the Young Men's Association, is a life member thereof, and has done
much in its aid. He is a member of St. Andrew's Society, and the Scottish athletic
organizations; he is a promoter of all healthy outdoor sports, and has also been president
of the Grand National Curling Club, and was presented with a valuable testimonial by
the society in token of its high appreciation of his services. Mr. Bell is still actively
engaged in carrying on his extensive business, which has developed to proportions of
great magnitude. His fame has spread far and near, and orders come to him from

distant points. His services have been called for in innumerable ways. He built three iron cutters for the revenue service; merchant steamers of large size for the trade to Cleveland, Detroit and Chicago; pleasure yachts and steamers; fleets of tugs; engines and locomotive almost without number; and the miscellaneous line of orders that find their way to such a representative establishment as his is. He is an American pioneer in numerous prominent features; he not only built the first tug-boat, the first elevator engine, the first marine engine for propellers, but it was he that built the first iron propeller on the lakes, and the first and only iron revenue cutter ever built in Buffalo; also the first locomotive in Buffalo.

Several years ago Mr. Bell invented and patented a new style of steam hammer, illustrated herewith, which has proved one of the most effective, useful and valuable labor, time, wages and fuel-saving mechanical devices ever brought out. The Bell improved patent steam hammer is made in four sizes, No. 1 being intended for the ordinary smith-shop. It is of very simple construction, having single column standard, with bed-plate and cylinder cast in one piece, very strong, self-acting, and taking steam at both ends of the cylinder, all of the sizes striking a square blow. Either of the sizes will strike a heavy or light blow ,as required, and can be worked either " double acting " or " single acting," the change being easily and quickly effected. It is the best and most economical hammer in use, far superior to all belt, trip, and helve hammers—easier to manage and keep in repair, and at least fifty per cent cheaper than any hammer yet invented that will do the same work.

Nos. 2 and 3 sizes will work up old car axles and make the best iron that can be produced for connecting rods, eccentric rods, and all parts of engines and other machinery where the best quality of iron is required. They will also work up old scrap, quantities of which are always to be found in a blacksmith shop, and produce the best of iron for all ordinary purposes.

No. 4 has been constructed with a view to furnish at a very moderate price a hammer that will forge large and heavy cranks and shafts, and the frames and other bearings connected with locomotives, not only with expedition but with the greatest accuracy and saving of labor, and it is claimed that twice the number of locomotive frames and bearings can be turned out in the same time that can be done with the appliances hitherto employed for doing the same work. With a heating furnace it will work up scrap into billets for making car axles, crank shafts, and all heavy forgings which have heretofore required large and very expensive hammers to accomplish.

EDWARD H. JENNINGS,

Successor to Warner & Jennings—Household Art Rooms—No. 263 Main St.

Most people of refinement in our day give great attention to the adornment of their homes, not for the sake of mere vulgar display, but for the pure pleasure it yields and as a tribute to the newly-aroused art spirit of the age. Among those who have contributed to this awakening of a commendable feeling and its gratification Mr. Edward H. Jennings of this city is quite conspicuous. His beautiful art rooms No. 263 Main street, Buffalo, present such an exposition of art goods for household adornment as can hardly be found west of New York city, embracing every variety of mural decorations, art paper-hangings, bric-a-brac, antique rugs, stained glass, artistic furniture, and a thousand pretty and useful things for which we have not space even for passing mention. This bazar of beauty is certainly the most elegantly fitted up place of business in the city, and the resort of the most cultivated people of all Western New York and of thousands of visitors from a distance. The building itself is a handsome one, of five stories and basement, 25 feet front by 150 feet deep, and the various departments of Mr. Jennings' business occupy the whole, every floor being a treasure-house of taste and beauty in color and form. The main, or ground floor, is divided into six separate departments, each devoted to some special line of goods, and arranged with faultless regard for what is most striking and appropriate, and each representing on a reduced b t compact and effective scale the resources of the establishment. We will not attempt a detailed description of the attractions here presented, but recommend every housekeeper and lover of what is best in household art to go and see for herself or himself.

Mr. Jennings is a native of Richmond, Mass., and has had the experience of a life-time in his vocation. The house now under consideration was established by Warner & Jennings in 1879, and has a reputation and trade coextensive with the Union. Mr. J. became sole proprietor in 1885.

DONALDSON & CO.,

Bankers and Brokers—Dealers in Foreign Exchange, Stock and Investment Securities, Grain and Provisions—Rooms 1 and 2, Hayen Building, Corner Main and Seneca Sts.

The vast volume of business transacted here in trade, commerce and manufactures render Buffalo one of the most desirable fields for banking operations to be found anywhere. True, the field is pretty well occupied just now, but it is extending, and the time is not far distant when double the amount of capital at present invested in this branch of business will be demanded and fully employed in legitimate channels.

This house was organized in 1880 by Abell & McNiven, and changed to the present style in 1884, and is composed of Messrs. J. A. Donaldson and W. R. McNiven, with Mr. C. Lee Abell as cashier. The office, formerly at No. 20 East Seneca street, was removed to its present quarters in 1885.

The house is prepared in the best manner with all requisite facilities for the transaction of any and all banking business, the purchase and sale of foreign exchange, etc., on as favorable terms as are consistent with legitimate business and safety to all parties. They also deal largely in stocks and investment securities, and, having direct communication by leased wire with the New York Stock Exchange, can buy or sell for cash or on margin any of the leading listed stocks, bonds or speculative securities. Special telegraphic connection afford them, besides, the best advantages for buying and selling grain and provisions on the Chicago Board of Trade for cash or on margins, and for furnishing late and reliable information relative to the course of the markets. They deal in petroleum through the New York and Oil City Exchanges, and have superior facilities for promptly executing orders and for carrying certificates at low rates of interest. In connection with their business in securities, grain, provisions and oil the firm issue a daily circular, which will be sent on application. They solicit correspondence from those interested.

The house is a sound, stable and responsible one, and has a superb patronage throughout the country. The members are in all respects first-class business men and public-spirited citizens. Mr. Donaldson is a native of Buffalo, as is also Cashier Abell. The former was for many years book-keeper of the Erie County Savings Bank, while the latter is part owner of the Marine elevator, and handles the cash grain business thereof through the banking-house. Mr. McNiven is of Canadian birth; has resided in Buffalo since 1870; was formerly with Pratt & Co., iron and hardware merchants, and was one of the originators of the banking-house with which he is now connected.

CHARLES BAYER,

Architect and Surveyor—No. 442 Main St.

However much Americans may excel in the mechanic arts, and in some branches of practical science, it must be conceded that in the matter of architectural taste the soundest principles and best training up to the present time are imparted in European schools. Our finest examples of public and private architecture are adaptations of European models, and our most successful and popular architects are close students of European styles and precedents. There are abundant reasons for this state of affairs, as the comparative newness of our country, the recent development of its resources, the rarity of colossal fortunes, the neglect of this branch of art, and the unsubstantial character of our first domiciliary improvements—all of which will be remedied in time, but the fact remains that in our day the architect who presents proofs of thorough training in the French, German and Italian schools, and of the ability to adapt his acquired knowledge to changed conditions such as govern in this country, enjoys great advantages over the average American in the same pursuit.

Such an architect is Mr. Charles Bayer, of No. 442 Main street, who previous to his arrival in the United States, in 1881, had for seven years been a practical architect and surveyor in his native Stuttgart, Kingdom of Wurtemburg. None who have read descriptions of that grand old city of palaces and cathedrals need be told of the superb opportunities for study it presents to the earnest seeker after perfection in architecture such as Mr. Bayer, who chose this profession in obedience to his natural bent. On coming to this country he proceeded to Cincinnati, where he remained seven months, and then removed to Buffalo. Since his arrival here he has been quite successful, particularly in the line of ecclesiastical architecture, among his most notable productions being the plans for St. Mary's church, Lockport, among the handsomest temples of worship in Western New York. He also furnished the plans for the elegant residence recently erected by Dueringer & Fassett on Walden avenue, and many other business and dwelling-houses. He gives prompt attention to plans, specifications and details for street, church and domestic architecture.

WESTERN BEEF CO.,

Wholesale Dealers in Swift's Chicago Dressed Beef and Mutton—Nos. 72 and 74 River St.

Whatever opposition formerly existed, arising from prejudice or selfishness, against the trade in Western dressed meats, has about died out in face of the fact that all classes of citizens, rich and poor alike, are by this system supplied with choice beef and mutton at moderate prices, and, while no reasonable objection is made to the consumption of New York or Kentucky-fattened short-horns by those who can afford it, yet the accessibility of ample supples of the cheaper (though scarcely less juicy, palatable and sustaining) Western beef is confessedly a great boon to the great body of the people—those who live by their labor and those who wish to practice economy. The Western Beef Co., Nos. 72 and 74 River street, is therefore a blessing to the community, purveying as it does to the wants of the masses.

This company is equipped in the best manner for the transaction of a large business, and was established in August of 1883. The members are E. C. Swift of Boston, G. F. Swift of Chicago, and Mr. Edward Smith of this city, who manages the Buffalo branch in a liberal and business-like manner which has popularized both the company and its goods.

All surrounding towns and villages also have the advantages afforded by the company through its branch houses, all of which are kept constantly-supplied with excellent Chicago meats, fresh, sweet, sound and cheap. The great River-street warehouse is 100 by 100 feet square, provided with stables for the company's horses and wagons, a handsome office, and an immense refrigerator, or, more correctly speaking, ice chamber, with capacity for the storage and safe-keeping of 250 quarters of beef and a corresponding quantity of mutton—beef being the leading specialty. None but the best grades of meats are sold, and as a consequence the enterprise has proved a wonderful success, involving large capital and making fair returns. The Swift brothers are live, wide-awake Boston men, while Mr. Edward Smith, the manager here, has bought and slaughtered hundreds of cattle himself, and is a Buffalo man of wide acquaintance and great business capacity. The trade, hotels, restaurants and others buying meats in quantities will find it to their advantage to visit the Western Beef Co.'s warehouse and inspect its facilities.

QUEEN CITY HAT MANUFACTURING CO.,

Manufacturers and Wholesale and Retail Dealers in Every Description of Men's Headgear, Furnishing Goods, etc.—A. H. & M. F. Babcock, Proprietors; Robt. H. Cranston, Superintendent—No. 87 Genesee St.

All mankind are directly interested in the subject of hats, and it is consequently a matter of importance to the public that they should be informed as to where they can obtain the best and most stylish head-covering for the least money. The Queen City Hat Manufacturing Co., No. 87 East Genesee street, established in the spring of 1886, is one of the most energetic and prosperous of Buffalo's new business enterprises, run upon the most liberal principles and enjoying the confidence and patronage of a rapidly growing circle of first-class trade. During its first season this enterprising company made sales aggregating over $40,000, with good indications that they will more than double that sum in 1887. The company employs four active travelers and twenty-eight skillful and well-paid operatives—all members of the Hatters' Union—and every article of headgear that leaves their store bears the union label, is guaranteed as represented, and is positive proof in itself that liberal wages does not mean high prices of products, as the Queen City Hat Manufacturing Co. is ready to compare goods and prices with any non-union establishment, guaranteeing to supply a superior hat or cap, made of the same or better material, by better and better paid workmen, at the same or lower figures than are demanded by their wage-cutting competitors.

The company has already extended its trade all over Western New York and Pennsylvania and Eastern Ohio. Their goods embrace every description of hats and caps for all classes and conditions of men, military, band and society uniform hats and caps, fine silk, felt and wool hats, cloth and straw hats and caps, etc. A specialty is made of fine silk hats to order, which they usually deliver complete in ten hours, though, if necessary, they can be made in four hours. They also have a large factory at Orange, N. J., whence they obtain their supplies for the trade.

In connection with their store at this point they also carry a splendid stock of gentlemen's fine and medium furnishing goods in all varieties.

Messrs. A. H. and M. F. Babcock came to Buffalo from Rochester three years ago. Mr. Robert H. Cranston, the superintendent, is a practical hatter, and a very skillful workman. All are young, capable, enterprising business men, and the success of the Queen City Hat Manufacturing Company is assured.

WALLACE JOHNSON,

Wholesale Produce—Dealer in Dried Fruit, Clover and Timothy Seed, Butter, Eggs, Beans, Peas, Bags, etc.—No. 110 Main St., Two Doors Below Canal Bridge.

For more than thirty-six years Mr. Wallace Johnson has stood in the front rank of Buffalo's dried fruit, seed and produce trade, beginning in 1850 on Seneca street, where he remained for three years, removing to 119 Main street. In 1865 he changed his location to No. 70 Main street, where he was burned out in 1886—immediately re-establishing himself at his present place, No. 110 Main street. It will be seen, therefore, that he has had vast experience in his business, and should be, as he is, master of all its details.

Mr. Johnson is an exclusively wholesale dealer in the goods he handles, comprising immense quantities of dried fruits of all kinds, clover and timothy seeds, etc. His trade is about equally divided between local buyers and exportations to Europe, and for thirty years has averaged $250,000 per annum. He also has a wide and valuable business connection throughout this State, Pennsylvania, Ohio and Michigan, maintaining a large and prosperous branch house at Hillsdale, Mich.

Mr. Johnson is an Ohio man of Yankee parentage, an energetic, enterprising, upright merchant and citizen, and well deserves the success and personal popularity he has achieved in his nearly forty years of residence in Buffalo. As an evidence of his standing, reliability and responsibility, he refers to the following well-known bankers and merchants, East and West: Bank of Commerce, Buffalo; George B. Ferris & Co., New York; Straight, Deming & Co., Cincinnati; Manran, Wright & Co., Chicago; T. W. Evans & Co., Cleveland; H. & L. Chase, Boston; Crabb, Billman & Co., Toledo; Albert Dickinson, Chicago; Root & Dow, St. Louis; Ira M. Davis & Co., Milwaukee; George Tait & Co., New Orleans; Littlefield, Webb & Co., San Francisco; Wooster, Shattuck & Co., San Francisco; E. H. Cowing & Co, Cincinnati; Ouerbacker, Gilmore & Co., Louisville.

HIBBARD BROTHERS, Agents,

Dealers in Jewelry and Silver-Plated Ware (Installment Plan)—No. 345 Main St., Up-stairs.

The plan of selling goods on installments has much to recommend it. In the first place, it enables tasteful people in cramped circumstances to make a respectable appearance on terms they can easily meet. Secondly, it encourages economy and thrift. And thirdly, it supplies customers with really good goods at prices which, taking into account the risks assumed by the seller, the expense of collection, interest on investment, etc., are actually but little higher than are usually demanded in spot cash by the regular trade.

The firm of Hibbard Brothers (J. W. & E. R. Hibbard), agents, No. 345 Main street, does the largest jewelry and silver-plated goods installment business of any house in Western New York, and gives unvarying satisfaction to its patrons. They established themselves here in a modest way in 1880, and gradually increased their trade until last year it reached an aggregate of $25,000, exclusively with Buffalo people, and entirely on installments. We are informed that the house is extremely lenient in its dealings with honest, responsible people, and has seldom resorted to harsh measures to make collections. All goods sold are delivered on receipt of the first payment, and the purchaser has the use of them pending the payment of deferred installments.

Repairing of all kinds of watches, jewelry, etc., promptly done and at reasonable rates. Out-of-town parties ordering goods or repairing will be at no expense for postage.

FISHER BROS. & CO.,

Maltsters—Proprietors of "City" and "Genesee" Malt-houses—Office, No. 283 West Genesee St.

Buffalo produces about five million bushels of malt per annum for export. Considering her advantages (including lake and railroad facilities, the near vicinity of the famous Canadian barley-growing region, etc.), this is not surprising. Unquestionably some of the largest malt-houses are located here, prominent among them those of Fisher Bros. & Co., two in number, known as the "Genesee" and "City," the former located at the intersection of Genesee, Canal and Erie streets, and the latter on West Genesee street, the capacity of both being 250,000 bushels per annum. In addition, the firm last December built a fine new storage elevator of 60,000 bushels capacity.

These great malt-houses are provided with every improved modern device in the way of machinery for the handling of grain and malt, and are among the most complete in the world, covering respectively ground 100 by 140 and 40 by 130 feet, each four stories in height. The new elevator is built upon the same scale of magnitude and completeness.

This conspicuous business enterprise was established in 1862 by Mr. George Fisher, and proved so successful that in 1865 he admitted his brother, Jacob P., and Mr. Philip Houck as partners. George Fisher is a native of France, born in 1820; Jacob P. Fisher was born in Erie county in 1835, and Philip Houck first saw the light in Germany in 1823.

FRED SCHULZ,

Custom Tailor—No. 78 East Eagle St.

Mr. Schulz, a recognized artist in all that pertains to the production of gentlemen's fine garments, established himself in 1885 at No. 385 Washington street, where, as "Our Custom Tailor," he became so popular and secured so liberal a run of custom, that he was obliged in October last to remove ro his present handsome place, where he has an elegantly appointed store and shop, 20 feet front by 40 feet deep, employs a strong force of competent cutters and tailors, and is better equipped than hitherto to meet the demands of a well-dressed public. Mr. Schulz is an artist in his profession, and has a well-earned reputation for correct taste, great skill, excellent judgment and the superior workmanship he furnishes his patrons, which, combined with promptitude in the execution of orders, and reasonable prices, render him popular and successful.

Mr. S. is of Prussian birth, and exhibits a medal earned in the Franco-German war, and presented by General Von Moltke. He has been in this country some twelve or thirteen years.

JOHN M. LUIPPOLD,

Proprietor East Side Brewery—No. 298 Emslie St.

One of the most striking features of the development of Buffalo's industrial resources is seen in the growth of the brewing business. It now ranks among the leading interests, both in the amount of capital invested and the number of men employed. Among those who have contributed largely to build up a reputation for the Queen City of the Lakes in this direction is John M. Luippold. The business was begun in a small way in 1868 by Mr. Luippold, on Emslie street, where his present magnificent brewery is located. The first year the number of barrels turned out did not exceed 2,000. An idea can be formed of the way the business has increased from the fact that the brewery now has a yearly output of 12,000 barrels. The East Side Brewery is one of the most complete in appointments in every particular of any in Buffalo. The buildings, which are of brick, and most substantially erected, cover an area of twenty-two lots situated on Emslie street, between William and Howard streets. It will not be inappropriate to state right here that the plant of the East Side Brewery represents a capital invested of $150,000. The brewery has all the modern improvements in the way of machinery, which includes an ice machine built by Lehmen & Son, of Cleveland. The consequence is, that Luippold's beer is conceded to be without any superior in Buffalo. It is mostly all consumed in the city.

Mr. Luippold has been a resident of Buffalo for the past forty years. He carried on the grocery business for sixteen years on the corner of Jefferson and William streets before starting the brewery. He is looked upon as one of the solid men of the city from a business point of view. His success has been due to strict attention to business and honorable dealing.

CITY LAUNDRY AND CUSTOM SHIRT FACTORY.

Established 1860—Miss M. E. Farmar, Proprietress—No. 9 West Eagle St.

The City Laundry, which claims the credit of being the oldest establishment of the kind in Buffalo, was first opened in 1850 by A. D. Sumner. His efforts were crowned with success, and the business steadily increased. In 1882 the concern passed into the hands of Miss M. E. Farmar, who for a considerable length of time had been employed as book-keeper. Since then evidences of her ability have become apparent in the improvements which have taken place. The laundry is fitted up with the most improved machinery to be found, and all work done is strictly first-class. There is a working force of thirty hands and the weekly pay-roll amounts to $160. An important feature of the business is the custom shirt work. The best of facilities are at hand for doing the finest work. Hand-work collars and cuffs are a specialty. In the entire direction of the business Miss Farmar has demonstrated the fact that woman's sphere in business is not so circumscribed as has been popularly supposed.

E. L. WINSHIP,

Wholesale Dealer in Foreign and Domestic Tobaccos, Cigars, Cigarettes and Snuffs—No. 11 Terrace.

Most Americans use tobacco in some form—we speak of the male biped, of course—and the trade in the weed is of astonishing proportions. Buffalo and the region tributary thereto chews and smokes and snuffs a fair proportion of the grand total, and consequently the trade here is very large. A representative house in this line is the great wholesale tobacco, cigar and snuff concern of E. L. Winship, No. 11 Terrace, which handles about $425,000 worth of goods per annum, embracing all grades, from the finest and most costly to the commonest and cheapest, the specialties being the renowned Kinney Bros.' cigarettes, fine imported Key West and domestic cigars, and the best and choicest brands of Virginia and Kentucky plug and fine-cut chewing tobaccos, together with Scotch and American snuff, smokers' goods, and fancy articles.

Mr. Winship is a native of Buffalo, established his present venture in 1874, and has made a study of the trade to which he caters. He carries an immense stock, selected especially for this market, sells only at wholesale for cash or to prompt time buyers, and offers the lowest market quotations. He deserves and has a liberal support.

JOHN KNEIS,

House, Sign, Fresco, Wagon and Carriage Painter—Graining, Kalsomining, Decorating, Wall Tinting, etc.—No. 21 Purdy St.

The house painter and frescoer may be fairly denominated the poet of architecture, bringing out, as he does, its beauties, softening its asperities, concealing or relieving its faults and adding to its effects. But the painter who would achieve fame and fortune thus must be a man of taste, skill and aptitude, conscientious and painstaking. Such a one is Mr. John Kneis, of No. 21 Purdy street, Buffalo. Mr. Kneis first established himself on Pearl street in 1881, removing to his present location in April, 1885. Here he has ample accommodations, comprising a fine lot 33 by 200 feet, upon which stands a commodious and convenient paint-shop 30 feet front and 60 feet in depth. Sixteen journeymen and apprentices are steadily employed, whose wages average $200 a week, Mr. Kneis' business footing up about $50,000 a year. His facilities are of the best, particularly for the doing of fine work. Among his recently completed contracts are : St. John's church, Buffalo Plains, painting; several residences for Mr. Hellriegel, president of German-American Bank, painting and frescoing; the Hayen building, frescoing, besides a number of superior jobs of frescoing for other parties.

Mr. Kneis was born in Sandusky, Ohio, in 1854. He was a member of the 65th N. G. S. N. Y. up to its disbandment, and is a good citizen in all respects. Among his references we note the name of Rev. Gerard H. Gyson, pastor of St. John's church, North Buffalo.

Mr. Kneis indulges his ingenuity occasionally on matters outside of his regular calling, and is the inventor of an improved incubator, manufactured by Axford & Bros., Chicago. Its capacity is forty-four dozen, which number of chicks it can turn out every twenty-one days, provided it is supplied with fresh, sound eggs and properly attended. It is a great thing, and will prove a blessing to the overworked hens of the country.

F. J. SCHAFER,

Merchant Tailor—No. 64 Arcade Building, Over No. 9 Clinton St.

Mr. F. J. Schafer has been engaged in the merchant tailoring business at his present location, Nos. 63 and 64 Arcade building, since 1878. He came to this city from Attica in 1875, having the advantage of a very thorough practical knowledge of the business in all its details. In everything pertaining to designing and making the most stylish garments for gentlemen's wear, Mr. Schafer is unsurpassed by any rivals in his line. The stock of imported and domestic suitings to be found on his counters is selected with the greatest care, and no pains are spared to please the most fastidious taste. When it comes to giving the greatest satisfaction for the money, it is simply giving the bald-headed truth the greatest publicity in saying in this connection that Mr. Schafer never allows any opposition to offer better inducements. The consequence is, when a good many other tailors are pining for something to do, Mr. Schafer is full of business. Hence, as a live, enterprising citizen, he finds himself represented in this work on the Industries of Buffalo.

VALENTINE GENTNER, JR.,

Manufacturing Jeweler—Plain, Chased and Seal Rings a Specialty—Badges, etc.—Nos. 16 and 18 East Eagle St.

The extent to which the manufacture of jewelers' specialties is carried on in this city is something remarkable. The representation is large and the volume of business done is of considerable importance. Among those engaged in the business who are already taking a leading position may be mentioned Mr. V. Gentner, jr. He started in the year 1883, and is now doing a business of $10,000 a year. The lines which Mr. Gentner represents are among the finest in the whole range of the jewelry business. The setting of diamonds is a feature in which this gentleman has achieved a well-earned reputation. Badges of all descriptions and plain, chased and seal rings are specialties with him, and for artistic finish and reliable material they are unsurpassed. He has been in the business thirteen years, and with several leading firms. A native of Germany, Mr. Gentner came to Buffalo in 1860. A working force of twelve men is required, and it is not a rash presumption that in time this establishment will acknowledge no superior, either in this city or elsewhere.

SAMUEL McCUTCHEON,

Steamboat and Engineers' Supplies—Copper, Tin and Sheet Iron Manufacturing—No. 18 Ohio St.

One of the important industries of this city is associated with handling the supplies needed by engineers and steamcraft generally. For more than a quarter of a century past the well-known house of Samuel McCutcheon has been identified with this branch of business at the old stand, No. 18 Ohio street. The premises here occupied consist of a well-equipped four-story building, where the manufacture of copper, tin and sheet iron work is extensively carried on. Special attention has always been given to steamboat, vessel, brewery and distillery work. In this direction Mr. McCutcheon claims that from his long and successful experience in the business, and intimate knowledge of the work and material required, he is able to guarantee the best results. His establishment is completely stocked with a superior line of goods, such as brass cocks, globe valves and couplings of all kinds, iron pipe and fittings, also leather and rubber hose and hose pipes, steam packing, and all kinds of rubber goods. The house is also agent for the Davidson steam pump, Amazon boiler compound, and Orme patent safety and relief valve. As may be supposed, the business of the house is widely distributed and aggregates a large volume annually.

Originally the style of the firm was Brown & McCutcheon. In 1875 Mr. Brown retired, and since then it has been as noted, Samuel McCutcheon. This gentleman is a native of New York city, where he acquired a knowledge of the business. His career in Buffalo has been one of uninterrupted success, due to the judicious management given the business.

A. J. GRAD,

Carriage and Wagon Manufacturer—No. 718 Broadway.

Mr. Grad is the direct successor of Eugene Hickman, who established this prosperous industry in 1875, Mr. Grad taking possession in 1886. He has a very commodious and well-appointed three-story factory, built of brick, the front building, 30 by 40 feet, containing the warerooms, paint shop and blacksmith shop, the rear, of same dimensions, containing the wood-working department. Nine men are steadily employed, who turn out from $8,000 to $9,000 worth of finished work per annum, most of which is custom work for city patrons.

Every description of fine and medium buggy and wagon work, together with repairing, repainting and blacksmithing, is done in the best manner at this establishment, at moderate prices and promptly.

Mr. Grad was born in this city—Sixth ward—in 1858, and has followed his present vocation since early youth. His is the leading concern of the kind out Broadway, and is growing in importance.

URBAN & CO.,

Proprietors of the Urban Roller Mill—Wholesale Dealers in Flour, Feed, Grain, etc.—Nos. 381 and 383 Ellicott and 324 and 326 Oak St.

George Urban established this firm in 1846 as flour dealers. The present mill has all the modern improvements in milling, as it was built in 1881, since the revolution in milling caused by the introduction of the roller system, and was the first complete roller mill in Buffalo. All new improvements are added as soon as discovered, and the flour kept in the front rank. Mr. Urban, senior, admitted his son, George, jr., as partner in 1870. In 1875 Mr. E. G. S. Miller was admitted to the firm, and in 1882 Mr. Urban's youngest son, William C., was admitted. In 1885 Mr. George Urban, sr., retired, and the remaining partners continued as Urban & Co.

The mill itself is a fine five-story brick building, 40 by 100 feet, on Ellicott street, opposite the Washington market, while a three-story office and warehouse, 40 by 90 feet, fronts on Oak street, Messrs. Urban & Co. making it a point to keep a full supply of everything in the flour line constantly on hand, the bakers' trade especially being able to get from their stock any kind or kinds of flour they may call for, while the product of the mill has from the first taken the lead. Their "Pearl" brand of flour, made from a combination of spring and winter wheats, is especially a favorite as a family flour, while only the finest of No. 1 hard wheat is used for their "Urban's Best" and "Bakers'" flour.

DR. JOHN T. CLARIS,

Veterinary Surgeon and Proprietor of the East Side Horse Infirmary—Nos. 627 and 629 Clinton St.

The importance of the successful treatment of the diseases of horses and cattle, especially the former, has been exemplified by the conspicuous position now occupied by veterinary schools. Probably the one with the most widely extended reputation is the Ontario Veterinary College, located at Toronto. Our neighbors across the border have taken an advanced position in this specialty, the institution referred to being under the direction of the Ontario government. Among the most successful graduates of this college is Dr. John T. Claris, who in 1882 located in this city. He immediately began business in a manner which indicated that he was bound to make a splendid success of his chosen profession. Securing a well-located site, corner of Clinton and Adams streets, Dr. Claris proceeded to erect a commodious horse infirmary which should contain features not possessed by any similar one in Western New York. When completed the new building met his expectations, and its record since demonstrates the utility of its design. It is a most substantially constructed three-story brick with cut stone trimmings, and is 30 by 110 feet in dimensions. The office and laboratory are elegantly and completely appointed. Coming to the interior arrangements, there are thirty-eight single and ten box stalls, all scientifically permeated with steam pipes, which insure the proper temperature. This feature is peculiar to this establishment, and is of vital importance during cold weather in the successful treatment of all respiratory diseases. The cost of the building complete was $15,000, and the results have amply justified the outlay.

Dr. Claris' success in the treatment of horse ailments has been remarkable, and his reputation has gone abroad as a skillful and accomplished veterinary surgeon. He has been ably assisted by Dr. E. W. Anderson since the infirmary was opened, and one or the other is always present. From the foregoing it can be inferred that any cases intrusted to this popular institution are sure of the best treatment. Dr. Claris is a courteous gentleman and will be found a reliable man of business. Among his preparations is Dr. Claris' celebrated veterinary ointment, a valuable remedy for scratches, cracked heels, sore backs and shoulders, cuts, wounds, and all surface diseases of horses and cattle. His anti-chill and fever medicine is invaluable for the cure of inflammatory diseases, particularly chills, fevers, congestion and inflammation of the lungs, coughs, colds, colic, staggers, etc.

12

(See opposite page.)

OF BUFFALO.

J. F. Moulton, President; James Adams, Vice-President; J. M. Brinker, Treasurer; W. S. Frear, Secretary; J. C. Weber, Superintendent—Works, Seventh, Wilkeson and Mohawk Sts.; Executive Office, Room 6, Coal and Iron Exchange.

Thanks to the progressive spirit of a few resolute and influential citizens, Buffalo enjoys the enviable distinction of being one of the best lighted, and consequently one of the safest cities, for life and property, on the continent, and her broad, handsomely-built thoroughfares are indeed an inspiring sight after nightfall, when hundreds of glittering electric lamps shed their far-reaching refulgence on every hand.

From the *Electrical Review* we glean the subjoined interesting summary of the early history of electric lighting in Buffalo:

The subject of electric lighting was first agitated in Buffalo early in 1881, and a company organized and incorporated March 28th of that year, known as the "Buffalo Electric Light Company," with a capital stock of $100,000; John F. Moulton, president; A. P. Wright, vice-president, and H. G. Nolton, secretary and treasurer.

Through the efforts of the Brush Electric Company of Cleveland, and before any operations had been commenced, the Buffalo Electric Light Company sold all rights of way, etc., to the Brush Electric Light Company of Buffalo, incorporated June 1st, 1881, with the following officers: John F. Moulton, president; James Adams, vice-president, and H. G. Nolton, secretary and treasurer.

The company first started a forty-light station on the "Island," where there were no gas mains, and subsequently lighted Ganson street with twelve lamps at $5,000 per year. Two additional stations were soon put into operation, and wires rapidly extended to accommodate the fast increasing demand for more brilliancy than the old illuminants were capable of furnishing. The prices adopted at the outset were fifty cents for half-night lights and seventy-five cents for all-night lights, yearly contracts being required and strictly adhered to, having no competing company to cut rates. In July, 1882, the capacity of the company was about two hundred lights, and at that time a contract was secured with the city to light portions of the most prominent streets, requiring forty lamps, for which the city paid sixty-five cents per light per night.

The opposition of the gas companies did not commence to be felt to any great extent until June, 1883, when, having further extended the plant, the electric light company were naturally desirous of an increased amount of the city's patronage, and made a bid to light the public streets at fifty-five cents per night per light. At the inception of the electric light company, gas cost private consumers $2.50 per thousand and $2 to the city for street lighting, and $2.25 for public buildings. Through the effects of electricity's advent this was forced to $2.25, $1 80 and $2 respectively in 1882. The city's contract with the gas companies expired in August, 1883, and the encroaching electric light company attracted the righteous indignation of the gas producers and war was declared. The fight in the common council waged hot and heavy. A majority favored electric light, and three times in as many months the mayor, favoring gas, vetoed the resolution of the common council authorizing contracts to be made with the electric light company for lighting a large amount of territory. In October a compromise was effected, by which the electric light company secured 125 additional lights at fifty-five cents per light, but not before the gas companies were compelled by their opposition to decrease the price of gas to $1.60 to the city and $1.80 to private consumers. At this time the price of gas is $1.50 per 1,000 to private consumers and $1.40 to the city, a reduction from $2.50 when the company started that the Brush Electric Light Company claim full credit for and generally receive. The present council and mayor are friendly to the extension of the district to be lighted with electricity, and numerous additions have been voted since January, 1886.

The plan of small or sub-stations was found to be too expensive, and steps taken to concentrate the power which have produced what experts are pleased to term "the best equipped electric lighting station in the country." The building, erected in 1884, is 120 by 180 feet in area, two stories in height, and the ground floor is devoted to the boilers and furnaces, the battery consisting of 12 steel 100-horse-power boilers of late improved pattern, provided with smokeless furnaces that consume soft coal slack. The smoke-stack is eight feet square at the base and 115 feet high. In the generator room, 40 by 120 feet, are 21 Westinghouse upright automatic engines of 65 horse-power each—one for each of the 21 Brush dynamos'and two incandescent machines—one the United States patent, the other a Westinghouse—designed for competition with gas in interior lighting. Adam, Meldrum & Anderson's dry goods establishment and the Tift house were lighted by this system in November—the first with 400, the latter with 200 lamps of sixteen-candle-power—a much better and safer light, at less cost than gas, however cheap the latter. The capacity of the Brush dynamo is 65 lamps of 2,000 candle-power each, or a power of illumination equal to 130,000 candles.

In this city the company has now in actual use about 300 miles of conducting wire and over six hundred poles for city lighting—a showing that will be vastly increased during the present year. In anticipation thereof a substantial new brick building, 100 by 100 feet, has been erected adjoining the old one, thus providing ample room for any required augmentation of plant. At present 50 or more men are required, including linemen, firemen, engineers, lamp-trimmers, repairers, etc. As a matter of economy a large stock of material is carried at all times to meet emergencies in the way of extensions and repairs. Mr. Albert J. Weber, a brother of the superintendent, is general foreman.

THE HINTERMISTER ORGAN AND PIANO CO.
(Limited),

Manufacturers of The Hintermister Organ and Piano—Nos. 198 and 200 Terrace.

Of Buffalo's more recently established industries, one of the most notable is the fine factory of the Hintermister Organ and Piano Co., Nos. 198 and 200 Terrace, established in 1884. The chairman of the company, M. J. H. Hintermister, a native of Zurich, Switzerland, is one of the most accomplished makers of these instruments in the world, having had an experience extending over forty years in Europe and this country. He resides at Oil City, Pa., while his son, Mr. F. A. Hintermister, is manager of the works here. The latter is a native of Ithaca, N. Y., has been connected with the organ trade all his life, is a practical workman, and a master of the business in all its details.

A visit to the factory and salesrooms is full of interest and instruction. The company occupy a handsome four-story building, 32 by 107 feet, with commodious basement, and at this time employ ten finished workmen, a force that will be added to as opportunity offers to secure competent instrument makers. A fine equipment of ingenious and costly machinery forms a valuable portion of the plant, and the capacity is sufficient to meet present demands. The sales for the past year aggregated about $15,000, but the prospect is that 1887 will see that figure more than doubled. The specialty of the house is the celebrated Hintermister organ, an instrument that has made for itself a splendid reputation in the face of the severest opposition from rival manufacturers. It is a singularly perfect organ, beautifully made and finished and remarkably sweet in touch and tone, and, though we do not profess a profound knowledge of music, we must say that we have never heard more delightful sounds than were evoked from one of these instruments for our delectation.

The house has a general trade all over the country, particularly in the oil region, Western Pennsylvania, Pittsburg and Detroit.

WILLIAM H. SLOCUM,

Official Stenographer to the Supreme Court, Eighth Judicial District of New York; Principal of Slocum's Stenographic School; Patentee of Slocum's Improved Type-Writer, and Agent for the Remington Standard Type-Writer—Rooms 50, 51, 52 and 53 Chapin Block, No. 17 West Swan St.

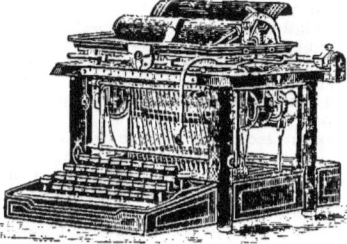

To the intelligent and industrious young man or woman having his or her own way to make in life and sufficiently cultivated and refined to care for superior associations, no other pursuit offers so many attractions as the study and practice of stenography; and when to a thorough knowledge of this most useful art is added a mastery of the type-writer and a liberal fund of general information obtained from books and current literature, no better equipment for the battle of life could be desired, for positions are always open to its possessors—positions in which good pay, and, what is better, habitual contact with practical men of affairs, bankers, merchants, capitalists, professional men, authors, editors, scientists, etc., are assured, and a vista of advancement at once opened to them, full of promise and of splendid possibilities.

Slocum's Stenographic School, rooms 50 to 53 Chapin block, No. 17 West Swan street, Buffalo, stands in the front rank of those institutions which fit the young men and women of America for careers of usefulness, independence and possible distinction. A complete and finishing course is given in the rudiments and higher branches of stenography in any of the popular systems of the day—Graham's being the standard—together with careful training in penmanship and type-writing, six months being the time usually required, and the fee in both branches being $50. A neat pamphlet containing all necessary information will be mailed to any address on application to the principal.

THE REMINGTON STANDARD TYPE-WRITER.—Mr. Slocum is general agent for the famous Remington Standard type-writer for Buffalo and vicinity. He carries a complete line of these popular machines, and is prepared to fill orders for the same at factory prices. It is unnecessary to either describe or praise the "Remington Standard," which is the best-known, most popular, oldest and most universally used of all typewriters. Catalogue and price-list mailed when desired.

SLOCUM'S IMPROVED TYPE-WRITER.— The Improved Type-Writer, illustrated herewith, is of Mr. Slocum's own invention, patented February 9, 1886. The cut was made from the original model, and a number of more or less important changes and modifications have been introduced previous to offering the machine to the public. *Sunday Truth* of February 28 prints the subjoined very clear and concise description of the new caligraphic instrument: The key-board is about ten inches in width and the extreme length of the machine about 13 inches, and its height, including carriage, 6 inches. Point A represents the fulcrum of the type levers, B the guide for the type bar, and C the joint of the type bar, and figure 2 shows a detached key on which D is the fulcrum and E the joint. Figure 3 shows the universal guide, against the under side of which each letter strikes as the key is depressed, causing the type bar to slide from the right

or left to the center, then rising vertically to the paper. Figures 2 and 3 do not represent the parts accurately, but show the principle, and how they operate.

A spring is placed under and forward of the fulcrum on each type lever, which carries the key upward and causes the type bar to follow the guide back to its normal position after the letter is printed. The feeding mechanism consists of two rack bars placed side by side, firmly attached to each other with alternate teeth pointing downward, underneath which is a vertical wheel with square cogs, against which the teeth of the rack bar are successively engaged. As the wheel is rotated, the cog which arrests a tooth of the first rack bar is passed by that tooth, which tooth then passes between the cogs of the wheel, and the double rack bar moves ahead and the second part of the double rack bar engages the same cog as the first rack bar tooth did.

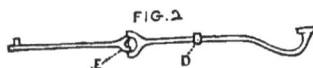

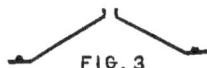

The next movement of the wheel allows the second rack bar to be released, and a tooth of the first rack bar is engaged by a cog as before, and so on, continuously. By this feed it is impossible to have any skipping of letters, or failure of the carriage to move, and it is capable of quicker action than any feed upon machines in present use.

Upon depressing a key the type bar follows the universal guide and delivers the impression. As soon as the finger leaves the key the type bar resumes its normal position, at the same time, by a simple mechanism, rotates the wheel one tooth, which allows the rack bar to travel one space.

It will be observed that while each type bar on its upward movement follows the universal guide shown in figure 8, on its return it does not follow that guide back, but drops directly into place between the individual guides, B.

This movement allows almost perfect freedom of operation of any two adjoining type bars, as one type bar following the universal guide to the center will not interfere with the other bar returning to its place of rest.

In all of the machines constructed with type bars in a concentric ring, each bar is compelled to describe an arc of nearly or quite forty-five degrees. In this machine the levers raise only about twelve degrees of a circle.

It will be seen that each letter is guided to the center by the positive universal guide, and there will consequently be an impossibility of any letter getting out of alignment after once having been placed in position, as the latter part of the guide is of only sufficient width to allow the type bar to pass.

The fulcrum joint is attached to a plate by two screws through slotted holes, allowing the lever to be moved forward or backward to place the letters in perfect alignment.

Perfect impression of the type can easily be made at an angle of 60 degrees. There are only about one-third the number of pieces used in the construction of this machine that there is in any other of the leading machines before the public.

Several parties formerly connected with the manufacture and sale of other type-writing machines now upon the market unhesitatingly acknowledge its simplicity, and that it possesses points of superiority over every other machine that has yet been exhibited. The principal points in favor of this machine are:

1. Rapidity and ease of action.
2. Impossibility of losing its alignment.
3. Simplicity of construction, all parts being made of metal, hence will not be affected by dampness.
4. All parts liable to wear are provided with simple adjustments, which unskillful operators can adjust.
5. It can be built and sold for one-half the price of other first-class machines.
6. Its weight is only ten pounds, and occupies less space than any other machine upon the market.

Mr. Slocum has had flattering offers for his patent, but prefers to either manufacture them here or allow them to be made on a royalty. He now has five other patents pending for improvements in type-writers, and his inventive genius is not confined to this branch of mechanics. A lead-pencil sharpener which does its work quickly and perfectly, and never breaks the points, will soon be placed upon the market by him.

Mr. Slocum is personally a very popular, public-spirited gentleman, and a good citizen. In addition to the arduous duties of his stenographic school and type-writer depot, he is president of the Buffalo Mutual Accident Association, noticed at length on another page.

A. H. BROWN,

Machine Shop and Brass Foundry—Copper and Sheet Iron Work, General Repairing, Engineers' Supplies—Nos. 16, 18 and 20 Elk St.

Owing to the vast amount of engine and machine-building done here, there is probably no better location in America for the skillful worker in metals than Buffalo, the terminus of lake navigation and of so many railroads stretching away to every point of the compass, and the seat of a vast manufacturing interest.

One of the oldest and most favorably known of Buffalo's machinists, brass founders and sheet-metal workers is Mr. A. H. Brown, Nos. 16, 18 and 20 Elk street, who has resided here since 1838. Up to 1854 he was a lake steamer engineer, then for four years chief engineer of the American Transportation Co., and in 1859 established himself in business at his present location. He is of Irish birth, removing at the age of three years, with his parents, to Montgomery county, Pa.

Mr. Brown's works occupy a convenient three-story brick building, 45 by 51 feet square, and give employment to from twelve to twenty-five hands, according to the requirements of trade and season, and does a steady and flourishing business.

Mr. Brown does every description of light machine work, sells one of the best steam governors in use, and has on hand a full line of water and steam gauges, copper and sheet iron work for tanners, brewers and others, gives attention to repairs of all kinds in his line, carries a superior stock of engineers' supplies, and makes specialties of railroad and steamboat brass castings, steam fitting, Cameron steam pumps, brass goods, rubber and leather hose and packing, crucibles, etc.

JOHN KAM,

Maltster—Malthouses, Nos. 410 and 436 Pratt and Corner Genesee and Pratt Sts. ; Office, No. 377 Genesee, Corner Pratt St.

Buffalo's maltsters annually produce and ship rather more than less than 5,000,000 bushels of superior malt, principally from the famous Canadian barley, which it is claimed has no equal for that purpose. Some thirty firms and individuals are engaged in this industry, employing hundreds of operatives and many millions of dollars capital. One of the most prosperous and successful of the Queen City's maltsters is Mr. John Kam, who began operations in a small way at No. 377 Genesee street some eighteen or nineteen years ago. Himself a skillful maltster, industrious and thrifty, he found ready sale for every bushel he could produce at the highest market prices, and soon found himself obliged to increase his facilities. In 1872 he built the fine malt-house No. 436 Pratt street, 40 by 50 feet square and three stories in height; eight years later he erected the large and commodious establishment at No. 410 Pratt street, at first three stories, 125 by 160 feet, but enlarged in 1884 by the addition of four floors, thus securing the advantage of vastly increased floorage without extra expenditure for land. He also continues to occupy his original stand, No. 377 Genesee street, where he has two malting floors and his office. He employs twenty to thirty hands and all necessary machinery of the latest improved kinds, and has ample facilities for the manufacture of 200,000 bushels annually.

Mr. Kam's skillfully made malt is in demand among brewers at home, and is largely shipped to the trade all over Western New York, to the metropolis, Brooklyn, Newark, Baltimore, Cleveland and elsewhere.

Mr. K. is of German birth, came to Buffalo more than thirty years ago, and has made malting the business of his life. He is ably assisted in the office and malt-houses by his sons, Henry and Joseph, energetic, enterprising, wide-awake young men.

F. S. PEASE,

Manufacturer of Refined Petroleum, Illuminating and Lubricating Oils, Paints, Artists' Materials, etc.—Nos. 65 and 67 Main, 82, 84 and 86 Washington Sts.

The subject of illuminating and lubricating oils is of direct interest to people of every condition and in every walk of life, for it is one that immediately c o n c e r n s and influences manufactures, commerce and domestic economy. Mr. F. S. Pease, the p r o m inent manufacturer of and dealer in refined petroleum oils for lubricating and illuminating purposes, whose commodious establishment at Nos. 65 and 67 Main and 82, 84 and 86 Washington streets, is widely and favorably known to the trade and consumers, may safely be called a public benefactor, since he has attained to a wonderful degree of perfection in the manipulation of this subtle and even yet somewhat mysterious fluid, removing from it by his peculiar and approved processes nearly if not quite all of its objectionable and dangerous elements. His high fire test, colorless, odorless, non-explosive illuminating oil, refined and prepared expressly for domestic use, is confessedly equal if not superior to any article of the kind ever offered to the public. As an evidence of its high grade, and, indeed, of all of Mr. Pease's products, it may be stated here that his goods were awarded prize medals at the world's expositions of London, 1862 ; Paris, 1867; Vienna, 1873; Santiago, 1875; the Centennial, 1876; Paris, 1878; New York, 1878 ; Baltimore, 1878; Chicago, 1878 ; Sidney, 1879; Melbourne, 1880, and the National Exposition of Railway Appliances, Chicago, 1883.

Mr. Pease has been established here as a refiner and dealer in oils, paints, artists' materials, etc., since 1848, and consequently has a high reputation, earned by a long and honorable career, to sustain; therefore the grade of his goods may be at all times relied upon as standard. His place of business, 50 by 150 feet and four stories in height, is one of the most complete and conveniently arranged in the country. Some fifteen or twenty men are employed in the various departments, and the annual output aggregates several hundred thousand dollars in value, finding a market not only in the United States but in Europe. No travelers are employed, and the sales of the house are based on merit only.

J. WIESBAUER,

Manufacturer of Jewelers' Findings—No. 410 Main St.

The variety of manufactures in the city of Buffalo demonstrates the fact that in the near future this city is bound to become one of the leading industrial centers of the country. In the pages of this work will be found reference to all the different lines. As an illustration, a few remarks will be made in regard to the business done by Mr. J. Wiesbauer, manufacturer of jewelers' findings. The term is a very comprehensive one, and calls for specific mention. As is well known, the jewelry trade requires a long line of articles, specially made for the purpose of displaying wares to the best advantage. This has created a branch of business of considerable importance. Mr. Wiesbauer gives his attention entirely to the manufacture of such specialties as fine trays, plush, velvet and morocco cases, etc. He is sole manufacturer of Fowler's patent material cabinet, which is one of the most useful cabinets known to the trade. Wood mailing and express boxes, tags, cords and the entire range of such and kindred requisites are among the goods which are manufactured. Mr. Wiesbauer has been in the business since 1877, and his is the only complete establishment of the kind west of New York. Possessing the best of facilities, he is able to meet competition from any quarter. The annual business amounts to about $25,000 a year, which indicates what its extent and possibilities are. He also keeps two travelers constantly on the road.

N. P. CHANEY & CO.

Feather Beds, Pillows and Hair Mattresses Renovated by Steam—Mattresses, Bedsteads, Springs, etc.—No. 818 Main St.

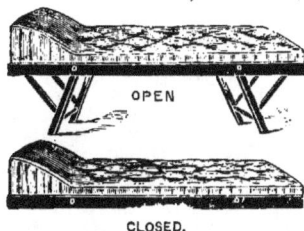

OPEN

CLOSED.

Around the city of Buffalo the chronicler of her various industrial interests can find ample material to write about. People are becoming more enlightened every day of the importance, from a sanitary point of view, of the frequent renovating of feather beds, hair mattresses, pillows, etc. Too much care cannot be taken in such a matter of vital importance to health and comfort. The firm of N. P. Chaney & Co., No. 818 Main street, have exceptionally good facilities for doing this work by a steam process. Mr. Chaney is the patentee of what is probably the most efficient renovating machine for this purpose in use at the present time. No chemicals are used, and after going through the process the goods come out as clean as when new.

This firm also manufacture Chaney's improved upholstered cot and lounge, which is conceded, by all who have seen and used it, to be the most complete cot ever introduced. It is light and easily handled, made with spiral springs, and is equal in sleeping qualities to any bed. It is a bed and lounge complete, and at one-half the cost of an ordinary lounge. There is also kept in stock a full line of mattresses made of the best hair. Fibres, husk, sea-grass and mixed mattresses, with bedsteads, cribs, cots, springs, live geese feathers and all bed furnishings, are constantly kept in stock. Mr. Chaney is a thoroughly practical man and fully understands all the details of the business. The trade is large and on the increase.

KEHR & DUFFY,

General Machinists—Builders of Steam Yacht, Stationary, Marine and Portable Engines, Pulleys, Hangers and Shafting—Dealers in New and Second-hand Boilers and Engines—General Repairers, etc.—No. 93 Washington St.

The building of steam engines for all purposes on land and water is an industry in which Buffalo mechanics excel and in which they are renowned throughout the length and breadth of the continent. One firm that is doing much to augment the fame of the Queen City in this specialty is that of Kehr & Duffy, founded by Mr. Geo. H. Kehr in 1881, and strengthened by the accession of Mr. James Duffy in 1885. This very skillful firm of machinists occupy the first and second floors, each 30 by 60 feet, of the commodious brick building No. 93 Washington street, where they have well-appointed shops provided with all required machinery of the latest improved kinds, and employ a competent force of first-class workmen, turning out many thousands dollars' worth of superior work every year, most of which is disposed of at home, but much is made to order for shipment to other States.

The specialties of the house embrace every description of yacht, stationary, marine and portable steam engines of modern pattern, embracing in their construction various practical and useful improvements devised or patented by the members of the firm. These engines are of all sizes, in all styles, and of the finest material and workmanship. The house also carries a large stock of new and second-hand boilers and upright engines of various sizes, and manufacture pulleys, hangers and shafting to order, besides giving prompt and careful attention to repairs of engines, boilers, steam pumps and machinery of all kinds, the testing of boilers and the purchase and sale of new and second-hand boilers and engines, and the construction of improved dredge machinery and friction clutches.

Mr. Kehr came to Buffalo from Connecticut, of which State he is a native, in 1850. Mr. Duffy was reared here. Both have devoted their entire active lives to their present pursuit, are ingenious and successful men and worthy citizens.

FROM M & CO.

Wholesale Manufacturers of Lounges—Nos. 360 DeWitt St. and 1335 West Ave., Black Rock.

This energetic young firm, formerly Fromm & Blandford, is coming rapidly to the front, and bids fair ere long to take rank with Buffalo's leading manufacturers. Founded as recently as March, 1886, it is already turning out goods at the rate of $30,000 worth per annum and of the best grades, making an exclusive specialty of lounges in all styles, of superior design, material and workmanship. The original firm was dissolved on the 18th of January by the withdrawal Mr. J. T. Blandford. A reorganization under the present firm name was at once effected, composed of Messrs. John W. Fromm, Clifford R. Orr and John R. Ash. Their factory occupies a commodious two-story frame building, Nos. 360 DeWitt street and 1335 West avenue, fronting 60 feet on the first and 15 feet on the last-named thoroughfare. This building is of irregular shape, and is in fact equal in dimensions to one 45 by 80 feet, with wings, one 30 by 50, the other 40 by 50 feet. Besides a full complement of woodworking and other machinery twenty-five workmen are employed, and every facility is at hand for doing a large and growing business. Mr. John W. Fromm is a native of Buffalo, and all members of the firm are men of push and industry. Mr. Fromm was for a time superintendent of the late H. J. Comstock's renowned lounge works on Court street. The house is therefore headed by a practical mechanic, who has worked his way to the position of employer by the exercise of push and skill. The firm already control much of the best trade of Buffalo and vicinity, and are extending their connections throughout this and adjoining States.

J. LANGDON & CO.—Incorporated.

C. J. Langdon, President; J. D. F. Slee, Vice-President; T. W. Crane, Treasurer; C. M. Underhill, Western Manager; C. N. Shipman, Secretary — Anthracite and Bituminous Coal—Office, Rooms 1 and 2 Chapin Block, No. 17 West Swan Street.

The coal transactions of the city and port of Buffalo aggregate about 10,000,000 tons, of which grand total the above-named corporation handles about one-tenth, or 1,000,000 tons, comprising the best grades of anthracite and bituminous fuel, shipping to the West.

The company has its principal office at Elmira. The branch office here, rooms 1 and 2 Chapin block, is in charge of Mr. C. M. Underhill, the western manager, who superintends the business of the company at this point in an able and satisfactory manner. The yards at the foot of Genesee street front 300 feet, with a like depth on the Erie basin, and furnish ample facilities for the storage and shipment of coal in cargoes or such quantities as may be desired. It is scarcely necessary to say that all orders receive prompt attention and are filled with dispatch at the lowest ruling quotations.

President C. J. Langdon is a native of and resides in Elmira. He is a conspicuous figure in business circles, connected with the La France Fire Engine Manufacturing Co. and several other well-known enterprises. Vice-President Slee and Treasurer Crane are also prominent citizens and business men of Elmira. Secretary Shipman also resides in Elmira. Mr. Underhill, manager of the company's western interests, has been actively engaged in the handling of coal for the past twenty years, fifteen of which were passed in Buffalo. He is a native of Wayne county, an upright gentleman and a business man of great executive ability.

BEALS & BROWN,

Successors to Pratt & Co.—Iron, Steel, Nails, Hardware, Bolts, Nuts, Washers —Contractors', Mechanics', Shop and Manufacturers' Supplies, etc.—The Old Stand, Terrace Square.

No more famous iron and hardware concern ever existed in this country than the old house of Pratt & Co., who for over half a century led the trade of Western New York. On the 30th of March, 1886, the renowned and ancient firm was dissolved, Mr. Pascal P. Pratt, the senior member, who had been identified with the house from its inception, withdrawing entirely from business life save in so far as his presidency of the Manufacturers and Traders Bank, while Mr. Edward P. Beals, the junior member, who had occupied that station for forty years, formed a new partnership with Mr. David E. Brown, who during the preceding twenty-four years filled satisfactorily and successfully the station of business manager, and thus the same day that saw the retirement of Mr. Pratt also witnessed the succession and installation of the new house of Beals & Brown, the entire stock, buildings, fixtures, good-will and established trade and high reputation of the former firm passing unreservedly into their hands. Referring to this important business change, the *News* of April 8, said:

"The brief announcement hitherto made of the dissolution of Pratt & Co., and the formation of a new firm under the name of Beals & Brown to administer its business, has challenged attention very generally throughout the country. The name of Pratt has for half a century been a very bright one in the commercial world, with its sales aggregating as high as the enormous sum of three millions of dollars a year, its customers scattered over every city and cross-roads in the country, and its reputation extending to every market for iron and hardware in the world.

"The succession has fallen into good hands. While the retirement of Mr. Pascal P. Pratt will of course be regretted, the advent of the former junior partner, Mr. Edward P. Beals, will give particular satisfaction. As the leading partner his invaluable experience and his ability as a financier will have a telling effect upon the fortunes of the new craft which seeks the popular favor under such auspicious breezes.

" The junior partner, Mr. David E. Brown, is none other than the urbane and progressive manager who for twenty-four years has made the success of the old house his daily and nightly study. No man in this country controls a larger *clientele* of friends or a wider acquaintance among the members of the hardware trade. He is all vigor and enterprise."

The new firm have enlarged the business with the addition of all classes of goods required in machine shops and for general metal manufacturing purposes, and established a supply depot patterned something after the large iron and steel supply establishments existing in New York and Boston.

The premises occupied by Messrs. Beals & Brown are 80 feet front on the Terrace, extend back to the canal, are four stories in height, especially arranged in every department for the storage, display and sale of all goods pertaining to the hardware and metal trade, and carry the largest, best and most varied stock of these commodities offered by any establishment west of the metropolis. Moderate profits and prompt attention to orders is the motto of the house, which cannot fail to lead it to greater triumphs in the future than it ever achieved in the past. Both partners are native Buffalonians.

JAMES COYLE,

Wagon-Maker and General Blacksmith—Nos. 150 and 152 Ohio St.

Mr. Coyle is a thoroughly accomplished mechanic, practically conversant with every detail of his trade, an unexcelled blacksmith and wagon-maker. He came to Buffalo from the north of Ireland more than thirty-six years ago, and has been busy ever since constructing first-class heavy vehicles for the merchants, teamsters, farmers and others of the city and vicinity, all of whom know and hundreds of whom patronize him. He began on his own account in 1869, and from the first has prospered, doing a business of $8,000 to $10,000 per annum. His leading specialty is the building of heavy wagons for transferring freight, hauling lumber, stone, brick, coal, etc., and his success therein is conceded. He also gives considerable attention to the manufacture of iron-box wheel-barrows, warehouse and propeller trucks, heavy drays, etc., for which class of work he has a steady demand, and gives unvarying satisfaction. Mr. Coyle employs a competent force of skilled help, and occupies two two-story buildings—one of brick, 70 by 150 feet, the other frame, 70 by 152 feet.

HENRY D. KELLER,

Successor to Keller & Boller—Importer and Jobber of Wines, Liquors and Cigars, and Wholesale Grocer—No. 458 Washington St.

The sales of wines and liquors in this market are very large in the aggregate, though the number of wholesale houses handling first-class goods is limited. One of the most extensive of these—perhaps, indeed, the heaviest of the kind in Buffalo—is that of Henry D. Keller, twenty-one years a wine and liquor merchant, No. 473 Main street. Mr. Keller was one of the founders of the concern —Ripont & Keller—who first opened it in 1865. In 1877 the firm of Keller & Boller was established, and remained so until Mr. Boller died. In 1886 Mr. Keller took sole control. From the first the venture was successful, and has prospered.

No. 458 Washington street is three stories high, with a great basement extending under the whole. The stock carried is one of the largest in the city, and selected with special reference to the requirements of this market, embracing all the leading brands of imported and domestic wines, brandies, whiskies, rums, gins, cigars, tobaccos, etc. Some of the wines in stock are very old and fine. Casks of delicious California and Ohio wines lie there tier upon tier, much of it so old and ripe that it would tempt an anchorite, while of the other liquors the stock is always kept up to the mark in quality and quantity.

A leading specialty of the house is the renowned " Old Petrie " whisky, a *fac-simile* of the brand of which we print herewith. This whisky is sold strictly upon its merits, and is known to the trade and experienced consumers as a strictly pure whisky of the best quality. It is popular with all who know good liquor wherever introduced. The brand belongs to Mr. Keller, and as he controls this brand the trade will do well to communicate with him. He is proud of this whisky and of its reputation, and will do all that is right and reasonable in filling orders for it.

BITTER & KASSON,

Sole Manufacturers of the " Buffalo " Railroad, Lubricating and Axle Grease and Harness Oil—Works, Foot of Brace St.; Office, No. 476 Main St.

Few persons outside of manufacturing, railroad and steam-navigation circles have any adequate idea of the cost of lubricating machinery and rolling stock. For many years constant and measurably successful efforts have been directed to the improvement of lubricants and the consequent effecting of a saving in this item of expense, and it cannot be denied that much has been accomplished, the actual cost of oils, wear and tear being now fully twenty-five per cent. less for the same service than it was twenty years ago—a result due to scientific research and a proper understanding of the relative value of various greases singly and in combination.

Of the more successful and popular lubricants, resulting of late years from intelligent experiment, few if any have given such general satisfaction to consumers as the famous " Buffalo " railroad grease, lubricating grease, axle grease and harness oil, manufactured by Bitter & Kasson of this city—greases that are unaffected by high or low temperatures and that combine perfect lubricating properties with the maximum of service and the minimum of waste. They have already been introduced very extensively among the railroads, machine-shops, ocean, lake and river steamers, manufacturers of leather and leather goods, etc., of this country, in all cases have given entire satisfaction, are growing in favor at a most gratifying rate, and it is the intention of the manufacturers to push them in all the markets of the world.

Messrs. Bitter & Kasson are well-known and popular citizens. The former was previously for some years a member of the firm of Kast & Co., now the Kast Copper and Sheet Iron Company. Mr. Kasson has been engaged in practical experimentation with lubricants for the past six or seven years, and is an energetic and capable gentleman. All of the firm's goods bear the buffalo bull's head as a trade-mark.

NIAGARA STOCK FARM,

Bronson C. Rumsey, Proprietor—Wm. H. Gibson, Manager—Delaware Ave., Adjoining the Park.

In few things has this country made greater progress during the past quarter century than in the improvement of its live stock. While it is true that the best strains of our domestic animals of all kinds were imported, it is equally true that the care lavished upon them has still further developed their good qualities, which are handed down from generation to generation in a constantly increasing degree, until it is a question if even the most advanced breeders of Europe can boast of better if as good strains as are exhibited by leading American fanciers, more particularly of neat cattle for market and dairy purposes. New York, by reason of her advantageous geographical and climatic position—and more especially Western New York—is contributing immensely toward this object, and it is only right that in a volume of this kind, dealing with the material resources of the city of Buffalo and vicinity, some mention should be made of this valuable interest—one of the most conspicuous, independent of manufactures, that has come under our notice.

The largest, most prosperous and most famous short-horn stock farm in this part of the country is the celebrated "Niagara," located at the head of Delaware avenue, adjoining the park, and about three miles distant from the City and County Hall, easy of access by street cars, stages and private conveyance. This farm is the property of Mr. Bronson C. Rumsey, and was established six or seven years ago for the purpose of supplying breeders with fine blooded short-horn bulls and heifers. The grounds include about 900 acres, are eligibly and beautifully situated, afford ample pasturage, running water and shelter, accommodate about 100 head of choice bulls and cows, and are under the personal supervision and management of Mr. Wm. H. Gibson, one of the most experienced and capable stock men in this country, a native of Leicestershire, England, born in 1845 of a family famous for its connection with the same industry, and reared to it himself from childhood. He came to America in 1869, in charge of a shipment of short-horns imported by Wolcott & Campbell, of the New York Mills, Utica. He remained with the firm named for several years, resigning charge of their herd not long previous to their great sale of September, 1873—the most noted event of the kind that ever occurred in this country, when 108 head of cattle were disposed of under the hammer, realizing $380,490, or an average of $3,523 per head. In 1880, when Mr. Rumsey became practically interested in the breeding of fine cattle, Mr. Gibson's services were secured, and from that time to the present he has devoted his best energies and thorough practical knowledge of the business to the improvement of the herd committed to his care, and whatever honors have been achieved by this renowned herd (now said to be the finest of the kind on the North American continent) is due, blood aside, to Mr. Gibson's intelligent and conscientious labors. The exercise grounds, stables, residence of manager, outbuildings, etc., all on the most liberal and complete scale, occupy about ten acres; from ten to thirty men are employed as the season may require, and the annual sales reach a very large aggregate, varying from year to year, but constantly increasing, mostly of bulls to Western breeders, who frequently come from the far-away Pacific slope, Colorado, Arizona, New Mexico, Texas and elsewhere, in order to secure choice specimens from this superb herd.

Of the magnificent animals now in stable and ready to begin the season of 1887 we make mention of the following because of their fine promise or established reputation, viz.: Bulls—Imported Grand Duke of Connaught, 56303; imported Knight of Oxford Second, 39549 (43440); Duke of Niagara, 69368; Third Baron Oxford of Niagara. Cows—Duchess of Niagara; Second Duchess of Niagara; Duchess of Leicester, imported; Thorndale Rose 19, imported; Wisdom Second, imported.

A specialty is made of breeding the celebrated Bates pure-blooded short-horns. Pedigrees are guaranteed. Complete catalogue and descriptive list mailed free to applicants.

GEO. N. PIERCE & CO.,

Manufacturers of Japanned and Brass Bird Cages, Refrigerators and Ice Chests—Nos. 6 to 18 Hanover St., Buffalo; New York Office and Salesroom, No. 195 Water Street.

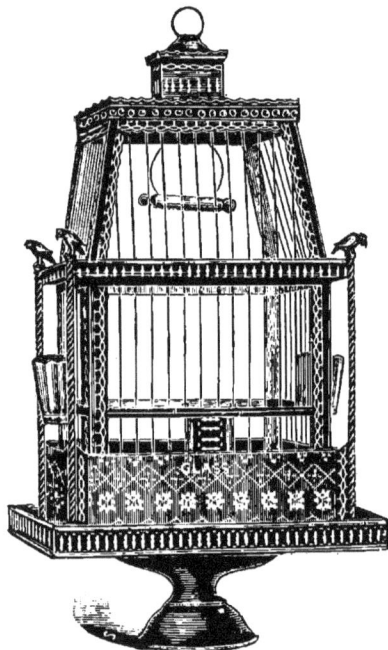

Few of those unacquainted with the trade have any idea of the extent of the bird cage industry, which doubtless foots up several millions of dollars annually in this country alone. Buffalo contributes largely to its volume, her leading house in this line, Geo. N. Pierce & Co., making no less than one hundred and sixty-five distinct patterns of these goods in japanned and brass wire, many of them real works of art, and all beautiful and well-made. These goods have made for themselves a first-class reputation, and are in demand all over the country because of the superior material and workmanship employed, and the good taste and originality displayed, embracing 165 styles.

Messrs. Geo. N. Pierce & Co. are also extensive manufacturers of superior refrigerators, of which they produce twenty styles and forty-eight sizes, covering the entire range of these indispensable adjuncts to comfortable and economical house and hotel-keeping. The "Empire" refrigerator is the best low-priced refrigerator in the market, charcoal filled, oak grained, overlapping doors, and porcelain casters—a favorite with housekeepers of small family. Other styles are the single, double and four-door "Polar," hardwood and water-cooler "Polar," all charcoal-filled, zinc-lined, with galvanized shelves, porcelain casters patent locks, best finish, best goods, with porcelain water-coolers where required, and in all respects A 1; the "King" made of clear oak lumber and elegant trimmed; the "Pearl;" the "Favorite" dry air refrigerator and ice-chest combined; the "Champion" sideboard refrigerator the "Economy" and other sideboard refrigerators—splendid goods; the "Triumph" and "Superb" refrigerators, and several patterns of improved domestic and grocers' ice-chests. We have not space here to set forth the many attractions and superior points of these several devices, but the trade will be supplied with catalogues on application.

The firm of Geo. N. Pierce & Co., in 1878, succeeded Messrs. Geselgen & Voght, who founded the business in 1864. Besides a fine complement of the best and latest-improved machinery the firm employ about 150 skilled mechanics, turning out $125,000 worth of goods per annum, which are sold all over the Union and in foreign lands. Five travelers are constantly on the road, and their orders keep the works in full operation from year's end to year's end, the output averaging 100,000 bird cages and 7,000 refrigerators and ice-chests.

Mr. Pierce is a Pennsylvanian who has resided in Buffalo for twenty-five years, twenty of which were devoted to his present line of business. He is a member of the Board of Trade in high standing. His late partner, Mr. N. S. Miller, died at Paris, France, July 15th, 1886. He was a capable, honest man, whose loss is deplored by the community.

JACOB VIERGIVER,

Wholesale and Retail Dealer in Paints, Oils, Varnishes, English, French, German and Pittsburg Window and Plate Glass, Wax, Artists' Materials, etc.—No. 9 Swan St., between Main and Washington.

The career of the above-named gentleman furnishes another striking illustration of what may be accomplished in this free country by persevering industry combined with intelligence and enterprise in a given direction. Mr. Viergiver was born in Holland, landing in the United States a little over forty years ago with little more than his ready and willing hands, his entire capital consisting of a single five-franc piece. Coming to Buffalo eleven years later, he began in earnest the battle of life. In 1863 he joined his fellow-countryman, Mr. John C. Post, in the paint, oil and glass business, the firm being Post & Co., changed in 1865 to Post & Viergiver. Mr. Post withdrew in 1871, since which time the concern has been conducted by Mr. Viergiver alone, occupying the handsome three-story store No. 9 East Swan street, 20 feet front by 80 feet deep, with commodious basement, and conveniently fitted up in every department for the transaction of a large and flourishing business, averaging of late years about $65,000 per annum.

Mr. Viergiver carries at all times complete lines of all goods pertaining to his trade, embracing superior grades of white lead, colors dry and in oil, fine imported and American varnishes, linseed oils, raw and boiled, artists' materials, wax, imported and American plate and window glass, glass globes, etc. He has the general agency for the celebrated Pittsburg Plate Glass Co., and is prepared to fill orders promptly and at factory prices.

Mr. Viergiver deservedly enjoys the confidence and a liberal share of the patronage of the painters, contractors and retail dealers of Buffalo and the country round about, and is popular with all who known him by reason of his well-known integrity, liberality and courteous manners.

THE MERCANTILE ASSOCIATION OF THE UNITED STATES.

F. M. DeCeu, Manager; Andrews & Hill, Attorneys—No. 30 East Eagle St.

Every branch of mercantile and professional business is victimized to a greater or less extent by persons who contract accounts and then, either willfully or through neglect, fail to settle. The losses thus occasioned aggregate many millions of dollars annually in this country, and it is for the benefit of the sufferers thereby that the Mercantile Association of the United States was organized during the past year, with headquarters at No. 30 East Eagle street, Buffalo; F. M. DeCeu, manager. The association, in brief, is a union of retail merchants, physicians, attorneys, dentists and others for mutual protection against non-paying debtors, and for the speedy collection of over-due accounts. The association maintains corresponding and collecting agents at all important points throughout the United States and Canada, and all business is transacted quietly, promptly and in the best shape. The demand for such an association, properly conducted, has long been recognized, but, so far as we are informed, the plan adopted here is the only one that has proved equal to the wants of a much-swindled and long-suffering community hitherto regarded as legitimate prey by the legions of dead-beats distributed all over this continent. Up to this time the Mercantile Association has proved unexpectedly successful, is now in a flourishing condition, and its prospects for future usefulness and profit are extremely flattering. Full explanations and particulars are mailed on application to the manager.

SCHNEIDER & BETZ,

Manufacturing Jewelers—Seal, Chased and Plain Rings, Badges and Emblems a Specialty—Nos. 114 and 116 Clinton St.

The steady growth of manufacturing interests of all kinds in this city is a feature of itself which calls for more than passing mention. Among the lines that are well represented none are more conspicuous than the jewelry business. Among the firms that have in a remarkably short space of time taken a prominent position is that of Messrs. Schneider & Betz, Nos. 114 and 116 Clinton street. This firm, composed of Henry G. Schneider and John C. Betz, was organized in January, 1886, and began business under the most favorable circumstances. Both members previously had an experience of seventeen years as practical jewelers. They began manufacturing with every needed facility, their specialty being seal, chased and plain rings, chains, charms, and all kinds of jewelry, made to order on short notice and at very reasonable prices. Being possessed of artistic talent in designing, the manufacture of badges for parades, conventions, etc., society emblems and similar work, soon became an important feature of the business. Gold and silver-plating and engraving is done on short notice and in the highest style of the art. The extent of the business can be inferred from the fact that during the first year of the firm's existence it amounted to $10,000, and extends all over Western New York and Pennsylvania. The results have exceeded the firm's expectations, and it is safe to presume that during the ensuing year the business will be doubled. Mr. Schneider is a native of Germany, and has resided in this city since 1856. Mr. Betz is a thoroughgoing Buffalonian by birth and education, and both gentlemen combine in a high degree all the essential qualities that go to make successful business men.

FRANK C. CHAMBERS,

Successor to Bartholomew & Chambers—Draper and Tailor—No. 385 Washington St., bet. Eagle and Clinton.

The first thought of the well-to-do gentleman of good taste, when he decides upon a new suit, is, "To whom shall I give my order?"—a question, usually, much easier to propound than to answer, for there are tailors and tailors, as there are lawyers and lawyers. Some of these alleged gentleman's costumers are mere mechanical automatons; another class are true artists and make of every suit they undertake a poem in cloth, an epic in textiles, "a thing of beauty and a joy forever." And of these latter Mr. Frank C. Chambers, No. 385 Washington street, is a shining example, famous for cultivated taste, the true artistic instinct, and a finished sense of the eternal fitness of things. Mr. Chambers has devoted his life to an exhaustive study of his art, which he has never regarded as a mere trade, with the result of achieving a reputation co-extensive with the Union for correct taste, remarkable skill as a cutter, and a perfect mastery of details. Mr. C. is a graduate of one of New York's most celebrated fashionable tailoring establishments, and has had great experience in leading Eastern and Western houses in the same line. In his own special field—the cutting of fine garments—it is doubtful if he has an equal in Buffalo or a superior anywhere. Importing the best and rarest weaves of French and English looms, giving conscientious attention to style and fit, and personal supervision to every stage of the work from measurement to finish, employing the highest skill in every department, making reasonable prices and demanding spot cash, while guaranteeing fit and quality, we have not far to seek for the secret of his success, and it will be found that the most elegantly attired gentlemen of Buffalo, Dunkirk, Titusville, and other neighboring and some distant cities are his regular patrons.

The firm of Bartholomew & Chambers, formerly of Dunkirk, removed to this city in 1885, locating at No. 14 East Eagle street. During the past year Mr. Bartholomew retired, and Mr. Chambers succeeded to the business on his individual account, removing to his present location on the 1st of February last. That he will continue to prosper there can be no question, for true merit always meets with reward proportioned to its deserts.

THE HOWARD STOCK FARMS.

City Farm (Trotting Stock), Tifft St., Thirteenth Ward; Meadow Farm (Jersey Cattle), near Big Tree Station, Buffalo & Southwestern Railroad.

Erie county is fast becoming, as a well-posted writer on live stock and sporting topics has aptly expressed it, "the Bluegrass Mecca of the North." Probably in no section of the country, Central Kentucky alone excepted, are to be found so many, so extensive, so well-conducted or so valuable and profitable farms devoted to the breeding and rearing of aristocratic equine and bovine stock as in Erie and Niagara counties— the former more especially. We have had occasion to refer to this important interest in another portion of this work, and in this place desire to make special reference to the two splendid farms of Gen. R. L. Howard—one located in the Thirteenth ward within the city limits, known as the Howard stock farm, the other within a mile of Big Tree station, B. & S. W. railroad, and called the Meadow farm, both of which we have personally visited and inspected.

The Howard stock farm (known also as the City farm) consists of 178 acres of superior grazing and gardening lands, all under substantial fence and handsomely improved—with manager's residence, large barns, stables, exercise track and grounds, pastures, running water, and every requisite essential and convenience. The display of blooded animals embraces about sixty-five horses and mares of renowned trotting pedigree, comprising the get of several of the most celebrated trotting stallions known to the American turf. At the head of this distinguished array stands the noted horse Wilkie Collins, bred by Capt. B. J. Treacy of Lexington, Ky. Wilkie Collins is a son of the great George Wilkes, the most celebrated son of Rysdyk's Hambletonian. On the dam's side Wilkie Collins is descended from Pilot, Jr., and seven thoroughbred crosses. As becomes his superb descent, he is a noble animal both in appearance and action. He is eleven years old, 15½ hands, is jet black with star and white heels behind, has a sensible head, fine neck, heavy middle piece, strong arms, muscular quarters, good bone, sound feet and pure trotting action; does not require boots or toe-weights, and, no doubt, in proper condition and handling, can beat 2:20. His colts possess good tempers, splendid action, are very stylish, fine size, and have plenty of bone and muscle. Several of Wilkie's get have shown better than three minutes at three years of age.

In the selection of his brood mares Gen. Howard has been guided by the established truism, "Blood will tell," and has availed himself of none but the best trotting strains. They were sired by such horses of national reputation as Ericsson, Allie West, Administrator, Howard's Mambrino by Mambrino Chief, Case's Norman, Field's Royal George, Aberdeen by Rysdyk's Hambletonian, Messenger Duroc, Wood's Hambletonian, Balsora by Alexander's Abdallah, Rochester by Aberdeen, Almont, Jr., by Almont, Stephen A. Douglas and others. The list includes Alice Grey, gray, 11 years old, sired by Allie West, bred by T. L. Coons, Fayette county, Ky., record 2.25; Aberdale, 9 years old, sired by Aberdeen by Rysdyk's Hambletonian; Almontress, bay, 9 years old, by Hamlin's Almont, Jr., bred by R. L. Howard, record 2.26; Annie Stephens, chestnut, 8 years old, by Administrator by Rysdyk's Hambletonian, bred by Capt. B. J. Treacy, Lexington, Ky.; Belle Messenger, bay, 11 years old, by Messenger Duroc by Rysdyk's Hambletonian, bred by R. L. Howard; Fanny, chestnut, 9 years old, by King George by Field's Royal George; G.psey, bay, 7 years old, by John Gilpin by Strader's C. M. Clay, bred by R. L. Howard; Josie Eaton, bay, 22 years old, by Ericsson by Mambrino Chief; Josephine, 14 years old, by Wood's Hambletonian, bred by F. H. Arnold, Port Allegany, Pa.; Laura Bassett, chestnut, by Balsora by Alexander's Abdallah, 15 years old, bred by S. Patterson, Jessamine county, Ky.; Lizzie Bassett, chestnut, 7 years old, by Rochester by Aberdeen, bred by R. L. Howard; Mollie Grey, gray, 15 years old, by Brayman's Young Norman by Case's Norman by Nottingham's Norman, bred by H. M. Starr, Medina, N. Y.; Maggie Patchen, bay, foaled 1879, by Pluto by Mambrino Patchen, bred by R. L. Howard; the Rebel Mare 2d, foaled 1869, by Howard's Mambrino by Mambrino Chief, bred by R. L. Howard, once a rebel cavalry mare with a romantic history; Reindeer II., chestnut, foaled 1874, by Howard's Mambrino by Mambrino Chief, bred by R. L. Howard; Nellie Gilpin, bay, foaled 1882, by John Gilpin by Strader's C. M. Clay; Gipsey Girl, bay, foaled 1877, by Stephen A. Douglas by Rysdyk's Hambletonian, bred by Capt. W Robinson, Chautauqua county. Sister to Nellie R., 2:22½.

These brood mares are all perfectly sound, and possess speed, size, action and finish. Their produce by Wilkie Collins have been pronounced, by disinterested parties, equal to the get of any other stallion in the United States. Over seventy-five per cent. of the

13

colts and fillies possess a striking resemblance of their sire in uniformity of color, style, speed and symmetry of form. The majority are rich blacks, bays or browns in color.

The following is a partial list of stallion colts sired by Wilkie Collins and bred by Gen. Howard: Almont Wilkes, bay, foaled May, 1883; Almo Wilkes, bay, foaled April 30th, 1885 ; Grey Wilkes, 4434, steel-gray, foaled April 19th, 1885; Medina Wilkes, brown, foaled May 29th, 1885 ; Royal Wilkes, 4436, bay, foaled 1884; Superb Wilkes, 4433, brown, foaled October 9th, 1885; Buffalo Wilkes, black, foaled August 22d, 1884, was bred by ex-Alderman Twitchell ; and Charlie Wilkes, gray, foaled 1885, was bred by Charles Newton, Hamburg, N. Y.

Gen. Howard has Wilkie Collins fillies of his own breeding as follows: Bella Wilkes, bay, foaled October 22d, 1885; Bertha Wilkes, bay, foaled May, 1883 ; Cornelia Wilkes, black, foaled 1883 ; Daisy Wilkes, chestnut, foaled July 10th, 1885 ; Georgia Wilkes, chestnut, foaled May, 1883; Josie Wilkes, black, foaled 1884; Kate Wilkes, bay, foaled March 27th, 1885 ; Louise Wilkes, bay, foaled 1883 ; Maud Wilkes, chestnut, foaled June, 1883; Nellie Wilkes, brown, foaled 1882 ; Norma Wilkes, bay, foaled 1883. All of the animals named in this article, with very few exceptions, are standard bred and registered. Winona Stanton, chestnut, foaled 1883, by General Stanton, bred by Geo. A. Chambers, Winona, Ont., also makes her home here.

Gen. Howard's line of geldings comprises numerous splendid animals; among them Allie Wilkes, black, foaled May, 1883; Golden Wilkes, chestnut, foaled 1881, and Willie Wilkes, bay, foaled May, 1883, all of his own breeding from choice mares by Wilkie Collins; Charlie Newton, bay, foaled October 30th, 1881, by S. J. Tilden, bred by Chas. Newton, Hamburg; Henry, bay, foaled 1880, by Rochester by Aberdeen, bred by Gen. Howard; Moonlight, gray, foaled April 12th, 1880, by Hero of Thorndale, bred by Chas. Alexander, Woodford county, Ky.

Of elegant and high-bred roadsters we note : Annie Wilkes, bay, by Wilkie Collins, foaled May 22d, 1881, bred by Gen. Howard; Highland Maid, chestnut, foaled 1879, 15¾ hands, by Kerr's Highland Boy, bred in Canada ; Miss Stanton, chestnut, 15¾ hands, foaled 1879, by General Stanton; Neppy, bay mare, foaled June 28th, 1880, by W. M. Rysdyk by Rysdyk's Hambletonian, bred by Henry Peterson, Seneca county, N. Y.; Nellie R., record 2:32¼, by Stephen A. Douglas out of a well-bred mare owned by Capt. Robinson, Fredonia, N. Y.—bought last year by Gen. Howard.

Mr. Howard Conkling, superintendent of this leading stock farm, is about 37 years of age. He has spent his entire life from childhood in the breeding and training of horses, and has no superior in his specialty. He took charge of Gen. Howard's horse interests in 1879, and has proved a most capable, faithful and successful manager, who thoroughly understands his calling in all its ramifications.

The farm itself has been established some twenty years, and is noted for the number and value of the fine harness animals it has produced and contributed to the turf and to the stables of admirers of fine horseflesh.

A large number of blooded colts of Wilkie Collins' get are offered for sale. Their dams were by such celebrated sires as Messenger Duroc, Allie West, Aberdeen, Wood's Hambletonian, Administrator, Almont, Jr., Ericsson, all standard, and other well-bred mares. The two-year-olds and over are well broken to single and double harness.

MEADOW FARM.

This is one of the most delightful rural establishments in Western New York, comprising 350 acres of fertile and highly improved land. 270 acres of which are devoted to crops and fruits, and 80 acres to the breeding and pasturing of Jersey cattle and the prosecution of dairy operations. The General owns a beautiful and conveniently arranged mansion here, where with his family he resides during the heats of summer, living upon the fat of the land, inhaling the pure breeze cooled by its passage across the limpid waters of Lake Erie, and storing up health and vigor sufficient to fortify against the influences of city life from year to year. A cordial welcome is here extended to all visitors, and a generous hospitality dispensed that carries one back in memory to the happy days spent with the big-hearted farmers of Kentucky's garden-spot, the Bluegrass region. On the occasion of our visit we were received and entertained in Gen. Howard's absence by his efficient and intelligent lieutenant and superintendent, Mr. Oliver Knapp, a native of this county, whose almost forty years of life have been spent upon the best farms in this portion of the State, who for the past three years has had charge of Meadow Farm, and who has a thorough practical knowledge of the requirements of his position, together with unusual executive capacity, an innate love of his occupation, and a conscientious desire to perform well and to the satisfaction of his employer every duty devolving upon him. Provided with all the assistants he needs and half-a-dozen magnificent farm horses, together with all the tools, machinery, vehicles, etc., required for the successful working of the farm, Mr. Knapp is noted for the yield and quality of his crops, the care lavished upon his stock, fences and outbuildings, and the superiority and quantity of the milk and butter produced from the splendid herd of pure-bred Jerseys under the care of W. A. Field, as well as the attractive appearance and fine condition of the cattle and their progeny. The sales of butter alone for 1886 reached 3,000 pounds, bringing the highest prices paid.

Gen. Howard's herd of Jerseys numbers at present forty-six head of bulls, cows and yearlings, which will be considerably augmented by natural increase during the approaching season. The value of this herd in money it would be difficult to estimate. The herd, as before stated, is of the purest strain without a drop of plebeian blood in its veins, and it is rather Gen. Howard's object to afford the dairy interest the means of improving their stock by the judicious introduction of fine blood than to realize large and sudden gains by extensive sales. The General is justly proud of his herd, and of the success that has hitherto attended his efforts to benefit the class referred to, and will continue to assist them in their praiseworthy war against shams, and for the education of the masses to a proper appreciation of rich milk and genuine butter.

Of this herd—of which every member is a royal prince or princess in his or her own right—the following with their pedigrees are registered in the American Herd Book, viz.:

Worthy Beauty 2d, 16635; sire. Bristol Brown, 6681, descended through a noble line from imported Prince of Jersey, 66, imported Jersey Queen, 1410, imported Splendid, 16, and imported Jessie, 28; dam, Worthy Beauty, 16632, out of Locust Blossom 2d by Winfield, 5005. She is a solid light fawn in color, with full black points, and has a pedigree and individual record equal to the best.

Duke's Lassie, 16890, dropped April, 1882; sire, Duke of Ghent 2d; dam, Midget, 14254; solid fawn, full black points. Pedigree in part identical with that of Jersey Belle of Scituate,

Emma Mc 5th, 13960, dropped October 13th, 1881; sire, Gilderoy 2d, 4037; dam, Emma Mc, 4649; solid fawn, black points, a premium heifer.

Cuddie, 17267; sire, Pride of the Island, 5416, imported October 6th, 1880; dam, Lady Warnock, 11909, imported October 6th, 1880. Pride of the Island was sired by Le Broeq's Prize. Cuddie is a solid fawn, black points.

Bright Lady 3d, 16451; solid fawn, full black points; dropped January 17th, 1882 ; sire, Prince of M. 2d, 5507 ; dam, Bright Lady, 5938. Bright Lady is one-fourth Albert, 44, and a very fine cow.

Bristol Bella, 15697; solid fawn, full black points; dropped February 13th, 1881 ; sire, Pompus. 2881 ; dam, Dolly P., 10129.

Cuddie's Prince, 11795, by Alphea Prince, 6337, by Mercury, 432. This bull took first premium at Erie county fair last fall over all on exhibition, and is considered one of the most valuable animals of his kind in the State.

Calves, both male and female, for sale. Pure Jersey cows and calves for sale at reasonable prices; also standard bred Wilkes colts and road horses at less than Kentucky prices. Address R. L. HOWARD, Buffalo, N. Y.

CHARLES P. RUPPERSBERG,

Manufacturer of Fancy Furs—Show Room, No. 383 Main St., over Hamilton & McCracken's—Seal Work a Specialty—Sacques Redyed, Refitted and Repaired.

In a climate like this furs are a prime necessary of life, without which comfort is simply unattainable by those who venture out doors in winter ; particularly ladies, who, accustomed to warm rooms and protection from even the rough winds of spring and autumn, are illy calculated to brave the fierce blasts of winter. Of the two practical furriers engaged in manufacturing in this city, one, Mr. Charles F. Ruppersberg, has an elegant show and salesroom at No. 383 Main street, second floor, McArthur building, where buyers will find in the season the largest, finest and most valuable stock of these goods in the State, outside of New York, fancy furs being Mr. Ruppersberg's specialty. Ladies and others interested are cordially invited and will be warmly welcomed. Mr. R. employs thirteen carefully trained and very skillful operatives, and is prepared to manufacture to order any description of seal cloaks, sacques, fancy furs, etc., in the neatest, best and most stylish manner and at short notice. Such are his facilities that he will engage to make to order fine seal sacques for $75 less than any other Buffalo house, fit, workmanship, style and material guaranteed. As a natural consequence of his skill and liberality he is building up a large business, though established only since the season of 1885.

Some of the finest work of this kind that has ever come under our observation we saw in his elegant rooms. Besides a superb line of seal furs we noticed a number of fur mats of most elaborate workmanship—one in particular, composed of over 9,000 distinct pieces, beautiful to look at and luxurious to the touch.

Mr. Ruppersberg came to Buffalo from New York some sixteen years ago, and for fifteen years was manager or Bergtold's establishment. He is quite popular.

H. M. BACKUS OIL COMPANY,

Manufacturers of the Celebrated Backus Shafting and Journal Grease and Machinery Oils—Office and Factory, Nos. 52, 54 and 56 Norton St., Corner Erie.

A good lubricant—one that does its work well and economically—is of the utmost importance to all who own or have the care of machinery, and has been the object of long and patient search, because it has long been known that unlimited sale awaited the discovery of a grease that would render entire satisfaction, both in effectiveness and price. The H. M. Backus Oil Company, of this city, has achieved wonderful success in this direction, its Backus shafting grease and cylinder oils and machinery oils having come into general use upon their merits, and their popularity at home and abroad increasing from year to year. A perfect knowledge of the requirements of the trade, great skill and ample resources have enabled this company to push its experiments and researches to a greater extent than most of its rivals, with the result named. From a vast accumulation of flattering testimonials in the possession of the company we select the following from Hardwicke & Ware, proprietors of the famous Buffalo tube works:

BUFFALO, December 23, 1886.—*H. M. Backus Oil Co.*: Gentlemen—It is now over eight months since we adopted the Backus journal grease for lubricating our shafting, and our superintendent, who was opposed to it at first, is so well pleased with it now that it would be hard to get him to go back to using oil, even if we got it for nothing, because the journals are always cool and there is no danger of fire by heating, and no dripping and wasting on the floor, as when we used oil. Yours truly, HARDWICKE & WARE.

The folowing are some of those in Buffalo who use their shafting grease : George W. Tifft Sons & Co., iron works; Hardwicke & Ware, tube works; John C. Jewett Manufacturing Co., refrigerator manufacturers; Pitts Agricultural Works; Farrar & Trefts, iron works; George H. Dunston, lithographer; Heinz & Munschauer, bird cage manufacturers; George Pooley & Son, rope walk; Dempster Engine Works, engine works; Niagara Elevator, elevator; Fountain Elevator, elevator; Swiftsure Elevator, elevator; Anchor Line Steamers, steam propellers.

The company's building, three stories in height, occupies the triangle between Norton, Erie and Peacock streets, and is quite extensive, equipped in the best manner, employs a large force of operatives, and turns out immense quantities of the goods named, which are shipped to all parts of the United States and Canada. A leading specialty is axle grease—a favorite grade with all who have tried it.

This industry was established in 1879 by Mr. H. M. Backus, who, for some years previously, had been engaged in the oil trade at Cleveland, Ohio. That he has made a grand and growing success of his Buffalo venture there is no room for question.

J. G. BALSAM,

Architect and Civil Engineer—Office, No. 511 Main St.

Mr. Balsam, who was born in Germany, is a graduate of the technical school of Liegnitz, as also of the polytechnic high schools of Dresden and Berlin. Having thus become thoroughly proficient in the theoretical knowledge of his chosen profession, he next turned his attention to more realistic labor by entering the service of the government of his native country, which position he held for a period of three years.

Considering the New World as affording a favorable field for more extended operations, we next find him in America, connected with the N. P. R. R. Co. for two and one-half years, and afterwards with the Union Bridge Co. of Buffalo for a term of two years. This considerable and somewhat varied experience, combined with remarkable vigor and energy of character, have served to place Mr. Balsam in a prominent position amidst his local compeers. In 1883 he established himself in business on his own account, and since that time, owing to his peculiar adaptability to varying and difficult circumstances, has deservedly received the liberal patronage of an appreciative public. The subject of this article is the type of a class who are ever welcome to the shores of America, inasmuch as the representatives of skilled labor, whether of the hand or the head, prove alike a credit and a benefit to their adopted country. Mr. B. has also evinced a laudable public spirit by identifying himself with philanthropic enterprises outside of his own vocation. He is at present engaged in contributing his share toward the task of resuscitating the Mechanics' Institute, and let us hope that through the united efforts of other earnest men and himself that worthy institution may rise Phœnix-like from its ashes, possessed of greater vitality and more perfect than before.

MRS. DR. L. BROAD,

Druggist—Corner Erie and Pearl Sts.—Proprietress Broad's Instant Pain Cure and Patent Fumigating Disinfectant.

The prominence attained by Mrs. Dr. L. Broad in Buffalo during the past twenty years is such as to warrant some mention in these pages. This lady has occupied a special sphere in the successful care and treatment of the sick and afflicted. Having been specially qualified in all that goes to constitute the successful nurse, Mrs. Broad devoted her energies to the study of medicine and the successful treatment of the afflicted. As a result of a long and valuable experience in different hospitals and other public institutions, and a thorough knowledge of the drug business, this lady during her residence in Buffalo has prepared and put within the reach of the public valuable and well-known remedies. Broad's Patent Fumigating Disinfectant was thoroughly tested in St. Louis during the cholera epidemic of 1866 and found to be the best in use. In cases of diphtheria and scarlet fever it is invaluable, preventing contagion and materially aiding the patient to recovery. It has been indorsed by the boards of health of Buffalo, Chicago, New York and other cities; by the International Cholera Conference, and by leading physicians and chemists throughout the country.

Broad's Instant Pain Cure entirely eradicates rheumatism, neuralgia, sprains, bruises, pains in the limbs, stiffness of the joints, swellings, freezes, chilblains, burns, ague in the breast or face, toothache, canker, nursing sore mouth, putrid or inflammatory sore throat, pleurisy, lameness of the back, kidney complaint or cramp, colic, dysentery, inflammation of the lungs, etc.

Mrs. Dr. Broad is a regular practitioner in medicine, and has confined her practice to the treatment of the diseases of women and children, and with great success. She also conducts an elegantly fitted up drug store at the corner of Erie and Pearl streets, and has enjoyed an unparalleled degree of prosperity. The demand for her preparations comes from all parts of the country. The following, from a number of testimonials, substantiate the claims set forth for the fumigating disinfectant, are selected:

NORTH BUFFALO, May 28, 1869.—With a knowledge of the ingredients of Broad's Fumigating Disinfectant, and the result of its use in the rooms of patients afflicted with malignant, sloughing, scirrhus diseases at the Erie county alms-house, I will say that its efficacy in removing the offensive smell of decomposing organic matter surpasses any substance with which I am acquainted. C. L. DAYTON, M. D., Physician and Surgeon to the Alms-house.

BUFFALO, May 31, 1869.—I have given Broad's Fumigating Disinfectant a thorough trial, and can fully indorse the views of Prof. George Hadley. G. E. MACKAY, M. D., Physician Erie County Penitentiary.

From the nature and well-known properties of the articles entering into the composition of Broad's Disinfectant I have no doubt but that it will prove very efficient where such an article is required. JOHN CRONYN, M. D., Physician Buffalo Hospital.

CHICAGO, June 27, 1867.—This is to certify that I have examined and submitted to trial, as a deodorizer, an article known as Broad's Patent Fumigating Disinfectant. I find it to be very efficient in removing unpleasant and noxious odors from the atmosphere of rooms contaminated by the presence of decomposing organic matter. In my opinion, it will also prove efficacious, if freely and frequently used, in retarding, if not in arresting, the putrefactive process, while burning it diffuses a grateful odor, without emitting any vapors which are hurtful if breathed by the sick. JAMES V. Z. BLANEY, Consulting Chemist.

CHARLES C. PENFOLD,

Designer, Engraver and Manufacturer of Fine Jewelry, Badges, Medals, etc.—Nos. 2 and 4 East Swan St.

Mr. Chas. C. Penfold, of Nos. 2 and 4 East Swan street, Buffalo, is conceded to possess rare taste and skill in the designing and making of badges. He has been wonderfully successful in his chosen specialty, and as a consequence he finds himself already in a flourishing condition from a business point of view, though established on his own account less than a year.

Mr. Penfold is a practical designer and engraver, and a successful manufacturer of fine jewelry of artistic and appropriate design. His services are in great and growing request for the designing of badges and medals of every description, club and class pins, jewels and pieces for prize presentations in gold and silver, etc. Among his most notable efforts in this special direction may be mentioned a silver bronze medallion of President Cleveland (for which he has an autograph letter of thanks from the Chief Magistrate), and the new parade badge recently adopted by the select knights, A. O. U. W., of New York State, which he has had patented. Besides these Mr. Penfold has on exhibition a great variety of badges and medals, fine jewelry, bronzes, charms, etc., of his own designing, all beautiful and interesting, which will be cheerfully shown to all who desire to inspect them. The souvenir badges worn by Utica Commandery Knights Templar at the Elmira conclave, October 12 last, were designed and made by him, and attracted universal attention and admiration for the taste, skill and artistic beauty combined in them. The badge consists of a passion cross, over which a banner is suspended by rings from a rod. The banner in turn bears on its field the raised figure of a horse, carrying a knight in full armor, between the words "Utica Commandery No. 3," and "Utica, N. Y." The arms of the cross extend from a quarter to three-eighths of an inch from under the banner. The hilts of crossed swords and the lower end of the scabbards appear at the upper and lower angles formed by the banner and cross. The whole is suspended from a metal bar on which are engraved the words, "73d Annual Conclave." Mr. Penfold was also the designer and manufacturer of the badges worn on the same notable occasion by Lake Erie Commandery No. 20 of Buffalo, St. Omer Commandery No. 19 of Elmira, Lafayette Commandery No. 7 of Hudson, and other organizations distinguished for their handsome appearance and tasteful equipment. In point of design and workmanship the decorations produced at this establishment are equal to any we have ever seen, and worthy of special attention from committees and individuals in search of unique and artistic productions in this line.

Mr. Penfold's equipment of late improved machinery is complete. He also has the requisite apparatus, and is prepared to do every description of gold and silver-plating in the best manner and at short notice.

Mr. Penfold is a native of Lockport, N. Y. He entered the jewelry trade in 1872, having resided in Buffalo during the previous fifteen years, with the exception of two years spent at Providence, R. I., in perfecting himself as a practical jeweler and designer. He is a popular gentleman, and for six years was inspector of rifle practice in the 74th N. G. S. N. Y.

HOWARD IRON WORKS.

Manufacturers of Hotel, Factory and Store Hydraulic, Power and Hand Elevators, also Grain Elevators, Printers' and Book-Binders' Machinery, Steam Engines, Shafting, Hangers, Pulleys, Bark Mills, Tannery Fixtures, Schlenker's Bolt Cutters, Howard Parallel Bench Vises, Taps and Dies, Set Screws, Every Description of Railroad Work, and Iron Castings in General—Agency for the "Otto" Gas Engine—No. 287 Chicago St.

The above is one of those great representative establishments that have contributed to the upbuilding of Buffalo, not only in the volume, variety and value of their products, but in spreading abroad an accurate knowledge of her manufacturing and commercial resources. Established in 1849 by Mr. Rufus L. Howard, who still remains at its head, this superb enterprise at once took rank with the leading concerns of this continent, and has always sustained a pre-eminent reputation for the material, ingenuity, skill, finish and general excellence of its machinery, tools, castings, and, in short, every item of work done on its premises. Ten years ago at the Philadelphia Centennial Exposition these works were awarded the first grand prize medal and diploma for superior machinery over all competitors—an award the value of which will be appreciated when it is stated that the most famous iron and steel manufacturers, engine and machinery builders and inventors of this country, England, France, Germany and Italy entered their best productions and were eager, determined rivals for the honors accorded this unpretentious, yet grandly substantial and deserving Buffalo house. Since then, as before, the course of the Howard Iron Works has been steadily and undeviatingly onward and upward, original and independent, always leading, never following, sustaining and strengthening its claim to superiority by the introduction of novelties in machinery and the improvement of old devices whereby they are rendered capable of faster and better work than ever. It has ever been the policy of the Howard Iron Works to encourage and employ inventive talent, the result of which is seen in the unusual number and recognized capacity of the ingenious mechanics found in its various departments, and the constant stream of new and improved devices designed and manufactured here.

The premises, fronting on Chicago street, the Main and the Hamburg canals and Granger street, embrace something over two acres of the most valuable ground in the manufacturing district, two-thirds of which is covered by commodious and substantial buildings, containing the immense foundry, machine and wood-working shops. Two fine blast furnaces of twenty tons daily capacity add to the completeness of the works and enable the proprietors to make their own finished iron direct from the pig—an advantage that will readily be appreciated by all who possess any knowledge of the business. The equipment in every department is as complete as long experience and practically unlimited means can make it, and is unsurpassed anywhere. A working force of nearly 300 skilled mechanics and laborers is constantly employed under the personal supervision of Mr. E. Schlenker, himself an accomplished machinist and inventor. The capital invested is between $200,000 and $300,000, and the annual output varies from $300,000 to $400,000.

It would be impossible in the limits of an article of this kind to more than glance at and mention by name the various products of this truly colossal concern. Among the more important are the Howard steam, hydraulic and hand elevator for hotels, stores and factories, grain and coal elevator machinery, printers' and binders' machinery, including hand and hydraulic presses, paper-cutters, stabbers, backers, etc. ; Schlenker's patent revolving bolt cutters of all sizes, Howard patent parallel bench vises, bark mills, centering lathes, railway frogs, switches, etc., iron and steel set screws, machine screw taps, bolts, and every description of small machinery and appliances for every conceivable purpose. They also have the general agency for the silent "Otto" gas engine.

Mr. Schlenker, who is the patentee of much of the machinery they manufacture, exercises constant and close superintendence of every department, and nothing leaves the works until it has passed a rigid inspection.

The Howard Iron Works enjoys the abundant confidence of the machinery-buying public everywhere, and its productions are in general use throughout this continent. Those interested are advised to send to headquarters for catalogue and price-list—a handsome book of over 100 pages—from which may be obtained much valuable information on the subject of manufacturing and machinery in general.

THE BUFFALO SATURDAY MERCURY,

W. J. McCahill & Co., Publishers—W. J. McCahill, President; John Fischer, Secretary and Treasurer—Office, Second Floor, No. 60 East Seneca St.

By reason of the rivalry of the dailies (which usually combine to crush out aspiring newcomers) the publication of regular weekly newspapers in the cities is attended with many and serious difficulties, and only those entering this field amply equipped with capital, energy, industry and brains can hope to succeed. So fortified, however, and with a fixed determination to win, success is most impossible, as has been repeatedly demonstrated—notably by the publishers of the *Buffalo Saturday Mercury*, established by W. J. McCahill & Co. in April last. The *Mercury* is an exceedingly bright six-column quarto, full to the brim of entertaining local notes, condensed news and literary miscellany, and has already achieved wonderful popularity, as is shown by the figures relating to circulation, as follows: First issue, gratuitous; at end of first month, *bona fide* paid circulation, 1,200; end of second month, 1,500; end of third month, 2,500; end of fourth month, 3,700; end of fifth month, 4,500; end of sixth month (September), 6,000; and on Saturday, December 4th, 10,000 copies were printed and sold in Buffalo and surrounding towns—a most gratifying exhibit, and one upon which the enterprising proprietors have every reason to congratulate themselves. Under a continuation of such capable management the *Mercury's* future is assured, and the problem of how to live and be happy in a bear's den will again be solved—for the struggling weekly, surrounded by rich and powerful dailies, occupies just that position. The *Mercury* has a large and growing circulation, not only at home but in all the adjacent New York and Pennsylvania towns—Erie, Bradford, Oil City, Dunkirk, Medina, Elmira, etc.—a special edition being printed for that special purpose, filled with news, society notes, etc., from over 170 local correspondents in the States of New York, Pennsylvania and Ohio.

December saw the opening, in connection with the *Saturday Mercury*, of a job printing office, under the same management, which is complete and well-appointed in every department, and is already doing a large and profitable business.

The *Mercury* occupies the entire second floor of No. 60 Seneca street, 26 by 80 feet. It is a flourishing establishment throughout. The capital invested is about $6,000, and is paying a fair return thus early. President McCahill and Secretary and Treasurer Fischer are well known and popular business men, endowed with tact and pluck sufficient to carry their enterprise to a successful issue in the face of any conceivable obstacle, and there is no reason to doubt that they will do so. The firm have just set up a first-class cylinder press from the Bagley & Sewell Co., Watertown, N. Y.

BUFFALO REFRIGERATOR MANUFACTORY.

Peter A. Vogt, Manufacturer of Vogt's Patent Refrigerators for Hotel, Restaurant and Family Use, Ice Chests, Beer Coolers, etc.—Nos. 81 and 83 Broadway.

Mr. Peter A. Vogt, head of the Buffalo Refrigerator Manufactory, has devoted thirty years of his life to this branch of industry. For a long period he was a practical workman in the shops of John C. Jewett, establishing himself as a manufacturer on a small scale in 1865. Ingenious, studious and industrious, he introduced improvement after improvement, taking out patents upon the more important and valuable, until at last a point of perfection has been reached which seems to leave nothing more desirable undone, and his goods are renowned throughout the length and breadth of the land for their beauty, economy and absolute reliability. Every ice-chest, refrigerator and beer-cooler turned out of this factory is carefully inspected previous to shipping, and all are packed with charcoal, well and substantially made, and finished in superior style. They are made of varying sizes, patterns and weights for different purposes, in styles as follows: Grained ice-chests, "Star" refrigerators, "Excelsior," "Reliable," "Standard" (illustrated herewith), "Monarch" refrigerators; "Grocers'"

ice-chests, lunch-coolers in several patterns, and beer and ale coolers in eight or ten different sizes and styles. The following are a few of the advantages presented by these chests, coolers and refrigerators :

1. They have been before the public for the past twenty years, and are manufactured under three distinct patents, granted May 23, 1866, September 24, 1867, and March 11, 1873.

2. A perfect uniform temperature.

3. A constant change of air in the provision chamber, without waste of ice or loss of air already cooled.

4. A downward current of cold air prevents the provision chamber from being filled with warm air on opening the door.

5. The cool air performs double duty of cooling and purifying the chamber and protecting it from warm external air.

6. The great convenience of the ice chamber.

7. The form of the provision chamber ; every portion of it can be used with equal convenience.

8. Articles of strong and unpleasant and of delicate odor can be placed in the provision chamber together without danger of mixing flavors.

9. They are lined throughout with zinc, preventing the absorption of offensive odors.

10. The stationary ice bottom is covered with galvanized iron, preventing taint.

11. The crowning feature of these refrigerators is one by which, with the aid of rubber strips, the doors are made nearly air-tight.

12. The wood-work portion is thoroughly kiln-dried, and in all particulars these are the best-made articles of the kind now offered the public.

Mr. Vogt's premises are quite roomy, embracing the entire six floors and basement, 40 by 100 feet, of the building Nos. 81 and 83 Broadway. The firm was formerly Geselgen & Vogt, Mr. Geselgen retiring in 1871. Mr. Vogt removed from the old stand, No. 31 Main street, to his present location in 1883. He employs from fifteen to twenty skilled workmen in fitting up and finishing the goods, all of the mill work being done by contract elsewhere. Three active travelers are steadily employed.

T. & E. DICKINSON,

Dealers in Choice Diamonds, Rubies, Sapphires, Emeralds, Pearls, Rich Jewelry, Watches, Clocks, Solid Silverware, Plated Ware, Brass and Optical Goods, Canes, Novelties, etc.—No. 254 Main St.

Beyond all question the above-named is the largest, best-equipped and most liberally patronized establishment of the kind between New York and Chicago. It is also the oldest, having been founded by its present head in 1849, occupying the noted old St. John's dwelling, then No. 370 Main street, used as a hospital in the war of 1812, and one of the few Buffalo residences spared by the British and their almost equally savage Indian allies when Buffalo was burnt. In 1866 Mr. Dickinson made a business as well as life partner of his estimable wife; the present location was purchased; little by little, as the requirements of their growing trade demanded, the building was enlarged and improved and their facilities increased, until now the one is a most desirable property, 20 feet front, 130 feet deep, and five stories in height, and the other, as already noted, is one of the most extensive and complete in this country. All of the latest improved machinery and special tools used in the trade are provided, some thirteen or fourteen skilled jewelers and watchmakers are regularly employed, and a vast quantity of superior goods are produced, the specialties of the house embracing choice diamonds, rubies, sapphires, pearls, emeralds, rich jewelry in original and standard designs, American and imported watches and clocks, solid silver and silver-plated ware, brass and optical goods, gold and silver-headed canes, and all the latest and most attractive novelties of the trade as fast as introduced.

The store is a truly elegant and inviting place, the resort of the best people of Buffalo and vicinity—the class who recognize and appreciate artistic taste, genuine value and the highest grade of workmanship. Of course the aggregate annual sales are very large, and the firm of T. & E. Dickinson is a prosperous one, a credit to the members and to the city.

BUFFALO RUBBER COMPANY.

G. D. Barr, Proprietor—Manufacturers and Jobbers of India Rubber Goods of Every Description—Pure Oak-Tanned Leather Belting and Mill Supplies—Agency of the Boston Belting Co.—Nos. 204 and 206 Main Street.

One of the most attractive establishments in the city of Buffalo is the splendid seven-story edifice occupied by the Buffalo Rubber Co., Main street, between Seneca and Exchange. The building was for many years occupied by the old established house of W. H. Glenny, Sons & Co. It was entirely rebuilt at a large outlay, two stories added, and especially adapted to the requirements of the Buffalo Rubber Co., which formally opened it with one of the finest displays in the country, during the past summer. Since that time the salesrooms have been remodeled and lighted with electricity throughout. It would be difficult through a pen sketch to give an adequate idea of what such a comprehensive assortment of goods, especially in the rubber line, consists of. The display is so varied and artistically arranged that it attracted crowds of visitors for several days after the opening. The facilities possessed for the manufacture of this company's celebrated pure oak-tanned leather belting and hose are unsurpassed, while the stock of rubber belting, hose, packing and mill supplies is conceded to be larger than that of any other house in the State. It is carefully selected from the best manufacturers in the country, of which the old reliable Boston Belting Co. of world-wide reputation stands at the head.

The trade of this company extends over a wide territory, having been built up by years of energetic effort. The firm was originally N. H. Gardner & Co., in 1853; in 1873 it was succeeded by Barr & Curtiss, and in 1877 by the present proprietor, Mr. G. D. Barr. The latter has demonstrated that he is one of Buffalo's leading business men in the line of progress—a wide-awake and liberal business man and good citizen.

SIDNEY SHEPARD & CO.

Buffalo Stamping Works—Manufacturers of Stamped, Pieced and Japanned Tin Ware, Metals, Tinmen's Supplies, Tools, Iron and Steel Cut Nails, etc.—Nos. 145, 147 and 149 East Seneca St.

The leading establishment of its kind outside the metropolis, and perhaps as extensive as any similar American concern, the house of Sidney Shepard & Co. was founded in 1836, and has pursued a steady upward and onward course to commercial distinction from its inception. The firm removed in January from No. 68 Main street to Nos. 145, 147 and 149 East Seneca street, where they occupy spacious and convenient quarters fronting 60 feet on both Seneca and Carroll streets, with a depth of 163 feet, four stories on the former and five on the latter thoroughfare. Here they have ample room for the transaction of an immense business, and largely increased facilities and opportunities for still further enlarging their operations. At the factory, No. 191 Clinton street, every department is completely fitted up with special reference to the demands of the specialties to which it is devoted, and each is complete in itself. The manufacturing plant and facilities are all that could be desired, including many devices and approved machines for economizing labor and producing the most perfect work rapidly and in large quantities. Much of this ingenious machinery was specially designed and constructed for and is covered by patents held by the firm; it is consequently peculiar to this establishment and beyond the reach of competing manufacturers. Steam power supplements and supplants hand-work wherever available, and the output is enormous in quantity, superb in quality, and almost infinite in variety. The equipment is valued at several hundred thousand dollars, in addition to which the house commands ample resources and is sound and responsible in all respects.

As before stated, the Seneca-street building is headquarters of the firm, containing the principal office and salesrooms, and is a hive of industry at all seasons. The stock exhibited here is one of the most extensive ever offered the trade, and embraces almost all items of stamped, japanned and plain tinware for which there is any demand, together with a carefully selected stock of metals, tinners' supplies and house-furnishing hardware of every description.

Necessarily, an establishment doing so widely-diffused a business enjoys many and important advantages over smaller concerns, and is prepared to fill heavy orders with the utmost promptitude, in the best and most satisfactory manner, and at rock-bottom figures; consequently, Sidney Shepard & Co. have the entire confidence and a large share of the patronage of the trade, not only of the region immediately tributary to Buffalo, embracing Western New York and Pennsylvania, but throughout the East, North, South and West.

Their branch house at Chicago, established some ten years ago, does a business to the full as extensive as that of the parent house here, and is increasing its sales and importance at a rapid rate. Here at home the firm employ several hundred skilled workmen in their various departments. It will be seen that Sidney Shepard & Co. confer as much indirect benefit upon the community in the way of providing remunerative employment to large numbers of people as directly in attracting hither buyers of merchandise from a distance. The house is one of which Buffalo should be and is justly proud.

SWAN-STREET CAFÉ.

J. A. Oaks, Proprietor—No 11 East Swan St.

The Swan Street Café was opened to public patronage by its present proprietor, Mr. J. A. Oaks, in April of 1885, and is truly a model establishment, conducted on the most liberal scale throughout. Mr. Oaks is an experienced caterer, brought up to the business of ministering to the inner man, and in his present venture has spared neither labor nor expense in the effort to please the public and render his house popular with, and the regular resort of, the best citizens of Buffalo, and of such transient sojourners as appreciate the good things of life, prepared in the highest style of the art and served in an unexceptionable manner. That he has succeeded is evident from the large and constantly increasing patronage extended, and the general air of prosperity and pleasant bustle that pervades the entire place.

Guests of the "Swan-Street" are provided with tempting meals, including every substantial and delicacy of the season, at any hour of the day or night, served promptly by polite and attentive waiters, at comparatively very low prices.

An elegantly appointed suite of dining parlors for the convenience of families, ladies and dinner-parties is provided on the second and third floors, reached by both stairs and elevator, where quiet and comfort add zest to the delicious viands. Lady visitors will find toilet rooms and other conveniences.

The Swan-Street is also the leading shell oyster house of the city, and patrons may have the luscious bivalves opened before their eyes, as all are opened on the premises, served promptly, neatly and in any style or quantity desired. Oysters are supplied to families and others by the hundred, quart or gallon, and delivered, fried, by the hundred or dozen.

Private consumers are also supplied with chicken and lobster salads, green turtle soup, dressed and cooked game and fowls in season, boned turkey, etc. In short, the establishment is first-class in every particular, and well worthy the liberal support it receives at the hands of a critical and appreciative public.

SLATE MANTELS.

Empire Slate Mantel Works—H. N. Warren, Proprietor—No. 169 Niagara St.

One of the principal slate mantel houses of Buffalo is that of Mr. H. N. Warren—the Empire Slate Mantel Works—No. 169 Niagara street, established by T. M. Ryan & Co. in 1885, Mr. Warren purchasing the plant in May of 1886. The factory is four stories in height, 30 feet front, 200 feet deep, employs eighteen men, and turns out about $25,000 worth of finished goods per annum, all of which are eagerly taken by the trade, principally in the West.

The object is to build up a first-class connection with builders, inside finishers and others more or less directly interested, and to that end the latest designs, novelties in patterns, superior material and workmanship and moderate prices are the rule. That this plan is a successful one goes without saying, and the products of the Empire Slate Mantel Works are already well and favorably known all over the country.

Mr. H. N. Warren was formerly engaged in the newspaper business, and later in merchandising. He is an old citizen of Buffalo, popular with all who know him. In the late civil war he served his country with ardor and distinction for three years, entering the service as a captain and returning a colonel. He was seriously wounded in the last battle of the war at Five Forks, Virginia.

A. T. KERR & CO.,

Wholesale Dealers in Wines and Liquors—No. 99 East Seneca St.

Mean and adulterated drinks supply the temperance apostles and prohibition fanatics with their most powerful arguments, and if it were possible to abolish the manufacture and sale of these abominable concoctions there would be little need for stringent laws for the restriction, much less the prohibition of the liquor traffic. Some men and women are so physically and mentally constituted that an occasional glass of stimulant is necessary to their health and comfort, and to them the maker and dealer in pure, sound liquors is a real benefactor and friend, supplying them with the means of maintaining health, strength and courage to enjoy life and overcome its ever-recurring cares and difficulties. Such a house is that of A. T. Kerr & Co., the well and favorably known importers and wholesale dealers in fine wines and liquors, No. 99 Seneca street. The house was founded by its present senior member in 1859 at No. 59 Main street. He removed to the present location in 1873, and in 1875 the firm of A. T. Kerr & Co. was organized, composed of Messrs. A. T. and A. D. Kerr and H. C. Green.

The firm have a handsome four-story building, 25 feet front, 165 feet deep, with ample cellars, conveniently arranged throughout, and stocked on every floor with superb lines of the finest wines of noted vintages, fruity old French brandies, and rich and fragrant rye and Bourbon whiskies of the most celebrated brands—conspicuous among which is exhibited a rare stock of the renowned "Old Amber" rye, their leading specialty, a bland, ripe, oily and delicious whisky that has few equals and no superior— the favorite with *bon vivant* and medical practitioner alike.

Messrs. A. T. Kerr & Co. have a very large and growing trade, extending over New York and adjoining States, averaging about $175,000 per annum. The house enjoys the confidence of and is popular with the trade and consumers wherever known. All of the members are natives of this county. Mr. A. T. Kerr was born in 1835, and has resided in Buffalo since 1854, clerking for Bidwell & Co. until 1857, subsequently keeping books for Renwick & Bissell, plumbers, for two years, when he embarked in the liquor business, first as a member of the firm of Kerr & Laing, and later by himself. He was a charter member of Neptune Hose No. 5, and is an exempt fireman. He is also an active Freemason. Mr. A. D. Kerr was born in 1842, and entered the firm in 1875, having been in his brother's employ previously. He served in the Sixty-fourth New York as a second lieutenant, and was wounded in the shoulder at Bristow's Station, October 14th, 1863, from which he has never entirely recovered. He is an Oddfellow, a Knight of Honor, and a member of the A. O. U. W. Mr. H. C. Green, born in 1838, came to Buffalo in 1859, and entered the firm in 1875. He is a Freemason, a Knight of Honor and a Workman. All are A No. 1 men, upright and faithful in every relation, and fairly entitled to their social and business prosperity.

JACOB F. KUHN,

Proprietor of the Union Brewery—Nos. 648, 650 and 652 Broadway.

The Union Brewery, of which Mr. Jacob F. Kuhn is the proprietor, is one of the pioneer breweries of the city, and for this reason alone is entitled to special mention. A noteworthy point is the fact that several of the leading Buffalo brewers either received their practical training at the Union Brewery or were connected with it in some capacity. This brewery was planned on the best principles, and the beer brewed there has always stood high. At the present time there is not a brand of beer in the Buffalo market that excels it for purity or flavor. During the last fifteen years Mr. Kuhn has conducted it, and with good success. He has been ably assisted by his two sons, and the practical working of the establishment has for some time past been in their hands. For the year 1886 the product was about 6,000 barrels. The brewery is now refrigerated with a fifteen-ton Kransch refrigerating machine, which was put in operation during the present season. The plant of the brewery is being remodeled and will, when completed, make the capacity at least 20,000 barrels per year. These improvements will consist of adding another story to the present brewery and additional storage rooms. The property occupied on Broadway affords plenty of accommodation for the improvements mentioned, which will tend to enhance the old-time reputation of this brewery.

The Messrs. Kuhn are all level-headed, practical business men. Their aim has always been to give satisfaction to their customers, whether in the trade or otherwise.

PETER G. STRAUB (Established 1873),

Dealer in all Kinds of Cut and Building Stone, Lime and Cements—Sidewalk Paver and Jobber—Manufacturer of Stone Burial Cases—Main Yard and Office, Nos. 918 to 930 Main St.; Branch Yards, No. 1151 Main and 938 Ellicott St.

Mr. Straub has been established in his present line of business here in Buffalo since 1873, having been a member of the firm of Bauer, Straub & Co., to which he succeeded in 1877. Among his most important recent building contracts were the Peoria (Ill.) postoffice, erected in 1885, and the Erie (Pa.) postoffice, now nearing completion. These are both splendid pieces of work, and reflect great credit upon the builder.

Mr. Straub is the most extensive layer of sidewalks in Buffalo, and his excellent work is seen in all portions of the city. He is also patentee and manufacturer of a new and improved stone burial case, which is rapidly coming into general use, since it affords perfect security and protection to the dead.

The burial case is made from the best sawed stone, carefully grooved and hermetically sealed, thus guaranteeing the preservation of the remains for a longer period than the old system. The prices are reasonable, and orders are executed and cases set on completion of the grave.

Mr. Straub has the contract for working the county almshouse quarry, employing otherwise idle pauper labor for excavating, and skilled labor for quarrying and dressing the stone, which is of superior quality and much sought by builders, to whom it is supplied in immense quantities, besides what he requires for the various improvements upon which he is himself engaged. This plan of employing pauper labor, while it does not bring it into competition with free skilled labor, saves the taxpayers a considerable sum annually, which would otherwise go for the maintenance of drones, who can but will not work, save under compulsion, besides which the county receives a handsome royalty for the quarrying privilege, which, lying within the city limits, is of practical value to the contractor.

Mr. Straub also handles all other popular varieties of building stone, Seneca and Ohio sandstone, etc., which he supplies to builders on reasonable terms. He carries large stocks of lime and cements, besides, and is prepared to fill orders promptly and in the best manner. His yards are three in number, viz.: One—where is also located his office—at Nos. 918 to 930 Main street, 140 by 150 feet; one at No. 1151 Main street, 80 by 150 feet, and the third at No. 938 Ellicott street, 80 by 230 feet. He employs about fifty men, and does an annual business of over $100,000.

C. J. DRESCHER & SON,

Paper Box Manufacturers—Wholesale and Retail Dealers in Printed Manilas, Straw and Rag Wrapping, Fancy and Print Papers, Straw and Wood Pulp Boards—Nos. 13, 15 and 17 Terrace.

The leading paper box factory of Buffalo is that of C. J. Drescher & Son, Nos. 13, 15, and 17 Terrace, where they have six floors, 40 by 60 feet square, employ thirty-five men and girls, besides a fine equipment of first-class machinery, and turn out from 4,800 to 5,000 boxes of all sizes per diem. They also make a specialty of strawboard tubes of all kinds and sizes for mailing maps, engravings, chromos, drawings, sheet music, etc., and are prepared to supply the trade with either boxes or tubes in any quantity desired at short notice and on reasonable terms. A fine steam engine supplies power for running all the machinery, paper and board cutters, presses, etc., required in the establishment.

C. J. Drescher himself is also an extensive dealer in printed manila wrapping papers for merchants, straw and rag wrapping, fancy and print papers of every description, and sole agent for the goods of several celebrated straw and wood pulp board manufactures, whose products he furnishes to the trade at mill prices. His warerooms are at all times stocked with full lines of goods of the kinds we have enumerated, and buyers and others interested will do well to call and see the samples and prices.

Mr. Drescher, sr., established the present business in 1867 at Nos. 188 and 190 Main street, over the Bank of Commerce, removing in 1877 to No. 15 Terrace. By industry and close attention to the demands of the trade he has made his venture a conspicuous and profitable success. His son, Mr. C. A. Dresher, an active, industrious, live young man, has charge of the establishment.

THE BUFFALO NATURAL GAS FUEL CO.

D. O'Day, President; O. G. Warren, Vice-President; John McManus, Secretary and Treasurer; C. N. Payne, General Manager—Office, Rooms 4 and 5 Coal and Iron Exchange.

No more opportune or valuable discovery has ever been made than that of natural gas. It has already revolutionized many branches of manufactures, and bids fair to prove in various ways the most beneficent of all the forces stored up in the bosom of Mother Earth, to be released and utilized when most needed for the comfort, convenience and profit of man. It has made a new, clean and healthful city of Pittsburg, reinspired Wheeling, warmed, lighted and beautified scores of towns throughout Western Pennsylvania, West Virginia and Eastern Ohio, and has at last been introduced to work its wonders here in Buffalo. Its cleanliness in use, economy and convenience, cannot fail to commend it not only to manufacturers but to housekeepers. First turned on at Wheeling in September last, the *Intelligencer* has this to say of it:

"Next to the Pittsburg of former days, Wheeling has an unenviable reputation for smoke and soot and all the debris of dirt and blackness that results from the universal use of coal in an unscientific way—that is, in a way that did not consume the smoke. It was here as it was in Pittsburg, that every house vied with every factory in belching forth columns of smoke from its chimneys that rained down endless flakes of soot on the town. The inside and outside of our houses too plainly suggested smoke and soot and dirt. No amount of paint could keep down this unprepossessing appearance. It would persist in asserting itself as soon as the paint was fairly dry. The roofs on the houses, the paper on the walls, the carpets on the floors, the curtains in the windows, the shrubbery and grass in the yards, the trees on the sidewalks, all conspired to tell the tale of sulphur and soot, and all took on the complexion of a damaged reputation. The sorrows of wash-days in Wheeling can never be told, especially of the clothesline part of it—the hanging-out-to-dry ordeal. The breeze that dried the linen would rain down the carbon that so provokingly besprinkled it. Until the news that natural gas was coming, we all expected to plod along in this weary housekeeping throughout our lives, after the manner of our predecessors. But a great change in this matter of soot and blackness is about to occur—the same sort of a change that has already occurred at Pittsburg. Pittsburg is now a clean town. A collar and a pair of cuffs can be worn a whole day, and an ordinary cake of toilet soap will last a lady a week. To many people who have not seen Pittsburg lately this may appear incredible, but it is a fact. And it is all owing to the substitution of natural gas for coal to such a general extent. As it now is up in that once "smoky city" so will it very soon be down here in Wheeling. In a year or so, when gas is burned in all our homes and only colorless carbonic air is seen issuing from our chimneys, we will scarcely recognize the complexion of the old town. And when in winter there is no kindling to provide and split up, no shivering over damp fuel that refuses to ignite, no smoke to be driven down the chimney by a gust of changing weather, no sulphurous cinders and dust scattering ashes to take up, no unsightly barrels or bins of refuse in the back yards waiting to be hauled away to the dump pile, we shall all thank Providence that while our lamps still hold out to burn we were permitted to see this new order of things. Really and truly it will revolutionize housekeeping in Wheeling and give numberless weary hands a rest from hitherto endless scrubbing, sweeping and cleaning. This of itself, putting aside all we expect of benefit to our manufacturers, is enough to create a boom in the old town."

Next to Pittsburg, Wheeling is the greatest iron and steel manufacturing point in the West, and all the mills and factories are using natural gas, which gives unqualified satisfaction. The same paper already quoted, interviewed Secretary Whitaker of the Whitaker Iron Company as to the value and acceptability of the gas. Mr. Whitaker said he was delighted with it. He could not say too much in its favor, for its advantages could not be overestimated. "There is no question about its making a better article of iron," said Mr. Whitaker. "No sulphur comes in contact with the iron as it is put through the various processes from the raw to the finished state. It cannot help but add to the durability of the product."

"The gas is a great thing for most of your employes, isn't it?"

"The gas was hailed with delight by the men employed at the furnaces. The sulphur and smoke from coal were annoying, and no doubt unhealthy. With natural gas all this is obviated. No grate bars are to clean, no clinkers to knock out of the furnace, the sulphur and smoke almost stifling the men in performing this work. In addition, there will be a great saving in furnace building. There are so many advantages that gas has over coal in the manufacture of iron that they cannot be enumerated. Wheeling is certainly fortunate in securing the new fuel. It means the continuance and increased output of her present manufactories, and unquestionably the erection of many more."

These extracts are sufficient to prove the advantages of natural gas over coal, and it only remains for Buffalo manufacturers' and housekeepers to stretch forth their hands, take hold of the new fuel, and at once and forever rid themselves of the annoyance and waste inseparable from the burning of coal.

The Buffalo Natural Gas Fuel Company was incorporated early in the past year with a cash capital of $250,000. The officers—well-known and popular business men—we have already named. The wells are located in McKean county, Pa., and the great supply main is eighty-seven and one-half miles in length, capable of delivering here 2,500,000 feet of gas every twenty-four hours. The principal Buffalo station is located at No. 13 Franklin street, and the company's office at rooms 4 and 5 Coal and Iron Exchange building, Washington street, adjoining custom-house. During the past summer and fall about three hundred men were employed in the work of laying pipes and making connections on the west side of the city, numerous factories and private residences availing themselves of the vapor fuel as soon as turned on, in December. It is already popular with our citizens, and the management is besieged with applications from people who are desirous of using it experimentally with a view to dispensing with coal. The entire city will be piped ere another winter, and the probability is that the present facilities will have to be multiplied for the accommodation of the public.

ORIENTAL BATH ROOMS.

Turkish and Russian Baths—Wagner & Nugent, Proprietors—No. 850 Main St.

The Oriental baths were opened by Mr. J. B. Wagner in 1882. He came here from New York highly recommended by leading residents of that city, and with an experience of sixteen years in this specialty—seven years with the Imperial Bath Co. and five years with Drs. Atwater and Angell, whose renowned baths are the resort of thousands from a distance, as well as residents of New York and surrounding cities, most of whom are sent to them by practicing physicians of high repute. Mr. Wagner has been remarkably successful with his Buffalo venture, and has gained the confidence of the medical profession and the general public in a marked degree. So large was his patronage, in fact, that in June of 1885 he was compelled to double his accommodations, so that at present, in addition to the original bath-rooms, the establishment occupies the entire ground floor of No. 850 Main street, which connects with the old quarters, and both are fitted up in the most complete and elegant manner for the reception and treatment of invalids and the general public. Every adjunct is modern, the baths located on the main floor, the heating and ventilating arrangements perfect, the baths equal to any in the world and superior to any others in this vicinity, and the entire concern is under the supervision of Mr. Wagner himself, of whose long experience we have already spoken. The subjoined letter speaks for itself:

To whom it may concern :   NEW YORK, October 1, 1881.

The bearer, Mr. John Wagner, had charge of the bathing department of the New York Racquet Club, of which I am a member. I think they would have voted him the degree of A. B. (artistic bather), had it been suggested or thought of. I consider him an adept in the matter of bathing and rubbing, and that he has reduced those processes as near as can be to perfection, and so recommend him.   JAMES BUELL,
Late President of Importers & Traders' Bank of New York, and also of the United States Life Insurance Co.

January 13th of the present year Mr. John A. Nugent, a native of Vermont, who has resided in Buffalo for the past seven years, became associated with Mr. Wagner as part proprietor and assistant manager, and the firm is now Wagner & Nugent.

Physicians furnish their patients written directions; otherwise Mr. Wagner exercises his own ripe judgment, the object being to please and benefit every patron. The firm enjoy a large and prosperous business, and expect to build up here one of the most famous bathing houses in the world. A fine pool and low charges—fifty cents per bath—tend to make the establishment popular, while the beneficial effects of medicated baths are universally conceded.

A separate ladies' bath, complete in every detail, and elegant and luxurious in appointment, is soon to be in operation on Main street, near the gentlemen's baths, and will be under the management of Mrs. J. B. Wagner, assisted by a corps of female helpers.

BUFFALO REAL ESTATE.

A Most Attractive Field for Investment—Values Rapidly on the Increase—Gigantic Improvements.

The growth of Buffalo has been so extensive within the past decade, particularly in the outlying districts, that it is necessary to get out a new map almost every year. .In that extensive section included in the term East Buffalo, extending through an area of several miles along the Belt Line railroad, the real estate boom has been a phenomenal one. During the past year there has been remarkable activity in the extensive tracts of this section available for building purposes. According to Mr. Joseph Bork, who is an unquestioned authority, values in the class of real estate referred to have more than doubled within a year. It is pretty safe to assert that nearly all the property between the Belt Line railroad and the city line has changed hands recently, representing an average advance of 100 per cent. This property is being rapidly divided up into building lots and taken by a very thrifty element among the laboring class, of whom there has been large influx to this city within the past few years, The extensive manufacturing, railroad and other industrial interests furnish lucrative employment for thousands of the new-comers, while the Belt Line gives convenient access to those seeking homes in this part of the city, and which can be had at a moderate outlay from their earnings. As an illustration of real estate improvement, it is credibly stated that on one tract east of Fillmore avenue, between Sycamore street and Broadway, within the past year Mr. Bork sold 800 lots, upon which 500 houses have been built. A large Polish immigration has settled here and built up considerable portions of East Buffalo as if by magic. These industrious people now have two splendid churches, one of which, nearly completed, represents a cost of $30,000. The owners presented this congregation with the half interest held by them in the twenty-seven lots which were secured as the church site on Rother street, between Sycamore street and Broadway. Mr. Bork, who is in a position to know, gave it as his opinion that at no late day that entire section from the Belt Line railroad to Cheektowaga will be entirely built up.

Among the transactions in this section in 1886, one piece of property sold in May for $12,000; later, in July, for $18,000, and finally, in November, for $34,000. This represents purchases by prominent real estate men exclusively. In that central portion of the city between Main, Michigan, Broadway and Seneca streets, the growing demands for additional business blocks makes this class of real estate gilt-edge for investment purposes. In fact, there is no city in the country to-day where there is so much inquiry from outside capitalists for investment, or where the same opportunities are afforded on such a magnificent scale as in Buffalo. Among the best posted and most active operators in real estate, Mr. Bork stands prominently to the front. He has had thirty years experience in the business, and is now the largest operator in the city. His office, at No. 363 Main street, is thronged every hour in the day. Any business intrusted to him is sure to receive careful and judicious attention. Associated with him is Mr. Henry H. Voght, a rising young business man of experience, who is also well and favorably known.

FOX & HOLLOWAY,

Dealers in South Shore and Canada Sand—Yard, Fourth St. near Wilkeson; Office, Room 2, Austin Building, Niagara, Franklin and Eagle Sts.

It is of the greatest importance to property-owners and builders, pavers and others that the sand used should be of the best quality, since the durability of the work in which it is employed depends thereon to a great extent.

The firm of Fox & Holloway, established in 1883, with extensive yards at the intersection of Fourth, Georgia and Wilkeson streets, and office in the Austin building, corner of Eagle and Franklin streets, are prepared with superior facilities in the way of teams and boats to supply contractors and builders with any desired quantity of the best lake sand, both South shore and Canada, promptly and on the most reasonable terms. It is unnecessary to explain the reasons for the superiority of this sand over all other kinds obtainable in this part of the country; the fact stands undisputed and is sufficient.

Mr. Charles W. Holloway has been in this business for a long period, his uncle, Mr. Isaac Holloway, having followed it for twenty years.

14

THE BUFFALO WOOD VULCANIZING CO.,

Largest and Most Complete Wood Vulcanizing Works in the World—J. F. Moulton, President; D. O'Day, Vice-President; F. A. Bell, Treasurer; F. T. Moulton, Secretary—Office and Works, Ganson St. near Michigan; Uptown Office, Coal and Iron Exchange.

Of late years one of the great economic questions of the day, which has puzzled the minds of leading scientists as well as statesmen, has been that of the rapid destruction of timber. Vast sections from whence came the great lumber supply of the country have been denuded to meet the enormous demand, and the question has gravely arisen as to what the result would be. As might be expected, inventive genius has solved the problem. In other words, a process has been discovered which renders wood of any kind as imperishable as iron, so far as the effects of temperature, moisture, etc., are concerned.

Heretofore the treatment of wood for durability has been confined to seasoning and kiln-drying. The effect has been the evaporation of the natural fluids, which deprived the fibre of chemical elements which ought to contribute to its strength and durability. The vulcanizing process herein referred to will revolutionize the old methods which have been in vogue from almost time immemorial. The principles involved in vulcanizing are simple and wonderful in effect. Wood subject to treatment is sumitted to immense air pressure, which prevents the escape of the fluid components when the high temperature is applied. The effect of the heat produces chemical changes in the fluids and other elements, which are thus retained, making it much stronger and more durable. All vegetable matter liable to generate decay is neutralized, and the consequence is the complete preservation of the wood.

The Buffalo Wood Vulcanizing Company, organized during the past year, has now in successful operation the largest works of the kind in the world. The process under which they are working was patented five years ago, and was first introduced commercially a year later by the United States Wood Vulcanizing Co. of New York City. The

Buffalo works rank among the most important of this city's industrial interests. They are centrally located on Ganson street near Michigan, adjacent to the Buffalo Creek railway, which connects with every railroad coming into the city. Being also situated on the Blackwell canal, they are equally accessible to the lake or canal. Hence all the shipping advantages of this great lumber market are at hand.

For the purpose of treating lumber or wood of any kind there are two large steel cylinders, 100 feet each in length by 6½ feet in diameter. These readily admit of an air pressure of 200 pounds to the square inch, supplied by a large air compressor built by the Ingersoll Rock Drill Co. of New York, the steam cylinders of which are 20 by 30 inches, and the air cylinders 18 by 30 inches. Within each of the large steel cylinders for treating the wood is over a mile of steam pipe coiled around the inner surface. Two of Moore's patent water-tube boilers, of 100-horse power each, built by the National Water Tube Boiler Works of New Brunswick, N. J., furnish the necessary heat and power. They are tested to carry a pressure of 300 pounds. The air and steam pressure varies for different woods. The works have a capacity of 100,000 feet per day, and it only requires from eight to ten hours to finish any lot. The ordinary pressure required is from 156 to 200 pounds at a temperature of 250 to 500 degrees.

From scientific tests made at the Stephens Institute of Technology, Hoboken, N. J., by Prof. Thurstone, it appeared that the strength and durability of wood treated by this process was from 20 to 23 per cent. greater than lumber seasoned the ordinary way. Green lumber especially exhibits the best results, as the fluids are coagulated, thus filling up the pores and cementing the fibres together. It will not shrink, swell or checks. Railway ties and heavy construction timbers are treated as successfully as the finest hardwood for finishing purposes. This is a great achievement for the railway interests of the country. For building purposes vulcanized wood is unapproachable. It is used entirely in the magnificent Mutual Life Insurance building ; Park & Tilford's up-town grocery house ; Osborne flats at Fifty-seventh street and Seventeenth avenue, and other noted buildings in New York city. The New York and Brooklyn Elevated railroad and the Erie and New York Central railroads have had vulcanized ties and stringers in use for several years, and they are as perfect as when put down.

GEORGE MONTAGUE,

Dealer in All Kinds of Coal, Hard and Soft Wood in Stick, Sawed and Split—Also "Magic Cleaner"—Yard and Office, No. 350 Virginia St. ; Branch Office, No. 573 Main St.

SOAP PLANT.

In referring to the local trade in coal and wood we might mention, as one of the oldest dealers, Mr. George Montague, whose office and yard are located at No. 350 Virginia street. This gentleman has been identified with the business since 1865, and by the judicious manner in which he has conducted it has built up a good trade. The best of facilities are at hand for supplying all demands, especially for family use. Steam furnishes the power used in sawing and splitting the wood by machinery, and large quantities are cut up. A specialty is made of kindling, and the coal handled is always of the best quality.

Mr. Montague is also the inventor of a cheap and valuable substitute for soap, called the "Magic Cleaner." This valuable compound consists mainly of an extract of the soap plant, combined with a few other simple ingredients, each and all of which are of a wholesome and cleanly nature. The offensive matter used more or less in the manufacture of soap in its various forms is happily absent from this truly excellent cleanser. It contains no acid, lime or potash, and can be used for cleaning paint, marble, oil cloth, glass, queensware, picture frames, sewing machines, or in fact, anything soiled by oil or grease. For washing clothes it is unsurpassed, as it dispenses to a great degree with the exertion and manual labor which may be said to have always made the washtub the terror of the average housewife. From the variety of uses for which the "Magic Cleaner" is available, it is certainly a most valuable article for the household. It has proved to be of great excellence for shampooing and the bath, and in case of cuts and burns is a safe and sure remedy. The finest fabric is not injured in the least by contact with it, and as a universal cleanser it deserves a prominent place. In addition it is a first-class disinfectant and deodorizer, while the price is within the reach of all, being but thirty-five cents a gallon. Since its introduction "Magic Cleaner" has met with universal favor as its qualities have become known, and every lady should give it a trial.

ROBERT AMBROSE,

Pisciculturist—Dealer in Building Stone, Groceries, etc.—Cor. Delavan Avenue and Avenue A.

Mr. Robert Ambrose came to Buffalo in the year 1828 at the age of two and one-half years, in company with his father and other members of the family. The elder was John A. Ambrose, a native of France, near the city of Strasburg. He settled on a tract of land in what is now the northeastern part of the city. It was then a wilderness, and wild animals were numerous, as were Indians. At that time the village of Buffalo had but sixty-five houses all told, and farming was carried on under difficulties unknown at the present day.

At the present time Mr. Ambrose resides at the corner of Delavan avenue and Avenue A, in a commodious residence replete with all modern improvements. Here he has for years carried on the grocery business. In addition, the valuable deposits of building stone on the tracts now owned by him have been worked. Sixteen years ago quarrying was begun on the corner of Delavan avenue and Avenue A, and a basin nearly an acre in extent was excavated to a depth of about fourteen feet. At a depth of six feet below the rock surface a stream of pure water was struck which flowed steadily. After the excavation was down to the depth mentioned Mr. Ambrose conceived the idea of transforming the basin into a miniature lake for the breeding and cultivation of fish. Drilling down to a depth of thirty-nine feet below the first vein, an artesian supply of water was struck, and the lake was soon ready. In June, 1885, Mr. Ambrose secured 15,000 California mountain trout. From Dr. Bissell, at Washington, nineteen German carp were secured, and from State Fish Commissioner Seth Green an additional supply of three-year-old carp for breeding purposes. Sturgeon, perch, rock bass, bullheads and other varieties have been added, and it is expected that about July of the present year the fishing will be opened to the public. The facilities for casting the fly will be unsurpassed, and lovers of rod and line will have some rare sport. The fish are all doing well, and the spawning facilities are first-class.

Mr. Ambrose owns three tracts of land, comprising twenty-three acres. It all contains excellent stone deposits, while the soil is unsurpassed for garden purposes. It is conveniently located, near the Belt Line railroad's driving park station. The old log-house still stands on the old homestead, and visitors are always sure of a cordial welcome. They will find Mr. Ambrose a rich mine of interesting and valuable reminiscences, while his fish project is so entirely novel that it cannot prove other than a source of satisfaction to the public and profit to its projector.

HOLMES & ADAMS,

Refiners of Petroleum and Paraffine Oils—No. 1070 East Seneca St.; Office, No. 47 East Seneca St.; Boston Office, No. 32 Broad St.

It is unnecessary to go into an extended disquisition on the subject of petroleum, this substance, its history, products and wonderful influence upon mercantile, manufacturing and commercial progress during the past twenty-five years being familiar to every intelligent reader who cares to inform himself. In this place we desire simply to make brief mention of one of Buffalo's conspicuous houses engaged in the refining of petroleum and shipment of the product—the firm of HOLMES & ADAMS, established originally by Lootz, Holmes & Adams in 1877, and changed to the present style in 1884 by the death of Mr. Lootz.

The works of this house are located at the junction of Seneca street and the Buffalo Creek railway, and comprises about six and a-half acres of land, upon which are erected all necessary buildings, equipped in the best manner with late improved machinery for the reduction and refining of petroleum and paraffine oils, naphtha, gasoline, etc., and the manufacture of superior grades of illuminants, wax and naphtha for export and home trade. From the first the object of the firm has been to establish for their products a high reputation and to maintain the same by every honorable means, the result being that by constant and watchful supervision, and the introduction of improved processes, they have attained a rare degree of perfection, and their oils are in steadily increasing demand at the highest market figures.

Both members of the firm are from Boston, and they maintain a branch office at No. 32 Broad street, that city. They ship large quantities of high-grade oils to all parts of this country and Europe, and are enterprising and successful business men.

THE BENNETT AND UNION ELEVATORS.

D. S. Bennett, Proprietor; R. M. Cannon, Superintendent—Bennett Elevator, Corner Water St., Ship Canal and Buffalo River; Union Elevator, Joy Street and Buffalo River; Office at Bennett Elevator.

In the historical and statistical portion of this work will be found a detailed account of the origin of Buffalo's grain trade and elevator interest, and a summary of the progress and development of these mutually dependent industries. In this place we desire simply to describe and detail the careers of two of the most noted of the elevators, viz.: The Bennett and the Union. The former of these was erected in 1862–63, at the intersection of Water street, the ship canal and Buffalo river, fronting 150 feet on the latter, with a depth of 98 feet. The bins, of 3,000 to 7,000 bushels capacity each, are 52 feet in depth, the roof being 60 feet above their tops, or 130 feet from the foundations. The bins of the Union elevator, built in 1867, are 52 feet in depth, the edifice being 40 by 54 feet square. An improved dry-kiln of 8,000 bushels daily capacity, and a complete outfit of the best and most ingenious modern machinery, give Mr. Bennett extraordinary facilities for the handling of grain, while the united capacity of the two elevators is about 15,000,000 bushels a year. The actual business of both is from 5,000,000 to 8,000,000, and seventy men are employed.

Mr. D. S. Bennett, the owner, is a native of Onondaga county, and has resided in Buffalo for nearly forty years. He is a public-spirited, liberal gentleman, and has served the people as a State Senator and in the halls of Congress.

Superintendent Cannon, the capable and experienced gentleman who has the practical management of the Bennett and Union elevators, has occupied that position since 1881.

THE OZARK PLATEAU LAND COMPANY.

Jewett M. Richmond, President; Lucian Hawley, Secretary; Absalom Nelson, Local Agent in Missouri—Offices, Lebanon, Mo., and No. 24 Erie St., Buffalo.

The Ozark Plateau Land Company was organized and incorporated in December, 1883, with a paid-up capital of $50,000, and owns 150,000 acres of superior farming and grazing land in that garden-spot of the Southwest, Southern Central Missouri—an undulating region of forest and prairie, intersected with running streams and numerous living springs of pure water, elevated 1,100 to 1,200 feet above tide-water and 1,000 feet above the Mississippi at St. Louis, with a mild and salubrious climate, where deep snows are unknown in winter, and torrid heats in summer; the air dry, pure and bracing, and malaria unheard-of. The average sunshine and rainfall are all that could be expected, forming an average between extremes, so necessary to the successful and profitable prosecution of farming operations. Crops seldom fail from either deluge or drought, while the rolling character of the country contributes to its healthfulness, and the beauty of the scenery, embracing every variety of hill and valley, woodland, open vista and shining river, make pleasant places for the homes of virtuous people.

The soils are among the best and most fertile known, principally magnesian limestone, which extend through the counties of Camden, Laclede, Dallas, Webster and others, and are dark in color, warm, light and productive. They produce black and white walnut, post, laurel, black and other oaks, and many trees of smaller growth, and, when cultivated, crops grow luxuriantly with reasonable attention throughout this favored region, and embrace corn, wheat, oats, tobacco, Irish and sweet potatoes, sorghum and all of the more palatable and useful garden vegetables. Fruits of all kinds, berries and grapes flourish there as well as in any portion of this country, and a ready market is found for all products of farm, garden and vineyard at St. Louis.

Stock-raising is a leading and profitable industry. Kentucky bluegrass grows luxuriantly, and cattle, sheep, horses and mules thrive and fatten upon it. As a wool-growing country it is equal to the best portions of Ohio, and it is capable of being made one of the richest dairy sections of the Union, the grass, the water, the topography and the climate all favoring that industry.

The State of Missouri holds vast bodies of school lands, making ample provision for educational advantages, and the school laws, modeled upon those of the older States, are unsurpassed for liberality in this respect.

The towns in the vicinity of the Ozark Plateau Land Company's lands are : Lebanon, the county seat of Laclede county, 185 miles from St. Louis, on the St. Louis & San Francisco railway, 2,500 inhabitants, bank, two newspapers, several school-houses, high school, five churches, court-house, flouring and saw-mills, factories and numerous dry-goods and grocery stores; Phillipsburg, Brush Creek, Conway and Niangua, railroad shipping points; Marshfield, county seat of Webster County, 1,400 inhabitants, 217 miles from St Louis, on St. Louis & San Francisco railway—much such a place as Lebanon, with equal attractions; North View, a railroad town, and many smaller villages. In short, these lands offer inducements to farmers such as are seldom found. Missouri is a rapidly growing State—a high-license State, where the laws are enforced —and the sober-minded, industrious tiller of the soil has opportunities equal to those found in any part of the world.

The company's lands are offered at very moderate prices, and all who think of investing in Western soil should address the secretary, Mr. Lucian Hawley, No. 24 Erie street, Buffalo, for full particulars, or call upon Mr. Absalom Nelson, local agent at Lebanon, Mo., and inspect the lands and their advantages.

BUFFALO FELT GOODS CO.,

Nos. 119 and 121 Chicago St.

The manufacture of felt and felt goods is rapidly advancing to a foremost position among the industries. This material has been found, upon trial, admirably adapted to a variety of purposes to which hitherto cloth and rubber were exclusively applied, as, for instance, the manufacture of snow and water-proof boots and shoes—felt being warmer, more pliable and more absorptive, and consequently more healthful than rubber, and in all respects superior to cloth.

Within the past year Buffalo has seen the establishment within her corporate limits of the first and only felt works in this section of the country—the Buffalo Felt Goods Company's factory at Nos. 119 and 121 Chicago street, of which Messrs. James Kerr and Edward Roos are the proprietors. Mr. Kerr is of Scottish birth, has resided in the United States since 1848, and in Buffalo about a year. He is an experienced woolen mill man. Mr. Roos, who for some years has been engaged in the manufacture of felt in the Dominion, came here in 1885.

The Buffalo Felt Company's works is the only woolen goods manufactory in Buffalo. The plant embraces a commodious three-story building, 80 by 125 feet, fitted up with a fine equipment of latest improved machinery, specially designed for the production of felt goods of the best quality, and employs some twenty-five or thirty operatives.

The leading specialty of the house is the manufacture of superior felt boots, for which there is a large and steadily growing demand throughout the North and North-west. These goods are supplied to jobbers and the wholesale trade exclusively, by whom they are furnished to retailers, and by them sold to consumers.

THE BUFFALO MUTUAL ACCIDENT ASSOCIA-TION.

William H. Slocum, President; J. W. Aldrich, Secretary; Charles A. Orr, Treasurer; Leroy Andrus, Attorney; Joseph Fowler, M. D., Surgeon; George A. Sanborn, General Manager—Home Office, Room 47 Chapin Block.

Disease, accident and death are conditions incident to this stage of existence that are certain to come to us all sooner or later. Against the consequences which would in the natural course ensue to our dependents from our being overtaken by prostrating disease, disabling accident or death, various fraternal societies and incorporated companies offer protection more or less ample and effective, and it is the plain duty of every respectable man of good habits while in the enjoyment of his faculties, health and strength to avail himself thereof and throw around his loved ones such safeguards as will secure them from the pinchings and temptations of want, in the day when he shall lie broken and helpless upon a bed of suffering, maimed past mending, or under the sod.

Of all the plans that have ever come to our notice for relieving the woes arising from disease and accident—from which none are exempt—we believe that of "The Buffalo Mutual Accident and Sick Benefit Association" is the most perfect, and presents the best claims to the consideration of thinking men and women, combining as it does the most commendable features with the greatest certainty of results. As its name implies, this association is conducted upon a purely mutual basis, every member contributing prorata towards the expense, and having a voice in the management. An admission fee of $5, to be paid to the agent, is required from all applicants. The dues are payable monthly as per table, directly to the home office, unless otherwise provided for, the death indemnity ranging from $250 to $5,000, and the weekly indemnity paid varies from $5 to $25, and the cost of the same per month to the member is from 30 cents to $3.50, according to occupation and amount insured. Ten per cent. of the monthly dues may be held in reserve until the association begins to pay full death benefits, after which time fifteen per cent. of the monthly calls may be set apart to the reserve fund, together with all the money received from re-instatement of delinquent members, and accrued interest on all investments. This fund will be held in trust for the exclusive benefit of the members, and to be used in case of excessive claims, or in case monthly dues are not sufficient to pay such claims. Sometimes the bulk of several months' losses will fall due in a single month, but by this system payments are so distributed as to avoid making a special assessment upon members in any such month. All surplus thus not used will be reimbursed to the members in the following manner: At the end of each five years, from January 1, 1887, the association will declare a dividend by setting aside for the use of the then present membership fifty per cent. of the entire reserve fund accumulated up to that date, which amount shall be ratably apportioned on the amount of monthly dues paid in by each surviving member in good standing on the books of the association on December 31st, prior to January 15th, that being the date of making such awards to all members who have paid monthly dues for one year or more. The method to be adopted in the division of this fund will be to issue scrip to each member for a ratable proportion due them. The scrip will be divided into five equal amounts, bearing the date of the next ensuing five years. Each amount will be subdivided into twelve coupons that may be used in part payment of the monthly dues during each year for five years after date of coupon. This method guarantees to the members all the advantage of gain realized from the Tontine system of insurance, where the profits and benefits of endowments are obtained. It is the only plan of accidental insurance equalizing the results as between those who live out their full expectation of life and those who prematurely allow their certificates to lapse. The Tontine feature stipulates a period of 5-10-15-20 years, during which all surplus interest on reserve funds, arising from deaths or lapses, are placed to the credit and benefit of surviving members, producing results that can be obtained by no other plan of accident insurance. We confidently believe there is no co-operative association that will insure its members at so low a cost for each five years as will this association under this method. The certificates of membership are non-forfeitable in two respects: By the above plans in this system of reserve fund a membership becomes nearly self-sustaining after the first five years of membership, because of the yearly dividends accruing from the Tontine fund, as heretofore explained. No extra charge for issuing permit for European travel. Should a member meet with an accident, fatal or totally disabling him, while engaged temporarily or permanently in any occupation of a more hazardous classification than that under which the member elected to be insured, or approximating thereto, if not mentioned in the association schedule of rates, the principal amount or weekly indemnity payable shall be such proportion of the amount therein as the amount paid by the member would insure for under such higher classification. All persons between the ages of 16 and 66, although they are not eligible for life insurance, can enter the accident class. Persons without visible means of support, drunkards, disreputable characters, the deaf, blind, demented or crippled, are not eligible to membership. Blank forms of application for membership are furnished, to be filled by the applicant, upon the receipt of which, with an admission fee of $5, a certificate will be issued by the association, as designated in the application.

The sick benefit feature has been adopted to meet the requirements of artisans, book-keepers, tradesmen, clerks, laborers and others who need a weekly allowance when ill. The plan is a practicable and well approved one, successful with other associations, and calculated to do much good.

The officers of the association, named above, are prominent business men, well known to the public. Mr. George A. Sanborn, the manager, has had long experience in both fraternal and regular insurance, and is a thoroughly practical man.

SCHWARTZ & CO.,

Manufacturers of Marbleized Slate Mantels, Grates, Fenders, Brass Open Fire-places, Brass Fenders, Andirons, Coal Hods, Fire Sets, etc.—Slate Work of Every Description—Tiles in all Varieties—Stoves, Ranges, Furnaces, etc.—Factory, Elk St. and N. Y. C. & H. R. Railway; Salesrooms, Nos. 89 and 91 Seneca St.

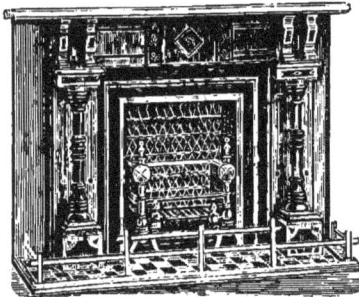

Progress is the watchword of our time, and few houses have done more to realize it, in its relation to the beautifying of the people's homes, than has that of L. Schwartz & Co., of this city, whose superb works in marbleized slate, brass, tiles and iron are found in the costliest modern residences all over this section of the Union. This now celebrated establishment was founded by Messrs. L. and B. Schwartz in the year 1867, and, owing to the skill and taste displayed, their enterprise has prospered from its inception—so much so, indeed, that in order to meet the constantly growing demand for their artistic and beautiful work they have been compelled to increase their facilities from time to time, until now they find themselves at the head of one of the largest industries of the kind in the country, employing some fifty trained workmen and turning out about $100,000 worth of finished goods per annum. Their ware and sales-rooms, Nos. 89 and 91 East Seneca street, occupy the entire building, five stories high, and here may be found at all times the largest, finest and most varied stock (to which additions are constantly being made) of marbleized slate mantels in original and classic design, slate goods generally, plain and glazed vitrified hearth and art tiles, grates, fire-places, brass fenders, andirons, fire sets, coal hods, etc., ever submitted to the trade, embracing hundreds of patterns, and the entire range of prices from the cheapest to the most elaborate.

The factory at Elk street and the N. Y. C. & H. R. railway is a large, well-lighted building, 82 by 125 feet, fitted up with special reference to the demands of the business to which it is devoted, and contains a fine assemblage of skillful artists and workmen, and a superior equipment of labor-saving devices which enable the house to execute the most extensive and intricate orders promptly and in the best manner.

The firm have a flourishing trade in their leading specialty of slate mantels throughout the United States, and are, in fact, the largest manufacturers of these goods in this country, filling orders for shipment East, West and South, and to Canada. Their first work of this kind was for the State Insane Asylum, located near this city. Since then they have become famous, and at the late New Orleans Cotton Centennial Exposition they were awarded the highest medal for beauty of design and finish of slate mantels. The firm is composed of live, energetic men, whose purpose it is to lead all competition in their line, and the trade may rest assured that novelty, taste and beauty, combined with exquisite workmanship, will ever characterize the work of L. Schwartz & Co. Correspondence solicited for all kinds of fire-place goods and slate-work of every description.

COATSWORTH ELEVATOR,

Thomas Coatsworth, Proprietor—Michigan St. and Buffalo River.

The receipts and shipments of grain at this port during the past year show a gratifying increase, and notwithstanding the efforts put forth by rival water and rail routes, the unquestioned supremacy of Buffalo and the Erie canal has been more than sustained. During the past year several extensive elevators have been erected, thus adding several million bushels to the elevator capacity of the city. In presenting a detailed account of these in this work we find among the most recent of the new elevator enterprises the Coatsworth, which is in course of completion as this work goes to press. This elevator, which is the property of Mr. Thomas Coatsworth, of this city, is located on South Michigan street and Buffalo river, and also adjacent to the Pratt & Wadham slip. A solid foundation has been secured on a base of 2,500 piles. The building is 71 by 160 feet, and will contain 65 bins, each 82 feet in height. As these are 20 feet higher than in any of the other elevators, it will be observed that the Coatsworth will be the tallest elevator in the city. It will have a capacity of 531,000 bushels of grain. The cost of the building will be about $250,000. The chimney is 145 feet in height. This elevator will receive both from vessels and cars, and will discharge both into canal-boats and cars, as a switch is to be laid connecting with the Buffalo Creek railroad.

The proprietor of this elevator, Mr. Coatsworth, has been a resident of Buffalo for about sixty years, and during that time he has been prominently identified with the grain interests of the city.

WILLIAM H. BORK,

Bookbinder and Blank Book Manufacturer—Nos. 263 and 265 Washington Street.

The prominence which Buffalo has gained in most industries has been well earned, and this applies with special force to bookbinding and the manufacture of blank books. Among the houses prominently identified with the business, none occupy a more advanced position than that of William H. Bork. The business was established in 1854, the style of the firm being Nauert, Engel & Co. In 1872 it become Nauert & Bork, and in 1874 W. H. Bork & Co. In 1878 Mr. Bork became the sole proprietor, and has remained so up to the present. The present location at Nos. 263 and 265 Washington street was occupied on May 1, 1886, and is well equipped for the business. The premises occupied are 32 by 135 feet, and a working force of from twenty to twenty-five hands is employed. About three years ago Mr. Bork began the manufacture of envelopes, making a specialty of chromatic or tint printed envelopes, and all sizes of catalogue envelopes. The bookbinding department is the main feature of the business, and the work turned out is unsurpassed in style and finish. Mr. Bork is a native of Buffalo, and learned the business here. Starting in at the foot of the ladder, he mastered every detail with a degree of tact that counted in his favor. By dint of honest endeavor he in time succeeded to the house which he entered as an apprentice twenty-four years ago.

JACOB JAECKLE,

Contractor and Builder—Manufacturer of Sash, Blinds, Doors, Frames, etc.
—No. 915 Genesee St.

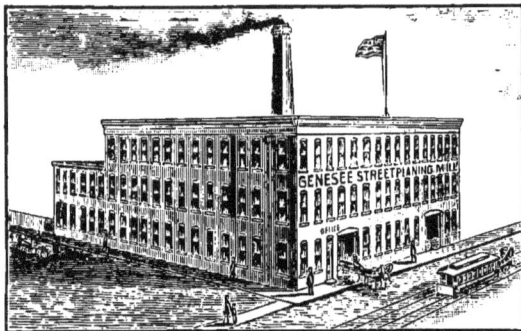

In treating of the industries of a city like Buffalo in detail, it is a remarkable fact that many of the most extensive establishments are located near the outskirts of the city. For instance, on the corner of Genesee and Guilford streets, Mr. Jacob Jaeckle carries on a business which employs, dependent on the season, from 80 to 100 hands, representing a weekly pay-roll in the neighborhood of $1,000. Such a business is one of the number contributing to make Buffalo what she is to-day. At the location mentioned is a large planing-mill, or, rather, two planing-mills. When Mr. Jaeckle started, in 1878, he began in an humble way. The business grew rapidly, and a couple of years later he added a building two stories high and 70 by about 100 feet in area. This, in the course of time, also proved inadequate, and another and larger structure of brick was added. These were fitted up with the best wood-working machinery and the manufacture of everything pertaining to building carried on. On the opposite corner is the lumber-yard, where a large and well-assorted stock is kept. Besides the above establishment, Mr. Jaeckle owns a lumber-yard, covering an area of about four acres of ground, on Genesee street, contiguous to the main line of the New York, Lake Erie and Western Railroad, which is known as Jaeckle's hemlock yard, and into which runs a switch 525 feet. Here can be found an immense array of hemlock timber and lumber at the lowest market prices.

As a contractor and builder, Mr. Jaeckle also does a large business. In this department about fifty men are employed. Among some of the buildings erected in part by this gentleman may be mentioned the High School, Insane Asylum, and others of equal note. As an illustration of the rapid expansion of the business, it now represents a capital of $80,000 and the annual business $150,000. The secret of this gentleman's success is largely referable to the fact that his personal supervision has always been given to the business in detail. He is a native of Buffalo and takes a deep interest in everything that pertains to the advancement of the city's interests. It should not be omitted, in conclusion, that on artistic decorative work, either exterior or interior, this establishment cannot be surpassed by any.

As above stated, Mr. Jacob Jaeckle is a native of Buffalo, where he was born in 1852, and learned his trade here. He has honestly earned the consideration in which he is held in this community, and the reputation he has established for integrity is acknowledged by all. We commend Mr. Jaeckle and his enterprise to those of our readers who may be interested, assuring them that business relations once entered upon will prove not only pleasant but profitable.

EDWARD MOELLER,

Dealer in First-Class Pianos—Nos. 24 and 26 Chippewa St.

Mr. Moeller is well known to the entire community, having been for many years a successful and popular teacher of music. He erected the handsome three-story block, the ground floor of which he now occupies, having thrown both store-rooms into one, or rather connected them, last spring, at which time he laid in the largest stock of fine pianos ever brought to this city, and, having floor space 60 by 72 feet, he is prepared with skillful workmen to repair all instruments sent him for that purpose. A handsome new front adds greatly to the attractiveness of the building. The block itself is a musical center, as a portion of it is occupied by Mr. Rottenbach, the most extensive dealer in music and musical merchandise in Western New York.

Mr. Moeller handles pianos exclusively, and none but those of the best makers, his stock embracing a superb assortment of grand, square and upright instruments from such renowned manufacturers as Decker Bros., New York; Henry F. Miller & Sons, Boston ; Kranich & Bach, Kroeger & Sons, Baer Bros., New York ; the Emerson Piano Co., and others. He has a large and growing trade in the city and throughout the adjoining counties, and his well-earned reputation among musical people is sufficient guarantee of his upright personal and business character. As a matter of accommodation, and to encourage the pursuit of the divine art, Mr. Moeller will sell pianos to responsible buyers on installments, and rent or exchange instruments when requested.

THE ARLINGTON.

Henry A. Roy, Proprietor—Cor. Exchange and Wells Sts., Opposite New York Central Passenger Depot.

One of the best appointed hotels in the city of Buffalo, beyond any question, is The Arlington. During the past year the firm of Mullen & Roy took the house in hand and expended several thousand dollars in refitting it from top to bottom. The building was entirely rejuvenated, and the transformation was so complete that it is practically a new building. The floors were newly laid with hard wood, the walls frescoed and papered, and the finest furniture, carpets and interior decorations put in. The house was reopened in June, and immediately became one of the most popular in the city. It is a great favorite with commercial men on account of the superiority of the accommodations and the further fact that the location is the most central and convenient in the city, being immediately opposite the New York Central passenger depot. On the first of September Mr. Mullen retired, and the house is now entirely in the hands of Mr. Roy.

Henry A. Roy was born in Albany in 1843, and came to Buffalo in 1865. He enlisted in the 177th New York Volunteers in 1862, and served with his regiment in several of the great battles of the late war. After the restoration of peace Mr. Roy went into railroading, and his extended acquaintance now redounds to his pecuniary advantage.

LIGHTNER & GOETTEL,

Merchant Tailors—No. 223 Pearl St.

As Shakspeare says: " The apparel oft proclaims the man," and he who would be regarded as a gentleman will do well to heed the teachings of all time and dress in character. A disregard of appearances is a sure indication of boorishness, and in no way is it more offensively exhibited than in carelessness and slovenliness in matters of attire. The tailor (when he is a good one) is man's best friend, in at least one respect —he brings out his physical perfections to the best advantage and conceals his blemishes as far as may be.

Prominent among Buffalo's best tailors are Messrs. Lightner & Goettel, No. 223 Pearl street, who opened their handsome establishment last summer, and have already secured a large and increasing run of first-class custom. These gentlemen carry a rich line of foreign and domestic suitings, cloths, overcoatings, etc., for the selection of their trade, and both are accomplished cutters of long experience. They employ about twenty journeymen, and expect to do a business of $30,000 for the first year. A visit to their neat and attractive rooms at the above number will prove both pleasant and profitable.

Mr. Lightner is from Reading, Pa., and has resided here five years. Mr. Goettel is a German, and came to Buffalo in 1883.

C. P. HAZARD,

Wholesale Dealer in Lumber, Shingles, Lath and Fence-Posts — No. 92
River St.

The lumber trade of Buffalo is one of its leading commercial interests, and happily
is in the hands of an enterprising, long-headed and liberal class of men who permit on
obstacle to withstand their energy or discourage their spirit. Prominent among the
leaders stands C. P. Hazard, No. 92 River street, a wide-awake Canadian who came to
Buffalo in 1864 and established himself, in partnership with his brother, in the same
line of business, about fifteen years ago. Mr. Hazard makes a specialty of Western pine
in cargo lots, which he sells to local dealers or ships to the Eastern cities as required.
His yards, bounded by slips Nos. 1 and 2, Erie basin, cover some three to four acres,
and are intersected by Palmer slip, which gives him unequaled receiving and shipping
facilities, and a storage capacity of some 10,000,000 to 12,000,000 feet. An average of
fifty men are employed during the shipping season. The tracks of the New York
Central, Michigan Central and Grand Trunk railways skirt the yards, and those roads
carry immense quantities of lumber from them to the various markets North and East,
the sales averaging 20,000,000 feet per annum, comprising a full line of choice pine
lumber, shingles, lath, cedar fence-posts and building material generally.

Mr. Hazard maintains a first-class planing mill at Rochester, where every description
of sash, doors, blinds, shutters, mouldings, etc., are made to order for the trade and pine
lumber of all dimensions prepared for the joiner. He is a member of the Buffalo
Merchants' Exchange and ranks with the solid business men of the city.

Mr. D. Y. Leslie is general manager for Mr. Hazard, and is an able and industrious
gentleman of fine address, popular with all who come in contact with him.

Builders, manufacturers, the lumber trade and all who require rough or dressed
pine in large quantities will do well to correspond with Mr. Hazard.

J. W. VICKERS,

Wholesale Manufacturer of Silk, Stiff and Cassimere Hats—No. 274 Main
St., corner Swan.

There are a number of diversified manufacturing interests in this city which,
although not conducted on a gigantic scale, yet in the aggregate tend to swell the
volume of Buffalo's industrial representation. Among them, for instance, may be
classed that of Mr. J. W. Vickers, manufacturer of silk, stiff and cassimere hats at wholesale. The location of this enterprise is at No. 274 Main street, corner of Swan, in the
building occupied by the United States Express Co. Here superior facilities are had

for conducting the business on an extended scale. All the modern appliances known to this time-honored craft are in operation, and a working force of from fifteen to twenty-five hands is employed. The business was established in 1874, the location originally being No. 215 Main street. Mr. Vickers' facilities are such that he has an extended business connection with the trade, not only in this city but throughout the contiguous territory. In the matter of styles, he always keeps up with the latest conceits, simultaneous with their appearance in New York. Samples are sent on approval when so desired, and no pains are spared to give entire satisfaction. In the matter of furnishing society uniforms, especially for Select Knights A. O. U. W., Mr. Vickers does a great deal of business ; in fact, for society organizations generally, any and all requirements are furnished on the shortest notice. The attention of the trade and all interested parties is directed to the advantages herein set forth. Mr. Vickers will be found honorable and straightforward in all his dealings, while the work he turns out complete is one of his best recommendations.

SHIFFERENS & SONS,

Manufacturers of All Kinds of Hand-Made Harness of the Best Oak Leather—Nos. 92 and 94 Broadway.

The City of Buffalo is gaining a great reputation for manufacturing. The extent and variety of the different lines represented is remarkable, as will be found from a glance at the pages of this work on the " Industries of Buffalo." In the manufacture of harness this city is becoming noted for the superiority of the goods turned out and the low prices as well. The house of Messrs. Shifferens & Sons is a pretty good illustration of what is done in this line, and the object of this article is to show what their work consists of. It has always been a ruling principle of this house since it was established in 1878 to make nothing but good honest harness, of the best material and of the very best workmanship. Then as an extra inducement to purchasers the prices are low, and the result has been, a large trade made up for the outlay. As an example, they turn out a single harness at $6.90 which they claim beats the world, and there is no doubt of it. Every man with a horse has a certain natural pride in having the animal show off to the best advantage, and when a harness can be secured for such a small outlay there is no excuse for driving a shabby-looking outfit. A splendid rubber-trimmed harness is sold at $16, and it is a beauty. Bargains on double harness are as numerous as bees in a clover patch on a July Sunday. Only the best oak leather is used, and there is no discounting the finish, of which it would take their catalogue to describe the different styles. Everything is hand-made, and the most skilled workmen are employed. Their harnesses are being used and handled in almost every State in the Union, including Canada, which speaks for itself. They send harnesses subject to approval, which goes to show that they do not sell a " cat in a bag," but that they do exactly as they agree. In light double and single harness for buggies, carriages, etc., they are not beaten anywhere.

The members of the firm are Peter J., William E. and John H. Shifferens. The location was originally on Ellicott street, but the business required better facilities, which have been secured at the present site, Nos. 92 and 94 Broadway, where three well-arranged floors, 30 by 100 feet, are occupied. About thirty hands are employed, and the business amounts to about $40,000 a year. The gentlemen composing the firm are live, enterprising business men, as their record shows. This firm will remove to their new factory, No. 102 Broadway, about May 1, 1887, and will enlarge same to about double its present size and employ from 50 to 100 men, their business having grown so large that the old factory was inadequate to supply the demand.

JEWETT M. RICHMOND,

Stock Farm Proprietor and Breeder of Registered Jersey Cattle—Buffalo Office, No. 24 Eric St.

Erie County, N. Y., has achieved a national reputation for breeding blooded stock of every description. Among the most noted stock farms worthy of a detailed account in these pages, that of Mr. Jewett M. Richmond is necessarily included. It consists of 200 acres of the most desirable land, lying near the shore of Lake Erie, elaborately improved and highly cultivated, with the special object in view of developing the highest qualities of that most valuable and interesting strain of cattle, the Jersey. Mr. Richmond's farm, which he took in hand for the purposes mentioned in 1880, is beautifully located one-half mile from West Hamburg, a station on the Lake Shore railroad, about nine miles west of Buffalo. The Nickel-plate and Buffalo & Pittsburg branch of the Buffalo, New York & Philadelphia railroad also pass through this station, while the Buffalo & Southwestern railroad taps Hamburg station, a distance of two and a half miles from the farm.

Mr. Richmond has demonstrated that for milk and butter purposes the Jersey is the most prolific and highest in quality of any; that they are full as hardy and stand the rigors of our climate full as well, if not better, than the common cattle of our country. Their availability for the dairy and for farmers located near good butter markets is a matter beyond any cavil or controversy. Then again the cost of feed is an important item decidedly in the Jersey's favor. If the farmers of the country who make a specialty of butter-making, would as a rule use only full-blooded Jersey bulls on their common cattle, they would greatly enrich the quality of the milk of their cows and the quality of the butter, and insure a certain profit to their business. Never use a grade bull, as a full-blooded animal can now be purchased at a low price, while a grade is not cheap at any price. No farmer who has had experience with a herd of grade Jerseys but will testify to the great improvement over common cows as butter producers.

Mr. Richmond's herd at present consists of over fifty head, of which a large number of cows, heifers and bull calves are for sale. They are all solid color with black points. As a rule these animals are all very large for this breed, fully equal to the common cattle of the country, and have been bred especially for their butter qualities. Quite a number of the cows have a record of fourteen pounds and over for a seven days' test, without forced feeding. Among the noted members of the herd there are of the bulls now in use : "Well Done's" Pedro, 15803, dropped April 26, 1885. The dam of this bull, imported Well Done, 25987, has a record of nineteen pounds four ounces in a test of seven days, recorded in the second volume of Major Campbell Brown's "Butter Tests of Jersey Cows." This magnificent young animal is a solid bronze fawn and gray, with dark shadings, full black points. Remarkable, 7662, as his name indicates, is an exceptionally fine animal, dropped June 13, 1881; solid color, full black points. The dam of this bull, imported Caroline, 12091, has a record of fourteen and a half pounds of butter in seven days in mid-winter, without forcing. This test is recorded in 1st volume of Maj. Campbell Brown's "Tests of Jersey Cows."

No bull has ever been used in this herd but whose dam had a record of fourteen pounds or over in a seven days' test. They have been selected and bred for butter qualities—descendants of and closely related to such noted butter families as St. Hillier, 45; Alphea, Coomassie, Khedive, Duke, 76; Albert, 44; Pansey, 8; Rioter, second; Eurotus; Pedro, 10588, etc.

Mr. Richmond invites correspondence or a personal visit to this herd, from breeders and others interested. The herdsman will be on hand to show the cattle and give such information as is required.

THE SCHOELLKOPF ANILINE AND CHEMICAL COMPANY,

Manufacturers of Coal Tar Dyes—Office and Works, Abbott Road and Buffalo Creek.

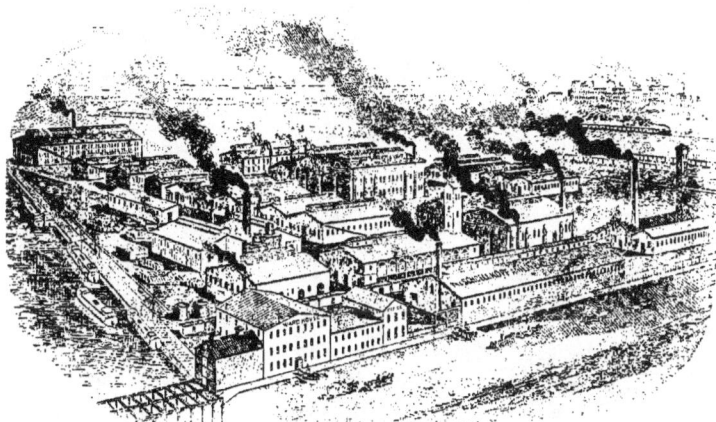

No discovery of the present age has had greater influence upon textile manufactures than that of the chemical properties of coal tar, from which are obtained many of the most brilliant dyes now employed. Not only has this discovery affected beneficially the beauty of all goods worn in our time, but the prices have been greatly reduced thereby on all fabrics, and thousands hitherto debarred by want of means from indulging their taste for texture and color are now enabled to revel in all the hues of the rainbow and in the richest weaves, because of the cheapening of materials and processes directly or indirectly brought about as the near or remote consequences of the introduction of aniline dyes.

The Schoellkopf Aniline and Chemical Company's works for the production of these dyes are the most extensive of the kind on this continent, and their reputation for high-grade dyes is unsurpassed by that of any similar concern in the world. These works, at the intersection of the Abbott road and Buffalo creek, were erected by Mr. J. F. Schoellkopf, one of Buffalo's most conspicuous citizens and business men, in 1879, and have since been greatly enlarged and improved. The company as it now exists was organized and incorporated in 1881 with a working capital of $150,000 ; J. F. Schoellkopf, sr., president ; J. F. Schoellkopf, jr., secretary and treasurer ; Dr. Koehler, chemist. The same gentlemen are members of the board of directors. The elder Mr. Schoellkopf is actively interested in many other important business enterprises—the manufacture of leather, brewing, milling, etc.—is a director of several leading corporations, and a member of all the more prominent German societies. He has resided in Buffalo for fifty years, and has done as much as any other one man toward developing her material interests.

The aniline and chemical works occupy a most favorable location with reference to the delivery of materials and the shipment of finished products. The plant embraces about six acres of land, upon which have been erected twenty-two distinct one, two and three-story substantial brick buildings, equipped in every department with the best and latest improved machinery and apparatus, several powerful steam engines, and everything required to render the establishment complete. Eighty men are employed, and wages are paid to the amount of $3,500 monthly. The shipping facilities are all that could be desired, and embrace, besides the Erie canal, which bounds the works on one side, switches and side-tracks from the Lackawanna, Nickel-Plate, and Buffalo Creek railroads, the latter communicating directly with all roads entering the city. The sales,

15

made principally to the New England cotton, woolen and silk manufacturers, aggregate $500,000 per annum.

There are many shades of each standard color, as all are aware, as reds, violets, yellow, orange, browns, scarlets, etc., and it requires a high degree of skill in chemistry and mechanics to produce these of satisfactory character as regards brilliancy and durability, hence the necessity for employing the best talent procurable. All processes are of course secret, and the company own patents upon most of the colors, not a few of which were devised by their own accomplished chemist, Dr. Koehler. This house manufactures all the colors and shades required by dyers, together with various acids and salts for the trade.

Mr. Schoellkopf, who has sole management and supervision of the works, is an earnest, practical and thoughtful man, "strictly business" and devoted to his calling. Mr. J. F. Schoellkopf, jr., the secretary and treasurer, is also a capable, energetic and pleasant gentleman.

J. LYTH & SONS,

Manufacturers of Sewer Pipe, Farm Tiles, Terra Cotta, etc.— No. 48 West Eagle St.

The various lines included under the above caption form an important branch among the industrial resources of Buffalo. Among the twenty-three firms composing the Sewer-Pipe Manufacturers' Association in the United States and Canada, that of Messrs. J. Lyth & Sons occupies a leading position. For this reason a glance at their operations, as showing the position this city occupies in this line, will be appropriate. The business was established in 1857 by the present senior member of the house. It has grown to be one of extensive proportions, and this house now owns and operates the Buffalo Sewer-Pipe Works, located on Puffer street, at Cold Springs, and the Ohio Sewer-Pipe Works, at Wellsville, Ohio. These employ in the aggregate a working force of from 80 to 100 men. In conjunction with the manufacture of sewer pipe

an important feature of the business is that of farm drain-tile. The extent to which the agricultural community are directing their attention to the question of proper drainage has created a large demand for this article. In architectural and general terra cotta ware, Messrs. Lyth & Sons make a very artistic and comprehensive showing. In addition to the foregoing, a very attractive line of encaustic tile, enameled brick, hollow brick, chimney-tops, flue-pipe, fire-brick and clay, and kindred lines, are exhibited at the warerooms, No. 48 West Eagle street. The articles enumerated are nearly all indispensable in modern buildings, and are extensively used, especially in fire-proof structures. When it comes to furnishing estimates on such work, this house is prepared to offer inducements which cannot be successfully underbid, when the quality and finish of the material furnished is considered. Their trade connections extend throughout this State, Pennsylvania, Ohio and New England. The individual members of the firm are John, Alfred, John, jr., and William H. Lyth. The house has been so long and favorably known that it is unnecessary to say the gentlemen composing it are A 1 business men in the best sense of the term. Personally they are the embodiment of courteous and straightforward dealing. Mr. Alfred Lyth is a member of the City Council for the Seventh ward, and has made an enviable reputation as an indefatigable servant of the people. His honesty, independence and rigid opposition to "jobbery" in any form have won the unqualified approval of citizens and taxpayers generally.

J. O. MEYER, MALTSTER.

Malt-Houses, Corner Eagle and Watson Sts.

We have had occasion in the preceding pages to refer quite frequently to the malting industry and its relation to the commerce of Buffalo—a relation which is of constantly augmenting importance in view of the fact that no other point in the United States enjoys such advantages in this connection—propinquity to the barley fields of Canada, ample transportation facilities, and an abundance of cheap skilled labor.

Of the more prominent maltsters here none have a higher or better deserved reputation for quality of product and upright business methods than has Mr. J. O. Meyer, whose extensive establishment, embracing malt-house and store-house, is conveniently located at the intersection of Eagle and Watson streets. The malt-house proper consists of a substantial two-story brick building, 156 by 138 feet in area, the store-house being connected therewith. The equipment is first-class in all respects, embracing all late improvements in machinery, apparatus and appliances, and a working force of eighteen men is steadily employed. The average output for the past eight years has been 250,000 bushels per annum, most of which is consumed in the manufacture of lager beer in this city and New York, though considerable shipments are made at times to various points in Pennsylvania, Ohio, Missouri and other States. It is hardly necessary to state that the malt made at Mr. Meyer's establishment is invariably of the highest grade and a favorite with brewers.

Mr. Meyer is a native Buffalonian and a self-made man in the best sense of the term. Previous to 1861 he was engaged in the lumber trade. At the outbreak of the rebellion he abandoned his business, entered the naval service and served faithfully for two years, when he was honorably discharged. Coming home to Buffalo with $90 in his pocket, he commenced the handling of flour and grain on a modest scale on Washington street. By the exercise of unflagging industry and close atttention to business he prospered, so much so that at the end of seven years he had accumulated sufficient capital to engage in his present calling. By slow degress he has built up his present large and growing trade, and has a right to feel proud of his honorable and successful career.

QUEEN CITY STEAM LAUNDRY.

E. D. Willsey, Proprietor—Nos. 487 and 489 Washington St., Tifft House Block.

Buffalo has plenty of laundries of every class, from the dingy Chinese washee-washee shop to the elegantly appointed establishment employing a powerful steam engine to operate the machinery, and a corps of bright-eyed, cherry-lipped girls to attend the same and wait upon customers. Of the latter class is the Queen City Laundry, Nos. 487 and 489 Washington street, Tifft House block. The proprietor is Mr. A. M. Willsey, formerly of Albany, who has been connected with the laundry business since 1879, having opened this establishment at Nos. 98 and 100 Pearl street in that year, under the name and style of E. V. Willsey & Co. The change of base and name was made in 1885. Mr. E. D. Willsey is general manager—a position for which his long and close connection with the business particularly fits him.

The Queen City Laundry occupies the entire ground floor at the above numbers, 53 feet front by 115 feet deep, and is fitted up in the best manner for the prosecution of the laundry business on a large scale, last year's receipts footing up $35,000, and the prospect being that those figures will be largely exceeded this year. Forty men and women are regularly employed, and the work done is of the best quality, people all over the city and in the surrounding country sending their more particular work, including shirts, collars, cuffs, etc., to this justly famous laundry. None but the best of washing and ironing is done, and patrons can depend upon promptitude and the utmost care in the execution of orders.

SCHAEFER & BRO.,

Maltsters — Commission Merchants — Importers of and Wholesale Dealers in Canada, Western and New York State Barley—Malt-House, Seventh and Jersey Sts.—Office, No. 178 Main St.

The firm of Schaefer & Bro. have been making malt and handling barley on this market for well-nigh twenty-four years, and have a most enviable reputation at home and abroad for square and liberal dealing, fine business capacity, great energy and enterprise, their operations extending throughout the Eastern States. Their fine malt-house at the corner of Seventh and Jersey streets is one of the most complete in the country, embracing all modern improvements of equipment and under the supervision of a competent and experienced maltster, the output averaging about 150,000 bushels per annum.

The firm are also leading importers, commission merchants and wholesale dealers in barley, Canadian, Western and New York State, of which they handle several hundred thousand bushels annually. Their grand specialty, however, is choice Canada barley malt, in the manufacture of which they excel, and have a ready sale for all they can produce, brewers holding their malt in the highest esteem.

Messrs. Gustavus A. and Henry L. Schaefer are natives of Germany, coming to the United States in childhood. They have resided in Buffalo for forty-five years, and are among her best and most respected citizens. For some years they were interested in the manufacture of vinegar at Tonawanda. Their handsome office on the second floor of No. 185 Main street, northwest corner of Exchange, is one of the most convenient and commodious in the city and the scene of many heavy transactions in barley and malt.

ZINK & HATCH,

Real Estate Brokers and Agents—Corner Franklin and Eagle Sts., Austin Building, Opposite City Hall.

One of the surest indications of a city's progress or retrogression (for to stand still is impossible) may be found in the activity or inactivity of the real estate market, and unquestionably the proper place to make inquiry on this head is at the offices of the real estate agents and dealers. In Buffalo, at least, all of this class of business men in good standing are doing a flourishing and profitable business—none of them being more actively and incessantly engaged in the care and transfer of property than are Messrs. Zink & Hatch, the famous firm of real estate brokers in the Austin block, corner of Franklin and Eagle streets. This house, composed of Messrs. Henry Zink and A. G. Hatch, experienced and capable gentlemen, was established in 1870 by the senior member, Mr. Hatch being admitted ten or eleven years ago. Their office was formerly located at Niagara and Pearl streets, removing to the Austin building in 1880, where they have commodious, convenient and handsomely appointed accommodations, and are doing a successful and fast augmenting business in the purchase and sale of property, the collection of rents, as agents for the non-resident owners of land, the payment of taxes, the furnishing of abstracts of title, and the negotiation of stocks, bonds, mortgages, government securities and commercial paper.

The firm is thoroughly reliable and responsible. Mr. Zink was born in this county in 1848, and has been handling real estate in this city and vicinity since arriving at manhood. Mr. Hatch is a native of Buffalo, forty-two years of age, and has pursued his present avocation for ten or eleven years. He was formerly a leather manufacturer.

E. B. WILBER & CO.,

Grain Commission Merchants—Room 49 Merchants Exchange.

The senior member of this firm, Mr. E. B. Wilber, was for some eighteen years a prominent railroad man, retiring about 1868 to enter the grain trade, which he has continued to prosecute. Mr. Henry F. Bagnall, his associate, an expert accountant, formerly employed in the Buffalo city and Erie county offices, joined Mr. Wilber six years ago, and his previous accurate business training and experience has proved of great value in his present calling. Both of these gentlemen are natives of Buffalo, and liberal, public-spirited citizens.

Their commodious and handsomely-appointed office in room 49 Merchants' Exchange, first occupied in 1882, is one of the most convenient for the purpose that could have been selected, and fitted up with every facility for the rapid and satisfactory transaction of business. The firm handle immense quantities of grain of all kinds—wheat, barley, oats, corn, etc.—and are large receivers of Western grain for shipment to the seaboard by canal, dealing extensively in the markets of New York and New England as well as at home. Close personal attention is given to all orders entrusted to the firm, either for buying or selling.

BUFFALO NOVELTY WOOD-TURNING CO.

C. F. Schell, Jr., H. M. Bardol—Manufacturers of Dowels, Broom Handles, and Every Description of Turned Wooden Goods—Office, No. 602 Broadway.

Conspicuous among the more recently established and prosperous manufacturing enterprises of Buffalo is the Buffalo Novelty Wood-Turning Company, whose office is located at No. 602 Broadway. This company was founded about a year ago by Messrs. C. F. Schell, jr., and H. M. Bardol, who continue to direct its operations in a capable and successful manner.

The buildings (some already completed others being erected) comprise, besides a convenient office, several handsome buildings sufficiently scattered to largely decrease the danger from fire. This is the situation at our time of going to press. At one corner of the premises are the turning and finishing shops, and the shed for dressed lumber occupies the front, at a short distance from the street, while the office stands flush with the sidewalk. Here may be found one of the proprietors and several assistants, book-keeper, clerk, etc., during business hours.

The turning shop, 40 by 60 feet, is one of the most complete and ingeniously arranged in the world, provided with the latest devices in automatic machinery, and capable of turning out a vast quantity of superior goods, such as dowels, broom, mop and tool handles, base-knobs, novelties of all kinds, and every description of light turned work in wood. A specialty is made of making to order, in quantities to suit, new forms of useful and ornamental conceits, and inventors or originators will find here every facility for producing their goods, either for experiment or to meet an already established demand. The company itself handles many desirable patented articles, thus furnishing agents with light, respectable and lucrative employment, among their goods the patent " Boss " cake, biscuit and doughnut cutter and " Handy " toilet case being specially popular. A great deal of job turning is done here ; all that is required is the model, and the order will be filled promptly and satisfactorily.

The Buffalo Novelty Wood-Turning Company supplies a long-felt and urgent want in this line of mechanical enterprise, and it is pleasant to know that it is already appreciated and largely patronized, the sales extending to all portions of the United States. The proprietors are wide-awake, enterprising, energetic and industrious men. In a recent circular to the trade they say :

" We would call your attention to the new novel article in the line of housefurnishing goods. It is called the Handy toilet-case, a combination comb case, match-safe, pin-cushion and looking-glass, made of iron, handsomely nickel, bronze and brass-plated, very attractive, and sells at sight. We are offering them to the trade at very moderate prices in order to introduce the same. Send for prices. A nickel sample sent to any part of the United States for $1. We are also making the ' Boss cake cutter.' It has a wood top and is very neat. It is the best-selling five-cent article in the market. Packed two dozen to a box, thirty-six and seventy-two dozen to a case. Sample sent for ten cents in stamps. Send for prices."

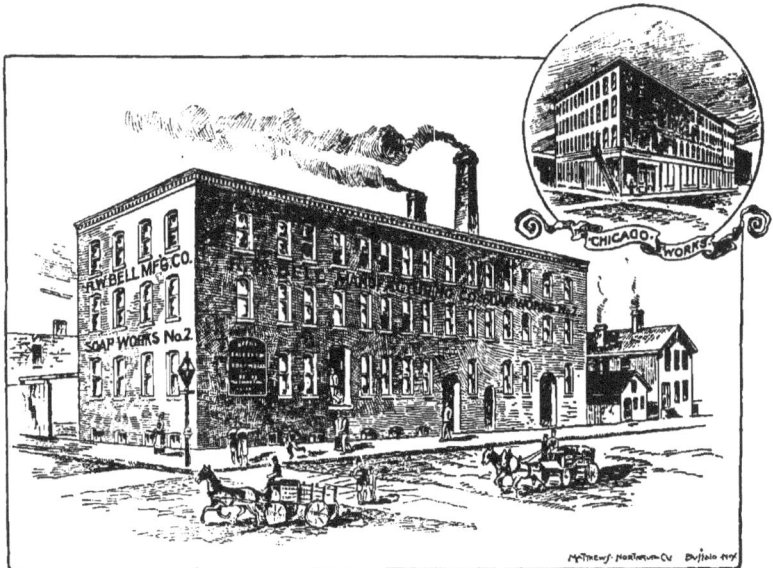

(See opposite page.)

THE R. W. BELL MANUFACTURING CO.

George H. Bell, President; Hector DeCastro, Vice-President; Edwin A. Bell, Secretary and Treasurer—Manufacturers of Toilet and Laundry Soaps, Soap Powder and Sal Soda—Nos. 77 to 89 Washington St.

Private Office of E. A. BELL, Sec'y & Tres.

"Cleanliness is next to godliness," says the inspired writer. Personal purity is the highest evidence of advanced civilization. Neatness is the watchword of progress, and soap is its emblem. Yet there are soaps and soaps. Not a few of the compounds sold under that name are infinitely more vile and loathsome than the dirt they are ostensibly made to remove, frequently causing troublesome diseases of the skin, and even blood-poisoning. The consumer cannot, therefore, exercise too great caution in this respect, or be too suspicious of the saponaceous preparations of the cheaper sort offered by family grocers and others whose only object is the realization of large profits without regard to consequences as they affect their customers.

Adulteration and debasement of quality has of late years reached the point from which a rebound became natural and necessary, and with the inauguration of reform those manufacturers who had steadily refused to join in the "swim" and produce worthless and disgusting trash began to reap their reward, the result being that fine goods are in unprecedented and rapidly increasing demand and the conscientious and high-toned manufacturer's soap is more popular among consumers than at any previous time.

Among the most extensive and famous establishments of this kind in the world, standing a head and shoulders above all local competitors and with a reputation broad as the continent, is that of the R. W. Bell Manufacturing Company, Nos. 77 to 89 Washington street, Nos. 8 to 20 Beaver street, Nos. 270 to 280 Perry street, and Nos. 233 to 241 Chicago street, Buffalo. The house was founded in February, 1865, by Messrs. R. W. and George H. Bell, who began operations on a comparatively small scale on State street, producing superior grades of toilet and laundry soaps. Their factory was destroyed by fire in 1872, and steps were immediately taken for the erection of the present large and commodious works on Washington street, in the construction of which neither labor nor expense were spared to render it one of the most complete of the kind ever built. Extensive improvements and a considerable enlargement were made in 1877, the factory at present being 4 stories in height, 120 feet front and 146 feet in depth. A vast number of male and female operatives find here steady and remunerative employment, the output reaches several hundred thousand dollars in value annually and is steadily augmenting in volume, and a small army of commercial travelers represent the houses all over the United States, the Canadas, Mexico and Central and South America.

The offices of the company are pleasantly located and conveniently arranged on the first floor of the building, the counting-room fronting on Washington street, the cashier, bookkeepers and clerks having their desks behind light railings. At the left of the main entrance is the private office of President George H. Bell, an amiable gentleman in the prime of life, aged forty-four. Beyond and adjoining is the large and elegant office of Secretary and Treasurer Edwin A. Bell, and in the rear, separated from the main office, is the private sanctum of Mr. J. D. Henderson, superintendent of advertising—a position which is no sinecure, since the company are strong believers in and patrons of printers' ink.

September 24, 1879, Mr. R. W. Bell died, leaving vacant his place as head of the original firm. Mr. George H. Bell continued the business under the old name and style until 1880, when Mr. Edwin A. Bell was admitted. In 1883 the style was changed to the R. W. Bell Manufacturing Company, with the officers above named. In June, 1885, the soap manufacturing plant of H. Thompson, corner of Perry and Chicago streets, was purchased, and has been run to its full capacity ever since.

The company maintain a branch house at Nos. 46 and 48 Michigan avenue, Chicago, under charge of Mr. B. O. Van Bokkelen, who has demonstrated his fitness for the place by building up a large and growing trade.

HAZARD & AREND,

Manufacturers of All Kinds of Dressed Lumber, Doors, Sash, Blinds, etc.— Dealers in Pine and Hemlock Lumber, Shingles, Lath and Fence Posts— Nos. 372 to 382 Massachusetts St.

Buffalo, by reason of her peculiarly eligible location at the foot of navigation on the great American lakes, is naturally the outlet through which the great volume of North-western lumber seeks a market in the East. Naturally, too, Buffalo is a superior point for the establishment of planing mills and factories for preparing lumber for the use of joiners and carpenters nearer the seaboard and for the manufacture of a variety of essentials to building, such as doors, sash, blinds, shutters, mouldings and other items that go to the completion and finish of houses large and small; hence the stranger within her gates will be struck by the number and magnitude of these mills and factories.

One of the latest and most promising ventures of this kind is the new firm of Hazard, Arend & Co., organized in the spring of 1886, and changed to Hazard & Arend in December, 1886. This establishment is known as the Queen City Planing Mill, Nos. 372 to 382 Massachusetts street—one of the finest and completest plants of the kind in the country, comprising a mill 56 by 145 feet, two stories high, with boiler and engine-room 32 by 32 feet attached. A wing 40 by 86 feet and shaving room 16 by 32 feet have been added since the firm name changed. A full complement of first-class machinery and some fifty men are employed, and the capacity is about $200,000 worth per annum of finished work. As yet, of course, most of Messrs. Hazard & Arend's patronage comes from the builders of Buffalo and vicinity, but they aspire to extend their connection all over the Eastern and Middle States, and if superior work and moderate prices can accomplish it they will succeed. They manufacture every description of plain and decorative inside finish, and, having unusual advantages in the matter of practically unlimited supplies of the best lumber and command of the best mechanical skill, they are prepared to offer excellent inducements to buyers of doors, sash, blinds, mouldings, etc., as well as rough and dressed lumber.

The members of the firm are W. B. Hazard and Fred. Arend. Mr. Hazard is a native of Prince Edward county, Canada ; he came to this city in 1870, and, besides his connection with the house now under consideration, is a prosperous lumber and real estate dealer, buying land and building houses for sale. Mr. Arend is a German and has resided here for many years. He has been connected with planing mills since boyhood.

UNION BRIDGE COMPANY,

Civil Engineers and Constructors of Bridges—Works, Athens, Pa., and Buffalo, N. Y.—New York Office, No. 18 Broadway.

The Union Bridge Company is the outcome of a consolidation of four leading American companies, viz. : The Central Bridge Co., of Buffalo, composed of Gen. Geo. S. Field and Mr. Edmund Hayes ; Kellogg and Maurice, of Athens, Pa. ; Thomas C. Clark, of Clark, Reeves & Co., Philadelphia, and Chas. Macdonald, of the Delaware Bridge Company, New York. The works of the new company comprise those of the late firm of Kellogg & Maurice, at Athens, Pa., capacity 14,000 tons, and those of the late Central Bridge Works, Buffalo, capacity 12,000 tons. The combination was formed in 1884, making the most extensive and most powerful bridge-building firm in America, the works being double the capacity of any other. The Buffalo shops and appurtenances cover six or eight acres of ground at the foot of Hamburg street, adjoining the Union Iron Company's rolling-mill and blast furnaces, convenient to railways, lake and canal, switches connecting with every railroad entering the city, and about a mile of tracks in their own yards furnishing every facility for the receipt of material and the shipment of finished work. The equipment of machinery and appliances is, of course, complete and on the most liberal scale, and a force of 200 skilled and well-paid mechanics find steady employment the year round. In all, here, at Athens and in the field, the Union Bridge Company employs about 1,200 men at all seasons.

The operations of the company extend throughout the United States, and even to foreign lands. At this time they are building an immense bridge at Hawksbury, New South Wales, the contract for which was awarded them in open competition with the most celebrated bridge-builders of England, France and Germany, and aggregates $2,000,000. They have also in course of construction across the Hudson river at Poughkeepsie an immense viaduct, which, when completed, will be one of the most important and costly in this country. It is a double-track railway bridge of five spans —two of 550 feet and three of 525 feet, besides 3,000 feet of trestle-work approaches— and is at the center 212 feet above low water-mark. This company has the contract for the entire work, foundations, masonry and superstructure. The company is also doing much work for the Canadian Pacific railway, and has contracts for bridges to be erected on the lines of nearly all American, Canadian, South American, Australian and Japanese railways. The magnificent cantilever bridge at Niagara Falls, built for the Michigan Central Railroad, is a specimen of their work.

The employment of steel in bridge construction is becoming more and more popular as the superiority of that material is demonstrated, and the Buffalo shops are specially fitted up with a first-class plant to meet this growing demand.

Messrs. Clark and Macdonald have charge of the New York office of the company, No. 18 Broadway. Messrs. Kellogg and Maurice direct operations at Athens, Pa., and Gen. Field and Mr. Hayes manage the Buffalo branch. All of these gentlemen are first-class engineers and eminent business men.

B. B. HAMILTON & CO.,

Dealers and Brokers in Real Estate—Buffalo Property a Specialty—No. 20 West Swan St.

The great value of this work, as its title in a measure suggests, will be in present-ing the material advantages of the city of Buffalo in detail as found at the present time. The fact that the city has nearly doubled in population during the past ten years, and is now one of the great railway centers, as well as controlling the commerce of the great lakes through the Erie canal, will in a measure indicate the material at hand and used in the preparation of this volume. As a manufacturing center, while Buffalo now takes a prominent position, yet when the fact is considered that the greatest water-power in the world—the Niagara river—right at her door, is as yet to be utilized, an idea can be formed of this city's future. That she is destined to be the greatest manufacturing center in this country, if not in the world, is no Utopian vision. Modern inventive genius will not long permit this great water-power to run to waste.

With the rapid increase in population and new enterprises of all kinds, real estate in and adjacent to the city has felt the effect of Buffalo's boom. This old reliable barometer of the business situation and standard of values has displayed remarkable activity, especially within the past year. There never was such a movement in the city's history on the part of the laboring classes to secure homes. Consequently the suburban sections are being built up at a rate which has astonished the old-timers. Within a quite recent period East Buffalo has undergone a transformation scene, and now Black Rock and vicinity are having a similar experience. Manufacturing and other enterprises, gigantic and otherwise, are springing into existence, and real estate for building purposes along the Belt Line railroad is being passed around like cider at a country wedding.

Mr. B. B. Hamilton, of the real estate firm of Hamilton & Co., a shrewd business man, enterprising and inclined to discount coming events on his own judgment, was requested to give an opinion on the prospects of the real estate market in Buffalo. Said he : " There was only once in the city's history when there was what might be called a genuine boom in real estate. After being incorporated, April 20, 1832, with five wards and a population of 10,000, the town grasped the situation and took a proper send-off. During the next three years the population doubled, and there was, to put it mildly, considerable activity about the place. At the time of the financial crash of 1837 real estate values had reached a point which in some sections of the city have never been touched since. I don't look for a repetition of that boom in 1887—fifty years later—but I must say real estate is pretty active. But it is on a sound basis. The city is growing so rapidly that real estate of any kind almost is a good thing to own, and is sure to advance. Outside capital, which is coming in pretty rapidly, seems to have dis-covered this fact, while some of Buffalo's sleepy old money-bags are looking askance and wonder what it all means."

During the past year Mr. Hamilton sold the Villa Park property, a tract of 185 acres located between Hertel avenue, the city line, and Delaware avenue and Main street, for $185,000. It is now held by a company, and being placed on the market for building purposes. This is one of a number of similar transactions in which Mr. Hamilton has figured. This gentleman, who was born in Buffalo in 1842, is probably as good a judge of the future of real estate in this city as any man living. His long experience in the banking business afforded the best opportunities in this direction. He first went with the International Bank in 1854, and remained until 1862, when he resigned as teller to enter the army. After his discharge Mr. Hamilton was two years in Chicago. Returning to Buffalo, he entered White's Bank, and remained there until the Third National was organized. In 1881 he was appointed cashier, and held that office three years, retiring to go in the real estate business. In the latter capacity Mr. Hamilton has had the success which his abilities were bound to command. His operations are on a large scale and backed by ample capital. As brokers, or agents for non-residents, this firm is competent and reliable. Abstracts of title and tax searches are furnished on short notice.

The other member of the firm, Mr. L. A. Smallwood, is in charge of the office, No. 20 West Swan street. He is the right man for the place.

LOUIS GOLDSTEIN,

Dealer in Boots and Shoes—No. 150 Broadway.

Among the new enterprises established with the opening of 1887, that handsome boot and shoe house of Mr. Louis Goldstein, No. 150 Broadway, is worthy of note, occupying as it does a fine four-story brick building, the premises being 30 feet front by 114 feet deep, and the store occupying the entire ground floor, displaying a very large, carefully selected, new and fresh stock of the best goods in all departments for men's, women's, boys', misses' and children's wear. The interior arrangements are all that could be desired for comfort and convenience, and when it is added that rock bottom prices will prevail in all departments, together with politeness and prompt attention to the wants of the public, it is reasonable to predict that Mr. Goldstein will score a great success from the start, and eventually build up an immense trade in that prosperous section of the city. The opening will occur March 26th, and those interested in the business development of the city, or in search of bargains, will do well to attend.

Mr. Goldstein has for some years been engaged in the manufacture of furniture, picture frames, etc., and in the restaurant and saloon business. He is a well-known and popular citizen, liberal and enterprising, owns the property he occupies, pays no rent, and will share that and other advantages with his trade.

Mr. G. is recognized as a solid and well-balanced business man, and enjoys the respect of his fellow-men, both in a business and social point of view.

WILLIAM S. BULL,

Paper Manufacturers' Agent—Nos. 84 and 86 Lloyd St.

The paper trade affects the comfort and pleasure of the general public as nearly, perhaps, as any other—it certainly has a more direct bearing upon the diffusion of intelligence than any other from the fact that it is the medium universally employed to convey expressed thought, whether written or printed.

One of Buffalo's most promising and useful business enterprises is the comparatively new but already popular and successful paper house of Mr. William S. Bull, Nos. 84 and 86 Lloyd street, established in 1882. It is a handsome four-story building, 50 feet front by 75 feet deep, and is stocked in every department with a large and varied line of superior book, news, writing and wrapping papers from the most celebrated Eastern makers, for whom Mr. Bull is manufacturers' agent. During the past year over $100,000 worth of these goods were supplied to the local trade through this house, and it is confidently expected that the present year's sales will exceed $150,000, and when Mr. Bull's experience and wide acquaintance and the character of his goods is taken into consideration this calculation does not appear extravagant. For over twenty-one years past he has been intimately and actively engaged in the paper trade, is a native of Buffalo, energetic, industrious and of pleasing address, and cannot fail to prosper in his present enterprise. He sells from the mills direct, and is prepared to fill orders to any extent, promptly and in the most satisfactory manner, at as low rates as can be offered by the manufacturers themselves.

McNEIL & KURTZ,

Wholesale and Retail Dealers in Hemlock Lumber, Lath, Shingles and Wood—Yard, corner Lord and South Division Sts. ; Office, Room 30, Coal and Iron Exchange, No. 257 Washington St.

There is a very strong demand in this market for the better grades of hemlock lumber, lath, shingles, etc., and the object of the firm named above is to aid in meeting the requirements of the trade. The house was established in 1877 by Mr. Peter McNeil, who admitted Mr. W. H. Kurtz in January, 1885. The yard, at the corner of Lord and South Division streets, comprises about an acre of land, with a storage capacity of from 10,000,000 to 15,000,000 feet, and is provided with a switch connecting with the various railroads, and all necessary facilities for the transaction of business on a large scale, the annual sales averaging $125,000. The leading specialty is hemlock lumber of all dimensions, of which the firm handles immense quantities, besides thousands of car-loads of lath, shingles, firewood, etc., most of their commodities being sold to local buyers and consumers.

Mr. McNeil is president of the Seneca Street and Franklin Way Stage Company, and was one of the originators of the Buffalo Herdic Company. He is also a member of the Allegheny Lumber Company.

This is Mr. Kurtz' first business venture, and he gives it his undivided personal attention.

C. D. ZIMMERMAN & CO.,

Dealers in Flour, Feed, Coal and Wood—Office, No. 50 West Eagle St.— Yards, No. 252 Maryland St.

The firm of C. D. Zimmerman & Co., composed of C. D. Zimmerman and R. D. Cursons, was organized in 1883. The house which they conduct dates back to 1840, and was begun by Michael Messmer, who was succeeded in 1872 by Frank Noell. Messrs. Zimmerman & Co. are wholesale and retail dealers in flour, feed, coal and wood. Their transactions are large, aggregating $40,000 annually. The firm are wholesale agents for the product of the Franklin flour mills at Lockport, and also for the New York Health Fruit Company's goods. In this department of the business the trade extends throughout Western New York and to portions of Pennsylvania and Ohio. The wood and coal branch was established in 1856, and since then it has grown to extensive proportions. The yards at No. 252 Maryland street are well arranged for the handling of stock, and are also quite commodious. A very extensive feature of the operations of the firm is included under the head of street sprinkling. In addition, a boarding stable is conducted on Franklin street, opposite the City Hall.

Mr. Zimmerman is a native of Pine Hill, this county, and was formerly one of the proprietors of the Pine Hill nurseries. He was also in charge of the Ohio State Agricultural Farm at Lancaster for two years, after which he returned to Buffalo.

Mr. Cursons is a native of Buffalo, having been born opposite where the High School building now stands. For more than thirty years he has been in the street-sprinkling business. Both members of the firm are thorough-going business men, and have the happy faculty of retaining and constantly adding to their circle of customers.

GEORGE MACNOE,

Official Stenographer of the Superior Court—Office, 21 Chapin Block.

Among the leading representatives of the profession we find Mr. George Macnoe, official stenographer for the Superior Court. He has also a large share of general reporting work in this and other places, and the accuracy of his work, and the promptness with which it has been furnished, has very often been suitably recognized. Mr. Macnoe has been a resident of Buffalo over thirty years. He was a student of the inventor of phonography, Mr. Pitman, and for some time followed the profession of stenographic reporter for the press.

During the past four years Mr. T. D. Macnoe has been identified with the business, having charge of the office and outside work. He is official stenographer for the grand juries of Erie county, and he has the reputation of being one of the brightest of the rising young members of the profession.

FLINT & KENT,

Wholesale Jobbers and Retail Dealers in Dry Goods, Notions, etc.—Nos. 261 Main and 268 Washington Sts.

The metropolitan character of Buffalo is in nothing more apparent than in the volume of her dry goods trade, both wholesale and retail, which foots up many millions of dollars annually. Some of the finest fortunes ever made here were amassed in this branch of business, and, judging from the activity apparent in the trade, other handsome fortunes are in process of acquisition by the same means.

One of the oldest and most reputable of the Queen City's great dry goods houses is that of Flint and Kent, Nos. 261 Main and 268 Washington streets, founded some fifty years ago by Ford & Howard, succeeded by Fitch & Howard, who were succeeded by Howard, Whitcomb & Co., and then by Flint, Kent & Stone, and Flint, Kent & Howard for one year, and they in turn by the present firm in 1865. As before intimated, Messrs. Flint & Kent are heavy handlers of dry goods, notions, etc., at both wholesale and retail. Their premises consist of a handsome five-story building fronting 30 feet on both streets, with a depth of 200 feet, with a basement of like dimensions, the whole being devoted to their use. An average of thirty-five clerks, salesmen and other help are employed, and the firm do a very large business, extending throughout Western New York. Their store is patronized by the best class of trade in the city and country, who find here vast stocks, infinite varieties, the most approved styles, reliable goods, and prices as reasonable as can be quoted by legitimate merchants anywhere. The arrangement of the salesrooms, while systematic and convenient, is elegant and attractive, while the polite and patient attention shown customers and visitors is a subject of enthusiastic remark, especially on the part of ladies.

Mr. Flint, the senior partner, now sixty years of age, came to Buffalo from his birthplace, Hancock, N. H., thirty-seven years ago. He has been connected with the trade in dry goods since boyhood.

Mr. Kent, sixty-three years of age, was born at Concord, N. H., and came to Buffalo in 1865. He, also, has devoted his entire business life to dry goods. Both are fully alive to Buffalo's great advantages and magnificent future, and deeply interested in all that concerns her welfare.

RICHARD EVANS & SON.

Established 1834—Manufacturers of Glue of All Kinds—Factory, Abbott Road near Iron Bridge—P. O. Box 66.

Manufacturers of all descriptions of goods which in use are protected from the elements are patrons of the glue manufacturer, who finds his best customers among the cabinet-makers, carpenters, trunk-makers, paper-box makers, carriage-makers, painters, etc. Glue is an article, indeed, of prime necessity to the trades and a standard item of commerce. The glue in general use is made from the horns, hoofs, waste bits of hide, etc., of neat cattle, and requires a high degree of skill and experience in the various processes involved ere it is ready for the market.

Among the most extensive and popular glue manufacturers in the United States are Messrs. Richard Evans & Son, whose works occupy an immense one-and-a-half-story frame building, 60 by 300 feet, on the Abbott road near the iron bridge. The concern employs some thirty workmen, and produces about 150 tons of glue per annum, which it is safe to say is of superior quality, and will compare favorably with any of domestic or foreign make, the specialty being fine glue for wood-working purposes. The firm have a very high reputation, and their product meets with ready sale at highest prices throughout the Eastern, Northern and Western States and Canada.

The senior Mr. Evans is a native of Ross, Herefordshire, England. He came to America when a child, and spent his earlier years in New York and Boston. Later he was in government employ, getting out live oak in Florida for use in naval construction. He came to Buffalo in 1834, and at once began the manufacture of glue on a small scale. By strict attention to business, great energy and the gradual improvement of processes for the production of superior glue, he has built up a first-class and steadily increasing trade. In this he has been most capably assisted by his son, Mr. R. Evans, jr., who now has entire charge of the works and sales, and is one of Buffalo's rising young business men.

D. R. & H. FOGELSONGER,

**Contractors and Dealers in All Kinds of Cut Limestone and Sandstone—
Quarry at Williamsville; Office and Yard, No. 215 Oak St.**

The remarkable increase of building operations hereabouts of late years has had the effect, among others, of developing the quarries of Western New York, and establishing as a regular calling the industry of supplying cut and dressed stone in quantities by contract. It is a great convenience to builders to be able to secure dimension stone ready for the mason, at such times and in such quantities as they may require. Consequently the reliable and responsible contracting quarryman and dealer in this kind of material is usually well patronized and prosperous.

Among the most prominent and successful of those who have invested their capital and business talents in this branch of business, is the firm of D. R. & H. Fogelsonger, whose large and busy yard, 118½ by 150 feet, with office attached, is at No. 215 Oak street, between Broadway and Sycamore. Their quarry, at Williamsville, is a very valuable and productive one, for which they have been offered $30,000 cash. The firm employ sixty-five men, pay an average of $800 weekly in wages, and do a business of about $100,000 a year in the quarrying, dressing and delivery of limestone and sandstone to builders and contractors in Buffalo and vicinity. That their material and workmanship are of the best is evidenced by the large and increasing volume of their sales, limestone being their leading specialty. The brothers are natives of Williamsville, D. R., forty-three and Henry thirty-seven years of age.

N. MOERSHFELDER,

**Cutler and Grinder—Wholesale and Retail Dealer in Concave Razors,
Tailors' and Barbers' Shears, Hones, Razor Strops, Combs, Barbers'
Supplies, etc.—Nos. 501 and 503 Main St.**

The above is the only fine cutlery and grinding establishment in Buffalo. It was established in 1850 by N. Moershfelder, senior, father of the present proprietor, both of whom in the year named emigrated hither from the then French province of Alsace, where the parent was born in 1806 and the son in 1834. The elder Mr. Moershfelder was a rarely skilled cutler in his own country, and brought with him his art, which he imparted to his son. Establishing himself here at first in a very moderate way, Mr. Moershfelder gradually built up a large and flourishing business, to which the son succeeded on the decease of the father in 1881.

The works now occupy the roomy three-story building, Nos. 501 and 503 Main street, 25 feet front and running back 85 feet, all the floors being devoted to factory purposes —the making, repairing and grinding of fine cutlery, razors, tailors' and barbers' shears, etc.—the concave grinding of razors being a leading specialty for which the house is famous. Mr. Moershfelder is also an extensive wholesale and retail dealer in the goods named, together with hones, razor strops, combs and barbers' supplies generally, which he is prepared to furnish to the trade in large or small lots at lowest prices, quality considered.

The works are run by steam, and orders are filled for shipment to all parts of the country. Eight men are employed, and sales average about $15,000 a year.

BUFFALO PRESSED BRICK CO.

**Edward J. Hall, President; George S. Metcalfe, Treasurer; Alfred Hall,
Secretary—Manufacturers of Pressed, Moulded, Stock and Common
Brick—Office, Room 1, Harvey Block, No. 7 Swan St.—Telephone 84.**

It were a waste of time and space to present a detailed argument in proof of the superiority of pressed and moulded bricks over the ordinary sort for building purposes, where beauty and durability are demanded. The bricks, and the work constructed of them, speak for themselves, and so effectively that the demand for this splendid building material multiplies season after season, while mammoth works for their manufacture are being established wherever clay of the proper kind can be found, and mechanical ingenuity is taxed to produce machinery that will turn them out fast enough and of good quality.

Among the great industries of this kind established of late years the vast yards, kilns and machinery plant of the Buffalo Pressed Brick Co., at Tonawanda, are conspicuous, comprising eighty-four acres of ground, several large brick buildings, an immense patent dryer, numerous kilns, and the finest collection of improved brick machinery of all kinds ever set up in this part of the country, with a yearly capacity of 5,000,000 high grade bricks. Railroad side-tracks intersect the yards, and the company owns a large number of small brick cars built expressly for the handling of bricks, which they sell in lots on the Buffalo market and throughout Western New York and Pennsylvania. Architects, property owners, contractors, builders and bricklayers unite in pronouncing these bricks equal to any ever made hereabout, a fact which is further evidenced by the rapidly growing demand. The leading specialty of the company is pressed brick for front walls, made to any desired pattern for irregular corners, copings, arches, cornices, or plain and of standard size. Sixty men are employed in the season, and the output for the first year exceeded $70,000, their first pressed brick being put upon the market in the fall of 1885. The bricks used in Gies & Co.'s fine business building, southeast corner Swan and Center streets, are of the Buffalo Pressed Brick Co.'s make, selected for their superiority in competition with those of many other local and foreign manufacturers.

The company is an outgrowth of Hall & Sons, manufacturers of fire and building brick, who were established in 1870. The Buffalo Pressed Brick Co. was organized with the above named officers in 1886. President Edward J. Hall is a New England man, who has been connected with ceramics as a brick manufacturer and agent of the Perth-Amboy Terra Cotta Works from boyhood ; while Mr. Alfred Hall is his son and partner in the firm of Hall & Sons. The elder Mr. Hall is a prominent Board of Trade man and vice-president of the Buffalo Telphone Co. Mr. Geo. S. Metcalfe, the treasurer, is a native of this city, formerly with the Anchor line of steamers, and a live, pushing business man.

LAKE VIEW MALT HOUSE.

White & Crafts, Proprietors—Lake View Ave. and Jersey St.

It is estimated that 1,000,000 bushels of superior malt is annually produced by Buffalo alone. Immense malt-houses are found in all parts of the city, and the importation, malting and shipping of barley is recognized as one of the leading industries here. It is a branch of manufactures demanding for its successful prosecution large capital, long experience, great skill and sound judgment, and the man who cannot bring ample resources of these to bear upon his business had better seek some other less exacting avenue of enterprise.

Among the more prominent establishments of this kind that dot the Queen City is the large and substantial Lake View malt-house of Messrs. White & Crafts, at the intersection of Lake View avenue and Jersey street, erected by the present proprietors in 1875. The main buildings front 115 feet on Lake View avenue, 240 feet on Jersey street, are four stories high, with spacious basement, and have an annual malting capacity of 300,000 bushels, all of which is taken by the trade of the Eastern States, where, because of its superior quality, Messrs. White & Crafts' malt is a general favorite with brewers, being carefully and skillfully prepared from selected grain and every process conducted under the personal supervision of the proprietors, who are famous maltsters, with a long-established reputation. Mr. White was formerly an extensive distiller, and has been connected with malting, directly and indirectly, for more than thirty years. He is of English birth, but has resided here since boyhood. Mr. Crafts was born in Chautauqua county, N. Y., came to Buffalo in 1871, at once became interested in the Niagara Malting Co., and only left it in 1875 to join Mr. White in the present venture.

The specialty of the house is malt of the highest grade. They employ forty capable workmen during the season, and pay from $350 to $400 in weekly wages. Their trade, as before stated, is altogether with Eastern brewers, and they have been unusually successful in the past and have excellent prospects for the future.

BUFFALO ELECTRIC COMPANY,

Manufacturers of Electric Work of Every Description—Annunciators, Speaking Tubes, Burglar Alarms, Electric Bells, etc.—No. 200 Pearl St.

The Buffalo Electric Company is an entirely new enterprise, established the present year, and one which in the nature of things must develop into a great success. The proprietors are Messrs. Wells Dygert and Fred. W. Schiefer, brothers-in-law. Mr. Dygert was formerly for some years superintendent of the Wagner Sleeping Car Company, a position which he filled satisfactorily to all concerned, and only resigned, because of failing health, to embark in farming near Detroit, abandoning that in January last to engage in his present venture. He is a capable and energetic business man. Mr. Schiefer, of German descent, ranks high as a theoretical and practical electrician, and is, besides, a skillful machinist. Both are natives of Buffalo.

The works occupy the entire second story of No. 200 Pearl street, formerly belonging to Liberty House Co. No. 1, and are fitted up in the best manner with all requisite machinery and appurtenances for the manufacture or repair of electrical apparatus of every description for the use of physicians, surgeons, philosophical students and experimenters with the subtle fluid. By means of ingenious yet simple devices erected in the office the working of all electric machinery, whether for the medical fraternity or others, is clearly shown and the principles of operation made plain. No more interesting exhibit can be found in Buffalo.

Those in any way interested in electrical science are invited to visit these works and witness the processes whereby the lightning is harnessed and made the servant of man. Special attention is given to the construction and repair of electric bells, annunciators, speaking tubes, electric lights, telephones, electric motors, etc., and all work done in the best manner and guaranteed.

SHANLEY BROS.,

Grocers, Dealers in Teas, Coffees, Spices, Fancy Groceries, Canned Goods, etc.—Tobacco and Cigars—No. 275 Swan St.

The above-named firm, composed of Thomas A. and James B. Shanley, was established in 1884, and has been remarkably successful, occupying a handsome and convenient three-story brick building 30 by 80 feet, with roomy cellar, fine stables attached, and all requisite facilities for the transaction of a first-class business. Their sales for the past year aggregated fully $30,000, and the prospect is that that figure will be largely exceeded in 1887, the reputation of the house being based on merit and its fame rapidly extending.

In addition to a large and carefully selected stock of all staple family groceries of the highest grades, the firm carry superior lines of choice teas, coffees, spices, etc., and extra fine popular brands of cigars and tobacco. They also make a specialty of leading brands of flour, selling to consumers at mill prices. The best goods only in every department are offered, the lowest prices asked, and politeness and promptitude characterize the firm in all transactions.

The senior member, Mr. Thomas A. Shanley, is an experienced insurance man, for ten years in the office of Smith, Davis & Co., No. 200 Main street. At this time he maintains an insurance agency on his own account at room No. 4, Board of Trade building, representing several leading fire and marine associations. He is a silent partner in the grocery house, the active management of which devolves upon the junior partner, Mr. James B. Shanley. The latter for seven years previous to 1884 was district circulator of the *Courier*, giving entire satisfaction in that position. Mr. George R. Shanley, a younger brother, renders able assistance in the house, and is regarded as a competent and rising young business man, "a host of himself." All the brothers are natives of Buffalo, but proud of their Irish descent, prompt and honorable in their dealings, affable, enterprising and liberal.

THE ASSOCIATED ELEVATORS.

S. F. SHERMAN, MANAGER.

International Elevating Co.: F. A. Bell, President; E. C. Hawks, Vice-President; G. H. Lewis, Treasurer; C. A. Gould, Secretary—Lake Shore Elevating Co.: F. A. Bell, President; Edward Michael, Vice-President; W. H. Sherman, Secretary and Treasurer—Dakota Elevator: Bell, Michael & Sherman, Owners—Office, Room 68, Board of Trade Building.

No other city in the world enjoys such advantages in connection with the grain trade as does Buffalo. Situated at the extreme eastern terminus of the great chain of lakes, and of the railroad systems on both sides thereof, and itself the western terminus of the Erie canal and the various railroads connecting with the Atlantic seaboard; with a vast and affluent grain territory upon the one hand from which to draw her supplies, and the markets of the world on the other—it would seem that neither nature nor man could do more to make her the granary and storehouse of this continent. Year by year her advantages in this connection become more and more apparent, year by year the volume of grain handled here becomes greater, aggregating for the season of 1885-86 over 120,000,000 bushels.

Hitherto all elevators erected here—nearly forty in number—have been designed and located with special reference to the receipt of grain by water, only two or three possessing facilities for receiving, elevating, storing and shipping by rail, and those totally inadequate to the demand, thus forcing the railroads to furnish not only transportation but storage until owners could sell or otherwise dispose of their grain, the cars standing loaded on the side tracks in great numbers, scattered along the lines of the Lake Shore, Michigan Central, Grand Trunk and Canadian Pacific, for distances varying from ten to seventy-five miles, awaiting the pleasure of shippers, sometimes for several months, ere being released. This was a great hardship, and the cause of serious inconvenience and loss to the railroad companies—a state of affairs that might have continued indefinitely, had not the idea occurred to Mr. S. F. Sherman, of The Sherman Bros. Co., Limited, that by the construction of capacious railroad elevators the abuse could be remedied, and an entirely new and profitable business enterprise inaugurated at the same time. The result we now have in the two magnificent structures known as the "International" and "Lake Shore" elevators—the former located upon and occupying two entire blocks of 95,000 square feet, bounded by Niagara, Wayne and Dearborn streets, the New York Central and Hudson River Railroad and Scajaquada creek; the latter upon a plot of 97,000 square feet fronting on the Hamburg canal, Alabama and Scott streets. The companies, officered as stated above, organized with a joint capital of $300,000. Work was begun July 1st last, and the "Lake Shore" began actual operations December 15th. Owing to delays in securing a firm foundation and the necessity for much excavation, the work on the "International" progressed less rapidly, and it was not completed until the practicability and value of the scheme had been fully demonstrated by the success and popularity of the "Lake Shore," which from the hour of its opening for business has been crowded to its utmost limit, as has also the "International" since its completion, and the management of the Associated Elevators have ample ground for self-gratulation in the indorsement and patronage extended them by the railroad grain trade of Buffalo. The sister elevators are so constructed and equipped with improved machinery as to insure promptitude in the handling of grain on track, grading, bulking and equitable delivery to all roads, each plant being provided with switches and private tracks, stationary engine and windlass for moving cars, cleaning and grading apparatus, power shovels, weighing hoppers and scales of thirty tons capacity, rubber belt conveyors with patent trippers, incandescent electric lights, and, in short, every requisite appliance and convenience for the handling of grain on a large scale, and in the best, quickest and most economical manner. Mr. S. F. Sherman, who may be fairly called the father of the enterprise, presides over the office, No. 68 Board of Trade building.

16

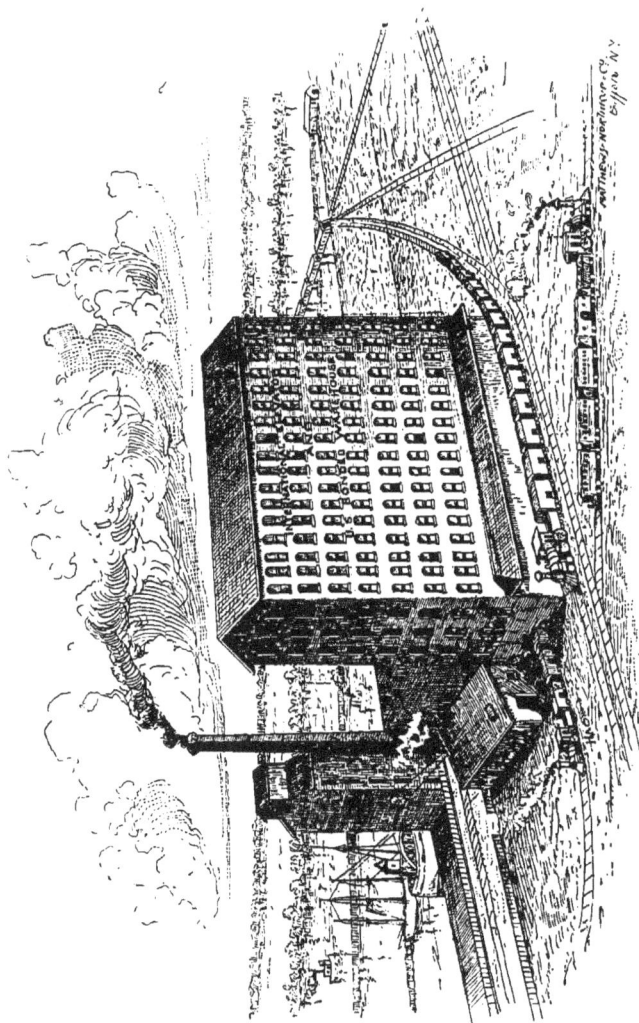

THE NEW "INTERNATIONAL" ELEVATOR.

The plan of operations differs materially from that hitherto pursued, and deserves notice. Previous to being stored all grain received is graded by the chief inspector and weighed by the official weighmaster of the Merchants' Exchange, a joint certificate being issued to the shipper for each car, and sent him by the receiver, as follows :

No. ...   OFFICIAL INSPECTION AND WEIGHT

OF THE

BUFFALO MERCHANTS' EXCHANGE.

———•◦•———

Buffalo, N. Y., ...188...

This Certifies, That there has been inspected and weighed,

Car No. ....into................Lake Shore Elevator,

Grade..

Weight..Bushels.

Junius S. Smith,   *C. W. Ball,*
Weighmaster.   Chief Inspector.

The manager of the Associated Elevators then issues to the railroad sending the grain a negotiable receipt, entitling the holder to the grain described, and which must be presented when it is desired to withdraw the same from store. This receipt reads on the face as follows :

No. ....   THE ASSOCIATED ELEVATORS,

This grain is subject   BUFFALO, N. Y.
to our advertised rates
of storage.   Kind of Grain ......

—   Bushels............ Buffalo, N. Y....188...

                         Grade.............

(Cut of Elevator.)   *Received in Store* in the Lake Shore Elevator

                         from....................................

                         ....bushels

                         of ....

                         subject only to the order hereon of.........

This grain is received   and the surrender of this receipt and pay-
and held in store subject
to the conditions printed ment of charges.
on the back hereof.
                                   ....
                                            Manager.

The subjoined conditions are printed on the back and provide a measure of protection to the elevator company : " It is hereby agreed by the holders of this receipt that the grain herein mentioned may be mixed with other grain of the same quality by inspection in accordance with the rules and regulations of the Merchants' Exchange of Buffalo. Loss by fire or heating at owner's risk. In case any grain in this elevator becomes heated or out of condition during the life of this receipt, said grain shall be deemed to be and shall be of and belonging to the receipt of like grade bearing the oldest date outstanding and uncanceled."

In making shipments the oldest grain of each grade is delivered first, thus holding fresh grain as far as possible and diminishing the danger from heating and other causes. Parties having lots of 5,000 or more bushels which they desire kept separately and the identity preserved must serve notice thereof previous to consignment, and no extra charge will be made for storage, but no guarantee of special care or equal

THE NEW "LAKE SHORE" ELEVATOR.

delivery to railroads can be given. All deliveries are made under the supervision of the chief inspector and weighmaster of the Exchange, who issue joint certificates therefor. The combined storage capacity of these elevators is 1,000,000 bushels, the "International" receiving from the Canadian roads and the "Lake Shore" from the Lake Shore, Nickel Plate, Nypano and B., N. Y. & P. railways. The Associated Elevators are already attracting much of the railroad grain heretofore sent to Chicago and elsewhere, and it is confidently expected that there will be a constant and growing increase of receipts in the future.

These elevators, constructed under the direction of Mr. Sherman, who expended much time in investigation and comparison before adopting plans, combine the best ideas utilized in the elevators at Brooklyn, Minneapolis, Chicago and Buffalo with several novel ones of his own. We illustrate both of these structures, and the engravings convey a fair notion of their general outward appearance. The "Lake Shore" has a superficial area of 11,446 square feet, two 104-foot towers, three receivers (two from tracks and one from canal), fifty bins 16 feet long, 10 feet wide and 45 feet deep, and can receive 100,000 or deliver 150,000 bushels per day. Cars of the New York Central, Buffalo, New York & Philadelphia, Nickel Plate, Buffalo, Rochester & Pittsburg, Erie, West Shore and Lehigh Valley railroads can be loaded here with the utmost ease and celerity, there being 1,600 feet of side-tracks on the premises, and from the opposite side canal-boats are loaded with the same facility. The power is furnished by a Rice automatic 100-horse-power engine, supplied with steam from a steel boiler 16 feet long by 66 inches in diameter. The yards belonging to this elevator embrace 85,000 square feet, furnishing ample room for cars and for the erection of additional buildings when deemed necessary.

The "International" is built in four sections. It has 104 bins, each 45 feet high, 10 feet wide, and 14 feet long. It has a machinery tower 104 feet high, 35 feet wide, 112 feet long ; a marine tower 104 feet high, 35 feet square, and connected with the main building by a truss bridge 100 feet long, 6 feet wide, and crossing Niagara street 45 feet above grade. It has five receiving elevators, one marine and four rail, with a daily receiving capacity of 320,000 bushels, and a delivering capacity of an equal amount. It is driven by a 200-horse power Buckeye automatic engine, taking its steam supply from two 60-inch by 16-foot steel boilers. It has 1,700 feet of side-track and can receive from vessels drawing 11 feet of water ; can deliver to canal-boats and the cars of the New York Central, West Shore, Lackawanna, Erie, Grand Trunk, Michigan Central, and Lehigh Valley railroads. One-half of the house will be bonded in order to hold grain in store in bond.

The processes of receiving and delivering grain at these elevators are somewhat different from those pursued at most similar establishments and quite interesting to the experienced grain handler as well as the novice. The railroad having placed a train of cars loaded with grain on the elevator switch, the men in charge of the shovels attach the rope of the car-puller to one or more of the cars, give the signal to the assistant, who presses down on the lever and starts the drum of the car-puller to winding up the rope and drawing the car into its position in front of the pit. From the bottom of the pit—which is 11 feet lower than the floor of the car—extending upward 110 feet to the top of the tower, are two stationary elevator legs containing an endless rubber belt, 17 inches wide, and revolving on iron pulleys at the top and bottom. Attached to this belt every 12 inches are tin buckets holding about eight quarts each. As this belt travels at the rate of 600 feet a minute, it therefore elevates 4,800 quarts or 150 bushels per minute. The car being in position, two men enter the car, each provided with a light wooden shovel about two feet square and connected by a rope with the shoveling machines. Each man goes to the end of the car, the machine revolves and winds the rope, thus drawing the shovels, with the grain in front of them, towards the car-door and thence into the pit. As the grain falls into the pit it is caught by the buckets and carried to the top of the tower, and as it passes over the pulley it drops into a large bin called the upper receiver, and thence into the weigh-hopper. After all the grain the car contains has been received into the weigh-hopper, the trap door in the upper receiver is closed, making it ready to receive the next car-load. The grain in the weigh-hopper is then weighed and a trap door in the bottom of the hopper is opened, allowing the grain to drop into the lower receiver, whence it passes through a short spout, dropping on to a 30-inch rubber belt which runs on rollers, placed over the partition of a row or section of bins holding about 5,000 bushels each. To take the grain from this belt at any desired point and not scatter or waste any of it is a feat that is accomplished by a little machine called a tripper, invented by George B. Mallory. This machine consists of an iron frame, traveling on wheels and running over the conveyor belt. On top of this frame is an iron roller over which the belt is made to pass, and thence under another iron roller in front and a little below the first. Before the belt with the grain on it passes under this roller an iron blade is pressed firmly against the belt, catching the grain and throwing it into a spout at either side, and thence into the bin. All that is required to empty the grain into any bin is to place the tripper in front of the bin, and the rest of the work is performed automatically.

To get the grain out of the elevator, almost the same routine is followed as to get it in, except that work is commenced at the conveyor first and ends at the car or vessel. Under each section of bins is a conveyor-pit 7 feet deep. In these pits are conveyors similar to the belt conveyors over the bins, but made up of 7-inch strips of rubber belt at the side and a strip of canvas in the center. The conveyors extend from the back of the elevator to the pits of the elevator leg. By opening a trap door in the bottom of any of the bins, the grain drops on to the conveyor, and is carried forward and emptied into the elevator pit, where it is caught by the buckets, carried up to the top of the tower, dropped into the upper receiver, thence into the weigh-hopper, where it is weighed, then into the lower receiver, and thence through a spout leading to the lower floor. At the end of this spout is a flexible or telescopic nozzle which casts the grain in any desired direction, providing for the trimming of cargo without manual labor. A custom-house *attache* at the elevator office facilitates clearances.

THE NEW DAKOTA ELEVATOR.

Work was commenced March 16, 1887, on what will be, when completed, the largest grain stores in the city. It is being built by Messrs. F. A. Bell, Edward Michael and D. A. Sherman. It will cover a plot of land 100 by 306 feet, with bins 100 feet deep, and three towers, each 140 feet high. The land is located on Blackwell canal and Hatch slip, having a frontage of 162 feet on the former and 335 feet on the latter and connecting with the Buffalo Creek Railway, and by it giving connection with all railroads entering Buffalo. The house when completed will have a storage capacity of 2,250,000 bushels, and will have three marine and six inside elevators. It will be provided with the Mallory system of belt conveyors, incandescent system of electric lights, steam fire extinguishers, Frisbie grain shovels, car pullers, "Buckeye" automatic engine, etc., and with sufficient track room to load twenty cars without switching. It will have six canal deliveries and will have a capacity for elevating about 175,000 bushels per day from vessels and 50,000 bushels per day from cars. It is expected the work will be so far completed by June 15th as to permit transfers from vessels to cars or canal-boats, and that it will be completed so as to receive grain for storage by October. It will be a part of the Associated Elevators system, and will offer to the grain trade the option of a graded negotiable receipt or a non-negotiable receipt with identity of grain preserved.

The Associated Elevators' schedule of charges is as follows :

Elevating from cars, including five day's storage and delivering to cars, boats or wagons .... Three-fourths cents per bush.	"	"
Storage each succeeding ten days or parts thereof...................One-fourth	"	"
Blowing and cleaning.. ....One-half	"	"
Grading and cleaning........... ....One	"	"
Separating and cleaning. ....Two	"	"
Running over and cooling..... ....One-fourth	"	"
Storing hot or damaged grain, commencing three days after same has been posted ....One-eighth cent per bush. per day.		

All holders of graded receipts will be entitled to delivery of grain on any railroad entering the city free of switching charges. The right reserved to amend or change these rates by giving thirty days notice to the Secretary of the Merchants' Exchange of Buffalo.

Grain becoming heated or out of condition will be charged one-eighth cent per day, commencing three days after it is posted.

The manager reserves the right to change the foregoing rates at any time by giving thirty days' notice to the Secretary of the Merchant's Exchange.

The officers of the associated companies are named at the head of this notice. President Bell, of the "International" is head of the firm of Bell, Lewis & Yates, coal miners and shippers; Treasurer Lewis is of the same firm ; Vice-President Hawks is a prominent lawyer, and Secretary Gould is of Gould & Stimson, proprietors of the Buffalo Steam Forge. Mr. Bell is also president of the "Lake Shore;" Mr. Michael, vice-president, is a leading lawyer; D. A. Sherman is president of The Sherman Bros. Co. (limited), commission dealers in grain, 58 Board of Trade building; Secretary Sherman is also secretary and treasurer of the same company, and Mr. S. F. Sherman, manager of the Associated Elevators, devotes his entire time to the successful management of the company. Mr. E. C. Loveridge, the assistant manager, has charge of the office details.

ROOD & BROWN,

Car Wheel Works—C. E. Rood, Henry M. Brown—Manufacturers of Railroad Car, Engine, Tender and Truck Wheels—Office and Works, Howard and Thomas Sts., near William St., Belt Line Station

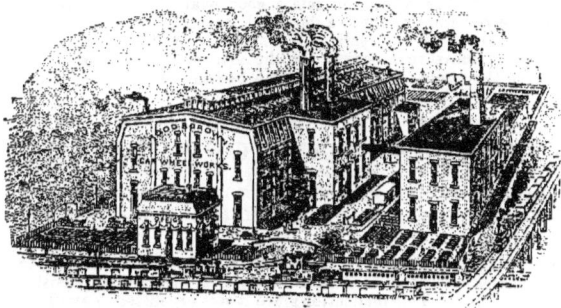

Buffalo taking as she does the front rank among the great railway centers of the United States, it is according to the law of natural selection that everything pertaining to railway rolling stock should be manufactured here on a large scale. For a long time this city has been a recognized headquarters for car-wheels. Among the firms engaged in the business, that of Messrs. Rood & Brown is here referred to. Their product consists of wheels for all kinds of railroad cars, engines, tenders and trucks. The works are quite extensive, as will appear from the accompanying illustration. They give employment to a large force of men and have the very best of facilities for turning out finished wheels in great quantities, their capacity being 150 wheels per day. The record of the wheels of this firm on a number of leading railroads has demonstrated their superiority over any others in use. All wheels are made from the best charcoal iron, by the chilled process. Before leaving the shops all wheels are thoroughly tested, so that any flaws or imperfections are readily detected, and back goes the wheel to be cast over again. The individual members of the firm are C. E. Rood and Henry M. Brown, both experienced and practical men in the business. Their establishment is one of a great number of industrial enterprises which have been opened up in East Buffalo quite recently, making that section of the city teem with the busy hum of progress.

FRANK H. KINNIUS,

Wholesale and Retail Grocer—Dealer in Flour, Feed, Corn, Oats, Hay, etc.— Telephone 2053 A—Nos. 1412 and 1414 Main St.

The phenomenal growth of Buffalo, so surprising to strangers, is, for obvious reasons, chiefly in a northerly direction, and Cold Spring may be termed a suburb of the city proper. Principal among the groceries in this locality is that owned by Mr. Frank H. Kinnius at Nos. 1412 and 1414 Main street, and occupied exclusively by himself as store and dwelling. It is a handsome three-story brick building, 42 by 60, with barns, stables and other out-buildings in the rear. The business was established in 1877 by John G. Langner & Co. The present proprietor was born in Buffalo in 1851, and having received the advantages of an ordinary school education, worked as clerk in different capacities till 1871. He then entered the freight office of the New York Central & Hudson River railroad. In 1877 he became a partner with Mr. J. G. Langner in the house of which he is now the head, and in 1882, at the death of Mr. Langner, took charge of the business of the firm on his own account. The store he now occupies was built by himself in 1885.

The store is divided into two distinct departments, one being set apart for flour, feed, grain and fodder of all kinds, while the other contains a large and well-selected stock of choice family groceries, a specialty being made of the finest brands of teas and coffees, a large assortment of which are always kept on hand, both for retail output and also to supply the trade. A public telephone may be mentioned as one of the many conveniences of this really well-appointed business house.

While the bulk of the goods sold are consumed in Buffalo and the surrounding country, still there are not wanting many orders from other towns and cities of the Union at long distances.

Mr. Kinnius is well and favorably known in Buffalo and recognized by all as a young man of good business habits and remarkable executive ability.

By putting his shoulder to the wheel, he sets a good example to his employes, and although at all times strict and prompt to a degree there is still a vein of kindness and liberality traceable throughout his dealings, an evidence of the live-and-let-live principle, which in a great measure accounts for the astonishing success that has attended his efforts during the comparatively short time he has been established in his present business.

GERMAN-AMERICAN BANK OF BUFFALO.

Henry Hellriegel, President ; Henry Breitweiser, Vice-President ; Henry W. Burt, Cashier—Capital, $100,000—No. 440 Main St., opposite Soldiers and Sailors' Monument.

Among the different fiduciary institutions of Buffalo there are none that are managed on sounder financial principles, with direct reference to the best interests of depositors, than the German-American Bank. This institution since it was organized, May 10, 1882, has steadily advanced in public favor. Among its officers and directors are to be found leading German business men whose names are synonyms for prudent, careful management of anything entrusted to their care. The board of directors consists of Messrs. Henry Hellriegel, Jacob W. Diehl, L. L. Lewis, Francis Handel, Michael Nellany, August Baetzhold, John Schaefer, Jos. Timmerman and Henry Breitweiser. These gentlemen are all well known to the citizens of Buffalo.

The cashier, Mr. Burt, is eminently qualified for his responsible position, and fills it to the entire satisfaction of the patrons and stockholders. Every facility is possessed for doing a general banking business, including making collections, issuing drafts, bills of exchange, etc., at the lowest current rates. The subjoined statement shows the condition of affairs for the quarter ending March 12, 1887 : Assets—Loans and discounts, $656.756.83 ; U. S. bonds, $1,000.00; bonds and mortgages, $7,500.00; due from banks, $87,136.45; cash on hand—currency, gold and silver, $23,426.70; furniture, fixtures, etc., $3,000.00; expense account, $3,070.99; real estate, etc., $5,750.00; overdrafts, $4,849.63; total, $792,490.60. Liabilities—Capital, $100,000; surplus account, $35,000; interest account, $11,794.63 ; amount due depositors, $645,695.97; total, $792,490.60.

INTERNATIONAL BOX AND HEADING CO.,

Manufacturers of Boxes and Heading—Foot of Hertel Ave.

The above company, formerly W. E. Plummer & Son, was founded in 1866. The members are W. E. Plummer, sr., and W. E. Plummer, jr., father and son. Their premises at the foot of Hertel avenue, embracing factory and yards, are 200 by 700 feet. The works occupy a substantial two-story building 100 by 110 feet, employ from 45 to 50 men, and are fitted up with a fine complement of machinery, comprising saws, planers, jointers, etc., run by a powerful steam engine.

Some idea of the quality and quantity of the work done here may be drawn from the fact that besides a steady and growing demand from the local trade—manufacturers, wholesale dealers and shippers of every description of goods, coopers, and others —large quantities of the company's boxes and headings are sent to Eastern markets, the total sales averaging $75,000 a year.

The Messrs. Plummer are industrious, enterprising gentlemen, and deserve the prosperity which has smiled upon their efforts. The father is a native of Windham county, N. H., born in 1822. He moved to Buffalo in 1846, and up to 1863 was engaged in the manufacture of woolen goods, abandoning that, for his present vocation. He is a plain, unassuming, straightforward man. W. E. Plummer, jr., was born in Buffalo in 1852, and has been in this line of business since boyhood. He is a wide-awake, hard-working, public-spirited young man, a freemason, and popular with all who know him.

DAVIS & BROWN,

Manufacturers of Superior Grades Fine-Cut Chewing and Smoking Tobaccos and Cigarettes—Northwest corner Pearl and Court Sts.

It has been sixteen years since Buffalo boasted a tobacco and cigarette factory, notwithstanding there is no better location for a business of that kind in the United States. The want is about to be supplied at last, however, by the above-named firm, who, having secured the splendid new five-story brick and iron building at the northwest corner of Pearl and Court streets, are fitting it up, as this work is issued, with a complete equipment of the latest improved machinery, and early in April will commence active operations with a large force of skilled hands, putting upon the market the finest grades of fine-cut chewing and smoking tobacco and cigarettes. The firm have ample capital, experience and facilities, and there can be no reasonable question of their ability to make Buffalo one of the most renowned and popular of American tobacco manufacturing centers. Only the finest Virginia, Kentucky and imported stock will be used, and every effort will be made to please the trade and consumers.

The building occupied is one of the most convenient and substantial in the city, and if specially erected for the purpose could not better suit the requirements of the firm. Each of the five floors constitutes a single immense room, 50 by 90 feet in dimensions, the ceilings supported by rows of iron columns.

Mr. William Davis, the senior member, has a thorough knowledge of his business, having had eighteen years experience. He is thirty-eight years of age, an active, energetic and enterprising business man. The junior member, Mr. William G. Brown, has had an experience of twelve years, and has a thorough practical knowledge of his calling in all its branches.

The firm have the neatest and best arranged factory in the country, and must succeed.

TROY LAUNDRY,

Mrs. Kate Fogarty, Proprietress—Hand Work Exclusively—Nos. 36 and 38 East Eagle St., near Washington.

The success achieved by the energetic, thorough-going proprietress of the above-named popular laundry shows what may be accomplished by a wide-awake woman when she is in earnest. Mrs. Fogarty came to this country from Scarborough, Yorkshire, England, when but five years old. Her parents, poor but industrious and respectable people, were unable to provide for their daughter further than to give her a plain common school education and a good example, and while still quite young she sought and obtained employment in one of Troy's great laundries, where she soon became noted for intelligence and capacity, and was elected President of the Troy Collar Laundry Union, which office she retained for five years, taking an active part in the strike of 1874. She then came to Buffalo, where she has remained ever since, attending strictly to her business, and gradually gaining the confidence and patronage of the public, and particularly of that class who recognize and appreciate first-class laundry work. At present Mrs. Fogarty occupies the entire three-story building, 46 by 60 feet, Nos. 36 and 38 East Eagle street, between Washington and Ellicott streets, where she employs some twenty-seven skillful laundresses, pays the best wages in the city for that kind of work, and does an annual business of nearly $20,000. No machinery whatever is used in the establishment, and consequently garments are done up in superior style and without injury. The specialty, of course, to which greatest attention is given, is the laundrying of gentlemen's shirts, collars and cuffs, both for the trade and for individual customers, though every description of men's washing is done to order in the best manner and at short notice. The Troy Laundry was established by Misses Mullany (now Mrs. Fogarty) and Carll in 1871, the former succeeding in 1875. Mrs. Fogarty has made the reputation of the laundry, and well deserves the prosperity that has attended her efforts.

GOULD & STIMSON,

BUFFALO STEAM FORGE,

Manufacturers of Locomotive and Car Axles, Engine Forgings, Heavy Shafts, Hammered Shapes, Boxes, Shanks, Links, Pins, etc.—Works, Across Ohio-st. Bridge; Office, Room 24 Hayen Building.

The Buffalo Steam Forge was established in 1863 by Henry Childs, the style subsequently changing for a short time to Childs & Saxton, then again Henry Childs, who in in January, 1885, were succeeded by the present firm, composed of Charles A. Gould and Henry B. Stimson. Mr. Gould, a native of Batavia, N.Y., born in 1849, has spent the greater portion of his life in Buffalo, where he is a well-known and popular citizen. He was deputy postmaster in 1879, a position which he resigned in 1881, having been appointed Collector of Customs for the district of Buffalo, an office which he retained until his term expired in 1885, when he joined Mr. Stimson in the present venture. Mr. S. first saw the light at New Lots, N. Y., in 1856. He came to Buffalo in 1874, and in 1876 became associated with Mr. Childs in the Buffalo Steam Forge. Both are energetic, earnest, enterprising business men, under whose administration this famous old forge property is becoming more valuable than ever before.

The works and appurtenances occupy more than four acres of land adjacent to the south end of the Ohio-street bridge, across the Buffalo river, and comprise two immense buildings—one 80 by 250 feet, the other 30 by 300 feet—and the necessary yards, sheds, etc. The works are very convenient to the various railroads and wharves, having direct connection with the Buffalo river, and are equipped in the best possible manner for the work they are designed to perform, the machinery including a number of monster steam hammers, lathes, etc., for shaping and finishing heavy work, and a wilderness of smaller machinery for light forgings of every description.

The specialties of the firm embrace locomotive and car axles of the highest grades, every variety of engine forgings, heavy shafts, hammered shapes of all kinds, boxes, shanks, links, pins—in short, any and every kind of heavy and light forgings for railroads, steamboats, mills, etc., railway work forming a leading specialty, their coupling links and pins being confessedly the very best made in this country.

The firm employ 100 men, pay some $4,000 a month in wages, and do an annual business of $500,000, which is increasing at a gratifying rate.

INDEX TO REPRESENTATIVE HOUSES.

ADVERTISERS' INDEX.

F W. HUMBLE,

ARCHITECT.

Nason & Son

NEW

Photo Parlors

Cor. Main and Clinton Streets,

OCCUPYING TWO ENTIRE FLOORS, COVERING AN AREA OF 11,000 SQUARE FEET,
BEING THE LARGEST ESTABLISHMENT OF THE KIND IN THE STATE.

o   o   o   o

We have the finest light, all the latest improvements, new instruments, experienced artists, and make strictly first-class work by the

NEW INSTANTANEOUS PROCESS,

Which is far superior to the Old Style.

o   o   o   o

☞ Call and see Sample of Work, and learn Prices.

o   o   o   o

MAIN STREET, No. 403,

NASON & SON, BUFFALO.

BLISS BROS., 368 Main Street, · · · ·
· · · COR. EAGLE, · · ·

Photographers,
Buffalo, N. Y.
· · ·

EXTERIOR AND INTERIOR VIEWS OF RESIDENCES, STORES, FACTORIES, ETC.,
TAKEN AT SHORT NOTICE. · · · COMMERCIAL AND RAILWAY · · · ·
· · · PHOTOGRAPHING WILL RECEIVE OUR SPECIAL ATTENTION. · · ·

✳ MOORE, ✳ ✳ ✳
THE FURNISHER AND SHIRT MAKER.

A Complete Line of Men's Furnishing Goods.
ORDERS BY MAIL WILL RECEIVE PROMPT ATTENTION.
315 MAIN STREET, BUFFALO, N. Y.

Superior Manufacturing Co.,
· MANUFACTURERS OF · · ·

FINE CASSIMERE PANTS AND VESTS.

~ ~ ~ FLANNEL SHIRTS AND OVERALLS. ~ ~ ~

· · · · · · OFFICE AND FACTORY, · ·

78 PEARL STREET, · ·

HENRY HAENLEIN,
· · · · · · Proprietor.
BUFFALO, N. Y.

17

◉

━ ━ ━━ ━ ━ ━━ ━Proprietors of Banner Mills━━━━━

SUPERLATIVE,
BEST,
EXCELSIOR,

FLOUR

◀BANNER,▶
STELLA,
◀BUFFALO▶

━━━━━Capacity, 1,000 Barrels Per Day━━━━━

◉

Roller Process,

OFFICE, NOS. 204 AND 206 MAIN STREET,
BUFFALO, N. Y.

WILSON CHEMICAL ══════THE══════ COMPANY, FIRE EXTINGUISHER

BUFFALO, N. Y.,
. . . . Manufacturers of . . . .
Chemical Fire Engines.

Double Globe Engines.—To be drawn by Horses. Two Sizes.
Double Globe Engines.—To be drawn by Men or Horses. Two Sizes.
Single Globe Village Engines.—Three Sizes.
   Warehouse Engines.—For Factories, Stores, Oil Works, Warehouses, Halls, Public Buildings, Flour Mills, Cotton Mills, Saw Mills, etc.
   Portable Fire Extinguishers. — "Useful Everywhere," for Fire Departments, Public and Private Buildings, etc.
   Stationary Globes.—With Standpipe and Hose connections on every floor. Especially adapted for high buildings.

    Send for Descriptive Circular and Prices, or call at their office, Buffalo, N. Y.

270

ADVERTISEMENTS.

1859 — ESTABLISHED - 1869

JOHN C ADAMS
J. HERBERT WHITE.
Adams & White
SUCCESSORS TO
YOUNG, LOCKWOOD & CO.

STATIONERS AND PRINTERS,

Binders and BLANK BOOK Manufacturers,

209 & 211 MAIN ST., BUFFALO, N. Y.

Book, Job, Railroad and Commercial Printing.

The Saturday Mercury,

AN EIGHT - PAGE WEEKLY PAPER.

Sworn-to Circulation, **16,000** Copies per Week.

SOLD IN EVERY VILLAGE WITHIN 500 MILES OF BUFFALO.

Book and Job Printing of Every Description.

Estimates on All Classes of Work Cheerfully Given.

W. J. McCAHILL, Prest.
JOHN FISHER, Sec. & Treas.

THE FRANCIS AXE CO.

BUFFALO, N. Y.

· · · MAKE THE · · · · · · · · ·

· · · · BEST AXE · · ·

IN THE WORLD

· · · · · ORDER THE ALL-STEEL AXE. · · ·

WRITE FOR ILLUSTRATED CATALOGUE
AND PRICE LIST.

"REGULAR."

HOWARD IRON WORKS,

· · · BUFFALO, N. Y. · ·

· MANUFACTURERS OF PATENTED

SAFETY ELEVATORS,

FOR
STORES, HOTELS
AND
MANUFACTORIES.

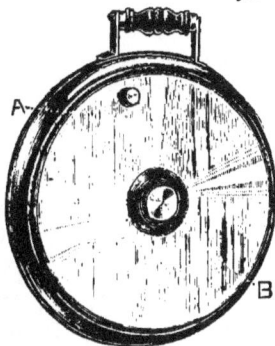

274 ADVERTISEMENTS.

J. S. EDWARDS,

DEALER IN Watches, Clocks
—AND—
... JEWELRY ...

No. 213 MAIN STREET,
BUFFALO, N. Y.

Watches. Clocks, Etc., Repaired and Warranted.

6. K. SUMMERHAYS,

*Steam and Water
Heating & Ventilating
Apparatus,*

226 PEARL ST., BUFFALO, N. Y.

TELEPHONE 296.   Formerly E. H. COOK Co., Limited.

A. R. KETCHAM,
FILLMORE AVENUE
Foundry,
OFFICE, 389 WASHINGTON STREET,
BUFFALO, N. Y.

Ketcham's Stop Valve Boxes for Street Water Mains and
Service Pipe.
Castings of all kinds furnished promptly, at
reasonable rates.

D. A. SLAGHT,
⊣American Billiard Hall⊢

394 Main St.,
BUFFALO, N. Y.

John H. Colgan,

Counselor at Law,

BUFFALO, N. Y.

ROOM 17,
404 MAIN STREET.

LAW OFFICES
OF
BAKER & SCHWARTZ,
ROOMS 30--33
HAYEN BUILDING,
COR. MAIN AND SENECA STS.,
BUFFALO, N. Y.

CHARLES A. GOULD.   HENRY B. STIMSON.

GOULD & STIMSON
BUFFALO STEAM FORGE.

LINKS,
ENGINE FORGINGS
HEAVY SHAFTS
HAMMERED
SHAPES,
BOXES, PINS
SHANKS
PINS

LOCOMOTIVE & CAR AXLES.

OFFICE: 24 HAYEN BUILDING.
WORKS: ACROSS OHIO ST. BRIDGE.

BUFFALO, N. Y.

JOSEPH BORK.   HENRY H. VOGHT.

JOSEPH BORK'S
Real Estate and ❀
❀ Insurance Office

NO. 368 MAIN STREET,

S. W. Corner Eagle Street,   BUFFALO, N. Y.
Opposite "THE RICHMOND,"

Suburban Building Sites a Specialty

ALONG THE BELT LINE RAILWAY.

Money Advanced for Building Purposes

ON LONG TIME AND EASY PAYMENTS.

Investments Made for Non-Residents.

AGENCY FOR

AMERICAN INSURANCE CO.,   -   Newark, N. J.
PHŒNIX INSURANCE CO., -   -   Brooklyn, N. Y.
LONDON ASSURANCE CORPORATION, England.

(See Page 217.)

www.ingramcontent.com/pod-product-compliance
Lightning Source LLC
Chambersburg PA
CBHW030346270326
41926CB00009B/976